The Mossad

ALSO BY MARC E. VARGO

*Women of the Resistance: Eight
Who Defied the Third Reich* (2012)

The Mossad

Six Landmark Missions of the Israeli Intelligence Agency, 1960–1990

MARC E. VARGO

McFarland & Company, Inc., Publishers
Jefferson, North Carolina

LIBRARY OF CONGRESS CATALOGUING-IN-PUBLICATION DATA

Vargo, Marc E., 1954– author.
 The Mossad : six landmark missions of the Israeli intelligence agency, 1960–1990 / Marc E. Vargo.
  p.   cm.
 Includes bibliographical references and index.

 ISBN 978-0-7864-7914-6 (softcover : acid free paper) ∞
 ISBN 978-1-4766-1966-8 (ebook)

 1. Israel. Mosad le-modi'in ve-tafkidim meyuhadim.
 2. Intelligence service—Israel—History—20th century.
 3. Secret service—Israel—History—20th century.   4. Special operations (Military science)—Israel—History—20th century.
 5. National security—Israel—History—20th century.   I. Title.

 UB251.I78V37 2015
 327.125694009'045—dc23   2014043234

BRITISH LIBRARY CATALOGUING DATA ARE AVAILABLE

© 2015 Marc E. Vargo. All rights reserved

No part of this book may be reproduced or transmitted in any form or by any means, electronic or mechanical, including photocopying or recording, or by any information storage and retrieval system, without permission in writing from the publisher.

Cover image © Dreamstime.com

Printed in the United States of America

McFarland & Company, Inc., Publishers
 Box 611, Jefferson, North Carolina 28640
  www.mcfarlandpub.com

For Addison Vargo,
With a wish for a wiser and more peaceful world.

Covert action should not be confused with missionary work.
—Henry Kissinger, 1975

Table of Contents

Introduction — 1

PART ONE: OPERATION EICHMANN — 9

1. Adolf Eichmann: The Man, the Manhunt — 11
2. Mission: Operation Eichmann — 26
3. Trial and Tribulations — 60

PART TWO: OPERATION WRATH OF GOD — 69

4. The Arab-Israeli Conflict and the Black September Organization — 71
5. Massacre at the 1972 Summer Olympic Games — 91
6. Mission: Operation Wrath of God — 116

PART THREE: OPERATION ENTEBBE — 151

7. The Emergence of Skyjacking as a Tool of Palestinian Terrorism — 152
8. Mission: Operation Entebbe — 161

PART FOUR: OPERATION OPERA — 187

9. Saddam Hussein and the Nuclear Program of Iraq — 189
10. Mission: Operation Opera — 196

PART FIVE: OPERATION PLUMBAT AND THE VANUNU AFFAIR — 223

11. Israel's Secret Nuclear Weapons Program — 225
12. The Quest for Uranium: Operation Plumbat and the NUMEC Affair — 233
13. Mordechai Vanunu: The Seduction of a Nuclear Whistleblower — 246

Chapter Notes — 275
Bibliography — 285
Index — 295

Introduction

Among the world's most formidable intelligence agencies is the Mossad, the organization that David Ben-Gurion, the first prime minister of Israel, established on December 13, 1949.[1] An inspired concept, the Mossad was designed to enhance the ability of Israel's intelligence community to gather information that would help protect the nation from attack, most notably invasion by its Arab neighbors. Certainly it was no secret that the Jewish state was in need of a smart, hard-nosed bureau of this type, national security being a paramount concern since the creation of the state of Israel.

It was on May 14, 1948, that the Jewish people celebrated the birth of their new home, the end result of a controversial resolution adopted by the United Nations General Assembly.[2] Across the country, streets teemed with jubilant citizens as Ben-Gurion, in a stirring ceremony at the Tel Aviv Museum, signed the Declaration of the Establishment of the State of Israel.[3] Yet the pride and grandeur of the occasion, the profound exultation of a newborn nation, was not to last. Within hours, the surrounding Arab nations greeted their young neighbor not with a handshake but with hostility, their militaries laying siege to the fledgling republic by land and sea. And these were not mere skirmishes, isolated and insignificant, designed to dampen the public spirit. Rather, the invaders, all of them charter members of the League of Arab States, were seeking to eradicate the Jewish domain before it had a chance to fully establish itself. To ensure a victory, moreover, the assailants boosted the number and reach of their sorties as the hours passed.

"Throughout the second full day of Israel's independence," writes historian Martin Gilbert, "Lebanese troops were advancing from the north; Syrian, Iraqi and Transjordanian troops from the east; Egyptian troops from the south."[4] And the number of aggressors continued to mount. "Even Saudi Arabia sent a small contingent," Martin adds, "that fought under Egyptian command."[5] Yet Israel was not without hope, its military being equal to the challenge.

Boasting nearly thirty-seven thousand troops, the Israeli armed forces counted among their fighters scores of former members of the Haganah, the Jewish paramilitary organization.[6] Then, too, the country's military strategists, a collection of shrewd tacticians, had anticipated the Arab offensive. So it was that the Israelis, their new nation's survival in the balance, fought brilliantly, driving back the assailants and preserving their country's sovereignty. In so doing, they earned the world's admiration, even the begrudging respect of their opponents. However, the latter's regard applied only to the skills of the Israeli military; it did not extend to reassessing, and accepting, the Jewish state's right to possess the land that the United Nations had placed in its possession. It was for this reason that Ben-Gurion, convinced that more attacks were on the horizon, set about assembling a national intelligence apparatus to maintain a watch on the region. His aim was to monitor all potential sources of threat—foreign and domestic, military and armed civilian—so that Israel could be forewarned about impending terrorist attacks and military strikes.

In Ben-Gurion's initial setup, Israel's intelligence system was designed to consist of five distinct yet interrelated components, each of which would perform its specific functions while collaborating with the other four units. But while the idea of a well-integrated intelligence community appeared feasible on paper, complications arose when it was put into practice, a situation that was due largely to the ambiguity of the units' boundaries and functions. "There was neither an absolute definition of responsibility nor a clear set of guidelines for action," writes Dennis Eisenberg.[7] All too soon, confusion and competition infected the system, with the attendant "rivalry, squabbling, and sniping" further diminishing the ineffectual network.[8] It was this dysfunctional state of affairs, then, that led to the creation of the Mossad, officially Ha Mossad le Teum, or "The Institute for Coordination."[9] Positioned in such a way as to transcend the malfunctioning machinery of the existent intelligence community, the new agency would nevertheless make use of the apparatus' five components, absorbing a portion of their responsibilities, conscripting members of their staffs, and conferring with their directors.

As to its formal purpose, the Mossad was to have two additional duties on top of coordinating the other intelligence units. First, it was to "gather and analyze information abroad," writes Eisenberg, "in any area that might be of interest to Israel."[10] Sensitive material pertaining to the surrounding Arab states was, of course, to be given precedence. And second, the organization was to conduct special operations at the behest of the prime minister, the character of such projects, by virtue of their covert nature, being undefined in the agency's mandate.

Introduction 3

A restructuring of the intelligence community on March 2, 1951, led to the Mossad being placed directly under the prime minister. Whereas it initially had been answerable to the foreign minister, its subsequent standing within the governmental hierarchy rendered it a freer, more flexible entity. In the same stroke, the agency's privileged position invited envy from certain quarters, along with tall expectations. The Mossad rose to the occasion, however. Sidestepping the internecine jealousies, it performed its duties with cool efficiency, thereby fulfilling the hopes that had been placed upon it.

In the course of the 1950s, the agency, under the guidance of Isser Harel, cultivated an impressive number of well-placed sources within the Arab world, in this way collecting information that could help prevent Israel's destruction. Alongside these efforts, the Mossad courted Western nations that were in a position to help ensure Israel's survival. Of these overtures, arguably the most productive occurred in 1954 when Harel traveled to Washington, D.C., to forge an alliance with Alan Dulles, the director of the Central Intelligence Agency. For Israel, the relationship proved to be a game-changer. "Dulles arranged for Mossad to have state-of-the-art equipment," writes Gordon Thomas, "listening and tracking devices, remote-operated cameras, and a range of gadgets that Harel admitted he never knew existed."[11]

During the ensuing years, the Mossad made use of this innovative technology to enhance its surveillance of its adversaries. And these foes were formidable by any standard. The preponderance, as noted earlier, was comprised of neighboring Arab forces bent on putting an end to the State of Israel, the principal argument being that the United Nations had awarded it a disproportionate amount of territory. But Israel's enemies also included several German scientists—"rabid and unrepentant Nazis," in the words of Zvi Malkin—who, after World War II, agreed to help certain Arab states advance their weapons programs.[12] The Mossad detected their presence in 1956, a period when Egypt, under the leadership of Gamal Abdel Nasser, was actively recruiting a number of Hitler's former experts in an array of disciplines.[13]

The Israeli government, for its part, was troubled by the participation of the German scientists, and justifiably so; their technical expertise coupled with their willingness to work for the Arab cause did not bode well for the beleaguered republic. Accordingly, Harel ordered his Mossad staff to monitor their activities. As the German scientists' involvement became even more worrisome in the ensuing years, however, he decided that his agents should do more than merely observe the situation; they should undercut the Germans' contributions to Egypt's burgeoning missile program. And his agents did so in a singularly sinister style. "[T]he Mossad," writes Ian Black, "waged a ruthless secret war of threats and assassinations against German scientists building rockets in Nasser's Egypt."[14]

It was, moreover, an effective campaign. But it was also where the Mossad's involvement with ex–Nazis ended. What Harel did *not* do at this juncture was to direct his staff to track down the much larger number of Nazi war criminals who were still in hiding, or in some cases living openly, in Europe and elsewhere in the world. Since these past offenders were not facilitating the Arab states' weapons programs, they were not considered an active threat to Israel. The fact is, the Mossad's resources were limited, and Harel knew that an open-ended pursuit of malefactors from the Holocaust was simply not feasible. "He had only one individual on his staff tasked with collecting intelligence on former Nazis," writes Neal Bascomb, "and this was, essentially, an archivist position, filing and cross-referencing information sent from various sources around the world."[15]

It is important to note, however, that the Mossad's inaction on this matter did not derive from indifference. If anything, its agents were galled by the fact that countless National Socialists who had willingly taken part in the most egregious mass murder in human history were still walking about with impunity. It therefore was buoying to many within the Mossad when, in 1960, Ben-Gurion authorized it to use its resources to apprehend a key figure of the Third Reich. Not only was the agency now in a position to better fund such a venture, but social conditions in Israel were ripe for an undertaking of this nature. In particular, the Jewish citizenry, including numerous survivors of the Holocaust, had become better equipped, emotionally, to revisit the horrors of the Final Solution than had been the case in the years immediately following the shattering ordeal. The moment had thus arrived for the Jewish state to sit in judgment of those who had readily contributed to the deportation, torture, and industrialized extermination of millions of Jewish men, women, and children. And it was the Mossad that would deliver the first of these desecraters of humanity to the State of Israel for prosecution.

In what was dubbed Operation Eichmann, the Mossad set out to capture the Nazi war criminal Adolf Eichmann, the man who helped devise and implement the Final Solution. In the postwar era, Eichmann no longer was an intimidating official holding the fates of millions in his palm; he was a mundane fugitive living under an assumed name in South America. Because he was hiding in such a faraway land, the Mossad would have no choice but to violate international law to carry out its mission. All the same, Harel considered the illegal endeavor to be justified on moral grounds, as did Israeli Prime Minister David Ben-Gurion. In their assessment, addressing a profound moral wrong committed against the Jewish people took precedence over the legal blowback that might result from breaching another country's borders. In the ensuing decades, this perspective would come to characterize the Mossad, this "sublime indifference to the niceties of international law or international opinion," as Tony Geraghty puts it.[16]

As to the reactions that Operation Eichmann produced, Harel had been spot-on: the mission, which consisted of kidnapping the former Nazi and flying him to Israel for trial, did indeed generate stinging criticism of both the Israeli government and the Mossad. Yet the undertaking also occasioned considerable praise, especially from Israel's supporters and from Holocaust survivors and their families around the world. And it did more: it cast the agency in a new light, serving notice that the Mossad was adopting a more hard-hitting approach to dealing with the adversaries of the Jewish people irrespective of the antagonists' whereabouts.

Adopting this bold new approach, the Mossad would become even more audacious in the following decade, a period when the agency would stun the world with a radical response to a terrorist attack on an elite squad of Israeli citizens. It happened in 1972 when the Palestinian extremist organization Black September abducted, held hostage, and ultimately murdered eleven Israeli athletes and officials at the Summer Olympic Games in Munich, Germany. Declassified documents have since revealed that German officials were alerted to the impending attack three weeks prior to the start of the Olympics but failed to take sufficient measures to prevent the assault or warn the Games' participants.[17] Israel, by comparison, proved to be proficient in its subsequent handling of the massacre.

In the days following the horrific ordeal, Israeli Prime Minister Golda Meir appealed to the Mossad for help. She and her advisors were determined to exact revenge from Black September while, at the same time, delivering a potent warning to would-be terrorists. So the Mossad went into action, launching a virtuoso scheme known as Operation Wrath of God. A twenty-year project that would span the globe, it represented a turning point both for the intelligence agency and the nation itself. "Israel would go on the offensive," writes Stewart Steven, "in the bitter, savage, merciless war being fought in the back streets of Europe and the Middle East."[18] As the maiden mission of this new approach, Wrath of God would prove to be an unprecedented cloak-and-dagger project.

It began with a team of Mossad agents tracking down scores of terrorists and their collaborators who had been involved, directly or indirectly, in the Munich attack. Rather than transport them to Israel for trial, however, the team took matters into its own hands: it neutralized the offenders wherever it found them and as swiftly as possible, in some cases shortly after placing the targets' obituaries in local newspapers so they would know that they were marked for murder. "The mission was not to capture anyone," write Dan Raviv and Yossi Melman. "It was out-and-out revenge—to terrorize the terrorists."[19] By all accounts, the strategy was effective in putting the extremists on the defensive, few of whom managed to escape their grisly fates. The public response to the

Mossad's ruthless approach saw many applauding it, praising it as shrewd, spirited, and morally defensible, while others decried it as tantamount to vigilantism.

Marginally less controversial, but a mission that would still result in a considerable degree of international condemnation, was Operation Entebbe, an undertaking in which the Mossad collaborated with the Israeli Defense Forces to help rescue scores of airline passengers who were being held hostage in an East African military dictatorship. Their plane was hijacked in Greece and diverted to Uganda. The passengers' rescue by the Israeli military, based on insights furnished by the Mossad and military intelligence, was both breathtaking and heroic. Because it entailed a violation of Uganda's borders, however, the mission would invite castigation from the United Nations as well as from numerous Arab states.

Even more debatable would be Operation Opera, a mission for which the Mossad would begin laying the groundwork in the mid-1970s when it detected a disturbing development in another Middle Eastern country.[20] The agency learned that Iraq, one of the Jewish state's longtime adversaries, had engaged a French company to design a nuclear research center near Baghdad, one that would house a seven hundred-megawatt commercial reactor ostensibly to produce electricity for the nation.[21] But the Israeli government was skeptical. Its officials worried that Iraq would use it to construct a nuclear weapon and employ it against the Jewish state itself, particularly since the Iraqis had been adamant, when forging the deal with the French, that the reactor use plutonium or enriched uranium rather than a more innocuous substance nicknamed "caramel."[22] The Israelis' concern hinged on the potential applications of the three substances: whereas all of them were capable of producing energy for domestic purposes, only plutonium and enriched uranium could also be used to make a nuclear weapon. And while this single piece of information, in itself, did not mean that Iraq was planning to assemble a nuclear arsenal, Israeli Prime Minister Menachem Begin, choosing to err on the side of caution, decided to green-light Operation Opera.

Unfolding over a period of four years, Opera was set into motion by a spectacular feat: the Mossad, posing as a French environmental group, blew up a warehouse near Marseilles that was storing nuclear core components awaiting shipment to Iraq. And this was only the beginning. The team next set out to eliminate an eminent Egyptian physicist who was involved in the Iraqi project and who had traveled to Paris on business. As to the method, the agents were neither subtle nor sophisticated when the moment arrived to remove him from the political equation. "They cut his throat," writes Gordon Thomas.[23] It would be in 1981, however, that the Mossad would deliver the coup de grâce: it would slip vital intelligence to the Israeli military enabling the air force to conduct an aerial strike on the nearly completed Iraqi facility, thereby obliterating it. Yet despite the fact that Operation Opera was successful in achieving, at least in part, its military and political aims—analysts interpreted the strategy as Israel's warning to the entire Arab world to abstain from pursuing nuclear weapons—the unprovoked attack would cost the Jewish nation the trust and respect of the global community. "The Israeli raid," writes Geoff Simons, "was almost universally condemned, with the new French premier, François Mitterrand, one of the first to protest."[24] International organizations objected as well, most notably the UN Security Council, which unanimously adopted Resolution 487 denouncing the attack. What many observers did not know is that Israel was itself no stranger to nuclear weapons even as it insisted that the Middle East remain free of them. In fact, it had already surpassed its Arab adversaries in the quest to possess them, with the Mossad having been instrumental in bringing about this state of affairs.

Despite the denials of its leaders, Israel had been pursuing a nuclear agenda as far back as 1956, when a French company delivered to the Jewish state its first nuclear reactor.[25] Although Israeli officials insisted it would be used solely for peaceful purposes, Ben-Gurion's government, once the reactor was installed, embarked on a clandestine drive to acquire enriched uranium for use in building a nuclear arsenal. Brushing aside the opposition of its chief ally, the United States, which warned that such a unilateral pursuit of nuclear arms threatened to upset the balance of power in the region, Israel pushed on with its plan. And it succeeded. Owing in large part to the machinations of the Mossad—Operation Plumbat, one of the agency's missions, would bring yellowcake uranium to Israel for use in its nuclear arms program—the Jewish state soon became the first Middle Eastern country to be in a position to launch a nuclear attack.[26] It would be twenty-five years later, moreover, that a former technician at Israel's nuclear facility would travel to Europe to reveal this volatile state secret to the Western media. By exposing the details of the country's arsenal, the whistleblower, Mordechai Vanunu, hoped to prevent a nuclear confrontation in the Middle East. As is now known, such a cataclysmic event would not, in fact, occur at that time, although a confrontation of sorts would take place between Vanunu and the Mossad.

It happened in 1986. Robert Maxwell, a prominent British publisher, purportedly tipped off Israeli officials that Vanunu was in England, where the onetime technician was offering a prominent newspaper a cache of photographic evidence of Israel's top-secret nuclear installation in the Negev Desert. Alarmed by this development, high-ranking Israeli officials decided to stop Vanunu in his tracks and, to this end, they called in the professionals. "The task was allotted to the Mossad with the provisos that Israel's good relationship with the British prime minister, Margaret Thatcher, was not to be jeopardized," writes Chris Chant.[27] And there was a second stipulation: "There was to be no possibility of a confrontation with British intelligence."[28] With these terms in mind, the Mossad activated a team in England which scrutinized Vanunu and found that he was attracted to one of its female members. Capitalizing on his susceptibility to her charms, the woman befriended Vanunu and lured him to Italy for a tryst, where the Mossad bundled him into a van, tranquilized him, and deposited him on a ship bound for Israel. A closed-court trial was subsequently held in Jerusalem, one that resulted in a controversial punishment, namely, Vanunu's relegation to solitary confinement for treason. As to the Mossad, it was yet another example of the agency accomplishing its mission quickly and without incident, but also one that raised profound moral questions since it was, and remains today, illegal for the Mossad to kidnap an Israeli citizen on foreign soil.

In the ensuing chapters, the covert missions highlighted in this overview—Operations Eichmann, Wrath of God, Entebbe, Opera, Plumbat, and the abduction of Mordechai Vanunu—are placed in their political contexts and examined in detail. Selected for inclusion because they are, in many respects, emblematic of the Mossad's evolution, the missions illustrate the expanding mandate of the organization, the ethical conflicts inherent in its covert operations, and the significance of technological advancements in contemporary spycraft. The aim is to provide an objective portrait of the Mossad, an agency that has increasingly found itself the target of criticism even as it continues to command the respect of those who recognize the vulnerability of the Jewish state and admire the supreme proficiency the organization has demonstrated in its efforts to protect the nation from harm.

Part One

Operation Eichmann

Introduction

It was May 1960, and the city of Buenos Aires was humming with activity. Preparations were under way for Revolution Day, a public holiday in Argentina, and the upcoming celebration promised to be even more extravagant than those of the past. This year it would be commemorating the one hundred fifty-year anniversary of the nation's transition from a monarchy to a republic, a point of pride that, for the past several months, had inspired the government to promote the event as an international affair. And the world was certainly listening. Delegations from around the globe were descending on the capital city to pay tribute to the democracy and share in its festivities. But what Argentine officials did not know is that another group of foreigners had also entered Buenos Aires and for an entirely different purpose, one that was truly hair-raising.

Unlike the event's planners with their focus on nineteenth-century Argentine history, the latter's attention was fixed on a more modern, and horrendous, occurrence: the slaughter of Jews during World War II. A Mossad team, it had slipped into the city to perform "one of the most difficult operations ever undertaken," in the words of Zvi Malkin, a participant in the project.[1] Like his collaborators, Malkin was banking on the holiday hubbub to serve as a distraction, drawing attention away from the team's comings and goings.

As to the mission's objective, the Mossad planned to kidnap a former Nazi official who had fled to Argentina after the war and smuggle him to Israel. Once he was behind bars in Tel Aviv, Israeli authorities would grill him about his wartime deeds, along with the whereabouts of his accomplices who had likewise managed to elude justice. Afterward, he would stand trial in Jerusalem, thereby being held publicly accountable for his crimes against humanity. First, though, he had to be abducted and transported in total secrecy to the Middle East, with this constituting an extraordinary challenge by any measure. The Mossad, however, was up to the task.

In recent weeks, Israeli operatives had been stealing in and out of Argentina, meticulous in their preparations for the capture of their prey. Nothing could be left to chance, since an unforeseen event could derail the precisely timed kidnapping, expose the Mossad's illegal project, and trigger an international incident. For that matter, the Mossad, together with the Israeli government, could face awkward consequences even in the absence of such a disruption. "[I]f the operation was successful," says Isser Harel, the scheme's mastermind, "there was still the danger of our being charged with having violated the sovereignty of a friendly state."[2] In the end, though, Israeli Prime Minister David Ben-Gurion deemed the mission to be worth the gamble since it could lead to the apprehension of Adolf Eichmann, a prominent figure in the Third Reich and the man who orchestrated the liquidation of millions of Jewish men, women, and children. As well, it could return the attention of the Israeli public to the Holocaust, the mass execution having been eclipsed by more recent developments in the Middle East, events that threatened the existence of the Jewish state itself. Then, too, the operation, if successful, could foster interagency respect for the Mossad, a boon for the young organization that had yet to demonstrate its virtuosity on the world stage. To be sure, it would be of both practical and symbolic value if the State of Israel, through its premier intelligence agency, were to seize and bring to justice the notorious Adolf Eichmann.

To fully appreciate the magnitude of the task faced by the Mossad in its quest to track down and apprehend the elusive war criminal, it will serve us well to begin with a brief examination of Eichmann himself. In the chapter that follows, three periods of his life will be revisited: his undistinguished years as a young adult, his subsequent rise as a National Socialist and architect of the Final Solution, and his postwar years spent secretly, and in relative poverty, in South America. The aim is to achieve an incisive understanding both of the man and of the challenges he presented to the Mossad in the course of its audacious mission to ensnare him, the amoral and obedient Nazi official widely regarded as the quintessence of evil.

1
Adolf Eichmann: The Man, the Manhunt

Long before he became a lieutenant colonel in the SS, a master of the logistics of genocide, and ultimately a prime focus of the Mossad, Karl Adolf Eichmann had been an aimless and unremarkable man. Born on March 19, 1906, in Solingen, Germany, he and his Lutheran parents moved to Austria a few years later, where he enrolled in the Kaiser-Franz-Josef School, the same institution from which Adolf Hitler had previously graduated.[1] Here, Eichmann's academic performance was far from stellar, with the question remaining as to whether he actually graduated. What is known is that he subsequently attempted to become a mechanic but dropped out of the training program. Also known is that a business venture with his father came next, and that it, too, proved unsuccessful. In fact, it would not be until Eichmann was twenty-two years old that he would land a job that endured, that of a traveling salesman for the Vacuum Oil Company, although he would not advance in the firm and would respond with indifference when the company terminated him five years later.[2] From such particulars about Eichmann's background, it is evident that his early adult life was anything but remarkable—until, that is, he discovered National Socialism.

It was in the spring of 1932 that Eichmann, like scores of young adults, joined the Nazi Party, an organization that was to his liking perhaps because it catered to his limitations. Tightly-structured and highly-regulated, it was one in which he could preserve his standing, and even advance it, largely by toeing the line. Also a plus, the party did not require that he spend a great deal of time engaged in critical thinking. More the opposite: it indoctrinated him into its simplistic political ideology, dictating to him the ideas he would embrace and thereafter espouse. It even furnished him with a community of comrades, like-minded men and women who, to his further advantage, displayed a distinctive mode of conduct he could adopt as his own. In short, the Nazi Party offered the faltering underachiever the conditions for his own reinvention, a fresh start in his heretofore dull and ineffectual existence.

"From a humdrum life without significance and consequence the wind had blown him into History, as he understood it," writes political theorist Hannah Arendt, "into a Movement that always kept moving and in which somebody like him—already a failure in the eyes of his social class, of his family, and hence in his own eyes as well—could start from scratch and still make a career."[3] Certainly Eichmann wasted no time ingratiating himself into the Party, complying with its directives and deferring without exception to his superiors. And he did more. Sensing the career prospects that lay in the Reich's escalating anti–Semitism, he set to work acquainting himself with the Yiddish and Hebrew languages. Along the same lines, he studied Jewish traditions and even scoured Europe for Jewish settlements into which he could insinuate himself, his aim being to scrutinize them at close range. In time, moreover, his labors bore fruit. Nine years later, in the summer of 1941, Eichmann's familiarity with Jewish life alongside his subservience to the regime and his compulsive traits—he had always been a martinet, the proverbial stickler for details—prompted the highest tier of the Nazi Party to select the thirty-five-year-old man to organize the Final Solution.

In addition to such tasks as confiscating Jewish-owned property, Eichmann now became responsible for systematizing the transport of millions of Jews and other "undesirables" to concentration camps and ensuring their extermination with Zyklon-B gas. It was a momentous assignment but one that he was quick to embrace, that of ensuring, from beginning to end, the ease and efficiency of the Third Reich's mass murder machine. "Eichmann took on his new job with characteristic vigor," says Neal Bascomb. "The more Jews he brought to the extermination camps, the better he looked to his superiors."[4]

As for his approach to the gruesome task, it was thoroughly businesslike and coldly efficient. "Eichmann managed genocide in the way that the director of a multi-national corporation manages production and distribution of [a] product," writes David Cesarini, "calibrating the supply of raw material to the capacity of [the] plant, monitoring output and quality controls and assuring prompt delivery."[5]

Certainly Eichmann was outstanding at his job. Perhaps more than any Nazi official other than the Führer himself, his deeds made possible the annihilation of European Jewry, an undertaking he often performed while sitting at his desk, far removed from the suffering and carnage he choreographed with such finesse.

"I spent years searching his personal history to find something that might explain why he became what he was," writes Simon Wiesenthal. "I didn't find anything."[6] Eichmann, he says, was not known to have had antagonistic encounters with Jewish people when he was a young man nor did he appear to have been inordinately anti–Semitic when he joined the Nazi Party. If anything, he was a grotesque exaggeration of the "organization man," an insecure drone who identified with, and vowed his allegiance to, an autocratic political entity while remaining oblivious to the moral ramifications of its aberrant principles and practices. As for feelings of pity or remorse that may have threatened to impede his job performance, he appears to have suppressed them, assuming, of course, he was capable of experiencing them at all. "Eichmann's great strength was that he treated the Jewish problem unemotionally," writes Wiesenthal. "He was the most dangerous man of all—a man with no human feeling."[7] The Nazi leader did, however, possess ambition. "Eichmann pursued the industrialised mass murder with great personal commitment," according to Zvi Aharoni and Wilhelm Dietl, the Final Solution being the only mission to which he appears to have devoted his energies wholeheartedly in the course of his lifetime.[8] It should come as no surprise, then, that his newfound demeanor, one that abounded with conceit, deflated in May of 1945 when the Allies brought to an end his lethal venture, with the former official reverting to the rudderless, unassuming man he had been prior to his empowerment by the fascist regime.

Flight to Argentina

At the war's end, American troops seized Eichmann and delivered him to a prisoner-of-war facility near the German city of Ulm. But there was a problem: the Americans did not realize who they had in their hands, nor, for that matter, could they have been expected to know so soon after Germany's defeat. At this juncture, the Allies were still collecting the facts about the Final Solution, with the name and physical appearance of its principal organizer not yet being known. Then, too, Eichmann told his jailers he was a colonel in the German army whose name was Adolf Barth, an alias he lifted from a local grocer.[9] The result was that his captors did not implement special measures to prevent his escape nor did they transfer him to a more secure facility. And, in due course, the foreseeable occurred. "Eichmann slipped away from the POW camp and disappeared," writes Ruth Sachs. "No massive search ensued for the escaped prisoner."[10]

Like numerous Nazi war criminals before him, Eichmann promptly went into hiding. Leaving behind his wife, Vera, and their three young sons—Klaus, Horst, and Dieter—he assumed the name Otto Heninger and passed himself off as a lumberjack and a chicken farmer in out-of-the-way German villages for the next few years.[11] Then, in 1950, he took to the road once again, this time bound for Italy. It was a country he would reach by means of a "ratline," a transnational escape network concocted for ex–Nazis on the lam.[12] Of the lines that still existed, Eichmann chose the "convent route," the one preferred by former SS officers and headed by Alois Hudal.[13] A Catholic bishop and fervent National Socialist, Hudal's extensive set-up furnished ex–Nazis with fabricated documents along with a web of monks and nuns to protect the fugitives from discovery. And Eichmann made use of Hudal's services, including the latter. "*En route* he was discreetly accommodated in monasteries and convents," says Cesarini.[14] The fugitive would not remain cloistered for long, however.

Taking a cue from those who operated the ratline, Eichmann decided to seek sanctuary nearly seven thousands miles away in Argentina. An unorthodox destination on the face of it, the draw was the receptiveness of its president, Juan Perón, who had long been infatuated with Hitler's radical ideology and was eager to welcome to Argentina those who had pledged their loyalty to the Nazi Party. Yet political sympathies were only a part of the picture. Perón was also an ambitious and opportunistic politician who knew that researchers in Nazi Germany had made remarkable strides in numerous fields and he was keen to exploit their knowledge. "Perón wanted to secure the immigration of Nazi scientists and engineers to benefit his country's military research and to promote industrialization," writes Bascomb.[15] For such reasons, his administration secretly arranged for the fascist émigrés to make the passage to its shores, among them the death camp physician Josef Mengele and the SS leader Klaus Barbie, although the latter pair would eventually resettle in Paraguay and Bolivia, respectively.

In all, officials in a handful of South American nations knowingly permitted an estimated thirty thousand ex–Nazis to enter and remain within their borders.[16] As it happened, Adolf Eichmann would be among the last to do so, after, of course, he had managed to exit Italy.

To make sure he absconded without incident, a Franciscan monk in the northern Italian city of Genoa secured for Eichmann fabricated identification papers through the Vatican, a backroom deal during which the name Ricardo Klement became the fugitive's permanent alias.[17] With these documents in hand, Eichmann proceeded to dupe the International Committee of the Red Cross into issuing him a refugee passport, the organization's staff believing the Church documents to be indisputable and thus dispensing with the customary background check. Then came the final affront: the fugitive persuaded a Catholic refugee group, unaware of his true identity, to pay for his passage by sea to Argentina. "Few SS men were better placed than Eichmann to know how to manipulate false papers and how to work the immigration systems of sovereign states and international refugee agencies," writes Cesarani.[18] And so it was that the engineer of the Final Solution boarded the *Giavanna C*, an emigrant ship, on July 17, 1950, at the port of Genoa.[19] After stopovers on the Iberian and African coasts, the ocean liner docked in Buenos Aires nearly a month later, on July 14, 1950.[20] At long last, Eichmann had severed his ties with Europe, a continent to which he would never return.

Life in South America

Upon disembarking, he felt reborn. "From being a shadow," he later said, "I was now a man again."[21] With only thirty dollars to his name, the forty-four-year-old fugitive presented himself to Argentine immigration officials as an unmarried refugee who had been born in Italy and brought up in the Catholic faith. In addition, he told officials that he was fluent in English, German, and Italian, and added that he was a skilled technician.[22] And the authorities, accepting his presentation at face value, granted him entry into the country without further inquiry.

In keeping with an arrangement that had been prepared in advance, a man by the name of Horst Carlos Fuldner approached Eichmann at this stage of the resettlement process, welcomed him to Buenos Aires, and set about fashioning the émigré's new life. Described by Guy Walters as "no model of rectitude," Fuldner was a German-Argentine banker who had served as an SS captain under Heinrich Himmler in Germany and subsequently befriended Juan Perón.[23] Now a top figure in Argentina's ex–Nazi underground, Fuldner secured lodging for Eichmann in Buenos Aires, on top of which he gave him a position in a duplicitous firm that Fuldner had himself founded. "He owned CAPRI," reports the German newsmagazine *Der Spiegel*, "a company that planned hydroelectric power plants where many Nazis were employed."[24] At this company, Eichmann's immediate supervisor was Armin Schoklitsch, a one-time SS leader linked to Heinrich Himmler.[25] And Schoklitsch was not the only such figure. "The upper echelon at CAPRI," writes Uki Goñi, "was a veritable Who's Who of Third Reich technocrats."[26] Regarding the business itself, the company made sure to deliver the hydroelectric services it advertised so as to avoid unwelcome scrutiny from Nazi hunters. It did, after all, employ over three hundred German émigrés, a figure alone that could attract suspicion.[27]

During the next three years, Eichmann worked for CAPRI without pause, even relocating to a town seven hundred miles away in order to continue doing so. In terms of his job performance, he carried out his role adeptly as the supervisor of a group of workers even though his relationships with the other employees were rather chilly. "Fellow workers recall that he was quiet and appeared unsociable," says Cesarini.[28] But countering Eichmann's aloofness on the job was his enduring attachment to his wife, Vera, who, along with their three sons, left Austria at this time to join him in South America. It was, by all accounts, a period of renewal and stability for the Eichmanns, with the couple bringing into the world their fourth son, Ricardo, during their stay in this remote, mountainous region of Argentina. Their favorable circumstances were not to last, however. In 1953, the hydroelectric company became entangled in financial troubles, the result being that the expatriate family had little choice but to move to Buenos Aires and into a lifestyle that Adolf Eichmann found both tedious and daunting.[29]

Settling in a district of the capital city where Josef Mengele also had a home, albeit a far more sumptuous one, Eichmann lunched with his wartime acquaintance from time to time at a German café. During such get-togethers, Eichmann's postwar angst was palpable. "Mengele found that Eichmann exuded an aura of fear and sensed that he was a broken man," writes Walters.[30] Not surprisingly, it was an apprehension, a suspiciousness, that infused the Eichmann household as well. "The cardinal rule in the family was: keep your mouth shut."[31] The last thing the fugitive wanted was to be noticed, his own continued existence being the preeminent concern of the man who had ensured that untold numbers of European Jews would not be afforded the same fundamental human right.

Lying low and continuing to pass himself off as Ricardo Klement for the remainder of the 1950s, Eichmann struggled to make ends meet. He worked as a foreman for a trucking company, a manager of a rabbit farm that went out of business, and a manual laborer at a warehouse that stored gas appliances. He also held positions at a fruit juice company and an auto parts store, and he opened a fabric shop and a laundry, both of which failed. At one point, he even strove to become a gaucho, which is not as far-fetched as it might seem given that horseback-riding was one of his few leisurely interests. The fact is, the draftsman of the Final Solution fared poorly when he was on his own and living as Ricardo Klement, the immigrant and everyman, the only position in Argentina that brought him any measure of success having been his initial one at CAPRI, the pro–Nazi firm. When that job fizzled, a period of bleakness ensued, one that lasted several years and was reminiscent of Eichmann's early adult years when he lacked a sense of identity, direction, and purpose.

Bleak, too, was the tone of the Eichmann household, emotional strain being constant and familial relationships, tense. Among the complaints were those of the sons, whose criticism centered on the regimentation that marked their days.

"Our father was very correct," says Klaus, the oldest son. "[E]verything had to be just so, everything had to be in exact order."[32] A compulsivity that had served the senior Eichmann well when he was scheduling cattle cars to carry Jews to the slaughterhouse, the same trait, in his present circumstances, served only to alienate his loved ones in what was, for all practical purposes, his South American safe house. And this brings us to the family's living arrangements in Argentina.

The Eichmanns' homes were invariably inadequate, being too small to comfortably accommodate the family of six and situated in neighborhoods that were less than desirable. Certainly this was the case in the late 1950s when the family settled in the town of Olivos, a scruffy suburb of Buenos Aires with careworn houses and streets of dirt. Yet Eichmann seems to have been amenable to living in such impoverished, out-of-the way locales, his adaptability in this regard contrasting with the much larger number of Hitler's former minions who insisted on basking in splendor in Argentina. The question is why he was so acquiescent in this regard, and the answer may perhaps be found in the comparative anonymity of such settings. That is to say, while it is easy to assume that Eichmann's humble living conditions were due solely to his meager earnings, it is also plausible that he believed such unremarkable circumstances would be less likely to attract the attention of Nazi hunters. If this was his assumption, however, then he was mistaken, since it was while he was living in Olivos that his oldest son, Klaus, bursting with braggadocio, sparked a chain of events that would plant the family firmly on the Mossad's radar screen and lead to an intriguing three-year manhunt. It was an endeavor that would forever change the face of the Israeli intelligence agency.

The Quest for Eichmann

The year was 1957. Adolf Eichmann was toiling at one of his nondescript jobs when Klaus, now in his early twenties, began dating a young woman by the name of Sylvia Hermann who lived with her parents in a predominantly gentile neighborhood in Olivos. Because she had not told him otherwise, Klaus assumed that Sylvia and her parents were gentiles, a belief that was, to say the least, wide of the mark. Not only were the young woman's parents German Jews, but the Nazis had imprisoned her father, Lothar, in Dachau in the 1930s because of his antifascist activities. And there was more: the Gestapo had beaten the elder Hermann so brutally that he was left with permanent damage, most notably blindness that was nearly total. Yet despite his ordeal, the senior Hermann's spirit remained unbroken, his aversion to the Nazi apparatus, if anything, intensifying as a result of the savage treatment he had suffered as a political prisoner. Klaus, however, was unaware of these harrowing features of Hermann's past, the upshot being that the younger man, a second-generation proponent of the vanquished Nazi Party, did not hesitate to voice his political opinions in the Hermann household presumably in the belief that he was speaking to a sympathetic audience.

"Klaus Eichmann visited Sylvia's home on various occasions, and made strongly anti–Semitic remarks," writes Uki Goñi.[33] Among Klaus' odious comments was his complaint that "the Nazis could not complete the extermination of the Jews."[34] Alongside his advocacy of genocide, he also boasted that his father had been a top official in the German military during the war. A position of great importance, Klaus said it had obliged the family to travel to several European countries in the course of the conflict, Occupied Poland among them. Yet Klaus' words, particularly as they pertained to his family, were at odds with his actions. Notwithstanding the pride with which he spoke about his loved ones, most of all his father, he kept his family at a distance from his girlfriend and her parents. "Sylvia was never invited to the young man's home," says Goñi.[35] Even more curious, Klaus would not tell her where he lived, nor did he share with her the fact that he and his father had different surnames, the latter still using the alias Ricardo Klement. As the war criminal's son had been trained to do, he took care not to divulge anything of substance about his family's circumstances. But although he succeeded in lowering a veil of secrecy over this side of his life, his caginess did not go unnoticed by Lothar Hermann, a retired attorney who was well-acquainted with the art of subterfuge. And, indeed, the former lawyer would find himself recalling, a year and a half later, the young man's overabundance of caution.

By this time, Sylvia and Klaus had dissolved their relationship and the Hermann family had moved to the town of Colonel Suárez, southwest of the capital. One morning as Sylvia was reading the newspaper aloud to her father, she shared with him an article about a war crimes trial that was being held in Germany. In the account, mention was made of a prominent National Socialist, Adolf Eichmann, who, the text explained, had been the architect of the Final Solution and was still at large. Lothar Hermann was thunderstruck. Until this moment, he had never known the name of this man. Now, however, he grasped the connection between Klaus and Adolf Eichmann, a familial relationship that accounted for the younger man's intense anti–Semitism, his refusal to tell Sylvia where he lived or introduce her to his parents, and his depiction of his father as a high-flying Nazi personage who had crisscrossed the European continent on matters of immense importance to the regime. The pieces of the puzzle falling into place, Hermann hurried into action.

A sensible man experienced in the ways of the political world, Hermann made a shrewd calculation early on, namely, the decision not to share his suspicions with the German embassy in Buenos Aires or with Argentine authorities. Knowing there were government officials in both Germany and Argentina who were well-disposed toward ex–Nazis and who therefore might be inclined to warn them about their impending arrests, he was determined to make sure Adolf Eichmann enjoyed no such tip-off.

Mulling over his options, Hermann decided to post a letter to a gentleman in Germany who, according to the newspaper article, was involved in the prosecution of war criminals. This fellow, in turn, passed the letter to Fritz Bauer, an antifascist lawyer, a public prosecutor in the German state of Hesse, and a man who, like Hermann, was both Jewish and a former victim of the Nazi regime. Predictably, Bauer proved eager to join in the pursuit of Eichmann, thus setting into motion what would turn out to be a three-year struggle to deliver justice to the nefarious war criminal.

The German attorney began by dispatching to Hermann a packet of materials to be used in verifying that the suspect was, first and foremost, the right man. Among the contents were photographs of Eichmann, a list of his distinguishing characteristics, and a description of his voice. At this juncture, Bauer was unaware that Hermann was largely blind. But no matter; Sylvia, whose vision was intact, planned to help identify the war criminal. Although neither she nor Lothar had ever met Klaus' father, the two were confident they could make an accurate appraisal as to whether he was the egregious coordinator of the Final Solution.

"Hermann and his daughter," writes Cesarini, "undertook the arduous journey to the capital," Buenos Aires being four hundred miles from their home in Colonel Suárez at a time when the nation's roadways were still quite primitive.[36] Arriving in the city, their first hurdle was to obtain the Eichmanns' address, an obstacle they overcame when Sylvia managed to wheedle it out of one of Klaus' friends. The Hermanns then traveled to the Eichmanns' residence in a ramshackle neighborhood of Olivos, where Sylvia had a rather astringent encounter with Klaus' parents.

When she knocked on the door and introduced herself as one of Klaus' friends, a standoffish middle-aged woman confirmed, if haltingly, that it was indeed the house in which the young man lived. As the woman was speaking, a man took shape behind her in the doorway. Asked if he was Klaus' father, the man, after a long pause, responded gruffly in the affirmative.[37] As to his presentation, the man's face, body, voice, and demeanor matched the description of Adolf Eichmann. And this, for Hermann, was "proof enough," says Cesarini. "[H]e sent a letter to Bauer with the address in Olivos."[38]

In Frankfurt, the arrival of the Hermann's verification presented a new challenge for Bauer, to wit, what to do with this volatile information. Like

Lothar, he harbored doubts about the integrity of Argentine and German officials when it came to ex–Nazis. He therefore decided to share his findings with the Israeli government, the Jewish state having the most to gain by ensuring that no leaks occurred. To this end, he sent a letter to the Foreign Ministry in Jerusalem divulging that Eichmann had been located. Dated September 19, 1957, the message stated only that the fugitive had been spotted in Argentina; it revealed nothing else, neither the witnesses' names nor Eichmann's address.[39] Bauer thought it wise to wait until he had forged a bond with his Israeli complement before disclosing such sensitive information.

In the ensuing days, the upper strata of the Israeli government, intrigued by Bauer's communique, decided to designate Isser Harel as the nation's collaborator in the case. Being the director of the country's premier intelligence agency, the Mossad, Harel was judged to be the most appropriate person for the task. It would not be an uncomplicated project, however. From the start, the Mossad chief would encounter stumbling blocks, the first centering on the accuracy of the sighting itself. Although Fritz Bauer's reputation was sterling, he was offering to the Mossad the eyewitness accounts of two unnamed civilians whose reliability had not been established and the agency found this state of affairs troubling. "[T]he Israelis had received many tips concerning Eichmann's whereabouts," says Walters, "all of which had led to naught."[40] Indeed, erroneous reports of Eichmann's presence had previously arrived from Syria, Egypt, Kuwait, Austria, Switzerland, and Germany. This meant, then, that it would fall upon the Mossad to travel to South America and confirm that the suspect was in fact Adolf Eichmann, a complicated, time-consuming task that raised the question of whether the organization should use its resources for such a purpose. It was a question that touched upon a more fundamental, and contentious, matter already brewing within the agency; that is, its proper role at this stage of its evolution.

Within the ranks of the organization was a knot of members who believed the Mossad would be wrong-headed to hunt down Adolf Eichmann, strong-willed opponents who conveyed their disapproval quite heatedly at times.[41] The agency's function, they argued, was not to pursue offenders from World War II, most of all at a time when Egypt, which flanked Israel, posed a grave threat to the Jewish state. National security, they insisted, should remain the Mossad's focus, with its funds being used exclusively to ensure the country's safety and survival. "If the decision was taken to bring Eichmann to Israel," says Cesarini, "it would tie up resources."[42] Yet side by side with these critics were those who believed the agency could effectively monitor the Arab states while, at the same time, broadening its scope of operations to collar a principal perpetrator of the Holocaust. And while both arguments had their merits, the latter position ultimately prevailed. So it was that Harel proceeded with the Eichmann case, thereby launching the Mossad's permanent transformation into a far more expansive entity. It would not be a smooth conversion, however, as illustrated by the start-and-stop nature of the investigation that led to the official Eichmann mission.

To activate the inquiry, Harel sent a member of Israel's security services to Germany in November of 1957 for the purpose of acquiring more detailed material from Bauer. A profitable meeting, the German attorney furnished the Israeli representative with reams of information, including Eichmann's address in Olivos.[43] Three months later, however, when the Mossad dispatched an agent to the Argentine suburb to scout the neighborhood and inspect the Eichmann residence, the operative was taken aback by what he discovered. Anticipating an opulent estate—conventional wisdom held that Adolf Eichmann, like other high-flying Nazi lynchpins, had fled Europe with a fortune pilfered from the Jews—the agent instead found himself standing in a seedy neighborhood staring at a shoddy bungalow. "The poverty-stricken suburb of Olivos, the unpaved street, and the wretched little house," says Harel, "could in no way be reconciled with our picture of the life of an SS officer of Eichmann's rank."[44] Forgoing further investigation, the operative, convinced an error had been made, flew back to Israel empty-handed while Adolf Eichmann remained in his Olivos home, unsuspected and untouched. The case subsequently fell into a slump on the assumption it had reached a dead end.

As the record reveals, it would be those outside the Mossad who would struggle most persistently to keep the inquiry moving forward, with the two leading figures in this effort being the same pair who started the ball rolling in the first place, Lothar Hermann and Fritz Bauer. In 1958, the indefatigable Hermann notified the Mossad that he had discovered that Eichmann had used a false surname, Clement, when applying for electrical utilities at the house in the Buenos Aires suburb of Olivos. Then, in 1959, Bauer informed the Mossad that he had found that Eichmann had adopted the pseudonym Ricardo Klement after the war, and, furthermore, the name was still being used by a German immigrant in Buenos Aires. To the principals in the investigation, most importantly Isser Harel, the uncanny similarity of these findings could only mean that Eichmann, under the aliases Clement and Klement, was alive and living in the Argentine capital—or at least he had been living in the faraway city.

The fact is, three years had passed since Lothar Hermann had sent his original letter to Bauer, the one bringing the case to life, and it was possible, even likely, that Eichmann had since moved to another location as Nazis-in-hiding were wont to do. If this were the case, it would mean the Mossad had made a mess of it, that it had failed to act with sufficient haste to nab one of the most wanted fugitives in the world. And Harel was painfully aware of the potential fall-out of such a debacle. So it was that the Mossad chief, humiliation looming, once again immersed himself in the Eichmann affair so as to ensure that his agency succeeded in capturing the war criminal. Harel's diligence now bordered on obsessiveness.

Bounding into action, the official's first order of business was to determine if the Mossad, in its inertia, had lost track of the ex–Nazi, and, if so, to reestablish the fugitive's whereabouts. With this aim in mind, Harel secured the expertise of a seasoned operative and investigator, Zvi Aharoni, who touched down in Buenos Aires on a chilly morning in May 1960, and set about searching for the target. Within days, moreover, he had a breakthrough. The operative discovered that the Eichmann family had moved, only three weeks earlier, from the town of Olivos to an even poorer district of Buenos Aires known as San Fernando. In accordance with Mossad procedure, Aharoni promptly sent a coded message to Tel Aviv notifying the agency that he was back on the trail of the war criminal. "THE DRIVER IS RED," his terse communiqué stated.[45]

Aharoni now struggled night and day to pinpoint the Eichmann house in San Fernando, scouting the neighborhood in which he suspected the family of living and speaking to its residents. It was in this way that he zeroed in on what he gathered must be the Eichmanns' house, an edifice, according to its neighbors, that was home to a German-speaking family. Equally telling, the tract on which it had been built was similar to the family's previous parcels in Argentina, being "an expanse of marshy, undeveloped land" with unpaved streets, according to Cesarini.[46]

A single-story, brick structure located at 14 Garibaldi Street, what would indeed prove to be the Eichmann house was remarkable for its shabbiness.[47] Resembling a bunker more than a family home, it had a flat roof, a fiberboard door, heavy shutters, and barred windows. It also lacked running water and electricity, and, perhaps by design, stood hundreds of yards away from the other residences in the area. "The house," writes Cesarini, "may have given Eichmann a sense of security because it was far removed from nosy neighbours and gave its occupants a clear field of vision for 360 degrees."[48] If seclusion were his goal, however, then the fugitive had missed the mark, since the dwelling had now entered the sights of the Mossad. And Zvi Aharoni, Eichmann's new nemesis, was fast converging on his prey.

On the morning of March 16, approximately two weeks after Aharoni deplaned in Argentina, he decided to approach the house, the reason being to take a crack at meeting face-to-face with its occupants. Accompanying him would be a Jewish architect, an immigrant from Israel, who had agreed to assist in a real estate masquerade. "[H]e helped me willingly without knowing the real reason for my investigations," says Aharoni.[49]

So it was that the operative and his accomplice, portraying themselves as

1. Adolf Eichmann: The Man, the Manhunt

land developers from the United States, knocked on the front door of the fortress-like structure, whereupon a young woman appeared and, visibly piqued, demanded to know the reason for their visit. Although Aharoni was not aware of it, nor did the woman did tell him, she was, in fact, Adolf Eichmann's daughter-in-law, a state of affairs that may have accounted for her defensiveness. Whatever its cause, the architect, in an effort to lessen her prickliness, began stitching together a fiction about property values in the neighborhood while Aharoni seized the moment for his own purposes. "I triggered the shutter of my secret briefcase camera several times," he says.[50] He was fortunate, moreover, in that he managed to net a serviceable photograph of the woman without her knowledge. All the while, her hostility continued to simmer—the architect's attempts to calm her were in vain—and, worse still, suspicion began to lace her anger. "I decided in favor of a hasty retreat," writes Aharoni.[51]

During the next forty-eight hours, the Mossad agent thrived on adrenalin. Around the clock, he kept the austere dwelling under surveillance, thereby gaining insight into the comings-and-goings of its occupants. Observing the house from various vantage points, he spotted in the yard a "drab and dumpy" middle-aged woman, presumably Vera Eichmann, as well as a boy he believed to be her youngest son, Ricardo.[52] Making use of his camera's telephoto lens, Aharoni studiously recorded these and other sightings on film. In the meantime, the architect, using his professional connections, obtained the registration records of landowners in the neighborhood. It was through these documents, moreover, that Aharoni struck gold. Listed as the owner of the property on Garibaldi Street was Vera Fichmann, a modified version of Vera Eichmann's real name.[53] The operative was now convinced he had the right house.

Then, on March 19, it happened. "On this day I saw him for the first time," says the Mossad agent.[54] Through binoculars, Aharoni watched as the fifty-three-year-old Adolf Eichmann took shape in front of the house on Garibaldi Street, then suddenly disappeared back inside of it. So brief was the episode that the operative did not have time to snap a photograph. But no matter; he had laid eyes on the target, thereby attaining his goal and completing the final leg of his assignment. Elated, he dispatched a message to Tel Aviv. "THE DRIVER IS BLACK," he wrote, a coded phrase meaning he had obtained direct visual confirmation of Eichmann.[55] Aharoni also recommended the next step.

"I suggest that I be permitted to return to Israel soon for the purpose of reporting in full and considering further action."[56] Certainly Isser Harel, upon receiving the communiqué, was in agreement, and the Mossad chief further realized the time had come to notify Prime Minister David Ben-Gurion that the draftsman of the Final Solution had at last been found.

As it stood, Ben-Gurion was already aware that the Mossad had been searching for the war criminal, Harel having discussed the matter with him three months earlier when seeking the prime minister's permission to send Aharoni to Buenos Aires to lead the hunt. Yet this previous meeting had another purpose as well: the Mossad chief needed to know Ben-Gurion's thoughts on how the agency should proceed if and when it found its target. It was imperative that Harel understand the parameters, the boundaries of action, that the head of state considered acceptable in dealing with the war criminal. In this regard, there were three methods of completing the operation and all of them carried formidable risks.

First, the Jewish state could pursue the matter legally, bringing the war criminal to Israel by means of an extradition agreement with the Argentine government and placing him on trial for crimes against humanity. Second, it could proceed illegally, abducting Eichmann without the Argentines' knowledge and transporting him to the Jewish state to face the same legal proceedings. Or third, the Mossad could assassinate him.

As for Ben-Gurion's decision at this point—it was December 1959—he instructed Harel that the Jewish state "should act covertly to bring Eichmann to Israel."[57] Assassination was ruled out for political reasons. Killing the fugitive would mean Israel had prejudged Eichmann and put him to death, an extrajudicial action that could galvanize the nation's critics. More to the point, opponents of the Jewish state could construe the murder as constituting a judge-and-jury approach not unlike the Nazis' own unilateral assault on the Jews of Europe. Extradition was also ruled out because Argentina, a nation known for its embrace of ex–Nazis, could not be counted on to cooperate. Certainly it was possible, even probable, that Eichmann would be tipped off and would vanish once again. Abduction, then, remained the only viable tactic.

Wrapping up his talk with Ben-Gurion, Harel subsequently sought the advice of three other figures in the Israeli government, concerned, as he was, about the legal ramifications of seizing and transporting a fugitive from a foreign land. These advisors consisted of the attorney general, the minister of justice, and the foreign minister, who, at the time, was Golda Meir.[58] The consensus was that Ben-Gurion's preferred method, abduction, held the greatest prospect of success, and that the strategy, although illegal, was morally justifiable. Harel was made to understand that the legal repercussions could be addressed once Eichmann was behind bars in Jerusalem, assuming there were, in fact, such troublesome consequences. At this point, the plan was to pin the kidnapping on a fictitious group of Holocaust survivors, with the Mossad and the Israeli government feigning ignorance of the mission.

Now, in March of 1960, it was time for Harel to confer once more with Ben-Gurion, the sole person in the Israeli government to whom he was accountable. In a private conversation at the prime minister's residence, the Mossad chief disclosed that the intelligence agency's search had succeeded in confirming Eichmann's presence in Argentina and the organization was readying itself for the abduction. "Bring him dead or alive," Ben-Gurion replied.[59] Of course, Harel already knew that the head of state preferred that Eichmann be alive so the Israeli state could mount a "show trial," in the words of Arendt, a widely broadcast event to further educate the public about the Holocaust.[60] "Ben-Gurion said it would be a lesson for the world."[61] So it was that the Mossad chief leapt into action, devising with remarkable speed a mission to bring the war criminal back to the Jewish state and, ultimately, to justice. By any standard, it would be a breathtaking project, an endeavor unlike anything the intelligence agency had heretofore undertaken.

2

Mission: Operation Eichmann

The Mossad's abduction scheme, the aptly named "Operation Eichmann," would unfold nearly eight thousand miles away from the Jewish state in a land that was, to a considerable extent, unfamiliar to the Israeli intelligence agency. A large-scale project, it would also be rather precarious, both technically and politically, and owing to its distinctive nature, labor-intensive. All the same, Isser Harel, undaunted by its formidable character, set about making a list of fundamental components the mission would require, then proceeded to address them.

First, transportation would be essential, most notably rental cars for travel within Buenos Aires and a plane or ship to deliver the prey, Adolf Eichmann, to Israel. Second, safe houses in the Argentine city would be needed, both for the team and its prisoner, with the latter's quarters approximating a detention cell. And third, the availability of emergency medical care would be a necessity, since neither the operatives nor their captive would be able to seek medical treatment in the customary fashion in Argentina without jeopardizing the mission. Then, too, the agents would probably find it necessary to tranquilize Eichmann when smuggling him out of the South American nation, the upshot being that the vital signs of the aging fugitive would need to be monitored during such periods of sedation. These and other requirements Harel resolved, at least in principal, as he sketched out the project in broad strokes, the details to be calibrated as more information became available in the ensuing weeks.

Next up, the Mossad chief began casting about for operatives whose talents promised to assure a successful mission. To acquire those most suited to the task, he conferred with Rafi Eitan, a veteran intelligence officer who was currently serving as the Chief of Coordination between the Mossad and Shin Bet, another security agency Harel was overseeing at the moment. Already an iconic figure in Israeli intelligence circles, the thirty-three-year-old Eitan was the right man to ask about such matters. "There had been no one like him for cold-blooded ruthlessness, cunning, an ability to improvise at ferocious speed, an inborn skill at outwitting even the best-laid plan and tirelessly tracking down a quarry," says Gordon Thomas.[1] Enthusiastic about helping the Mossad pin down Eichmann, Eitan was generous is offering suggestions for the team's composition, and the Mossad chief, in turn, gave serious consideration to all of those the venerated officer recommended.

As could be expected, the preponderance of the men and women Eitan proposed were already agents of the Mossad or Shin Bet. Yet he also offered the names of a handful of non-operatives who possessed exceptional skills, some of whom had collaborated with the Mossad or Shin Bet in the past. It was from these candidates that Harel drew up a list of eleven individuals, ten men and one woman, and invited them to take part in the operation. Owing to its illegal and potentially deadly nature, along with its focus on the principal designer of the Final Solution, he did not compel the candidates to participate. He wanted their involvement to be voluntary. And come forward they did. Not only were the eleven willing to serve on the team, they were eager to do so, which perhaps is not surprising given that among their number were Holocaust survivors who still bore on their forearms the identity tattoos they had received in the concentration camps. Their yearning to make accountable Adolf Eichmann, the bureaucrat who had engineered their torture and imprisonment along with the liquidation of their loved ones, was at once personal and intense.

Harel designed the team in such a way as to ensure group cohesiveness, an aim he achieved by reviewing the covert activities of the candidates and, in large measure, selecting those who had previously served together in the Mossad or Shin Bet. Such backgrounds increased the likelihood that the participants knew and trusted one another, which, for Harel, were essential criteria. It was imperative that the team live and work together harmoniously, since personal discord or a lack of trust could compromise the project and spell disaster for everyone involved. For that matter, it could damage the reputation of the State of Israel.

In assembling the team, Harel's first step was to select three people to lead the mission, and the trio he chose possessed impeccable credentials in the intelligence arena. They consisted of the following:

- Rafi Eitan—Commander of the operation and, as previously noted, the intelligence officer who assisted in identifying prospective members for the team. Born on a kibbutz in Palestine to Russian immigrant parents, Eitan boasted a lifetime of experience in the clandestine world. At the age of twelve, he joined the Haganah, a paramilitary organization created for Jewish self-defense. Six years later, he advanced to the role of commando in the Palmach, a guerrilla strike force within the Haganah. Next came a post in Army intelligence, followed by leadership roles in Shin Bet. Known to kill with his own hands those he regarded as enemies of the Jewish people, Eitan was held in high esteem by his colleagues in the Israeli intelligence community.

- Zvi Malkin—associate commander. Born in Poland, Malkin emigrated to Palestine and became a member of the Haganah. He next served in Shin Bet, where, among other tasks, he trained Israeli embassy personnel to detect letter bombs and take defensive action. Described as the "best spy-catcher" in the business, Malkin was respected for his strategic thinking, adeptness at disguises, and proficiency in surveillance techniques.[2]
- Avraham Shalom—deputy commander. Born in Austria, Shalom, as a nine-year-old boy, was attacked by thirty anti–Semites during Kristallnacht. Traumatized, he was left with an aversion to National Socialism and those who embraced it. Emigrating to Palestine with his parents, he joined the Haganah and still later Shin Bet, where he served as a commander in its counterintelligence division. Shalom's expertise centered on planning and logistics.

As to the remaining members, Harel picked eight men and women who possessed the unique skills necessary to execute the multifaceted mission. Most were also endowed with talents above and beyond the ones for which they had been chosen, meaning they could assume additional roles in the project if necessary. Certainly this was a plus, since Operation Eichmann, an intricate endeavor set to unroll on foreign soil, might well encounter unforeseen problems, in which case it would be advantageous to have in place a team distinguished by its versatility. The eight consisted of the following:

- Moshe Tavor. A Lithuanian-born strongman—tall, beefy, bald, and blunt—Tavor's role would be to lend a hand in the abduction itself. A member of the British Army during the war, Tavor subsequently joined the Avengers, a death squad that hunted down and dealt decisively with ex–Nazis. A few years later, he assumed a prominent role in the surveillance of Egypt's missile project. Although the straight-talking Tavor agreed to help kidnap Eichmann, he has been quoted as asking, "[W]hy don't we kill the bastard on the spot?"[3]
- Shalom Dani. A Hungarian-born artist and first-rate forger, Dani and his sister, during the Holocaust, escaped from Bergen-Belsen concentration camp using permits he fabricated on scraps of paper. After the war, Dani created documents to help Moroccan Jews resettle in the newly-established State of Israel. Described as "always reserved and calm," he was based in Paris but would slip into Buenos Aires to serve as the forger for the Mossad team.[4]
- Yaacov Gat. Born in Transylvania (Romania), Gat was a former Shin Bet agent who was selected for the mission because he spoke Spanish fluently and was experienced in creating and maintaining support structures for covert missions. His job would include procuring safe houses and performing vehicle maintenance. Like Dani, Gat was known for being "cool-headed," a desirable trait in an operative.[5]

- Yehudith ("Judith") Nissiyahu. Born in the Netherlands, Nissiyahu was a devoted Orthodox Jew and the Mossad's top female agent. In Operation Eichmann, her role would be to use her gender to help create a façade of normalcy at the team's safe houses. Otherwise, the occupants would be exclusively male, thereby inviting suspicion.
- Zvi Aharoni. Born in Germany, Aharoni was a former investigator with Shin Bet who improved and expanded the organization's fact-finding division. As noted, he was the Mossad agent who located Eichmann in San Fernando, Argentina. Aharoni's role in the forthcoming stage of the operation would include that of interrogator, he being the only member of the team who spoke Eichmann's native language, German, and the only one who would be permitted to talk to the fugitive in the course of the mission.
- Yitzhak Nesher. Born in Czechoslovakia, Nesher was a young man noted for, and deliberately used for, his innocent face and guileless demeanor. In the present operation, he would pose as an extravagant European businessman traveling in Buenos Aires, a pretense that would allow him to obtain essential materials for the team, including a villa, safe houses, automobiles, and various types of equipment.
- Yona Elian. A prominent physician in Tel Aviv, Elian's task would be to provide on-site medical care if the team or its captive required it. He would also examine Eichmann's physical body for identifying features, as well as tranquilize and monitor the health of the captive.
- Efraim Ilani. An expert locksmith and scholar whose knowledge of the Argentine capital and its customs was encyclopedic, Ilani's duties would include serving as the sole point of contact between the team and the Israeli embassy in Buenos Aires.

In addition to the team's eleven agents, Harel decided that he, too, would travel to Buenos Aires and remain in the city throughout the undertaking. A leader whose concern for his subordinates had always been paramount, he did not wish to place his operatives in a politically awkward position in a distant land. Realizing that international complications could arise in the course of the mission, Harel believed that such a possibility, however slight, called for his presence alongside his agents. "[I]mmediate decisions at the top level would need to be made," write Michael Bar-Zohar and Nissim Mishal. "It was therefore crucial that the Israelis be led by someone who could make political decisions if necessary."[6]

Determined, as Harel was, to keep in close contact with his team members while in the Argentine capital, he set to work crafting a rather industrious scheme to ensure he would have unfettered access to them. The result: an extensive roster of locations in the sprawling city, most of them cafés in which he could linger without inviting suspicion. "Every member of the team was given an itinerary of the cafés in Buenos Aires which Harel would use as a kind of mobile headquarters," explains Stewart Steven.[7] It was the official's intention to rendezvous frequently with his operatives at these locations, in this way receiving updates on the team's progress while furnishing it with instructions for further action. If the agents were to encounter an intractable obstacle or find themselves in a crisis, they could get in touch with him night or day at one of his scheduled stops across the restive city. It was an inspired arrangement, albeit a taxing one for the Mossad leader, since it would require him to be in nearly constant motion.

Having settled on the basic structure of the mission, lined up the team, and devised a method of communicating with it, Harel began pondering how best to utilize the group before its historic journey to South America. "I decided," he writes, "that it should be divided into two sections: an advance party to go to the target site and establish that Ricardo Klement [Adolf Eichmann] was still there and that conditions for carrying out the capture were reasonably good, and the main body to be primed and ready for action but waiting for the advance party's call before setting out."[8] And so it began.

Buenos Aires, April 25–May 5, 1960. The advance team that Harel dispatched was essentially a reconnaissance squad composed of four operatives: Zvi Aharoni, Avraham Shalom, Yaacov Got, and Efraim Ilani. The strategy was for three of the agents to travel to 14 Garibaldi Street in San Fernando to verify Eichmann's presence, while the fourth, Ilani, would break away from the pack and function independently. He would, in effect, serve as the point of contact between the advance team and the Israeli Embassy in Buenos Aires, through which he would communicate with the Mossad in Tel Aviv. "That was an immensely important role," says Aharoni, "because we were not allowed to go near the embassy, not even to call it on the telephone."[9]

Renting a car the following day, Aharoni, Shalom, and Gat waited until nightfall to drive to San Fernando, the reason for their delay having to do less with observing Eichmann and more with avoiding being observed themselves. Reconnoitering under cover of darkness would help to obscure their movements. What the three did not know is that the fugitive, punctilious as ever, returned home from work at exactly the same time each evening, and it was a time that would correspond to their initial scouting expedition to his neighborhood. And sure enough, the agents, shortly after arriving, spotted Eichmann stepping off a bus and trudging to his house. As to the team's reaction, it was a bit farcical, most notably that of Zvi Aharoni, who was driving the car. It seems he became so *verklempt* that he slammed on the brakes, stalling the engine. "I got out and lifted the bonnet," he recalls, "which is always the best excuse if one stops in the middle of nowhere."[10] Fortunately, the roadside drama did not attract the eye of the war criminal, who continued his walk homeward.

Repeating the reconnaissance procedure the next evening, the operatives once again observed Eichmann at the same time and the same bus stop, a consistency of movement that would make his abduction easier and more assured. With these details in hand, Aharoni established contact with Ilani, who, in turn, cabled the Mossad in Tel Aviv. The agency's prey was still present in San Fernando, Ilani's message stated, adding that conditions for Eichmann's abduction were favorable and further planning could therefore proceed. In keeping with the intelligence agency's arrangement, the reconnaissance team would remain in Buenos Aires and keep Eichmann under surveillance while preparing for the arrival of the full Mossad operational group. In addition, Yitzhak Nesher would now travel to Argentine capital and begin securing safe houses.

Tel Aviv, April 24–April 27, 1960. At Mossad headquarters, mission commander Rafi Eitan and his right-hand man, Zvi Malkin, were tackling further operational challenges during this same period. For starters, they wrestled with a rather intricate piece of business, namely, how to insert the Mossad team into Buenos Aires. "Special care had to be taken to avoid the impression that the group was organized and sent from Israel," says Dennis Eisenberg.[11] Certainly it is true that a single point of departure for all of the operatives, especially one originating in the Jewish state, would be highly incriminating if the team were to be discovered. It would bind the agents to one another and tie them collectively to the Middle Eastern country. Better for them to arrive from diverse foreign cities and on disparate schedules, Eitan and Malkin decided, since this would allow for greater deniability.

Along the same lines, the two operatives devised an escape plan for the team in the event that Operation Eichmann went awry in Argentina. As well, they formulated a separate strategy for departure if the mission proved to be successful. Like the team's method of entry into Buenos Aires, the operatives in both exit scenarios would leave the Argentine city at different times and, in some instances, by different modes of transportation. Furthermore, they would pass through other countries, including those flanking Argentina, rather than travel directly to Israel.

Having settled on the methods of passage to and from Buenos Aires, Eitan and Malkin turned their attention to the equipment that would be needed to perform the mission. Summoning those team members who were still in Tel Aviv, the pair asked them to compile a list of paraphernalia that would be indispensable to the operation, with emphasis on those materials the members would need to carry with them into Buenos Aires. "[S]ince the purchase of certain items in Argentina would likely arouse suspicion," says Malkin, "[we] had to think our way through the operation step by step and day by day."[12] The result was an intriguing inventory, one that included makeup kits, wigs, handcuffs, two-way radios, burglary tools, binoculars, and even a compact laboratory for forging documents.[13] Subsequent to this, the team members came up with false identities and cover stories that would permit them to travel with such gear without raising eyebrows.

Meanwhile, Isser Harel, elsewhere in Tel Aviv, brainstormed about how best to smuggle Eichmann out of Argentina and into the Jewish state. A reliable method had to be devised, otherwise there would be no mission; the question was how to pull off such a daring transport. Conveying Eichmann by sea, Harel realized, would be rife with problems. An ocean voyage, if only because of its length, would render it more likely that Israel's role in the affair would be detected. Such a discovery could occur aboard the ship during its long journey to the Middle East or it could happen in Argentina, where authorities would have several days to investigate the fugitive's disappearance before the vessel docked in Israel. Then, too, a journey by sea would require that Eichmann be sedated for long stretches of time, with this constituting a potential health hazard for a man of his age. And equally disconcerting was the threat of international complications, since Israel would be concealing an abductee aboard an ocean liner that would be docking in the ports of other nations *en route* to the Middle East. If the Jewish state's illegal deed were to be exposed, the Israeli government could expect to face formal objections not only from Argentina but also from the other countries in which the ship had berthed. For these reasons, Harel replaced the nautical notion with a more modern method, one that would be comparatively safe and mercifully swift. "It was masterful," declares Malkin.[14]

Until this moment in the preparatory process, Harel had been unaware that Israel's Ministry of Foreign Affairs was about to send a delegation to Buenos Aires to attend the Revolution Day festivities, Argentina's one hundred fifty-year anniversary celebration. When he did get wind of it, however, he seized the opportunity. Eichmann, he decided, would be flown to Israel. Within a matter of hours, the Mossad chief managed to buttonhole two men, the deputy director and the managing director of an airline, and secure their help. "Not for the first time in an intelligence operation, the national airline, El Al, was pressed into service," says Stewart Steven.[15] The company's role in the Eichmann kidnapping would go down in history as its most audacious contribution to the shadowy world of covert operations.

In short order, Harel persuaded the airline to fly the Israeli delegation to Buenos Aires, this at a time when El Al had no air service to the South American nation. Long distance air travel was still a luxury in 1960 and comparatively few international routes had been established. As for those malcontents within the Israeli government who might be inclined to find fault with such an extravagant means of transport, the Foreign Ministry would contend that its representatives should travel to South America in a high-status manner so as to impress the Argentine leadership and the world at large. The Ministry would further argue that the Jews of Argentina would find it inspirational if representatives from their spiritual homeland were to arrive with such panache. And paralleling this deception, the Mossad would let loose with a tale of its own, namely, that El Al was exploring the prospect of introducing air service to Buenos Aires. The delegates' flight, in this scenario, would be a trial run. Of course, critics of the travel arrangements could not be told the truth about Operation Eichmann or the airline's contribution to it. Subterfuge was essential.

And this would be the case in regard to the flight crew, too. The El Al personnel who would play a vital role in the perilous mission were not to be made aware that they would be doing so. It was an aircrew, moreover, that Harel would have a hand in choosing, the Mossad chief coaxing El Al's top tier into granting him this unheard-of privilege. And his specifications were clear. "He wanted only Israelis to be selected for the flight, cabin, and ground crews," says Neal Bascomb. "They were to be trustworthy and extremely capable."[16] Although there were other requirements as well, the most important one pertained to the plane's departure from Argentina. "The flight crew would also need to be prepared to take off quickly from Buenos Aires and, potentially, to make evasive maneuvers."[17] True to form, the single-minded Harel secured his crew.

The fact is, the Mossad chief's lightning-fast arrangement with the airline was a coup for the fastidious spymaster, a leader whose determination to control the fundamental elements of the transatlantic escape plan was unremitting. Yet his tenacious approach to the El Al agreement came at a cost to the forty-eight-year-old official. "His eyes were bloodshot and his skin slack," says Malkin of the director's appearance after his marathon of meetings with airline executives and government officials.[18] What Harel achieved, however, a guarantee of Eichmann's nearly nonstop conveyance to the Jewish state and into the hands of legal authorities, was, in the Mossad chief's opinion, well worth the exhaustion.[19]

Predictably perhaps, fatigue would become a problem for all of the operatives in the course of the mission, jet lag being one factor and the lengthy stretches of time required to set up the operation in Buenos Aires being another one. Furthermore, the team would need to keep Eichmann under surveillance, with this being an around-the-clock responsibility. For such reasons, some of the operatives, anticipating the weariness that lay ahead, decided to prepare for it. Zvi Malkin was one of them.

In his written account of the mission, *Eichmann in My Hands*, Malkin reveals that he began exercising at a gymnasium in Tel Aviv in the days preceding the mission.[20] He intended to be in suitable shape when he stepped off the plane in South America, stamina being crucial to the mission. But equally critical to Malkin's role, in particular, was his need to be adept at overpowering and restraining Eichmann, since the operative would be one of those to actually abduct the fugitive. Strength, speed, and skill were essential to the task. Accordingly, he cooked up an effective, if unorthodox, strategy to ready himself for the ambush.

The thirty-two-year-old operative, galvanized by the prospect of netting one of the most prominent ex–Nazis in existence, figured it would be best to hone his skills on familiar turf: Mossad headquarters in Tel Aviv. "[A]n office tower on King Saul Boulevard," in the words of Victor Ostrovsky, the building was emblematic of "those gray, bare concrete things popular in Israel."[21] Within its walls, however, the goings-on were anything but colorless, which is why Malkin chose it for his practice site. Here, his deeds—or misdeeds, as it were—would be accepted or at least tolerated; he wouldn't be arrested, at any rate. And this was a legitimate issue, since he intended to rehearse his abduction technique on unsuspecting men and women; specifically, the Mossad's office staff and operations officers.

"I began catching them unawares," writes the inventive agent, "leaping at them as they strolled down the hall whistling or rounding the corner reading a memo, and seizing them round the throat."[22] Women, he discovered, were instructive targets because their gender offered him the chance to fine-tune his movements. Through them, he learned to apply a chokehold that was firm enough to muffle their shouts but not so firm as to produce lasting harm.[23] This was of great importance, moreover, since it was precisely the outcome he hoped to achieve when subjugating Eichmann; muzzling, but not maiming, the fugitive. As for the strength required, Malkin turned to other men for practice, and the beefier the better. "My very favorite subject was a guy named Mikael," he recalls, "a mountain of an agent, 260 pounds of muscle, who soon took to fleeing at the very rumor of my presence in the vicinity."[24] But even as Malkin was refining his skills in these one-on-one encounters, he knew that he would not be acting alone when the time came to seize Eichmann and that he should therefore practice with the other members of the abduction squad. According to the Mossad schedule, he would soon be in a position to do just that, since he and three of his fellow operatives were about to spend a few days together in France in what would be, in effect, the first leg of their journey to Argentina.

Paris, April 28–May 3, 1960. It would be in the Bois de Boulogne, a lush, rambling park situated across the Seine from the Eiffel Tower, that the four men would coordinate and polish their abduction skills. Joining Malkin would be Eitan, along with a pair of team members whose identities have not been reported in public accounts of the mission. Each of these operatives would be playing a part in the Eichmann capture, either a direct role or a supporting one, despite the fact that certain aspects of the procedure had not yet been finalized. In fact, it was to be during the group's five-day interlude in the French capital that the men would iron out such details. So it was that the agents, preparing to put the finishing touches on the ambush plan, rented a Citroén, purchased wine and cheese for a meal *al fresco*, and drove to the park.

"Once a royal hunting preserve," writes Earl Steinbicker, Bois de Boulogne had since become a park beloved by Parisians of all social classes.[25] And for good reason. One of the largest metropolitan parks in the world, it offered a lake for boating as well as a "vast belt of greenery for strolling, cycling, [and] horseback riding."[26] The Mossad agents, however, would not be walking, biking, or riding; they would be snatching one of their own and wrestling him into the back seat of the idling Citroën. A scenario they would rehearse over and again, they would improvise several aspects of it so as to prepare for the unexpected. Malkin, for instance, the one who would actually be taking hold of Eichmann in Argentina, would practice on his teammates as each of them pretended to be the war criminal and reacted in different ways to being seized. To speed up the abduction process, the operatives would time their run-throughs with a stopwatch, shaving off seconds whenever possible.

And the agents' teamwork paid off. By the time they wrapped up their practice sessions, they had vastly increased their pace until they were able to pull off the kidnapping in a mere thirty-five seconds. Impressive, too, was the fact that they were able to repeatedly carry out the coup in a public park and in broad daylight—it was a spring afternoon in Paris—without being noticed by passersby or confronted by the police. This should not be taken to mean that there no close calls, however. Far from it. One daunting incident occurred when Malkin, as he was about to place a chokehold on another team member, heard a fellow operative shout a warning. "I stopped in my tracks just in time to spot a group of jodhpur-clad French people on horseback," Malkin recalls.[27] It was to the men's credit that their attention to their surroundings was such that they were able to avoid being observed by the party of equestrians.

In a similar vein, the operatives were attentive to the details of the San Fernando district of Buenos Aires in which they would be seizing Eichmann. In a stately apartment in a fashionable district of Paris, they pored over street maps of the Argentine capital, paying close attention to the suburb in which the war criminal lived and the area in which he was employed. Eichmann, the Mossad had discovered, worked as an assembly line foreman at a Mercedes-Benz plant southwest of Buenos Aires, a factory whose personnel was composed mainly of German émigrés, among them numerous ex–Nazis.[28] Tellingly, only one Jew was employed at the plant.[29] The agents therefore denoted the factory on the map, along with the fugitive's house on Garibaldi Street, the bus stop from which he disembarked each evening, and the surrounding streets that could be used as getaway routes after they seized him. They also noted secondary features that could prove significant as well, such as the location of a nearby railroad, the presence of which could put an end to the whole enterprise if a train were to block the team's path at a critical moment. It was because Operation Eichmann could be upended by such mundane factors that the four agents were so meticulous in their preparations, working night and day to minimize the possibility of any untoward surprises.

After rehearsing the kidnapping, scrutinizing the maps, and streamlining their plans, the men packed their equipment and set off for their flights to Buenos Aires. It was at this point that they assumed their disguises as non–Israeli citizens. In Malkin's account, he recalls posing as a German named Maxim Nolte, and he adds that his trip to Argentina was wearying.[30] Certainly this is no surprise. From Paris, he flew to Geneva, Switzerland, and from there to Recife, Brazil, before landing in Buenos Aires. A twenty-two hour journey, it was punctuated by punishing air turbulence as if to foreshadow the tumultuous events the Mossad team was about to experience in South America.

Arriving on May 5, 1960, Malkin was heartened to find that most of the other members of the team were already on the ground in the Argentine capital. Besides Harel and nine of the eleven core agents, many more men and women were available behind the scenes to assist, if needed, with various aspects of the operation. In fact, many of them had already contributed to secondary elements of the project since its inception several weeks earlier, even though virtually none of them were aware of its true purpose. As to their number, Dennis Eisenberg, a foreign correspondent and author, has placed it at upwards of twenty people, while a more recent report contends that fifty-six individuals were involved in both Israel and Argentina.[31] Surely the willingness of such a sizable number of men and women to contribute to a Mossad undertaking about which they knew essentially nothing is impressive, and it stands as a testament to their support for, and trust in, the State of Israel's preeminent intelligence agency.

Remarkable, too, was the determination with which the team's logistics experts struggled to rent safe houses and cars in Buenos Aires, an arduous assignment fraught with problems. Again and again, the operatives found that a potential residence, if it was spacious enough to accommodate several Mossad agents—a villa, for example—it invariably came with a staff, including servants, a cook, and a gardener. Often, these people were live-in employees. The Mossad, however, could not permit them onto the premises during the mission, but instead would have to refuse their services. And this, in turn, risked confounding the Argentine real estate broker who would be negotiating the terms of the lease. Given that the logistics operatives, most of all Yitzhak Nesher, were presenting themselves as wealthy foreigners, the broker might be inclined to view with suspicion their decision to eschew an entire household staff. It was a conundrum, to be sure.

It would not be the only quandary, however, as the same operatives came to realize when they tried to get their hands on reliable automobiles. Rental cars were scarce in Argentina, and those that were available tended to be poorly maintained and undependable in a pinch. The rental fees were also exorbitant; so steep, in fact, that purchasing a car was often a sensible alternative. For such reasons, the agents became exasperated as they struggled to complete their preparations.

Ramping up their stress levels, moreover, was the Mossad chief himself. Adamant that no room be left for error, Harel ordered them to secure double the number of houses and cars needed to carry out the mission. "Harel, who was fanatical about detail and ultra-cautious, insisted that there should be a back-up for each house and car," says Cesarini.[32] For the logistics experts, it was, by any measure, a considerable number of business transactions to conclude in a very short period of time.

The operatives, however, were not alone in their anxiety. Harel was himself at wit's end owing to a snag in his setup with El Al Airlines, one that centered on scheduling. It was a hitch that came about because the Israeli airline had never before flown to Argentina and therefore the airport in Buenos Aires would need to make special accommodations for it. Yet this would not be as simple as it appeared at first blush; certainly not as cut-and-dried as Harel and his collaborators at El Al had assumed would be the case. The fact is, the circumstances of the visit—Argentina's colossal anniversary celebration—meant there would be more planes than usual at the airport, thereby increasing the demand for refueling and parking on its aprons. The upshot: El Al, like the airlines of the other nations flying delegates to the festivities, could not choose the dates of its aircrafts' arrivals and departures. Argentine officials who would schedule the flights. And therein lay the problem.

The Mossad had planned to kidnap Eichmann on May 10 and fly him out of Buenos Aires the following day. But Argentine authorities now rolled back the date of the El Al flight to May 19, meaning the operatives would have to keep the fugitive locked up on foreign soil for well over a week. Of course, Harel knew that Eichmann's family might alert law enforcement officials during this stretch, thus raising the chilling specter of a police search for the missing man while the covert team was still on the ground in the South American nation. It was precisely the sort of situation the Mossad chief had tried to avoid, and its last-minute reemergence caused him to become apoplectic. And worsening matters, he could do nothing to alter the schedule. "If he asked the Israeli embassy to try to get the Argentinians to change their timetable," writes Guy Walters, "it would only draw attention to the special flight."[33] Delaying the abduction was also out of the question, since the fugitive might slip through the Mossad's hands if it were to postpone the kidnapping, particularly since the agency was not privy to the Eichmann family's plans for the upcoming national festivities. What

Harel did do, however, was to move back the date of the abduction by one day, to Wednesday, May 11, so as to give his agents more time to complete their preparations. Still, he remained frazzled, his lack of control over the team's air travel leaving him on edge.

Fortunately, the logistics experts who, as previously noted, were inundated with a rush of responsibilities, were about to enjoy a well-deserved respite. This is because they would finally succeed in obtaining seven safe houses for the team and its captive, including back-up residences in case of an emergency. Among the properties was a villa—Harel assigned it the code name *Tira*, or "palace"—which was a roomy estate capable of accommodating a considerable number of residents.[34] *Tira* would serve as the team's base and would contain Eichmann's detention chamber. A second residence, one that likewise contained a fortified room for the ex-Nazi, was reserved as well. And the operatives rented a third house, along with two apartments in Buenos Aires and two standby apartments in the suburbs. As for automobiles, they were able to obtain a handful of vehicles that, while not in prime condition, would suffice for the purposes at hand. And with these tasks behind them, the beleaguered agents attempted to rest, the aim being to restore their energy for the forthcoming capture and confinement of their target.

As the day of the abduction approached, the team tried to unwind but found it difficult. Certain matters were still unsettled, preparations were still incomplete, and two operatives had still not made it into Argentina. Through sheer persistence, however, the team members managed to put the finishing touches on most of the mission's elements, while the pair of remaining members, physician Yona Elian and female operative Yehudith Nissiyahu, finally arrived in Buenos Aires. Whereas the former touched down as scheduled, the latter, faced with an unforeseen twenty-four hour delay at an airport in Spain, arrived on the date of the kidnapping itself. It would be a day unlike any other in the history of the Israeli intelligence agency.

The Abduction

The morning of May 11, 1960, was windy and cold in Buenos Aires. Being situated south of the equator, the seasons in Argentina were the opposite of those in the Northern Hemisphere, meaning it was autumn. Unfortunately for Isser Harel, the chilly and damp weather also meant a head cold.

The Mossad chief started his day by checking out of his hotel and traveling by taxi to the city's train station. Although warm with fever, he decided not to tell the operatives about his malaise.[35] He wanted their thoughts to be on the mission, not on him. So he pushed on, proceeding unaccompanied to the train depot.

"I deposited my belongings in a locker and set out ... on a long tour of the cafés of Buenos Aires," he writes.[36] The team members knew where to find the dynamic, if diminutive, official—Harel was four feet, eight inches tall—since they had in their possession a list of venues through which he would be passing in the coming hours. And during this period, the most crucial phase of the mission, he would be in the city's flourishing entertainment district. Its cafés were plentiful and located side by side, a situation that, like most other aspects of Operation Eichmann, carried a strategic benefit: the close proximity would allow the Mossad chief to spend less time walking to and from the various establishments and more time stationed within them, poised for his operatives to make contact with him.

As Harel was setting off on his stroll through the entertainment quarter, Adolf Eichmann, in a barren neighborhood elsewhere in the city, began readying himself for work at the Mercedes-Benz factory.[37] It was the ex–Nazi's morning ritual. On this day there would be a slight difference, however, because his wife Vera had awakened during the night from an unnerving dream and felt she should share it with him. "Before he left," says Bascomb, "his wife told him about her nightmare."[38] She also advised him to be cautious. The fugitive then traveled two hours by bus to the automobile factory, where he began what would be, unbeknownst to him, his last day of work.

The blustery May morning would also be the last opportunity for the Mossad team to tie up loose ends before the abduction later that evening, the kidnapping being set to occur at 7:40 p.m. as Eichmann disembarked at a bus stop near his home. Eager to get started, the operatives arose early to check their equipment and make sure they had a hefty supply of food and medicine. Fearing a possible police siege, they had made it a point to overstock as much as possible. While some of the agents were examining their provisions and gear, others set about inspecting the cars that the team had rented, a task that would turn out to be a frustrating one, at least for Zvi Aharoni. It was he who examined the principal vehicle to be used in the kidnapping, a black Buick limousine that Harel, in a rare splurge, had selected and financed for the mission. The Mossad chief wanted the abduction squad to have a roomy, reliable vehicle in which to transport the fugitive. But while there was no doubt about the roominess of the car, Aharoni discovered it was far from reliable, and, indeed, would not be transporting anyone in its present condition. "[D]espite all our technical efforts, the battery was almost flat," he writes.[39] Flustered, the operative hit the streets in search of a solution, and fortunately came upon another battery remarkably fast. "I was lucky and found a repair shop that sold me a new one at a horrendous black-market price," says Aharoni.[40]

It was this same limousine that Moshe Tavor, on a more heartening note, had equipped with a device to help prevent the team's detection by Argentine police. "Tavor," write Raviv and Melman, "installed a rotating license plate panel on one of his team's cars—several years before the James Bond movie *Goldfinger* had a similar gimmick—so that the vehicle's identity tag could instantly be changed if the Israelis were spotted."[41] One side displayed an Argentine license plate while the other brandished a diplomatic plate, connoting an embassy vehicle. To be sure, it was an inspired invention.

After inspecting the vehicles, a handful of operatives returned those cars that were no longer needed for the mission. The automobiles were simply in the way at this point. Yet there was a second reason for relinquishing them: unburdening themselves of the spare cars was a way for team members to begin "covering their tracks," write Bar-Zohar and Nissim, the fewer ties they had to Buenos Aires, the better.[42] By mid-morning, only three vehicles remained in the team's possession; one to be used for the abduction, another to serve as a backup during the abduction, and the third to be available for the agents' own needs in the coming days. It would be during this stretch that the operatives would be confining Eichmann to the safe house.

Although the team had prepared two houses capable of detaining the war criminal, *Tira*, owing to the villa's size and location, was the preferred one. It was at *Tira* that Tavor had designed a room expressly for the infamous Eichmann. The operative had also built a separate hideout on the premises in case the police entered the estate, as well as crafting a concealed room to function as the team's arsenal. And he did more. "Tavor," writes Raviv and Melman, "built a metal cart where a folded-up Adolf Eichmann could be secreted."[43] By any standard, the set-up at the villa was a sophisticated one, and it is striking how quickly Tavor, with Malkin's help, constructed it.

Because of the thoroughness of the Mossad's preparations, the only task that remained in Eichmann's detention room was completed by Malkin within a matter of minutes on the morning of the planned abduction. The agent laid three items for the fugitive's use on a table next to the low-slung, iron bed. "I placed a pair of striped pajamas, a towel ... and a pair of dark motorcycle goggles on top," writes Malkin.[44] Once Eichmann was in custody, an operative would fit the goggles over his eyes so he could not see the team members. To its credit, the Mossad team had taken into account all aspects of the war criminal's confinement so as to ensure the agents' security as well as the health and safety of the captive himself.

By noon on this fateful day, the operatives had inspected the cars, safe houses, equipment, and provisions. They also had scrutinized the route to and from Eichmann's house on Garibaldi Street to make sure there was no road construction, police blockade, or other development that might hinder traffic or otherwise obstruct their movements later that evening. To their relief, the route was unimpeded and therefore no access problems were anticipated.

With these tasks behind them, the operatives traveled to a café in the entertainment district for a final meeting with Harel. The time was 1:00 p.m. The sky was overcast, the wind was gusting, a chill was in the air, and a rainstorm threatened. Although the conditions were far from ideal for a kidnapping, the weather was one factor over which the Mossad had no control. The only recourse would be to postpone the mission, and this was out of the question.

At the café gathering, the agents reviewed with Harel the details of the abduction plan, as well as concocting a contingency plan lest the police pursue the car that was carrying Eichmann. Whereas Harel, Eitan, and Malkin had already decided that two cars should be present at the scene of the kidnapping, it was now determined that the second vehicle would be used to transport Eichmann if Argentine authorities gave chase to the first one. After finalizing this arrangement, the meeting came to a close.

At 3:30 p.m. the operatives parked the two vehicles to be used in the kidnapping in the driveway at safe house *Tira*.[45] "Car One" was the Buick limousine, the vehicle in which Eichmann would be transported. The limousine would hold four agents: Aharoni, who would drive the car; Malkin, who would snatch Eichmann and restrain him; Tavor, who would help Malkin immobilize and hoist the fugitive into the back seat; and Eitan, who would be hiding inside the car and would help gag, blindfold, and conceal Eichmann once the war criminal had been bundled into it. As for the back-up team, it would be in "Car Two," a Chevrolet sedan, which would be driven by Shalom, with Gat and the doctor, Yona Elian, as passengers. The latter would be present in order to attend to any medical emergencies that might arise. He would not tranquilize Eichmann on the scene, however, nor would he authorize the operatives to do so. "Unsupervised sedation could kill him," Elian warned.[46] Instead, tranquilization would come later, at the safe house, and the physician would be the one to administer it.

An hour later, at 4:30 p.m. the operatives held an impromptu meeting at *Tira*, following which the two agents who would be visible to Eichmann at the moment of the kidnapping, Malkin and Tavor, began changing into their disguises. Both men were careful to ensure that their new appearances corresponded to the fabricated identity papers that the team's forger, Shalom Dani, had skillfully prepared for them.

The burly and towering Tavor, whether by accident or by design, wore an overcoat that made him appear "even more gargantuan and imposing than usual," says Bascomb.[47] He also pulled on a wig, which was probably a wise decision considering that the operative's bald pate was both noticeable and memorable and thus a potential problem. Due to the covert nature of the mission, it was imperative that Tavor avoid drawing attention to himself, that he escape being noticed and remembered by any passersby. As it stood, the tall, hairless operative tended to attract the eye in the same way that Isser Harel, due to his short stature, tended to draw unwanted notice.

Malkin wore a wig, too, along with a blue sweater and black pants. At the last minute, he stuffed a pair of gloves in his pocket as well, which he would wear when clutching Eichmann. "The thought of placing my bare hand over the mouth that had ordered the death of millions, of feeling the hot breath and the saliva on my skin, filled me with an overwhelming sense of revulsion," says Malkin.[48]

Although five other operatives would be at the abduction site with Tavor and Malkin, these other men did not require disguises because they would not be in Eichmann's presence until after he had been apprehended and blindfolded. That said, one of them, Aharoni, the driver of the limousine bearing the diplomatic license plates, donned formal clothing so his appearance would be accordant with that of an embassy staff member. If the car were to be stopped by the authorities, he wanted to look the part of a chauffeur.

And now the time had come to act. Rafi Eitan, the squad's commander, gathered the team members and reviewed the abduction plan one last time. "He offered no eloquent words of inspiration," says Bascomb. "Each of them knew what he needed to do."[49]

At 6:30 p.m. the abduction squad climbed into the two cars that sat idling in the villa's driveway. As the seven agents raced across the South American city, thunder rolled and the wind whipped their cars but, in a bit of good fortune, there was still no downpour.[50] Providential, too, was the fact that the men encountered no obstacles on the road during their drive to San Fernando. The Mossad plot, it seems, was off to a promising start.

Certainly the strategy itself was sensible enough, as Aharoni's account illustrates.[51] Based on the fugitive's past movements, the abduction squad was banking on Eichmann stepping off a bus at 7:40 p.m. at a depot on Highway 202. It was the same bus that Aharoni and two other members of the reconnaissance team had been keeping under surveillance, the one that Eichmann rode each evening. As a matter of course, the fugitive would then walk alongside the highway until he reached Garibaldi Street, turning onto it and proceeding the remaining few yards to his home. The Mossad had designed its abduction strategy, part and parcel, on these routine movements of the war criminal.

The blueprint called for the team to station its resources near the intersection of Garibaldi Street and Highway 202. Car One would be parked on Garibaldi Street and Car Two on Highway 202. As Eichmann walked down the highway and approached the intersection, the driver of Car Two, which

2. Mission: Operation Eichmann 43

would be directly ahead of, and facing, him, would switch on its headlights. A deceptively simple act, it would serve three purposes. It would alert Car One, the kidnap vehicle, that Eichmann was just around the corner and about to turn onto Garibaldi Street. It also would blind Eichmann temporarily so he could not see the two-car setup. And it would distract other drivers in the vicinity, rendering them less likely to notice the abduction.

Parked curbside on Garibaldi Street, meanwhile, would be Car One, the limousine, and it would be pointing away from Eichmann with its hood lifted so as to suggest the engine had malfunctioned. The driver, Aharoni, would stand in front of the raised hood and thus be hidden from Eichmann's view, while Eitan would lie down in the back seat, likewise out of sight. Only Malkin and Tavor would be visible to the ex–Nazi, the two agents standing beside the vehicle as though they were awaiting roadside assistance. As Eichmann came toward the limousine from behind, Malkin would step in front of him and act as if he were about to ask a question. When Eichmann paused, Malkin would overpower him and, with Tavor's help, fold the war criminal into the backseat of the car. Eitan, at this point, would join his comrades in restraining the fugitive, following which the two Mossad cars would exit the scene.

The plan was for the operatives to park in their designated spots at 7:25 p.m., fifteen minutes before Eichmann was expected to disembark from the bus. They knew that a broken-down limousine with an embassy license plate would look suspicious in the remote, dilapidated San Fernando neighborhood, just as the Chevrolet parked alongside the Highway 202 might seem a little odd. And the longer the vehicles remained in place, the greater the likelihood that a passerby would become curious and start asking questions or, worse still, notify the police. It was for this reason that the team planned such a swift abduction; it did not want outsiders to become involved.

Unfortunately, such an untoward turn of events did occur, if briefly, while the agents were waiting for their target. At a most inopportune moment, a youth on a bicycle, his jacket snapping in the wind, glimpsed the limousine with its hood lifted and offered to lend a hand. Startled, the car's driver, Aharoni, wasted no time shooing away the charitable lad. "Thank you! We do not need you. Please get lost!" the operative barked in broken Spanish, the baffled youth retreating in response.[52] Certainly the boy's presence at the scene, a presence that would have been irrelevant on any other day, could have obliterated the Mossad's costly and complicated mission, such was the gamble of carrying out the kidnapping in such a public spot. But even though the youth's arrival did not spoil the mission, it did generate a bit of irony in that he came upon the abduction site, unbidden and unwelcome, even as Eichmann, the "wanted man," seemed to be a no-show.

More precisely, the operatives, at 7:40 p.m. were in place and awaiting the appearance of the scheduled bus, the one believed to be carrying him. The time came and went, however, and no bus stopped at the depot. Then, at 7:44 p.m. a bus did pull up, but Eichmann was not on it, which caused the agents to worry that he may have been tipped off. Heightening their tension, more buses arrived and departed, but, as before, none of them carried the fugitive. The operatives had no way of knowing, of course, that their target had been delayed at the Mercedes-Benz plant, where a brief meeting had been slated for the end of his shift. So they pondered their options.

As it stood, Harel had already issued instructions to be followed if the ex–Nazi failed to show up by 8:00 p.m.: the squad was to abort the abduction attempt and return to the safe houses. Yet when the hour actually rolled around and Eichmann still had not appeared, Eitan, as the team commander, decided not to comply with Harel's directive. Instead, he ordered the agents to remain in position and stay primed for the fugitive. "There was no argument from the team," says Bascomb. "Not now, at this critical hour."[53] And then it happened.

At 8:05 p.m. a bus ground to a halt at the depot. A heavy-set woman stepped off, followed moments later by a middle-aged man, bespectacled and clad in an overcoat. It was Adolf Eichmann. As he walked down the highway in the gloom, Shalom, sitting behind the steering wheel in Car Two and looking directly at the fugitive through a pair of binoculars, turned on the headlights. Car One was thus alerted to Eichmann's proximity.

Turning the corner onto Garibaldi Street, the fugitive continued walking toward his house. But he did something else, something unexpected, which Aharoni noticed as he peered around the raised hood of the limousine. Eichmann placed his right hand in his coat pocket. Aharoni suspected at once that the former SS official might have detected the Mossad's scheme and was reaching for a pistol. In reality, Eichmann was reaching for a small flashlight he used occasionally when walking home in the dark. Unaware of this practice, however, Aharoni mouthed a warning to Malkin that their target might be armed. This meant that Malkin, who had planned to place a chokehold on the fugitive, had to reconsider the maneuver, since Eichmann could shoot him while being throttled. So it was that Malkin, in a flash, decided he would grab Eichmann's wrists in case the war criminal was indeed clutching a weapon. And it was precisely at this moment that the ex–Nazi neared the limousine.

"I could hear his footfalls, regular as ticks on a clock," says Malkin.[54] When Eichmann reached the car, the agent strode directly into his path. "*Un momentito, senõr*," Malkin said, nose to nose with his prey.[55] "Behind black-rimmed glasses, his eyes met mine," the operative recalled.[56] Instinctively, Eichmann stepped backwards, but the agent lunged at him and grabbed the fugitive's arms.

2. Mission: Operation Eichmann 45

As the two fell to the ground and tumbled into a shallow ditch, Tavor launched himself into the fray. While Malkin pinned Eichmann's upper body to the ground—to muffle the war criminal's shrieks, he now used the chokehold he had practiced on his colleagues in Tel Aviv—Tavor clutched the fugitive's legs. Restrained head to toe by the pair of agents, Eichmann appears to have grasped the futility of his situation. "Eichmann went slack and stopped screaming, surrendering himself," says Bascomb.[57] Together, the two operatives dragged him into the limousine, where they and Eitan taped a pair of motorcycle goggles over his eyes and a cloth over his mouth before depositing him on the floor of the car and tossing a blanket over him. "Do not move and no one will hurt you," warned Aharoni from the driver's seat.[58] And with this admonition, the abduction was complete. The limousine sped away, tailed by the Chevrolet, the kidnapping having been carried out in record time and with no witnesses. As for Eichmann, he dutifully complied with his captors' orders. "For the entire trip, he didn't budge," write Bar-Zohar and Mishal.[59]

Fifteen minutes later, the car carrying the captive approached the vicinity of the safe house. As it neared the villa, the limousine's license plates were rotated so the embassy designation would no longer be visible. The sedan then pulled up to the estate, where Yitzhak Nesher, the Czech-born agent who had leased the house, greeted the abduction squad at the front gate. He had been waiting anxiously for the operatives to return with what he hoped would be the Mossad's quarry.

After the car eased into the garage, the agents pulled Eichmann to his feet. "He appeared to be intimidated but was able to walk," says Aharoni.[60] The captive did need support, however. Because he was overcome with fear, Malkin and Shalom bracketed him as they led him into the kitchen, where the other agents had their first look at the mastermind of the Final Solution. Before them slumped the man whose directives had led to the liquidation of millions of Jews, among them their own loved ones. But now, in the kitchen, the same Adolf Eichmann was "utterly rigid, except for hands that kept opening and closing spasmodically," says Malkin. "The man was terrified."[61] The ex–Nazi would later reveal that he suspected it was a foreign intelligence service that had snatched him. "No drugs, no ropes, no handcuffs were used," writes Arendt, "and Eichmann immediately recognized that this was professional work, as no unnecessary violence had been applied; he was not hurt."[62] The captive was further aware that the implications for his future were direr than would have been the case if it had been a simple robbery pulled off by local thugs. His distress was a realistic response.

Moments later, the agents led Eichmann up a staircase to the room that would serve as his detention cell for the next nine days, being careful all the while not to speak to him or even to one another. It was important that he not hear their voices lest he be able to identify them if the Argentine police were to lay siege to the villa and arrest them. Only Aharoni, whose native tongue was German and who had been trained as an interrogator under the auspices of the CIA, would speak to him.[63] Not only would this help protect the identities of the other team members, but it also would restrict Eichmann's contact with his environment, the Mossad team making it a point to limit the detainee's external stimulation as much as possible.

The detention room, for instance, was stark. In the center stood the iron bed to which the captive would be cuffed at the ankle, while the windows, two of them, had been overlaid with mattresses. The thick padding was intended to serve multiple purposes: it would shut out any sunlight Eichmann might detect through the goggles and muffle any sounds he might hear from outside of the house, while also preventing anyone in the surrounding neighborhood from hearing him shout for help. The furnishings consisted of a nightstand and a couple of chairs positioned beside the low-slung bed; otherwise the chamber was bare. With forethought when constructing the room, Yaacov Gat also had installed an alarm in case an operative who was guarding Eichmann required emergency back-up. As things stood, three agents would be assigned to the dispiriting task of monitoring the prisoner—Aharoni, Malkin, and Tavor—with the trio slated for rotating eight-hour shifts to make sure he remained under direct observation day and night. The door to the room would remain ajar as well, the light would stay on around the clock, and the adjacent room would hold an agent primed to respond instantly to a "situation" in the Eichmann cell.

Having consigned the prisoner to the detention room, Aharoni ordered him to disrobe so the doctor could examine him. By all accounts, the war criminal's garments and body made for a pathetic sight. "I can still recall exactly how I was touched, even a bit disgusted, when I saw his shabby clothing, particularly his underwear," says Aharoni. "I could not help it and asked myself spontaneously: is this really the Great Eichmann, the man who decided the fates of millions of my people?"[64] And Aharoni was not alone in his reaction. Many of the team members had a similar response upon first glimpsing the prisoner, unclothed and weary, under the glare of the light bulb that dangled from the ceiling. As will be discussed shortly, some of the members, throughout Eichmann's lengthy detention at the villa, would struggle with feelings of pity, fury, and disgust, among other intense and conflicting emotions.

Conducting the physical exam, Dr. Elian first checked to make sure Eichmann had no cyanide pellets concealed in his dentures or ears for the purpose of committing suicide and that his vital signs were satisfactory given the traumatic circumstances. Once the physician determined that the captive had no poison on him and that his pulse and blood pressure, although elevated, were not at critical levels, he compared the prisoner's measurements to the known dimensions of Adolf Eichmann: height, head circumference, shoe size, and so forth. All of them corresponded. He then inspected him for the scars Eichmann was known to have acquired over the years, most notably one below his left eyebrow and another over his rib cage. Again, both were present. Lastly, the physician scrutinized the prisoner's armpit, the spot where the SS routinely tattooed its members' blood types in case a transfusion was required. And it was here, and only here, that a discrepancy arose in that captive did not have the tell-tale illustration. He did, however, display a small and rather odd patch of scar tissue in the same location suggesting he had tried, if haphazardly, to expunge the tattoo. So it was that Dr. Elian, in light of the exam's results, concluded that the prisoner's physical characteristics matched, from top to bottom, those of the inglorious fascist.

After Aharoni dressed the captive—the goggles were still taped over Eichmann's eyes—he sat him in a chair and ordered him to answer a series of questions. It was 9:15 p.m. The other agents remained in the room, silent and observant. In the book *Operation Eichmann*, Aharoni's account of the abduction and interrogation, he recites his line of questioning.

"What is your name?" Aharoni asked.
"Ricardo Klement," the captive replied.
"What were you called before?"
"Otto Heninger." It was Eichmann's first alias after the war.[65]

And so it began, the cat-and-mouse game. Relentlessly, Aharoni posed question after question, short ones he delivered brusquely. It was his modus operandi. "He never used force, knowing it only led to false confessions," says Bascomb. "Instead, he wore his subjects down with staccato bursts of questions, twisting them in their own lies and hammering them with known facts until the truth was the only way out."[66]

With a masterful touch, Aharoni corkscrewed his questions increasingly toward information about the war criminal's Nazi identity. Along the way, he adopted the tone of a man who already knows the answers to the questions he is asking, the assumption being that Eichmann would realize the futility of attempting to mislead such a well-versed interrogator. And sure enough, the captive dispensed with his efforts at obfuscation as the session moved steadily toward questions about his dubious past.

"What was your number in the SS?" snapped the operative.
"45 326," came the reply, the answer being the correct one.
"Place of birth?"
"Solingen." Once again, a factual response.[67]

After only a few minutes, Aharoni had managed to maneuver the prisoner into the position of having furnished a succession of truthful responses. And this, in turn, permitted the inquiry to proceed quite naturally to the final, inescapable question:

"Under what name were you born?" asked the operative.
"Adolf Eichmann," replied the captive.[68]

For Aharoni and the other agents in the room, it was a glorious moment. "[L]ike the sun coming out at night," is how Gat described it.[69] The war criminal had acknowledged his own identity, thereby confirming that the Mossad had netted its man.

With Eichmann's admission, the interrogation ended. Aharoni would resume the inquiry the next day, and, during the ensuing week, spend many more hours grilling the prisoner. But the Israelis now had what they needed most: physical evidence of Adolf Eichmann along with verification by the man himself.

Before bringing to a close their extraordinary day, Aharoni and Shalom drove the limousine to a parking lot in the heart of Buenos Aires where Yitzhak Nesher, who had rented it, would retrieve the car following morning and return it to the dealership. It was imperative that the Mossad be rid of the conspicuous sedan in case a passerby had spotted it during the abduction in San Fernando. Subsequent to this, Aharoni and Shalom tracked down Isser Harel at one of his scheduled café stops, the Mossad chief having endured a long, nerve-wracking night. "I sat waiting and wondering," says Harel, "drinking tea and coffee at rendezvous after rendezvous until it was nearly midnight and the café I was sitting in started to close."[70] It was therefore a relief when the two agents walked into the establishment, especially when Harel sensed the news was good. "They were tired and their clothes were rumpled, but one look at their faces was enough," he recalls.[71] Shortly thereafter, the two operatives returned to the safe house while Harel checked into a new hotel. At this turning point in the mission, the Mossad chief instructed Efraim Ilani to dispatch a communiqué to David Ben-Gurion and Golda Meir in Tel Aviv, a coded message notifying them that the architect of the Final Solution was, at long last, in the hands of the Israelis. It was a perfect ending to an extraordinary day.

At dawn the next morning—the date was May 13, 1960—Harel set off once more on his café rounds, a "secure spycraft technique that could be called roving headquarters," write Raviv and Melman.[72] Elsewhere in Buenos Aires, the eleven members of the Mossad team settled into the various safe houses. The base, *Tira*, lodged Eitan, Tavor, Nesher, Nissiyahu, and the doctor, while Aharoni and Malkin, the two agents who would be interacting most closely with the prisoner, adopted another residence. The remaining operatives likewise boarded away from the villa. Being dispersed in this fashion, the covert team was less likely to be ensnared in its entirety if the police were to raid the villa. At least some of the members might evade arrest.

Adolf Eichmann, on this same morning, remained leashed to the bed with the goggles still taped over his eyes. Just as the operatives were determined that he would never be out of their sight, they were equally determined that they would never be in his view, which is why the goggles were to remain in place until he was out of Argentina. They did not wish for him to be able to identify their faces or, for that matter, became aware of his whereabouts. The less he knew, the better. Then, too, existing in such an indeterminate state allowed the Mossad to better manipulate him. Aharoni, for instance, when speaking to Eichmann, would not tell him the date or time, not even if it were night or day, the aim being to foster in the captive a sense of disorientation so as to throw him off-balance. The seasoned interrogator believed a protracted state of uncertainty, coupled with Eichmann's mounting concern over his wife and sons, would prompt the war criminal to comply with the interrogation in the hope, however slim, that he would be released and reunited with his family.[73]

So it was that Aharoni, on this, the first full day of Eichmann's confinement, walked into the detention room with a special directive from Harel: extract from the detainee actionable information about Josef Mengele. Harel, it seems, had reached a decision overnight that the team should add the deranged Auschwitz physician to its abduction list if, like Eichmann, he was hiding in Argentina. Better to smuggle two Nazi war criminals into Israel rather than one. But the team balked. Its members considered Harel's ambitious plan to be well-intentioned but hastily hatched and a threat to the unfinished Eichmann project.[74] As it came to pass, however, the controversial proposal would not proceed since Aharoni would be able to obtain only a couple of pieces of information about Mengele, neither of them useful. This was because Eichmann's postwar existence had not lent itself to the kind of social discourse that would bring him such updates. "He had really lived a very withdrawn life," says Aharoni, "and always tried to avoid any contacts with other people."[75]

As for what Eichmann did reveal about Mengele, he explained that he and the Nazi doctor had met at a café in Buenos Aires a few years earlier and that Mengele had offered to take him on as a patient, an invitation he turned down. The captive also revealed that Mengele, whose surgical experiments on unanesthetized children and adults at Auschwitz were unparalleled in their ghastliness, had lived and practiced medicine under his own name in Buenos Aires in the 1950s, an assertion that was borne out by other sources.[76] Had the Mossad, or the CIA or MI6 for that matter, earnestly pursued him during those years, it is doubtful Mengele would have lived out his remaining days in South America, prosperous and surrounded by his family. As noted earlier, however, the Mossad's mandate during the previous decade centered exclusively on the safety and security of the nascent State of Israel, not on the hunt for Nazi war criminals.

Now, however, it was the 1960s, Eichmann was in the Mossad's custody, and Aharoni was about to interrogate him for the second time. And, as before, the operative would have company. Zvi Malkin, the agent who had tussled with the fugitive in San Fernando, had since become fascinated by the infamous figure and decided to attend the session as well. Like his comrades, Malkin was confounded by the ex–Nazi's insipid demeanor and wished to know more about the internal mechanisms, the inner world, of the man who had devoted four years of his life to effecting the mass murder of European Jewry.

"I had expected more of this most honored representative of the master race," says Malkin. "At the very least I thought there would be bearing, dignity, pride."[77] The operative then offers an insightful observation about the once-powerful Nazi official. "Stripped of power," he says, "Eichmann seemed a classic weakling, lacking the character even to accept his fate."[78] Surely it is true that behind the ostentatious armor of National Socialism cowered the same man whose young adult years had been marked by ennui and passivity, a man lacking a source of strength or power other than that which the Nazi Party had loaned him. In this regard, the anemic war criminal stood in stark contrast to those men and women of the Mossad who had apprehended him, possessed, as they were, with fortitude beyond measure. Notable, too, is the fact that the operatives, despite their aversion for the prisoner, had the self-control and professional discipline not to act on their emotions.

Malkin, for instance, spoke of being "caged under the same roof with a man whom we all despised—indeed, whom several among us would have loved to kill with their bare hands."[79] Among these agents, it would seem, was the mission's lone female operative, Yehudith Nissiyahu, whose role was to reside at *Tira* on the pretext of being Yitzhak Nesher's lover. But she had another responsibility as well. While it was the duty of Malkin and other agents to attend to Eichmann's personal needs, such as bathing and shaving him, it was Nissiyahu's job to cook for him, a task she found appalling. "She was disturbed by the fact that she would be nourishing a mass murderer and enemy of the Jewish people," write Raviv and Melman.[80] Even so, Nissiyahu kept her qualms in check as she fulfilled her assignment, preparing and serving to the detainee numerous light, kosher meals. She refused to wash his dishes, however, and instead tossed them into the garbage. By her own admission, she also gave serious thought to poisoning him.[81]

It was not simply a matter of the operatives' hatred, however, and their remarkable ability to contain it under the circumstances. Because Eichmann appeared pathetic and defenseless, a broken man, some of the agents, as mentioned earlier, had difficulty reconciling their pity for him with their revulsion over his deeds as a master of genocide. And their inner turmoil, which was intense, threatened to become problematic for the mission owing to its effects on group morale. "This conflict," writes Bascomb, "cast a pall over the house."[82]

It was for this reason that Harel became concerned when he met with a handful of operatives at an out-of-the-way café two days into Eichmann's detention. "That was my first glimpse into the heavy oppression hanging over the guards of our loathsome criminal," he says.[83] To lift their spirits, he urged them to take breaks, suggesting, for instance, that they travel around Buenos Aires and enjoy the sights. And indeed, they would do so in the coming days. They also would play chess, listen to music, read books, and stage apple-eating contests, the villa's gardens boasting an abundance of the ripe fruit.

The Mossad chief, however, continued to be concerned about his operatives and the strain that creased their faces, a team of diligent agents who still had ahead of them a week at close quarters with Eichmann. To better understand their situation, he decided to observe the ex–Nazi himself. Until this time, Harel had deliberately kept a distance from the safe houses and especially from the captive, but now he traveled to *Tira* and looked in on him.

"When I actually saw Eichmann for the first time, I was amazed at my reaction," Harel says, referring to the fact that he was not blinded by a gut hatred for the war criminal. "If I met him in the street I would see no difference between him and the thousands of other men passing by."[84] In his written account of the mission, the Mossad chief expresses the perplexity he experienced when confronted with "the miserable runt," as he refers to Eichmann.[85]

> Was *this* the personification of evil? Was *this* the tool used by a diabolic government to slaughter millions of innocent people? This nonentity, devoid of human dignity and pride, was *this* the messenger of death for six million Jews?[86]

As a result of his observations, Harel found himself sharing his agents' perception of Eichmann as an aging man whose lack of a robust physique and absence of a high-voltage personality flew in the face of the long-standing image of the top-tier Nazi leader. Like his operatives, he also found the captive's overly compliant behavior to be at odds with the self-important, defiant posturing so often attributed to Eichmann and other notables in Hitler's administration. And it is true, the ex–Nazi was, by all accounts, meek and unduly deferential. "He was obedient to the point of subservience," writes Bascomb.[87] Aharoni adds that Eichmann never raised his voice or failed to answer a question, nor did he express a complaint or even make a request.[88] And an observation by Harel seems particularly astute: "He behaved like a scared, submissive slave whose one aim was to please his new masters."[89]

The need for approval to which the Mossad chief refers brings us to the forces that may have driven Eichmann's behavior both during and after the war. While the operational team considered his presentation at safe house *Tira* to be inconsistent with his conduct during the Nazi era, it is likely that a more fundamental consistency did, in fact, exist and could be found in his underlying personality traits. More precisely, the subservience the Mossad observed in him, the need to "please his new masters" as Harel put it, may well have been present throughout his adult life and influenced his behavior as an instrumental member of the Third Reich. He simply may have transferred the object of his obedience from what he regarded as his German masters to his Israeli ones. The fact is, the available records reveal that Eichmann not only surrendered himself fully to the fascist regime and its demands, but he also appeared keen on impressing his superiors with his proficiency, which helps to explain why he devoted himself to perfecting the Final Solution even when it became obvious that Germany would lose the war. On this subject, it is instructive to note that the ex–Nazi articulated this same notion, that of deference to a more powerful entity, when Aharoni interrogated him about the past.

In the pair's daily question-and-answer sessions, marathon meetings during which the captive remained "calm and collected throughout" despite the grisly subject matter, Eichmann sought to justify his deeds during the Holocaust.[90] First and foremost, he insisted he was blameless. Portraying himself as "a small cog in the mighty and tyrannical machinery of the Nazi regime," the orchestrator of the Final Solution depicted himself as a pawn of the Nazi leadership, one who had been "unable to exert any influence on its decisions."[91] In his version of events, his job duties were handed to him by higher-ups and therefore he was not answerable for his actions. "Eichmann maintained that he had never committed a wrong," says Aharoni."[92] It was the National Socialist administration that should be held accountable for any atrocities committed against the Jewish people, the ex–Nazi argued, while implying that he, too, had been a casualty of the Third Reich.

Eichmann also sought to diminish the significance of his role in the Final Solution. Downplaying the herculean task of organizing and managing the largest genocidal apparatus in human history, he insisted that he had merely arranged deportations to the concentration camps, as if this were somehow an inconsequential contribution. The Mossad knew, of course, that he had done far more during Hitler's reign.

Then, too, Eichmann infused his account under interrogation with a purported concern for his victims, claiming he was sorry for the difficulties his position had required that he inflict upon the Jewish people.[93] Unbeknownst to Aharoni and the Mossad, the ex–Nazi's assertion flew in the face of his previous on-the-record statements to Willem Sassen. A Dutch journalist and former SS member, Sassen, like Eichmann, lived in Argentina during the 1950s, and it was at this time and place that the Dutchman interviewed the fugitive on several occasions in the hope of publishing the final product. To Sassen, Eichmann expressed regret over his actions during the Holocaust, but in a direction which was the polar opposite of that which he now conveyed to the Mossad. Eichmann told Sassen he was sorry he had not succeeded in exterminating the entirety of European Jewry. "I could have done more and should have done more," Eichmann said.[94] Although Aharoni and his colleagues were unaware of these earlier admissions and therefore could not confront Eichmann with his own words, they were astute enough to recognize that his professed pangs of conscience were calculated to save his own skin.

A few days later, self-preservation came to the fore even more urgently when Aharoni asked the war criminal to sign a letter confirming that he was, in fact, Adolf Eichmann, and that he agreed to face legal proceedings in Israel. The idea had originated several weeks earlier while Aharoni was still in Tel Aviv, where the Attorney General advised him to obtain such a statement before leaving Argentina with the prisoner. "This letter," writes David Cesarini, "was to be of significance in the trial in establishing whether Eichmann had come to Israel entirely under duress or with a degree of consent."[95] As well, the document could prove useful if the covert mission were to be exposed while the team was still in Buenos Aires.[96] And it could make a legal difference if the agents were apprehended *en route* to Israel with the war criminal in their possession, semi-conscious from sedation. In the absence of such a document, transporting Eichmann would be deemed a kidnapping since he was presumably being taken against his will, whereas it would be classified as smuggling, a lesser offense, if the agents had in hand his statement of consent for the journey. But as Aharoni would come to realize, securing the letter would not be an easy matter.

The fact is, the operative found it quite difficult to persuade the otherwise accommodating captive to sign the document confirming that he was Eichmann, and even harder to obtain his agreement to appear before an Israeli court. Alarmed and defensive, Eichmann turned down both requests. "I do not owe Israel anything," he said.[97] Three days later, however, and owing to Aharoni's persistent prodding, the ex–Nazi did agree to sign the statement and stand trial in the Middle Eastern nation, although he proposed, futilely, that the proceedings be held in Germany or Argentina. As to why he consented at all, he may have feared a lethal outcome if he refused, or it could have been as he claimed: he considered himself innocent and wished to defend himself in a public forum.

Whatever the case, Eichmann went on to say that he hoped to use the opportunity to warn the world about the dangers of unbridled animosity during wartime. To Aharoni, it was apparent that the captive, once he arrived in Israel, planned to continue promoting the idea that he was being maligned; that, in truth, he had merely been an instrument of Hitler's regime, the drone who had done the master's bidding. During the Nuremberg Trials several years earlier, many of the defendants had used this same argument, albeit unsuccessfully, since the alternative would have meant admitting to having willfully committed crimes against humanity. In any event, the captive, until his transport to Israel and his day in court, would remain locked away at *Tira*, where he would continue being peppered with questions about his deeds during and after the war.

Just as Eichmann faced an interrogation session each day at the safe house, the Mossad team combed the Buenos Aires newspapers each day, both the Spanish and German editions, for any news of his disappearance. No one knew how the Eichmann family would react to his absence, coming, as it did, seemingly out of the blue. And this was among the Mossad agents' top concerns, pertaining, as it did, to their immediate future in Buenos Aires. For this reason, Aharoni spent a considerable amount of time, especially during the opening days of Eichmann's detention, questioning him about his wife and sons' probable response to his disappearance. Today, of course, their course of action is known.

The morning after the kidnapping, eighteen-year-old Dieter rushed to the workplace of his brother Klaus, who was twenty-four, and blurted out that their father had gone missing. Shocked, Klaus, standing on a roof scaffold, dropped the screwdriver he was holding.[98] Having spent most of his life as the first-born son of a Nazi-in-hiding, he intuited the situation instantly. "My first thought was: Israelis!" he says.[99] Rushing into action, the brothers sought the advice of their father's closest friend, a former SS man widely assumed to have been Carlos Fuldner. As for the remaining Eichmann sons, they did not play a role in the drama, Horst being away at sea—he worked as a merchant marine—and Ricardo being too young to become involved. Instead, the latter, along with his mother Vera, left their house on Garibaldi Street and lodged with a family whose patriarch had also been an SS officer.

Dieter and Klaus, meanwhile, mulled over the various scenarios that might account for their father's abrupt disappearance and, with the input of his most trusted friend, arrived at three possibilities: the senior Eichmann had been kidnapped by those he had wronged—the Jews—as Klaus had initially suspected, or he had been in an accident or gotten drunk and wound up in jail. To rule out the latter two hypotheses, the sons checked the city's hospitals, morgues, and jails but found no trace of their father. They also spoke to his supervisor at the Mercedes-Benz plant, but again to no avail. No one, it seems, had a clue as to

2. Mission: Operation Eichmann 55

Eichmann's whereabouts. It was on the third day of his absence, then, that Dieter and Klaus concluded that Jews, almost certainly from the State of Israel, had indeed made off with him, and they became further convinced when they discovered his glasses in a ditch, broken and caked in mud, near the family home. It seems the spectacles had fallen off while he was struggling with the Mossad operatives.[100]

Realizing they were probably up against the professionals of the Israeli intelligence service, the sons turned to the ex–Nazi community in and around Buenos Aires. They were confident its members would help rescue their father. To their annoyance, however, the National Socialists who had settled in the Argentine capital after the war, a sizable and shadowy club of émigrés, were anything but obliging. In fact, some of them now high-tailed it to neighboring Uruguay, as an embittered Klaus would later complain.[101] The Eichmann sons did, on the other hand, receive the unsolicited, yet welcome, support of the Tacuara, a fascist youth group that eventually would expand into a significant political movement and produce Argentina's first crop of urban guerrillas. Extremist and anti–Semitic, the group adopted the Nazi salute, extolled the virtues of Hitler and Mussolini, and favored violence over dialogue. Upwards of three hundred of its adherents now volunteered to help the distraught sons locate and liberate their father.

Fanning out across Buenos Aires, the Tacuara members, scores of them young men on motorcycles, searched tirelessly for the infamous war criminal. At airports, railroads, harbors, synagogues, and major roadway intersections they kept their eyes peeled for the missing man. And they ached to do more. One of them suggested seizing the Israeli ambassador and torturing him until Eichmann was released, while another proposed bombing the Israeli embassy itself. When these ideas were presented to Adolf Eichmann's former SS cohorts, however, they balked, dismissing the propositions as reckless and apt to worsen the situation. These same figures, one could surmise, may have been equally concerned about worsening their own situations, their fear being that such radical measures might expose their personal histories in the SS.

It was at this juncture that a rumor emerged, one claiming that the war criminal was being confined in the cellar of a synagogue. Frantic, fatigued, and therefore willing to grasp at straws, Dieter and Klaus promptly pawned some of their belongings to purchase weapons, and, along with a band of Tacuara members, stormed into the house of worship. What they found, of course, was an empty synagogue with a vacant cellar. And this proved to be a turning point. The Eichmanns realized they had exhausted the available means of locating their father, except for one course of action, a course that, under normal circumstances, would have been the first and most sensible strategy. Throughout the ten-day ordeal, it seems that Dieter and Klaus refused to notify the police, steering clear of the law enforcement establishment entirely. Apparently, they considered it far too risky in light of his history. As a result, the Eichmanns would not find their father, and the Mossad, much to the relief of Harel and his covert band of operatives, would not have to contend with the police when whisking the captive out of the country. That said, the team's South American exit would still be a courageous, and a complex, endeavor.

Escape from Buenos Aires

On May 19, the El Al flight carrying the Israeli delegation to Argentina's anniversary celebration touched down on the tarmac at Ezeiza Airport in Buenos Aires. Nearly everyone on the plane, from the flight crew to the delegation itself, was in the dark about the Mossad operation. One who was in the know, however, was Abba Eban, the Israeli delegation's leader and a man who was presently beside himself with worry. He would later claim that he knew nothing about Operation Eichmann and was outraged the Mossad would place him in the midst of such an undertaking.[102] The other person on the plane who was aware of the mission was a flight navigator that the Mossad had brought into the fold because of his resemblance to Adolf Eichmann in terms of his build, age, and facial features.[103] He was, in effect, the fugitive's doppelgänger, his look-alike.

Upon donning civilian clothes, the navigator handed over his sky-blue uniform and identification papers to a Mossad agent, then vanished into the sprawling Argentine capital. Two days later, under a new name, he would depart for Chile and from there, Israel. In the meantime, Shalom Dani would alter the navigator's identification documents, among other conversions replacing his photo with that of Eichmann dressed in a shirt and tie in the style of El Al Airlines. By the end of the day, the captive would be reborn as the fictitious Ze'ev Zichroni, Israeli flight attendant.[104] The idea was at once inspired and audacious.

The next morning, Buenos Aires awakened to yet another cold front, but all the same the day the city bustled with activity in anticipation of the forthcoming festivities. While the capital was opening its arms to the world, however, the Mossad team was closing down its operational sites across the city. Rental apartments and houses were being shuttered and all traces of the agents and their captive, removed. Only *Tira* would remain open, where a handful of operatives would remain until the El Al plane was aloft. Afterward, they too would scatter.

Isser Harel, this same day, checked out of his hotel, steered his way through various cafés to meet with his operatives, then hailed a taxi for the airport. Here he secured a booth in a cafeteria, his makeshift office for the next several hours. "He sat at his table with his forger," write Raviv and Melman, "checking and distributing the identity documents his operatives would need to make a safe and unimpeachable departure from Buenos Aires."[105]

With Harel at the airport and the Mossad team at the sole remaining safe house, it was now a matter of waiting until nightfall, which, for several agents, was not as effortless as it might seem. Although Malkin distracted himself by playing chess with a comrade, his colleagues found it more difficult to relax.[106] "The nerves of some," says Aharoni, "were stretched to the breaking point."[107] Certainly Aharoni was relieved when the moment neared to depart from safe house *Tira*, a point at which he began readying the captive for the long journey to the Middle East.

At 9:00 p.m. he led Eichmann into the kitchen, where he set about dressing the ex–Nazi as an El Al steward. Aharoni did not put the jacket on him, however, a seeming oversight that prompted the captive to speak up. "He told me immediately that he too should have a jacket so as not to attract attention," says Aharoni.[108] It was a curious moment, since one would expect Eichmann to root for the scheme's failure, not its success. The fact that he tried to help his captors suggests he may have found himself drawn into their conspiracy despite it being contrary to his own interests. Alternately, he may have been resorting to type—that is, he may have trying to "please his masters" once again—or, by playing the role of the obliging prisoner, attempting to curry favor in the hope of receiving a lighter sentence down the line. Of course, it may also have been a complex combination of these motives driving his compliance. Be that as it may, Aharoni instructed him not to wear the jacket, and he told him why.

At this stage of the preparatory process, the doctor was about to inject Eichmann with a sedative that would render the captive unable to speak coherently although he would still be able to walk with support. Furthermore, the hypodermic needle would remain inserted in Eichmann's arm until he was out of Argentine airspace in case the physician needed to boost the medication to ensure continuous sedation. It was to avoid obstructing this medical procedure, Aharoni explained to Eichmann, that the jacket was to be draped over his shoulders. And with this, the agent placed a pair of sunglasses over the captive's eyes so that airport security officials, if they were to observe the ex–Nazi, would write him off as an intoxicated El Al attendant, half-asleep and with bloodshot eyes.

In these, Eichmann's last moments in Argentina, he broke down. Tearfully, he lamented leaving his wife and sons impoverished. Yaacov Gat and the doctor, meanwhile, hoisted him to his feet—the captive was becoming woozy from the tranquilizer—and guided him to a sedan parked in the garage. As before, it was a limousine displaying a diplomatic license plate. Airport officials, the Mossad assumed, would be less inclined to stop and inspect a VIP vehicle.

Placing Eichmann in the backseat, the doctor took his place on one side of the ex–Nazi while another operative sat on the opposite side. Aharoni was in the driver's seat, with Gat, the strongman, installed beside him in the passenger seat. All were decked out as El Al crew members apart from Aharoni, who was dressed in diplomatic attire. As the villa's gates swung open, the limousine passed through and made its way to Ezeiza Airport.

In accordance with the Mossad's strategy, a second car carrying a backup team trailed the sedan, Eitan and Shalom being among the passengers. And in an exquisitely-timed maneuver, a small bus carrying the real El Al crew, a group that had been ensconced in a hotel in downtown Buenos Aires since landing in the city the previous day, left their lodgings at this time, the plan being for all three vehicles to arrive simultaneously at the airport. In this way, they could pass through the airport's security checkpoint together, with the car carrying Eichmann sandwiched between the other two vehicles. Even now, it should be noted, the Mossad had not briefed the actual El Al crew about the mission, although these employees were fast catching on to the fact that a covert operation was afoot. For this reason, they were uneasy, and understandably so.

It was 10:30 p.m. when the convoy pulled up to the security gate at Ezeiza Airport. Perhaps it was because the security officers were already on friendly terms with the real El Al personnel sitting in the lead vehicle that none of the cars were stopped. For those in the limousine which was carrying Eichmann, this was, as one would expect, heartening news. "The car was waved through security and cruised right up to the waiting plane," writes Cesarini.[109]

Lifting the ex–Nazi from the back seat, Aharoni, Gat, and the other agents clustered around him, concealing him from public view as they dragged him up the boarding stairs and into the first-class cabin. Here they placed him in an aisle seat, while the doctor occupied the seat directly behind him and the remaining operatives and El Al relief crew filled those that were still vacant. To discourage Argentine officials from passing through the compartment before takeoff, a Mossad agent dimmed the cabin's lights. Eichmann, for his part, slid in and out of consciousness.[110]

"The hour that followed was by far the most difficult and nerve-wracking time," recalled one of the operatives. "We had nothing to do except wait for take-off."[111] Further escalating the tension, the Argentine passport clerk, apparently for benign reasons, delayed endorsing the group's travel documents until the last moment. As the airliner prepared to depart, the sheepish clerk, apologizing for his sluggishness, hurriedly stamped the men's passports so they could leave the country.

As the El Al plane, a Bristol Britannica, taxied down the runway, Harel pretended to sleep, as did the other three Mossad members on the flight. Among the latter were the doctor, whose medical expertise was essential; Aharoni, whose fluency in the captive's native tongue, German, was indispensable; and Gat, whose physical might was vital since it could be brought to bear if the captive tried to bolt. At four minutes past midnight on May 21, the plane lifted off the runway.[112] Once it was airborne, a flight attendant, still unaware of the passengers' historic feat, offered Aharoni a snack. "I gratefully declined," he says, "but asked for a double whisky."[113]

Meanwhile, Harel, in another part of the plane, explained to the pilot, Zvi Tohar, that the elusive Adolf Eichmann was aboard and being smuggled to Israel.[114] Given the possibility that the Argentine military might attempt to intercept the aircraft, the Mossad chief decided the pilot should be aware of Operation Eichmann and prepared to take evasive action. Yet this was not the only reason for Harel's disclosure: he also needed Tohar to re-route the plane. Although the flight plan called for the airliner to land in Brazil, where it would refuel prior to embarking on the trans–Atlantic leg of its journey, Harel thought it wise to bypass all South American countries and instead traverse the ocean before landing. In light of the circumstances, Tohar agreed. The pair therefore changed the refueling stop to Dakar, Senegal, "the most out-of-the-way city imaginable," on the assumption that Argentine authorities would not think to alert officials in the remote African city to the ex–Nazi's disappearance."[115]

As for the flight to Senegal, it was a northeasterly, thirteen-hour trip that would tax the aircraft's fuel reserves, but Tohar believed the Bristol Britannica could cover the distance without difficulty. And it did. The aircraft then continued on to Israel, with this second leg of the journey requiring it to be aloft for another eleven hours.[116] As before, it was a trouble-free flight.

Touching down in Tel Aviv on May 22, Harel and his three agents were elated as they returned home with one of the world's foremost war criminals in their possession.[117] By any standard, Operation Eichmann had been a resounding success, a stellar achievement for the young spy agency. For the aging war criminal, on the other hand, it had been a terminal defeat, with Israeli authorities bundling him into a waiting sedan, rushing him to judicial headquarters, and placing him under house arrest.

3
Trial and Tribulations

With Adolf Eichmann behind bars in Tel Aviv, Prime Minister Ben-Gurion decided the time was ripe to release a public statement. As things stood, the global community had no idea that the architect of the Final Solution had been apprehended and was now on Israeli soil, nor, for that matter, were the Israeli people aware of this historic development. Not even the members of the Knesset, the Jewish state's parliament, were privy to it. The embargo, however, was about to be lifted.

"At four o'clock on the afternoon of 23 May 1960 the seats in the Knesset were filled to capacity, as was the public gallery," writes Martin Gilbert. "Word had spread throughout the building that Ben-Gurion was about to make an extraordinary statement."[1] And, indeed, he did.

Standing before the packed assembly hall, the Prime Minister announced that Adolf Eichmann had been located and transported to Israel to appear before a court of law. Mindful of the politically sensitive nature of the capture, Ben-Gurion made it a point not to mention that the ex–Nazi had been abducted in Argentina; this he would do two weeks later in a letter to the Argentine government.[2] He also did not mention the Mossad's role in the affair, an omission that was designed to protect the Israeli government from criticism. In fact, the decision to withhold this crucial piece of information had been made, with Isser Harel's agreement, several months in advance.

As to the assembly's reaction to the Prime Minister's announcement, the statement hung in the air, a deep silence filling the cavernous room, followed by shouts of approval as the audience leapt to its feet. Those in the great hall were clearly taken aback by the news. And they were not alone: the whole world was stunned, including that handful of Mossad agents who had remained behind in South America. The latter's surprise, however, stemmed from the timing of the announcement. Ben-Gurion, it seems, was not supposed to have revealed the capture until all of the operatives had made it back safely to Israel.

"We stood there with silly smiles on our faces," says Zvi Malkin upon catching sight of a newspaper headline in Santiago, Chile, one that trumpeted Eichmann's arrest.[3] In the three days that had passed since the El Al plane carrying the fugitive had taken off for Tel Aviv, the men who had led the Mossad team in Buenos Aires—Eitan, Malkin, and Shalom—had traveled nearly a thousand miles westward to Santiago. A thirty-hour journey, the train on which they were passengers had traversed the South American continent, crossing the Andes along the way, before pulling into the depot in the Chilean capital. By all accounts, it had been a punishing ordeal. All the same, the weary trio welcomed the news that Eichmann was now incarcerated in Israel, although Malkin adds that they worried that Ben-Gurion's premature announcement might have compromised their safety.[4]

In the ensuing days, the operatives managed to secure airline tickets to Uruguay and Brazil, and from these nations eventually to Israel. Even so, they remained on edge throughout their journeys, an angst illustrated by Avraham Shalom's behavior when the plane on which he was traveling had a layover in Buenos Aires. The normally imperturbable Shalom, says Malkin, "was a wreck for the entire hour and a quarter we were on the ground, not only refusing to leave his seat but to even momentarily lower the newspaper he was pretending to read."[5] And the team members' apprehension was not to be short-lived. Nearly three weeks would pass before all of the operatives, including Nissiyahu, Ilani, and Nesher, touched down in Israel, or in Dani's case, France. In the meantime, the international community weighed in on the Jewish state's spectacular accomplishment. The verdict, however, was not a pretty one.

"International reaction to the capture of Eichmann and his transportation to Israel was overwhelmingly negative," says Ruth Sachs.[6] At issue: Israel's illicit methods, specifically its infringement of Argentina's borders and subsequent kidnapping of a resident. Once it became public knowledge that the elaborate abduction had taken place in a remote suburb of Buenos Aires, the Argentine government, like the international community, assumed the Jewish state had been behind the caper. Accordingly, the Argentine administration voiced its outrage and recalled its ambassador from Tel Aviv, while the world looked on in solidarity with the South American nation. "Even the United States ambassador to the United Nations, Henry Cabot Lodge, soundly denounced Israel's action," writes Sachs.[7] It seems the Jewish state's strident actions were seen as setting a dangerous precedent, as flying in the face of the values and principles that were supposed to characterize friendly nations in the postwar era. Honorable countries, Israel's critics insisted, respect one another's borders; they do not violate them. "[A] threat to world peace," is how one dignitary depicted Israel.[8] As noted earlier, such sweeping condemnation had been one of Harel's main concerns when envisioning the mission.

Ben-Gurion, for his part, attempted to absolve the Jewish state by claiming that Eichmann had been seized by volunteers—a band of Holocaust survivors turned Nazi hunters—who had acted apart from the Israeli government. Of their own accord, he asserted, these individuals had removed Eichmann from the South American city and handed him over to the Israeli secret service.[9] The Prime Minister further claimed that the war criminal had willingly accompanied his captors to the Middle East, and he pointed to Eichmann's signed statement as proof, the one that the Mossad had obtained from him in Buenos Aires.

The Argentine government, however, would have none of it. Wasting no time striking down Ben-Gurion's version of events, officials in Buenos Aires insisted that the bold abduction was imbued with the unmistakable scent of a sophisticated covert operation, the type that only a state-sponsored intelligence agency could devise. They also made it known that they had no intention of dispensing with the matter. Not only had Israel violated the sovereignty of the South American country, it had done so amidst the nation's celebration of its 150-year anniversary, thus constituting an affront to the nation and its people.

As for resolving the conflict, officials in Buenos Aires instructed Israel to return Eichmann to Argentina, to which Ben-Gurion, to the surprise of virtually no one, responded with a resounding "no." He did not intend to permit the man who had systematized the mass murder of European Jewry to retreat to his tropical sanctuary, Ben-Gurion's position being that Israel, irrespective of how it had come to be in possession of the former Nazi mastermind, would not set him free.

So it was that Argentina, having reached the limits of its authority, appealed to the United Nations for help. It was an appropriate avenue, of course, given that a fundamental purpose of the global assembly was to intercede in such disputes. And indeed, the UN promptly accepted the request, reviewed the case, and handed down a judgment that was at once unanimous and unequivocal. "The subsequent resolution, passed by 8 votes to 0 on 23 June 1960, condemned Israel's actions," writes David Cesarini.[10]

The United Nations resolution notwithstanding, the two countries would not settle their differences until August 3 of that year, the result of weeks of negotiations between their representatives, Golda Meir speaking for Israel and Mario Amadeo for Argentina. In the end, Israel, it seems, held the advantage because Eichmann was not, and had never been, an Argentine citizen. Because he had adopted a false identity, that of "Ricardo Klement," when entering and residing in the South American nation, the Argentine government was under no legal or ethical obligation to protect him. It was this same lack of citizenship, moreover, that would prove instrumental when the Jewish state subsequently asserted its right to prosecute him, a point of contention since he had not committed any crimes on Israeli soil. "[I]t was Eichmann's de facto statelessness, and nothing else, that enabled the Jerusalem court to sit in judgment of him," writes Hannah Arendt. "Eichmann, though no legal expert, should have been able to appreciate that, for he knew from his own career that one could do as one pleased only with stateless people; the Jews had had to lose their nationality before they could be exterminated."[11] It was a case of poetic justice.

Ultimately, the governments of Israel and Argentina issued a joint statement criticizing those nameless volunteers who had allegedly trespassed and abducted the war criminal, with the Jewish state going a step further and formally apologizing for these same stand-alone Israelis and their illegal acts. And Argentina, for its part, abandoned its demand that Eichmann be returned.[12] At last, the hatchet had been buried, and the Mossad had been kept completely out of picture.

Ben-Gurion, even in the midst of issuing Israel's official statement of regret, persisted in denying the Mossad had carried out the mission. Such disavowals frustrated Isser Harel, however, who took pride in Operation Eichmann, his agents, and his own leadership in the historic undertaking. He deeply regretted that the agency could not enjoy the public recognition he felt it deserved, although he did take comfort in the fact that the global community had little doubt that the kidnapping had been the Mossad's doing. The agency's fingerprints were all over it, and for this reason intelligence organizations around the globe took the mission's provenance for granted. Furthermore, the Mossad's stunning proficiency in the Eichmann affair was universally acclaimed when the operation was appraised on its own merits, distinct from the thicket of political and ethical questions the endeavor engendered. Of course, the agency's role would, in due course, be made public, and Harel would among those facilitating its propagation. Fifteen years later he would publish an account detailing the dramatic mission, with his book serving as a testament to his agents' courage, cleverness, and compassion.[13]

Compassion, unfortunately, would be in short supply on the streets of Buenos Aires in 1960. Although Israel's apology quelled the indignation of the Argentine government, the anger of the Argentine public did not diminish as quickly, at least not that of young anti–Semites in the capital city. Worse still, their fury intensified in 1961 as the Eichmann trial took shape in Jerusalem. The fact is, there had existed in Argentina, long before Operation Eichmann, those elements that nurtured an irrational hatred of the Jewish people as evinced by the mounting number of young adults who had taken to joining neo–Nazi movements and organizations. To them, the Mossad's abduction of Eichmann and his ensuing trial in the Jewish state offered an opportunity to vent their rage, which is why they brushed aside Israel's expression of regret. It was an inconvenience, one that threatened to cloud the pretext for their wrath.

Without provocation, mobs of extremists now attacked Argentina's Jewish citizenry in what were truly horrific assaults. From shooting a Jewish boy to carving a swastika on the breast of a Jewish woman, the assailants' deeds were wanton and sadistic.[14] In other countries as well, anti–Semites rose up, prompting Jewish leaders in those nations to advise Ben-Gurion to jettison the trial or move it to West Germany. Among these figures was Joseph Proskauer, the head of the American Jewish Committee, whose overarching concern was for the safety of Jews in the Diaspora.[15] The Prime Minister, however, held fast to his conviction that Eichmann be brought to justice in the State of Israel. As it turned out, it would not be until after the war criminal's case had been heard, and his sentence delivered, that conditions would stabilize in those nations that were home to such fierce anti–Semites.

As for the trial itself, it commenced on April 11, 1961, and lasted nearly four months. It was a towering event by any standard. Each day, nearly eight hundred spectators pressed into the auditorium in the heart of Jerusalem where the trial was held, in the course of which over a hundred Holocaust survivors were slated to testify against the defendant.[16] Not only was the event imposing in its scale, but it also held the distinction of being the first trial in the world to be broadcast on television, the product of Israel's collaboration with an American company. Then, too, the proceedings were unique in terms of the security provided to the defendant. Owing to his volatile identity, officials in Jerusalem went to unprecedented lengths to ensure Eichmann's safety, a consideration that carried more than a touch of irony in light of the defendant's own actions against the Jewish people during the Holocaust. Most conspicuous of the security measures was a glass booth the Israelis constructed specially for the occasion, a bulletproof compartment in which Eichmann would be positioned during the proceedings. "It protected him from survivors of the death camps who might seek their own revenge," writes Sachs, "and it made it easier for the police to ensure that the SS underground did not make a rescue attempt or slip him cyanide."[17]

From the glass chamber, Eichmann, in the weeks that followed, struggled to justify his deeds, but his central assertion, the one he hoped would absolve him, was flimsy at best. "Eichmann's defense amounted to him arguing that he was merely a cog in the wield, dutifully obeying orders passed down from his scheming superiors to carry out this mass genocide," says Ishaan Tharoor.[18] It was the same position Eichmann had originally adopted during his Mossad interrogation in Argentina a year earlier, as well as one that he reasserted during a pre-trial interview in Israel. In the course of the latter, he said,

> All my life I have been accustomed to obedience, from early childhood to May 8, 1945—an obedience which in my years of membership in the SS became blind and unconditional. What would I have gained by disobedience? And whom would it have served? ... I realize of course that I cannot wash my hands in innocence, because the fact that I was an absolute receiver of orders has undoubtedly ceased to mean anything. Though there is no blood on my hands, I shall certainly be convicted of complicity in murder.[19]

In his statement, Eichmann not only asserts that he was merely a conduit in the Final Solution, a "receiver of orders," but adds that he had "no blood" on his hands. And just as the former notion formed the basis of his defense strategy, so the latter emerged during the trial as well, with the ex–Nazi portraying himself an erstwhile bureaucrat whose actions had been solely administrative, not physical. He had not killed anyone himself, he explained; organizing the extermination program had been a desk job, a colossal clerical task. Not surprisingly, the prosecuting attorneys saw the matter very differently and were quick to knock down Eichmann's naïve depiction of his lead role in the genocidal nightmare. "A cattle car could be a murder weapon in the same way the gas chamber was," they pointed out. "Both made up parts of a lethal arsenal that had been unleashed for the sole purpose of slaughtering as many Jews as possible."[20]

In the end, Eichmann was unable to put forth a convincing argument to mitigate the fact that he had chosen to join the Nazi Party, and to accept, with obviously relish, the top position in its program to exterminate European Jewry. And this brings us to his longtime claim that he felt no animosity toward the Jews. An episode recounted in William Shirer's landmark work, *The Rise and Fall of the Third Reich*, suggests the contrary by illustrating the supreme self-satisfaction Eichmann gained from his contribution to the mass execution of the Jewish people.[21] According to the war correspondent, an Eichmann confidante in the Nazi Party recalled that, shortly before Germany's surrender, the implementer of the Final Solution set about reconciling himself to the nation's impending defeat, and in the process reflected on his own personal, and unparalleled, triumph during the war. With pride, Eichmann exclaimed that "he would leap laughing into the grave" because of his successful liquidation of the masses, which he had found to be "a source of extraordinary satisfaction."[22]

As the historical record reveals, Eichmann would not, in fact, leap laughing into his grave. On December 11, 1961, the court convicted him of crimes against the Jewish people and condemned him to death by hanging, the first and only death sentence ever to be delivered by the State of Israel.[23] And although Eichmann, who was beside himself with anguish at his point, filed an appeal, the

Supreme Court rejected it three months later. Frantic to hold onto his life, he thereafter submitted a plea for mercy to Itzhak Ben-Zvi, the president of Israel, but the leader denied it. So it was that two days later, on May 31, 1962, Adolf Eichmann was executed at Ramleh Prison in Israel and his body sent to a crematorium.[24]

As Ben-Gurion had hoped would be the case, the Eichmann proceedings were effective in redirecting public awareness to the Holocaust, most importantly that of Jewish youth in the State of Israel and beyond. In so doing, it helped plant in the consciousness of a new generation the discrimination and death faced by those who had come before it. And it did this, in part, through the educational system itself. "After the Eichmann trial," writes Thomas Friedman, "Holocaust survivors were invited to speak in high schools, and for the first time the subject of the Holocaust was included in the Israeli twelfth-grade high-school curriculum."[25]

In addition, the case, which was covered by media outlets across the globe, put ex–Nazis on notice once again. "The Eichmann affair had a great effect not only on the public in Israel, but also on the attitude towards the Holocaust and its perpetrators around the world," reads a statement in the Israel State Archives, a summary of a research report centering on post-trial developments.[26] The document continues,

> [I]n the year after Eichmann's capture and transfer to Israel, there was a dramatic increase in the number of arrests of Nazi criminals throughout the world—in Germany and in other countries. In addition, [there was] a sharp rise that year in the number of trials, carrying out of death sentences and extradition procedures of Nazi criminals, and even in the elimination of Nazi elements in West Germany.[27]

To be sure, the State of Israel had confronted, and disposed of, a phantom from its past, and it had done so owing to the prowess of the Mossad. The intelligence agency, by all accounts, had done its job, and it had done it exceptionally well. Furthermore, it had no intention of losing either its edge or its momentum.

In the years immediately following Operation Eichmann, Isser Harel established within the Mossad a special unit devoted exclusively to locating former high-powered figures of the Third Reich. Based in Paris, Zvi Aharoni served as its manager, the operative not only coordinating the unit's activities but also reprising his hands-on role as a Nazi hunter in the field.[28] This special unit, from 1961 to 1964, was Harel and Aharoni's passion.

The Mossad as a whole, owing to the success of Operation Eichmann, now came to be viewed worldwide as a formidable player in the realm of intelligence. A young and inventive organization, the controversial affair in Argentina had proven that it was adept at executing a precarious mission in a faraway land, and, just as impressive, that its proficiency did not depend on the use of highly sophisticated technology. In fact, it was due to the latter attribute that Operation Eichmann was heralded as "a pure example of *humint*—the human intelligence skills at which Israel excelled," write Raviv and Melman.[29]

As to the reason that the Mossad was reliant on its agents' wits, or "humint," it was because the agency, unlike the CIA, MI-6, or KGB, lacked the financial, and therefore the scientific, resources required to produce innovative technology. The Mossad had no choice but to make use its agents' ingenuity in devising operational strategies that could be carried out using the organization's less than state-of-the-art technological capabilities. It would be this distinctive fusion of creativity and chutzpah, moreover, that would characterize the Mossad throughout the remainder of the 1960s and into the early 1970s, at which point an element of cold-bloodedness would enter the mix. It was an unscrupulousness that would surface when Prime Minister Golda Meir called upon the agency to avenge one of the most horrendous terrorist attacks of the twentieth century, the Black September massacre of Israeli athletes at the 1972 Olympic Games in Munich, Germany. The Mossad's response to this bloodbath, calculated to be both conspicuous and brutal, would seal its reputation as a top-notch intelligence agency while also revealing a newly-acquired ruthlessness in its dealings with the nemeses of the Jewish state.

Part Two

Operation Wrath of God

Introduction

In traveling to Argentina to seize Adolf Eichmann and smuggle him to Israel, the Mossad, as shown in Part One, made it a point to avoid harming him at any point. And this was not necessarily for moral or philosophical reasons. The fact is, it was imperative that the operatives treat the war criminal humanely, otherwise the State of Israel could expect its critics to accuse it of hypocrisy for abusing the captive in the same way the Nazis had abused the Jews. On top of that, it was not the Mossad's task to assume the role of judge; Israel's legal system was in place precisely for this purpose. But then came the Black September attack at the 1972 Summer Olympics in Munich, Germany, and everything changed. First and foremost, the horrific event prompted the Jewish state to reconsider the Mossad's function in dealing with known assassins, with special attention given to expanding the scope of its covert actions in such cases.

Whereas Adolf Eichmann's deeds had taken place nearly two decades before his abduction in Argentina, the ex–Nazi having long stopped his murderous ways and fallen into a life on the skids in his South American hovel, the young and robust perpetrators of the Munich Massacre were still free, willing, and able to assassinate more Jewish targets in Europe and elsewhere. It would have been futile for the Israeli government to try to track down each one of them, seek his extradition to the Jewish state, and force him to stand trial before the public, as did Eichmann. No doubt other nations, most notably the Arab states in which some of the terrorists had sought sanctuary and been lauded as heroes, would not honor an extradition request. And even if the assassins were to be transported to Israel for legal proceedings, there was no question but that Arab-sponsored attacks inside the Jewish state would rise dramatically in an effort to terrorize the country into releasing the defendants.

For this reason, the Mossad was given the task of delivering justice to the members of the Black September cell, wherever it might find them. And this meant targeted assassinations. Since the terrorists could be expected to engage in future killings, the Israeli administration of Prime Minister Golda Meir decided they had to be removed from the scene as swiftly as possible. A permanent change in the Mossad's mandate, it was an expansion of permissible interventions that, even today, remains the subject of considerable debate.

4

The Arab-Israeli Conflict and the Black September Organization

Of the numerous terrorist operations of the twentieth century, the Black September Organization (BSO) holds the dubious distinction of having been the most diabolic. Even in the Middle East, a region long regarded as a cauldron of political and religious extremism, the tenor and scale of the group's savagery was beyond compare. "In its rejection of any limits on the scope and methods of warfare, its willingness to destroy itself along with the enemy, the BSO represented a quantum leap in the level of conflict," writes John Amos in his incisive study, *Palestinian Resistance: Organization of a Nationalist Movement*.[1] As for its archenemy, the State of Israel, the young nation found itself in the crosshairs of the lethal organization from 1971 to 1973, the entirety of the BSO's existence.

To understand the emergence of Black September and what has been called its "logic of total violence," this chapter will begin by looking back at the formation of the Jewish state and the development of the long-standing Arab-Israeli conflict.[2] This will show the context in which the BSO came into existence, as well as the reasons behind its radical and explicit approach to political change.

The Promised Land

When an independent state for the Jewish people was originally proposed, a principal aim was the creation of a homeland in which Jews would be free from persecution. It was a quest that began in 1896, when a handful of progressive Jews, faced with yet another wave of demonization and injustice in Russia and Europe, set out to forge a state of their own. At this juncture, Theodor Herzl, a Hungarian-born journalist, proposed in his book, *The Jewish State*, the establishment of a Jewish land where "[w]e shall live at last as free men on our own soil, and die peacefully in our own homes."[3] It was the birth of Zionism, the international political movement that, from the outset, called for a self-ruling Jewish homeland that would be welcoming to Jews of all nations and whose residents would live safely and securely. Among other benefits, such a harmonious home, Herzl believed, would enhance its residents' self-regard, their pride as a people. "There we can expect the award of honor for great deeds, so that the offensive cry of 'Jew!' may become an honorable appellation," he writes.[4] And the Jewish people were not the only ones who would benefit. "The world will be freed by our liberty, enriched by our wealth, magnified by our greatness," he adds.[5] Although Herzl considered Argentina a candidate, he preferred the Middle Eastern region of Palestine, where Jews and Arabs had long lived side by side. In fact, it was because the two groups had coexisted peacefully in Palestine for several centuries that Herzl did not foresee a problem with allocating a portion of the land to those who were Jewish. As it turned out, the homeland he advocated would not come into existence in his own lifetime, nor would the ensuing pursuit of it be without bloodshed.

During the interval between Herzl's death in 1904 and Israel's birth in 1948, Great Britain presided over Palestine, a state of affairs that came about during World War I when the British military defeated the Turkish (Ottoman) forces in the region and took control of the land. At this time in 1917, Britain's Foreign Secretary, Alfred Balfour, dispatched an official letter to Baron Walter Rothschild, an influential figure in Britain's Jewish community, announcing that the British government was in favor of adopting a policy that would make Palestine the formal home of the Jewish people. The letter became known as the Balfour Declaration. As for the motive behind this seeming act of generosity, the British government was, among other things, protecting its own interests in the strategically-situated region. "[B]ehind it all was the knowledge that, if Britain promoted such a policy, it would necessarily be up to her to implement it, and this would in turn mean that she would have to exercise political control over Palestine," writes John Grainger. "One aim of the Balfour Declaration was thus to freeze out France (and anyone else) from any post-war presence in Palestine."[6]

As for the centuries-old Arab presence in the territory, Balfour considered it a nuisance, and his solution was to brush aside any concerns the Arab population of Palestine might voice. "[In] Palestine, we do not propose even to go through the form of consulting the wishes of the present inhabitants," he wrote to his colleague, Lord Nathaniel Curzon, a former viceroy of India.[7] Curzon, unlike Balfour, was against the appropriation of land on which Palestinian Arabs, like Palestinian Jews, had made their home for several generations, and he conveyed his opposition to the Foreign Secretary on numerous occasions. Balfour continues,

> The four Great Powers are committed to Zionism. And Zionism, be it right or wrong, good or bad, is rooted in age-long traditions, in present needs, of far profounder import than the desires and prejudices of the 700,000 Arabs who now inhabit the land.[8]

Through such statements, it is evident that Balfour, a fervent Christian who considered his religion to be indebted to Judaism, believed that Jewish culture was superior to that of the Palestinian Arabs and that such supremacy entitled the Jewish people to take possession of a swath of territory they had heretofore shared with its Arab residents. As to the how Balfour's proposal was received, his perspective, imbued with the values of colonialism, came to be embraced by many of his British colleagues, eventually including Winston Churchill. And, of course, an arrangement for a Jewish homeland in Palestine would indeed be formulated, with British rule persisting in the region until such a time that the plan could be enacted.

In July of 1922, the League of Nations, the forerunner of the United Nations, officially approved the continued British presence in the region, with the organization's fifty-one member states unanimously endorsing the provisional occupation. Ratifying a document known as the Mandate for Palestine, the alliance called for Britain to preside over Palestine, which was viewed as a protectorate, until the region could function as the national home of the Jewish people.[9] As conceptualized by the League of Nations, this Jewish home would be respectful of the rights of Arabs and Jews alike. The Mandate states,

> [T]he Principal Allied Powers have agreed [to] ... the establishment in Palestine of a national home for the Jewish people, it being clearly understood that nothing should be done which might prejudice the civil and religious rights of existing non–Jewish communities in Palestine, or the rights and political status enjoyed by Jews in any other country.[10]

As the historical record reveals, profound discord would eventually erupt between Arabs and Jews on the subject of Palestine. Before this, however, conflict would arise between Palestinian Jews and British officials owing to the latter's death grip on the region. In the wake of the Mandate's ratification, it seems that the Jewish people expected efforts to begin toward the foundation of their homeland, but a mounting number of them came to be both skeptical and frustrated as they watched Britain maintain possession of the region. In their view, no serious effort was being made to transfer Palestine to them. Instead, the powers-that-be in Britain were perceived as being indifferent, even inimical, to the Jewish voices calling for control of the land. Not surprisingly perhaps, it was an impasse that would lead to armed conflict, with spasms of violence erupting during the 1930s between Jewish activists in Palestine and representatives of the British government. Despite such clashes, however, no handover was forthcoming.

Then came World War II and the Final Solution. In the wake of the Holocaust, Zionist aggression in Palestine escalated as a multitude of survivors made their way to the Middle Eastern territory, rapidly expanding its Jewish population and highlighting the need for a sanctuary for these beleaguered arrivals. In the eyes of many Jews, the creation of a Jewish state was now imperative. Never before had such an obvious justification for its existence presented itself. Yet Britain stood firm in its provisional occupation of the region, while condemning the mounting ferocity of the Zionist movement in Palestine. From June 1946, onward, British forces bore down heavily on Jews who were demanding an official state, incarcerating, physically attacking, and even executing those perceived as threats to the region's stability. All indications were that the struggle was approaching a flashpoint.

In what would stand out as one of most horrific terrorist attacks in the Middle East in the first half of the twentieth century, Menachem Begin, a fervent Zionist and the future Prime Minister of Israel, presided over the bombing of the King David Hotel in Jerusalem. The date was July 22, 1946, and the luxury establishment was serving a dual role as the headquarters of the British administration. Casting the British presence as outmoded and oppressive, the Irgun, an insurgent organization which Begin commanded, packed five hundred pounds of dynamite into large milk canisters, hauled them through the hotel restaurant and into the building's basement, and set the bombs' timers for thirty minutes later. The Irgun then dispatched three separate messages to British authorities insisting they evacuate the hotel, but the latter refused to heed the warnings, according to Begin's account of events.[11] "We are not here to take orders from the Jews," a high-level British officer purportedly said. "We give *them* orders."[12] Right on schedule, the bombs detonated, killing or wounding over two hundred people.[13]

"There was a shock of horror among Jews and Arabs alike in Palestine," writes Martin Gilbert, "and among critics of Jewish terrorism throughout the Diaspora, and in the non–Jewish world."[14] Such widespread disapproval notwithstanding, the attack had made its point. "The blowing up of the King David carried a message for the whole world," writes David Hirst. "A new nation had arisen in Palestine; conceived in the Balfour Declaration, nurtured in the Mandatory womb, it was delivered in the just violence that historic events always engender."[15]

4. The Arab-Israeli Conflict and the Black September Organization 75

British forces cracked down instantly, imposing curfews and pursuing the bombings' perpetrators in scores of buildings in Jerusalem and Tel Aviv. Their efforts, however, were to no avail, with those behind the hotel attack not only slipping through the fingers of British authorities but proceeding to launch further assaults.

So it was that the discord persisted, an animosity fueled by the ongoing actions of the British, Arabs, and Jews. On July 11, 1947, for instance, British officials in Palestine refused to permit a passenger ship, the *Exodus 1947*, to dock. The vessel, which had sailed from France, was packed with over 4,500 passengers, mostly children and adolescents, with nearly everyone onboard being a Holocaust survivor. Owing to their circumstances, the preponderance of these refugees also lacked formal immigration certificates. To be sure, they were a people in need. But Ernest Bevin, the British Foreign Secretary, decided that the refugee ship would not be allowed to berth in Palestine ostensibly because Zionist extremists might be among its passengers.[16] The British Royal Navy therefore commandeered the vessel and returned it to France, where many of its long-suffering passengers, upon arrival, struggled to remain on the *Exodus 1947* even in the face of its increasingly unsanitary and deprived conditions. British officers forcibly removed them, however, after which all of the ship's passengers were sent to Germany and placed in British-run camps where officials pored over them in search of potential troublemakers. Not surprisingly, the world was aghast that Britain would not only refuse to allow a shipload of Holocaust survivors to disembark in Palestine but would transport them to holding camps in the former Nazi Germany. An infamous ordeal, it captured international attention, brought reproach upon the British government, and helped turn public opinion in favor of the establishment of a Jewish state in Palestine. More dangerously, though, it further enraged Zionist guerrilla fighters, whose violence persisted unabated.

Arguably the most egregious expression of the latter's rage came in 1948 in another Irgun assault, this one staged in conjunction with a fellow insurgent-terrorist organization, the Stern Gang. Together, the two groups carried out a massacre at Deir Yassin, an Arab village near Jerusalem, that killed 245 Arab men, women, and children.[17] Afterward, the perpetrators humiliated the village's survivors by parading them through the streets of Jerusalem.

Once again, criticism was swift and scathing, and it included that of such Jewish luminaries as Albert Einstein, who was appalled by the bloodbath and abruptly ended his association with a pro–Sternist organization in the United States. It was the day after the massacre that the theoretical physicist penned a seething letter to the executive director of the American Friends of the Fighters for the Freedom of Israel. "When a real and final catastrophe should befall us in Palestine," writes Einstein, "the first responsible for it would be the British and the second responsible for it the Terrorist [sic] organizations built up from our own ranks."[18] Two days later, Einstein added Arabs to the mix in a letter to the *New York Times*. "Both Arab and Jewish extremists are today recklessly pushing Palestine into a futile war," writes the scientist. "While believing in the defense of legitimate claims, these extremists on each side play into each other's hands."[19] His words would prove prophetic four days later when Arab militants ambushed and killed 77 Jewish doctors and nurses en route to a hospital.[20] The attack was in retaliation for the mass murder at Deir Yassin, and was yet another instance of the deadly cycle of terror perpetuating itself.

It would be a month after the Deir Yassin massacre that Israel would officially become a nation, the Mandate for Palestine being allowed to expire. A transfer of power that had been in the works for many months, it was formalized in United Nations General Assembly Resolution 181.[21] To be sure, it had been an ugly journey to this point, and it was no secret that all parties had committed atrocities along the way. Even British dignitaries acknowledged this fact.

"The revolting way in which Britain was terminating her thirty years of rule in Palestine," write Michael Bar-Zohar and Eitan Haber, "was denounced with disgust by Winston Churchill as 'the dirty war' against the Jews."[22]

Recalling his and his compatriots' wrath during this period, as well as attempting to justify their terrorist activities, Menachem Begin writes,

> We had to hate—as any nation worthy of the name must and always will hate—the rule of the foreigner ... the barring of the gates of our own country to our own brethren, trampled and bleeding and crying out for help in a world morally deaf.[23]

"There are times," Begin adds, "when everything in you cries out: your very self-respect as a human being lies in your resistance to evil."[24]

Unfortunately, the hostility did not end with Israel declaring its statehood. Within hours of the announcement, the surrounding Arab states, refusing to accept Israel's existence, launched an across-the-board assault on the nascent nation and ignited a costly conflict in terms of blood and treasure. In what would become known as the 1948 Arab-Israeli War—in Israel, it is referred to as the War of Independence—the Israeli military fought valiantly to keep the aggressors at bay while Count Folke Bernadotte, a Swedish nobleman and the first mediator of the United Nations, toiled day and night to craft a cease-fire between the warring parties. But while the diplomat did indeed succeed at this intricate task, he soon discovered that the agreement he had brokered would not last—nor, for that matter, would he himself survive. A month later, a terrorist triumvirate in Tel Aviv, one that included Yitzhak Shamir, another future prime minister of Israel, ordered the Stern Gang to assassinate the UN mediator.[25] And the consequences were predictable: the Israeli government decried the murder, as did the greater number of Jews and Arabs in the region, while fighting between Israel and its neighbors resumed.

For the next several months, war raged as the Israeli military, over and again, hammered the Arab forces, evincing a might that surprised the world. Finally, in March, 1949, the conflict came to an end, with a triumphant Israel signing peace treaties with Jordan, Egypt, Syria, and Lebanon in the ensuing months. Only Iraq refused to sign a treaty with the Jewish state and so, on paper, remained in a state of war with it.

According to the U.S. State Department, the Jewish state, owing to its superb military, had managed to retain nearly all of the territory that UN Resolution 181 had granted the nation during its formation. Not only that, it had taken possession of an extensive amount of land that the same resolution had granted Palestine's Arab population, thereby increasing Israel's overall size. "Israel was in control of about one-third more territory (some 2,500 square miles) than it had been allocated by the United Nations partition plan," writes historian L. Carl Brown.[26] The Jewish state subsequently imposed martial law in the territories it had captured.

Of course, this remarkable development meant that the most of Palestine was now in Jewish hands, whereas Arabs had largely inhabited it prior to the war, according to Israeli-British historian Ilan Pappe. "Palestine was still very much an Arab country by the end of the [British] Mandate," he writes in his book, *The Ethnic Cleansing of Palestine*.[27] Not only was the Arab population in the majority, Pappe explains, but it also possessed the lion's share of arable property. "Almost all of the cultivated land in Palestine was held by the indigenous population—only 5.8 percent was in Jewish ownership in 1947."[28] Not surprisingly given the long-standing territorial dispute in the region, competing claims have been made, most notably that only a tiny number of Arabs lived in Palestine before the advent of the Jewish state. In a similar vein, Golda Meir, quoted in *The Washington Post* in 1969, claimed that while there were people living in Palestine before Israel came into being, they were not a Palestine-identified population; hence, there was no Palestinian people. "They did not exist," she said.[29] Such conflicting claims aside, the reality is that an enormous number of Arabs and Christians had lived in Palestine for centuries, a fact with which Israel would have to contend after winning the 1948 Arab-Israeli War.

Having benefited from the battle, the Jewish state was now in a position to move forward with its development as a nation. But there remained a problem, one that would eventually lead to the emergence of groups like Black September and a dilemma that persists even today. At its core was the plight of those Arabs, and to a lesser extent Christians, who had been living in Palestine between 1946 and 1949, the period encompassing the end of the Mandate for Palestine, the establishment of the State of Israel, and the 1948 Arab-Israeli War. Because violence ravaged the region during this time, hundreds of thousands of these residents had fled Palestine to escape the fighting. On top of this, Jewish fighters had forcibly expelled innumerable Arabs and Christians from Palestine with the intention of taking their land for the Jewish people. And while a handful of Jewish leaders were disheartened by these evacuations and evictions, a much larger number saw distinct advantages in the mass flight. "[O]nce the Palestinian exodus began," writes David Margolick in the *New York Times*, "Jewish leaders, struck by their good fortune, first encouraged it, then coerced it, then sought to make it stick."[30] Foremost among these benefits, says Margolick, was the fact that the departures would allow the State of Israel to make room for the Holocaust survivors who continued to arrive on its shores.[31] As it turned out, most of the Arabs, in particular, who evacuated Palestine would never return to the land they had left behind, a substantial share of which had been destroyed at any rate. "About 400 villages and towns were depopulated in the course of the war and its immediate aftermath," writes Benny Morris. "By mid–1949, the majority of these sites were either completely or partly in ruins and uninhabitable."[32]

As for the number of displaced people, it was set at 711,000 by the UN Conciliation Commission for Palestine.[33] Some of these individuals were loath to go back to a land where they no longer felt welcome or, more dauntingly, where they could face intimidation or expulsion. Others had lost their properties and livelihoods in towns that had been devastated and therefore had little reason to return. Still others thought it best to remain where they had ended up, since in their new locations they would be governed by fellow Arabs, not by Jewish officials, which would now be the case if they returned to their former homes. So it was that a sizable share of the dislocated Palestinian Arab population settled in areas such as the West Bank (Jordan) and the Gaza Strip (Egypt), situated alongside the Mediterranean Sea. Because so many of these people, being uprooted, lacked the essentials for life, the United Nations formed an organization tasked with building refugee camps in the locations where they had come to rest. A humanitarian operation known as the UN Relief and Works Agency for Palestine Refugees in the Near East (UNRWA), it offered, and continues to provide today, support services to displaced Palestinians dwelling in the West Bank, Gaza Strip, and other such areas.[34]

As for Israel, it flourished in the years immediately following the 1948 Arab-Israeli War, and it continued to thrive in the 1950s and 1960s despite the fact that relations with the surrounding Arab nations remained tentative at best. Its alliance with the United States, by comparison, was as strong as ever, and was bolstered when the Cold War began to infect the Middle East. During this period, the United States backed such strategic nations as Israel and Iran, the latter being under the dictatorial thumb of the pro–American shah, Mohammad Rezā Pahlavī. The Soviet Union, meanwhile, threw its weight behind Syria, Libya, and Egypt (United Arab Republic), among other countries. As it happened, it would be during this same period, in 1967, that another Arab-Israeli war would break out, and it would spring from faulty Soviet intelligence pertaining to one its client states in the Middle East.

It was during a meeting in Cairo on May 13, 1967, that Soviet diplomats unwittingly delivered a cache of erroneous information to Egyptian officials.[35] The inaccurate intelligence claimed that the Israeli military had stationed nearly a dozen contingents along the Israeli-Syrian border in preparation for an attack, according to Chaim Hertsog and Shlomo Gazit.[36] Since this was not true, the Israeli government sought at once to set the record straight. "The Soviet Ambassador to Israel was invited by the Prime Minister of Israel, Levi Eskhol, to accompany him to the area bordering the Syrian frontier so that he could convince himself that the concentration of Israeli forces was totally untrue," write Hertsog and Gazit.[37] The Soviet diplomat's response, however, was puzzling at best in that he turned down the invitation. And so war loomed.

Scrambling into action, Arab nations, most notably Egypt, set about whipping up war fever and arming for battle. In turn, Israel, alarmed by this development, followed suit and began readying for war, too. What ensued was a taut stretch, one that lasted the rest of the month of May, during which Israeli and Arab forces waited to be attacked by one another. For the Jewish state, it was a particularly nerve-wracking period, evoking, as it did, Nazi Germany's campaign to exterminate the Jewish people, a fear that was stoked by the apocalyptic rhetoric of Egyptian officials.

"[W]hen Egyptian President Gamal Abdel Nasser began beating his war drums, established a joint military command with Jordan, and threatened to wipe Israel off the face of the earth, many Israelis became convinced that their borrowed time was up," writes journalist Thomas Friedman. "It was the month when for the first time the widening awareness of the Holocaust among Israelis would begin to merge with their immediate predicament."[38]

It was a predicament that would soon come to an end, however. In a showdown that commenced on June 5, 1967, Israel launched a preemptive strike against Egyptian forces. Its rationale was a pragmatic one: facing what many considered to be an inevitable war, it would be more advantageous, tactically, to be on the offensive rather than the defensive.[39] Israel knew it would probably incur less damage to Israeli property if it were to fight the war on foreign soil instead of its own.

Combat lasted only a few days—it ended on June 10, 1967—in what came to be known as the Six-Day War. It was a conflict in which the Jewish state, in a stunning display of military prowess, prevailed handily over its Arab enemies. And the people of Israel were ecstatic. "Many described the victory as a miracle, as if they had been sprung from hell and borne up to the summit of salvation," writes Tom Segev. "The sense of total doom all but disappeared; history was about to begin again."[40] But not only had the Jewish state won the war and managed to retain nearly all of its land, it had also seized a staggering amount of Arab territory. This included the entire West Bank (Jordan), Gaza Strip (Egypt), Golan Heights (Syria), and Sinai Peninsula (Egypt). These lands became known as the Occupied Territories. "A new map of the Middle East came into being, with Israel three times larger than it was in 1949," write Ian Bickerton and Carla Klausner.[41] It was, however, a map that would be marked by contention.

The controversy stemmed from the fact that the Jewish state, despite its claims of self-defense, had been the nation to actually kick off the fighting and thereafter take possession of its neighbors' land. In response to this action, the United Nations Security Council adopted Resolution 242 in November of 1967. Unfortunately, it was an imperfect document, one that has been called "a masterpiece of diplomatic ambiguity" and which lent itself to differing interpretations.[42] The unanimously-approved resolution called for, in the wording of the document, the "[w]ithdrawal of Israel armed forces from territories occupied in the recent conflict."[43] A debate soon arose over the meaning of this statement, however, since the English-language version, unlike the French one, did not include the word "the" before "territories." The upshot: Israel used this inconsistency as wiggle room to argue that the resolution did not necessarily mean that *all* of the land it had captured should be returned.[44] The resolution also called for "respect for and acknowledgment of the sovereignty, territorial integrity and political independence of every State in the area," a condition that rankled certain Arab nations since it meant they must acknowledge Israel and accept its right to exist.[45]

In the end, Israel did not abide by the UN resolution, nor did Syria, which rejected the document because, among other reasons, it failed to address the plight of millions of stateless Palestinians. And pro-Palestinian organizations, although they were not parties to the resolution, dismissed the resolution as well, rejecting it, in part, "because it referred to the Palestinians merely as 'refugees,'" says Yehuda Lukacs.[46] The document, by comparison, required Arab nations to recognize the people of Israel.

For the dislocated Palestinians, the Six-Day War worsened matters, and rather significantly. Displaced to the West Bank, Gaza Strip, and other Arab-governed regions in the 1940s, the same lands to which they had fled now were being occupied by Israel. It was this distressing state of affairs, that of being overtaken by those of another religion, language, and culture, that would jump-start the drive for an independent Palestinian state. Front and center in this campaign, moreover, would be the fearsome Palestinian Liberation Organization.

The Palestinian Liberation Organization (PLO)

It was in May 1964, that over four hundred Palestinian Arabs gathered in Jordan-controlled East Jerusalem and formed the Palestinian Liberation Organization, or PLO.[47] A confederation of pro–Palestinian groups, the organization sought to bring together those who were determined to establish a self-governing Palestinian homeland. And while the PLO did indeed clamor for an autonomous state during its formative years, it became far more militant in the wake of the Six-Day War when the bellicose Yassir Arafat took the reins as its chairman. Joining him in the PLO was an extremist group he had established a decade earlier, Fatah (*al-Fatah*), which quickly became its military arm and most influential faction. It was now that the PLO, more than ever, became fixated on winning Palestinian statehood at any cost and with little regard for the difficulties the struggle might bring to the region's Arab nations. And the organization did, by all accounts, create profound havoc in the area as illustrated by its tenure in Jordan, a kingdom whose population was composed of both Trans-Jordanians and Palestinians.

Whereas the PLO, in the mid–1960s, had occasionally used the monarchy as a point from which to slip into, and then attack, Israel, it stepped up such infiltrations after the Six-Day War. It did so, moreover, without the support of Jordan's ruler, King Hussein, whose relationship with Israel was comparatively constructive. Coinciding with this development, the PLO also heightened its aggression within Jordan itself. Specifically, the organization struggled for authority over the large Palestinian community in and around Jordan's capital city, Amman, between 1967 and 1970. Stridently promoting its political agenda, the PLO strong-armed the local population into supporting it, as well as engaging in extortion to fund itself. It also vied for control of the streets, being determined to usurp the power of the Jordanian police. The predictable result was substantial damage to the kingdom in key spheres of its functioning and an unsustainable situation that would, in due course, lead to a bloody civil war. A merciless, largely urban battle, it would be sparked by a spectacular piece of theatre, a large-scale PLO operation in the Jordanian desert. Unfortunately for King Hussein, it was one that would implicate him and his monarchy in an audacious series of air piracies.

Skyjack Sunday. The Popular Front for the Liberation of Palestine (PFLP), the second largest faction in the PLO, orchestrated a mission—it was nicknamed "Skyjack Sunday"—to free pro–Palestinian fighters being held in prisons around the world.[48] The group also hoped to draw global attention to, and gain public sympathy for, the broader Palestinian cause. Unparalleled in its scope, the plot called for terrorists to commandeer four airliners representing Israel, the United States, and Switzerland, and divert them to an airfield in the Jordanian desert. As for Jordan's role in the criminal plot that was about to unfold inside its borders, it was entirely nonexistent. Knowing that King Hussein would order the Jordanian army to prevent the air piracy, Palestinian militants kept the monarch in the dark about their plans.

So it was that on September 6, 1970, the PLO faction launched its mission, a "swift, orchestrated operation that left the international community stunned," in the words of Samuel Katz.[49] Only two of the four aircraft touched down in Jordan, however. One proved too large for the airstrip and was re-routed to Cairo, while the other aircraft, an El Al plane, landed safely in London. The latter skyjacking had been foiled in mid-air, with those aboard the plane killing one of the perpetrators and British authorities taking into custody another one when the plane put down in London. A twenty-four-year-old woman by the name of Leila Khaled, the incarcerated extremist was a well-known figure in the shadowy realm of guerrilla warfare who recently had undergone plastic surgery so as to become unrecognizable.[50] In response to her arrest, terrorists swiftly seized another British airliner, essentially a replacement, and flew it to Jordan. In all, then, three planes were on the ground in Jordan and a fourth at an airport in Egypt.

Scores of the passengers who were being held in the Jordanian desert were released shortly after landing and transported to safety in Amman. However, over three hundred American, Swiss, British, German, and Israeli passengers, as well as Jewish passengers of any nationality, were not permitted to deplane, but instead were kept aboard as hostages.[51]

"The Jordanian government was powerless and humiliated," recalls David Raab, one of the captives. "Other than condemning the hijackings 'in principle,' ringing the site with troops, and providing food and first aid, it was helpless."[52] Owing to the large number of hostages, a raid on the airport was ruled out. It would be far too risky.

In the parched Jordanian wasteland, the hijackers forced the captives to remain on the aircrafts for nearly a week. "Inside the planes, the heat became oppressive as temperatures rose to 120 degrees Fahrenheit with no electricity and no air conditioning," recalls Raab.[53] It was during this grueling stretch that the extremists issued their demands. "These were that Swiss nationals would be released upon release of the three Swiss [pro–Palestinian] prisoners; German nationals upon release of the three German prisoners; British nationals upon Leila Khaled's release; Israeli nationals and 'dual nationals' ... upon the release of *fedayeen* in Israeli prisons; and, nondual American citizens when all demands were met."[54] In Arabic, *fedayeen* means "men of sacrifice." It was not until September 11 that the hijackers removed all of the hostages from the planes and sent them to Palestinian refugee camps temporarily. It was part of an exchange that would include the release of seven prisoners several days later, Leila Khaled among them. As a parting shot, the terrorists blew up the vacant airliners.

"The audacious Skyjack Sunday operation dramatically demonstrated the PFLP's ability to strike at numerous targets in different locations in a single day, with few repercussions," writes Katz.[55] Predictably, the success of the multiple hijackings inspired further acts of air piracy in the years ahead. Side by side with its momentary triumph on an isolated airstrip in the desert, however, would be a staggering setback for the PLO and its PFLP and Fatah factions.

It seems that the Jordanian episode infuriated King Hussein, since his kingdom had been used as the base for an international terrorist plot, one that had endangered the Jordanian people and caused the monarch himself to be viewed as a possible accomplice or, alternatively, as a cipher in his own land. For the Jordanian ruler, then, Skyjack Sunday was the last straw.

On September 17, 1970, Jordan's military stormed into the city of Amman and set about subduing those extremists whose deeds had been harming the monarchy.[56] A bold action, it swiftly escalated into a full-scale civil war during which Yasser Arafat and the various PLO factions called for Hussein's assassination and the seizure of the Kingdom of Jordan. But this was not to be. Instead, the Jordanian army overwhelmed the PLO, forcing Arafat and his network out of the country. For the cavalier PLO, it was a bleak and demoralizing experience, a stunning reversal of fortune for the once proud, even arrogant, umbrella organization. Alongside the humiliation, moreover, was a jarring structural collapse. "The Resistance was militarily shattered, its leadership in disarray," says Amos.[57] It was, to be sure, a dark phase in the life of the PLO and the Palestinian movement, one that would come to be known as "Black September," an allusion to the month it had begun. Before long, this would also be the name conferred upon a ruthless commando group that would emerge from the PLO's ashes of defeat.

The Black September Organization

"The Jordanian civil war ushered in a whole new phase of Palestinian violence—pure, unbridled terrorism," says Hirst.[58] Dumbstruck by the outcome of the war, the PLO moved to Lebanon, where Arafat and other top figures lingered in a state of discouragement and confusion in that country's Palestinian refugee camps. In time, Lebanon, like Jordan, would also find it necessary to expel the PLO, with the organization fleeing to Tunisia. For now, though, it was based in Lebanon and its leaders were in shock. Certainly they were not alone. For the masses of foot soldiers devoted to securing a Palestinian state—fifteen thousand PLO members had likewise bolted to Lebanon—they, too, were disillusioned and disoriented. "The contrast between the inflated claims prior to the war and the total disarray which followed produced an enormous emotional and perceptual dislocation for this rank and file," writes Amos. "[T]he seemingly solid and defined universe, the ideological framework of action, was shattered."[59] As a result, many members were in need of a lifeline, a chance to regroup and renew, and for some this would come through the creation of the Black September Organization. Intended to furnish a much-needed shock to the system of the Palestinian liberation movement, this new terrorist operation hoped to re-energize the drive for a Palestinian state by staging over-the-top, high-profile operations in the Middle East and beyond. Yet the BSO served other purposes as well: it was a means by which young Palestinian extremists could deny the PLO's recent drubbing, pushing it aside and thus minimizing the pain of disgrace, even as they visited revenge upon Jordan and attempted to lay waste to Israeli interests.

Although the roots of Black September remain vague in certain respects, the consensus is that it was an offshoot of the PLO's leading faction, the Fatah, a sizable number of whose members had become skeptical of Yasser Arafat's abilities as a leader owing to the fiasco in Jordan. The Fatah is believed to have encouraged the disgruntled militants to form the BSO, and for three reasons. First, it would provide these members with a target outside of the Palestinian Liberation Organization itself, meaning they would be less inclined to direct their hostility inward, toward Arafat and his deputies. Second, Black September, the Fatah leaders assumed, would serve as their own proxy militia, engaging in international guerrilla activities that the Fatah's own policies forbade. At the same time, both the PLO and its Fatah faction could outwardly appear to be unrelated to Black September and thus not be held accountable for its deeds. It is for this reason that the BSO has been described as a "'deniable' special operations force" of the Palestine Liberation Organization.[60] And third, the Fatah's leaders were counting on Black September to bolster the Fatah against its main competitor within the PLO itself, the Popular Front for the Liberation of Palestine. More specifically, the Fatah hoped Black September would "counteract the success and publicity generated by the PFLP's brazen airline hijackings," says Bruce Hoffman, referring to the Skyjack Sunday spectacle in the Jordanian desert.[61] And so it began.

At the outset, Black September was a fluid and unruly operation. As such, it was a departure from the usual Palestinian resistance organizations, with their well-defined structures, centralized leaderships, and distinct chains of command. "Originally, the BSO was an amorphous series of loosely connected terrorist groups (cells really)," writes Amos.[62] Arising from profound emotional turmoil, its originators were impetuous and experimental, throwing off the shackles they believed had stifled the PLO. It was for such reasons that historian David Hirst and others have described Black September as being "less an organization than a state of mind."[63] Surely this was an accurate depiction of the BSO during its formative months, although its character would change as the organization evolved, better defining itself and focusing its objectives. "[W]ithin a year or so the BSO had acquired an extensive organizational sophistication," writes Amos, "and its tactics and targeting displayed considerable calculation and expertise."[64] Although the organization's structure remained largely decentralized, key people would emerge occasionally to make critical decisions for particular operations.

Black September was composed of one hundred to three hundred people, most of them men. At any given time, approximately sixty members were actively involved in guerrilla activities. Besides these participants, the organization made use of intermediaries on other continents. While publicly appearing to be unaffiliated with Black September, such go-betweens lent a hand to the organization's cells operating in European, Asian, and Middle Eastern nations. And while detailed information about the nature and extent of this assistance is sparse due to its clandestine nature, it is known that BSO cells, among other things, received instructions near their attack sites by means of coded messages embedded in radio transmissions. Presumably, these communications were the handiwork of such local intermediaries. Then, too, Black September is believed to have had the off-stage backing and cooperation of certain pro–Arab nations. An example of such collaboration: it purportedly received intelligence updates courtesy of the Soviet Union and Eastern bloc nations.[65]

The BSO's strike units were typically four-person cells that received their assignments immediately before an operation. For security reasons, cell members were not given advance knowledge of their missions; the less they knew, the less they could reveal if caught and interrogated. For the same reason, members were kept in the dark about other Black September deeds and prospective missions, since such information was too vital, too incriminating, to be placed at risk. It was a classic "need to know" approach. If a cell were to be captured, the BSO's other cells would not be in jeopardy since all of them would be working independently of, and in ignorance of, each other.

Research reveals that Black September's members tended to be smart young adults, most of whom who had been born in refugee camps.[66] Educated in traditional universities in Egypt, a significant share of the male participants also belonged to the Muslim Brotherhood. Most Black September members were also socially adept and able to integrate easily into Arab communities in European, Asian, and Middle Eastern nations. And, as noted, they harbored an intense resentment of Arafat and his leadership of the PLO, dismissing it as outmoded and ineffective and as having set back the movement for Palestinian statehood. In the end, their hostility over the Palestinian loss in the Jordanian Civil War, along with Israel's ongoing occupation of former Arab lands, powered the members' willingness, if not their wish, to commit truly savage acts. Unlike many Arab terrorist organizations in the decades to come, Black September did not arise from the precepts of Islamic fundamentalism.

It would be on November 8, 1971, that the BSO's pageant of death would be introduced to the world with the assassination of Wasfi al-Tal, the prime minister of Jordan.[67] In Cairo to attend an Arab League conference, the Jordanian head of state was shot and killed by a four-person cell as he descended the stairs at the Sheraton Hotel. It was a revenge slaying, one conducted in retaliation for the PLO's expulsion from Jordan. As it came to pass, Egyptian forces managed to capture the assassins, but the government ultimately released them.

A month later, a Black September terrorist shot and wounded Zaid al Rafai, the Jordanian Ambassador to the United Kingdom.[68] In the ensuing months, the organization targeted additional Jordanian officials, along with numerous Israeli officials and at least one PLO member on Black September's internal enemies list. It also attacked Israeli interests in other nations, although it did not conduct operations inside the Jewish state itself. This is because the organization, by selecting its victims in parts of the world other than the ever-watchful, heavily-armed Israel, could better use the element of surprise, cornering its prey unawares and under-defended. In due time, however, the State of Israel would become a direct target, too.

Besides gunning down Jordanian and Israeli officials in the streets, Black September took to sabotaging the infrastructures of those nations that conducted business with Israel. It also launched letter bomb campaigns aimed at Israeli embassies and their staffs in European and Asian capitals. And like the PLO's Popular Front for the Liberation of the Palestine, Black September seized hundreds of civilians in the course of its skyjackings.

On May 8, 1972, for instance, a four-person BSO cell commandeered a Sabena Belgian Airlines jet en route from Vienna to Tel Aviv.[69] According to the British Broadcasting Corporation, two men and two women hijacked the aircraft, forcing its one hundred passengers and crew to remain onboard at Tel Aviv's Lod (Ben-Gurion) Airport until Israel released a hundred Arab inmates being held its prisons.[70] The BSO vowed to execute the hostages if its demands were not met. But while officials on the ground pretended to negotiate with the terrorists, an Israeli military squad charged the plane, killing the pair of male hijackers, capturing the two females, and freeing the hostages. Undeterred, the organization continued its attacks, most notably the Munich Massacre in September of 1972, its most nefarious operation and the subject of Chapter Six. But Black September's "shock days" were, in fact, numbered.

By 1973, many Arab nations and Palestinian resistance groups were starting to become disenchanted with the feral organization. Besides murdering Arab officials in Arab nations, Jordan foremost in this respect, its growing refusal to accept what many considered to be the much-needed guidance of the PLO caused it to endure mounting ostracism in the Middle East. Then, too, its excessiveness seemed to be lessening the public's sympathy for the Palestinian cause and increasing its support for the State of Israel. And this was not surprising. Terrorism frequently backfires when it is used to draw attention to an issue, since it unwittingly contaminates the subject it hopes to publicize by associating it, in the public mind, with physical and emotional violence directed at those who are innocent. It was for such reasons that the BSO was fast becoming the albatross of the Palestinian Liberation Organization and the movement for Palestinian statehood.

During this same year, 1973, two further events contributed to the weakening of Black September. One was the historic decision by Yasser Arafat and the PLO to denounce terrorism as a political tool and replace it with diplomacy. A dramatic change of course, it left no place in the organization for an outfit like Black September, either overtly or covertly. And hammering the final nail in the BSO's coffin would be a second development: its blood-soaked operation on March 1, 1973, in the Sudan's capital city.

It happened at the Saudi Arabian embassy in Khartoum during a party for George Curtis Moore, an American chargé d'affaires who held strong pro–Arab views.[71] The gathering was to have been an opportunity for Moore's friends and colleagues to bid farewell to the highly respected and affable foreign service officer who was returning to the United States for reassignment. Among the guests were Cleo Noel, United States Ambassador to the Sudan; Sheikh Abdullah al Malhouk, Saudi Arabian Ambassador to the Sudan; Guy Eid, a chargé d'affaires at the Embassy of Belgium; and Adli al Nasser, a chargé d'affaires at the Embassy of Jordan.

"Reports say eight hooded gunmen entered the building firing guns," reads a BBC statement from that day, adding that the terrorists promptly seized the five diplomats.[72] Leading the Black September cell was Rizk al-Qas, who also served as its spokesman. "He was twenty-seven, of medium height and build, with dark hair, a mustache, and a kind of wild good looks," writes former United

States ambassador David Korn. "But he was a firebrand, a crazy, a man whose anger spewed in every direction, a man who would say or do anything."[73]

The terrorist cell tied up the five men, one of whom, Guy Eid, lay bleeding from an injury suffered during the gunfire. The extremists refused to help him, however, and instead kicked him, denied him water, and otherwise abused the chargé d'affaires until he begged to be killed.[74] His death would come later, however, since al-Qas had another task in mind at the moment.

In accordance with Black September's plan, the cell leader issued its demands, foremost among them the immediate release of an improbable number of pro–Palestinians imprisoned in Israel and elsewhere, along with a group of German terrorists incarcerated in West Germany. Some of these individuals were given special weight, such as Black September leader Abu Daoud who was in jail in Jordan. Other names on the list attracted attention because their presence on it seemed, on the face of it, inexplicable. Most notable was that of Sirhan Sirhan, who was imprisoned in California for the assassination of Senator Robert Kennedy.[75] One can surmise that Black September decided to include him on its list because Sirhan Sirhan, a Palestinian Christian and citizen of Jordan, had long opposed Kennedy's support of Israel.

Of course, it was virtually assured that the BSO's demands would not be met, a turn of events that would furnish the terrorists with an excuse to murder the hostages. Some have posited that this may have been the real objective all along. It should be noted, too, that diplomats from other countries also attended the party—Hungary, Yugoslavia, Japan, and the Soviet Union sent their representatives—but the cell did not target them and so they remained unharmed.[76]

When it became apparent that a deal would not be forthcoming, the eight extremists approached the three male hostages from Western nations—Americans Curtis Moore and Cleo Noel, and Belgian Guy Eid—and began preparing to take them to the basement. As the diplomats started the walk to their deaths, Moore had a brief word with their Saudi host. "Cleo Noel stopped momentarily beside al-Malhouk," writes Korn. "Graciously, Noel thanked the Saudi ambassador for the hospitality of the reception."[77] The Saudi diplomat was surprised and impressed by Noel's composure given the circumstances, as well as moved by the American's thoughtfulness. "[Noel] assured Malhouk that he and Moore did not hold their host responsible for what had befallen them."[78]

In the basement, the terrorists lined the captives against the wall and began machine-gunning them. "Reportedly, the gunmen shot first for sport—aiming at their feet and legs—before aiming to kill," writes Andrew Wilson in the conservative newsmagazine, *The American Spectator*.[79] It was needless cruelty, not unlike the killers' refusal to permit the men to say goodbye to their wives who were upstairs in the embassy.

4. The Arab-Israeli Conflict and the Black September Organization 89

It would be three days later that the takeover would end, with the BSO releasing the remaining two hostages, the Saudi ambassador and the Jordanian chargé d'affaires. Surrendering to the authorities, the terrorists' punishments would range from none whatsoever to a few years in prison. Such light consequences does not mean, however, that the attack on the Saudi Arabian embassy did not spark outrage in the Arab world. It did.

The Sudanese government called for its fellow Arab nations to place restrictions on Palestinian resistance activities, Jordan re-confirmed the death sentences for the Fatah and Black September inmates it held in its prisons, and Saudi Arabia threatened to cut off financial support to the PLO's Fatah faction. For that matter, a collection of Arab states pondered de-funding the PLO altogether, the umbrella organization ultimately being held responsible for the Black September mission. And there was more regional aftermath. The seizure of the embassy and the killing of American and European diplomats enraged the Nixon administration in the United States at precisely the moment when certain Arab states were attempting to form productive relationships with this most powerful of Western governments. Black September's reckless operation therefore threatened progress in this important endeavor. So it was that the PLO and other Palestinian groups quickly distanced themselves from Black September, thereby isolating the unbridled organization and hastening its demise. And while minor BSO offshoots and imitators would continue to spring up from time to time, the original organization itself faded out of existence at this juncture.

Arguably the most heartfelt reaction to the operation that brought Black September such disdain—the Sudanese ordeal—was that of Gaafar Nimeiry, the President of the Sudan. Infuriated by the damage the terrorist group had inflicted on his nation's guests and his country's reputation, Nimeiry assessed the guerrillas' mettle with devastating precision. There is, he insisted, "no heroism in seizing defenceless men, when you yourself are armed to the teeth, bargaining with their lives for impossible demands, slaughtering them like sheep, and keeping their corpses for 24 hours to rot."[80]

As it happened, it was precisely this scenario, that of heavily-armed extremists intimidating and finally murdering unarmed civilians, that had characterized Black September's most monstrous episode, the Munich Massacre, a year earlier. An orgy of malevolence, segments of the Arab world applauded this unprovoked slaying of sportsmen at the height of their athletic glory. Not only that; young Palestinian men became fired up by the slaughter and sought in large numbers to locate and join Black September. But the same event was regarded as atrocious and disgraceful throughout the rest of the world. A murderous binge, it partially alienated the international community from the Palestinian cause and brought profound sympathy and support to the State of Israel. And the Munich Massacre did more: it triggered a stunning twenty-year retaliation program against Black September, and the PLO more generally; a program conducted by the Mossad and involving the pursuit and execution of those believed to have been directly or indirectly responsible for the Olympic carnage. Chapter 5 discusses this unprecedented mission.

5
Massacre at the 1972 Summer Olympic Games

The Black September attack at the Games of the XX Olympiad should never have happened. In the years that have passed since the commando raid on the unarmed Israeli delegation, it has come to light that German officials received ample warning about the assault and neglected to act on it.

It was on July 14, 1972, that a West German embassy official stationed in Beirut, Lebanon, chanced upon an alarming piece of information: Palestinian extremists were planning an attack at the Olympic Games that were set to commence in weeks in the Bavarian city of Munich.[1] Alerting German authorities to the impending terrorist strike, the Foreign Office advised them to take all measures necessary to avert it. Yet officials in charge of Olympic security did not follow up on the warning. They failed to notify the probable target of the attack, the Israeli team, and they did not beef up security at the Olympic site itself. Instead, it was business as usual for those in charge.

At first, it appeared that their response to the warning—or lack of—would not become an issue. As scheduled, the Olympic Games began on August 26, with the event drawing the largest viewership in television history. Approaching the one billion mark, the worldwide audience delighted in the opening ceremony, with its salute to peace and camaraderie among nations. It was an image of goodwill that the host country was fostering with great enthusiasm.

For Germany, the 1972 Summer Olympics offered the long-awaited opportunity to bury a far more sinister impression, one that the same event had conveyed when it was last held in Germany. During this earlier time—the year was 1936—the Third Reich was on the ascent, and Adolf Hitler's arrival at Olympiastadion Berlin to attend the Games' opening ceremony had crowned the occasion, a spectacle enlivened by the thunder of cannons, the arm salutes of the masses, and the snap of the stadium's swastika-emblazoned banners. So it was that the 1972 Games were designed to be wholly different from those of the Nazi era: the present event was to serve as a testament to a new age in Germany, a nonmilitaristic era of freedom and tolerance and accessibility. And this sweeping makeover extended to the security personnel at the Olympic site as well, cordial men and women who were outfitted in cheery, sky-blue blazers instead of military-style uniforms and who carried two-way radios rather than weapons. "To erase any memory of the 1936 Berlin Games, the German authorities decided to keep the security measures as discreet as possible," write Michael Bar-Zohar and Eitan Haber. "The number of policemen and other security guards was reduced to a strict minimum."[2] Presumably, it was also for this reason—to reassure the world of a fresh and nonthreatening Germany—that officials were unwilling to heed the warning about the forthcoming terrorist attack. The prospect, even the whisper, of such an assault, particularly one aimed at those who were Jewish, could unravel the carefully crafted image the rehabilitated Germany was straining to express during this fortnight when the eyes of the world would be upon it.

    Consistent with this mindset, it is now known that German security experts, while preparing for the large-scale event, pondered the types of crises that might arise, one of which was designated Situation 21.[3] At its heart was a group of Palestinian terrorists who would sneak into the Olympic Village at night, overpower the Israeli athletes and take them captive, murder one as a warning to the others, and demand the release of Arab prisoners being held in the State of Israel. According to Georg Sieber, the psychologist and terrorism expert who devised this scenario and presented it to security officials for study, the powers-that-be were put off by it. They also were displeased with some of his other emergency situations, since the potential crises he foresaw did not fit into the open, accessible event they were busily planning. "The organizers asked Sieber if he might get back to them with less-frightful scenarios," writes journalist Alexander Wolff, "threats better scaled to the Games they intended to stage."[4]

    Notwithstanding the security officials' distaste over the prospect of a terrorist attack and their desire to shield both themselves and the public from such a disturbing thought, the latter would in fact learn about the impending strike on September 2, 1972, when the Italian magazine *Gente* reported that Palestinian terrorists were preparing to launch a spectacular assault at the Games.[5] With such a claim being published in a popular magazine at the height of the Summer Olympics, German officials, it would seem, would be hard-pressed to ignore the warning. Yet once again they managed to dodge it, later claiming to have been unaware of the Italian report. In the end, German authorities, as internal documents obtained by *Der Spiegel* confirm, received "several warnings prior to the Games that an attack was imminent."[6]

Three days after the Italian magazine hit the newsstands, a Black September cell broached the Olympic Village in Munich in what would mark the beginning of one of the most dramatic terrorist strikes of the twentieth century. It was, in effect, Situation 21. And while some aspects of the assault may never be known, since all but one of the perpetrators are now deceased and the German government has worked assiduously to conceal the evidence of its own negligence, there is still a substantial amount of information that has been made available to the public in recent years. The attack, for instance, was several months in the planning, with the requisite paramilitary training taking place a few weeks before the Black September cell surfaced in Munich.

The masterminds behind the attack were Abu Iyad (birth name: Salah Khalef), a cofounder with Yasser Arafat of the Fatah in the 1950s and thereafter Arafat's right-hand man in the PLO and its Fatah faction; Abu Daoud, a close associate of Arafat and Iyad; and Ali Hassan Salameh. The latter was nicknamed the Red Prince, and it was he who would handle the details of the Munich operation.[7] Because the trio was vital to the Black September Organization, they would not take part in the attack itself. Rather, an eight-man cell would carry out the massacre, although it could contact Iyad, Daoud, or Salameh if it became necessary.

To select the most qualified men for the job, the trio of leaders drew up a list of approximately fifty members of the Fatah, most of whom were in their late teens or early twenties. The candidates were then sent to a guerrilla training camp in Lebanon, where they set about honing their skills while being sized up for the Olympic attack. From this pool, the leaders selected six young men, all of whom were kept in the dark about the impending operation other than being told that it was of the utmost importance to Black September and the Palestinian cause. The six next traveled to Libya to undergo advanced guerrilla training.

Two additional Black Septembrists, as the organization's members were known, would complete the eight-man cell. One would serve as its Palestinian commander on the ground in Munich, the thirty-five-year-old Luttif "Issa" Afif, whose mother was Jewish and father, Christian. "Afif was a natural choice as leader because he was a seasoned fighter—a veteran of the 1970–1 war in Jordan—and, having studied engineering in Berlin, was fluent in German," writes Paul Taylor.[8] The other commando, twenty-five-year-old Yusuf "Tony" Nazzal, would serve as Issa's deputy and would be conspicuous during the Munich raid because of his distinctive cowboy hat. Tony's background was similar to that of Issa in terms of his experiences in Germany and Jordan.

As top-notch, seasoned BSO guerrillas, Issa and Tony, unlike the six commandos under their direction, were well-informed about the forthcoming mission. They had, in fact, spent a considerable amount of time preparing for it, Issa having worked as a civil engineer at the expansive Olympic Park during its construction and Tony employed as a cook at the same site. Their aim was to understand the Park's layout and services, information that would be invaluable when the time arrived to devise the operation. In the same way, the other six commandos' familiarity with German society was expected to be useful during the execution of the mission itself.

As things stood, everyone in the cell possessed similar backgrounds when it came to Israel, Palestine, and Germany. "[A]ll eight terrorists selected for the operation had suffered at the hands of the Israelis," writes journalist Simon Reeve based on statements made by Abu Daoud.[9] Most had grown up in impoverished Palestinian refugee camps, in particular the Chatila camp in Beirut, where, as boys, they had played soccer together. "But although the fedayeen chosen for the attack were all children of the camps," adds Reeve, "the reason most were selected seems to have been their previous familiarity with Germany."[10] Certainly it is true that among their ranks were those who had lived in Germany and studied in that country. One had even become engaged to a German woman.

After weighting the cell with young men familiar with Germany who possessed basic fluency in its language, the organization set about ensuring that the guerrillas' weapons would be in place in Munich prior to the assault. In this facet of the operation, the BSO collaborated with German neo–Nazis, who agreed to supply hand grenades and assault rifles for the raid.[11] Because the weapons were delivered to the organization outside of German borders, however, slipping them into Germany for the attack would be another hurdle, and it would fall upon Black September to pull it off. Yet the organization would do so without a hitch.

It was on August 23 at a busy airport in Cologne, Germany, that a well-dressed couple, a man and a women carrying Libyan passports, arrived from Tripoli with four suitcases. The urbane pair were couriers for the terrorist organization. After scrutinizing the couple's documents, a customs officer ordered the man to open one of the bags, but the man, posing as a haughty entrepreneur, refused to comply. "He began to yell and scream," writes Aaron Klein, adding that the purported businessman insisted he "had never been so thoroughly embarrassed in all his travels throughout Europe."[12] Unimpressed, the customs officer once again demanded that he open one of the bags, any of the four sitting on the counter between them. Pretending to be exasperated, the courier grudgingly snapped up a suitcase and unlatched it, one that was chockfull of women's lingerie. With this peculiar turn of events, the officer, finding no reason for further inspection, waved the couple through the customs service. Little did he know that the remaining pieces of luggage were packed with AK-47s, hand grenades, and ammunition. Then again, neither did the couriers. The two had not been informed of the contents of the baggage or the gist of the BSO mission itself.[13] Evidently, they were only told which suitcase would be safe for inspection. Leaving the airport, the couple drove to Munich, where they stored the luggage in a locker at a train depot and returned from whence they came.

A week later—it would be the same day that Olga Korbut, the elfin gymnast, snared a gold medal for the Soviet Union—the remaining six commandos arrived in Germany. Carrying forged Jordanian passports, they arrived by train from Belgrade and by air from Rome, and they promptly established contact with Issa and Tony. During the ensuing days, the six would visit Munich's attractions and tour the Olympic Park, since they still were not privy to the nature of their mission and thus had nothing else to do. In accordance with Black September procedures, the operation would be revealed to them at the last possible moment, which, it turned out, would be the evening of September 4, 1972, just hours before the attack was slated to transpire.

It was at a restaurant in the Munich Central Train Station that the entire group gathered, Abu Daoud and the eight members of the cell. Here, Daoud disclosed the details of the forthcoming raid. A one-time math teacher and a notorious figure even among terrorists, Daoud was a man who had seldom been seen to experience remorse during his lifetime of violence. And this would include the Munich Massacre, which he looked upon as an act of political communication. "He saw the attack as instrumental in putting the Palestinian cause on the map," says *The Telegraph*.[14] To Daoud's way of thinking, a seismic shock was necessary to bring international attention to the suffering that the Palestinians had withstood for decades. He was correcting a problem, in his view, and he was using the dubious reasoning that was, and remains today, prevalent among extremists: violence attracts attention, and attention leads to political and social change. "From the terrorists' point of view," writes Iranian-born, British-trained psychologist Fathali Moghaddam, "terrorism is a rational problem-solving strategy."[15] More often than not, the fact that it usually fails to achieve its goal is sidestepped by those who embrace it, and this proved to be the case for Abu Daoud and the Black September Organization.

At this juncture, it is important to note that the BSO insisted throughout the Munich Massacre that its grievance was not with the Jewish people or Judaism itself. Its complaint was against the State of Israel for its ongoing occupation of what remained of Arab Palestine and its subjugation of the millions who subsisted in the sprawling refugee camps. It was for this reason that the Munich raid was code-named Iqrit and Biri'm, in remembrance of a pair of "ancient Arab villages in northern Israel that had been violently cleared by the

Israeli army in 1948 to make room for the Jews," in the words of historian David Large.[16] Thus, Black September's actions, the organization maintained, were political, not religious and not anti–Semitic.

In the train station restaurant, Daoud explained to the commandos that the immediate objective of the Munich raid was to take prisoner a group of Israeli athletes housed in the Olympic Village as the first phase of a hostage-exchange deal. "The prisoners were to be held captive in the Village pending agreement by the government of Prime Minister Golda Meir to release Palestinian 'prisoners of war' being held in Israeli jails," says David Large.[17] Despite the near-zero possibility of this happening—it was common knowledge that the Jewish state did not negotiate with terrorists—it does appear that Black September was counting on a deal to take place, even though the process itself might become protracted. Thinking ahead, the BSO had a contingency plan in place in the event that an arrangement was not reached quickly: the terrorists, after holding the hostages for twenty-four hours, would load them onto a plane and order it to be flown to an Arab nation, where negotiations would recommence.

The Black September leaders also believed, or claimed to believe, that no Israeli athletes or Palestinian commandos would be harmed in the attack. In this regard, Daoud told the cell members not to kill the captives, that only in self-defense could violence be employed.[18] Such claims notwithstanding, it appears that those at the vanguard of the raid may have anticipated bloodshed. "We knew that achieving our objective would cost lives," recalled a surviving terrorist, "but since the day we joined up, we had been aware that there was a possibility of martyrdom at any time in the name of Palestine."[19]

After the meeting at the train station had drawn to a close, the eight-man cell spent the final hours before the attack at a nearby hotel in the heart of Munich gearing up for the assault. Shortly before 4:00 a.m., the Black Septembrists, dressed in red tracksuits and lugging duffel bags so as to look like athletes returning from a night of celebrating, departed by taxis to the site of the operation. Contained within their duffel bags were amphetamines, first aid supplies, ski masks, AK-47s, and thirty-bullet magazines.[20] The first order of business, once they arrived at the Village, would be to overcome its security apparatus.

Black September had already observed the Village's safety measures to be rather lax during this, the second week of the Games. During nighttime, moreover, security precautions were scandalously slack, which is one reason that the attack was scheduled for 4:00 a.m. Other protective measures included a chain-link fence around the Village's perimeter, one that was ten feet tall but did not contain barbed wire and was no longer guarded at night. As to the Israelis' dormitory, it was clearly vulnerable to attack because it stood a few yards inside the fence, a distance away from the Village's main housing sector

5. Massacre at the 1972 Summer Olympic Games   97

where most of the other nations' athletes were lodged. It seems that Olympic organizers, prior to the Games, had given Israel the choice of dormitories, but rather inexplicably the Jewish state's security officials had found no problem with this one. They also had no qualms about some of the apartments of the Israeli athletes being situated on the ground floor of the building, with easy access from the street. The fact is, the Games' security arrangements were flaccid at best, due to decisions by both Olympic and Israeli officials. And this was a matter that deeply concerned the head of Israel's Olympic delegation, Shmuel Lalkin.

Worried about these conditions, Lalkin sought permission from an official at the Israeli embassy to carry a gun, but his request was denied. Lalkin also sent a letter outlining his concerns to Arie Shumar, the chief of security of Israel's Education, Culture and Sports Ministry, but Shumar replied with what amounted to a turf-war smack-down. His two-sentence note said, tersely,

> As Manager of the Israeli Olympic team it would be advisable for you to concentrate on sports. Leave security to the security personnel.[21]

Given that protective measures for the Israeli delegation were discernibly deficient, it should come as no surprise that members of the Israeli Olympic team were apprehensive. "Many of the athletes feared they would be attacked during their events," writes Klein.[22] Because they had trust in the security staff that was responsible for safeguarding them, however, they did not request more or better protection. "They didn't act, they said, because they assumed that the security forces must be working undercover," reads the Koppel Report, a summary of the ensuing investigation of the attack.[23] So it was that the athletes and their coaches and judges, in the early morning hours of September 5, were asleep and, in effect, unprotected in their suite of apartments at 31 Connollystrasse, while just outside the Village the eight Black Septembrists prepared to scale the fence.

Their entry, it turned out, was problem-free, being eased when they spied a group of Canadian athletes returning from a night of partying. The tipsy Canadians, mistaking the commandos for fellow athletes, lent them a hand, hoisting them and their duffel bags over the fence. And while one of the surviving terrorists later claimed it had been a group of Americans who provided this help, a member of the Canadian water polo team, in 2012, came forward to clarify the situation. "It's possible there was an American or two in the group," recalls poloist David Hart, "but the vast majority of us were Canadians."[24]

Inside the site, the commandos walked a short distance with these bona fide athletes and then parted ways, after which the Black Septembrists divided into two groups so as to be less conspicuous. Peeling off their tracksuits, they donned ordinary clothing, put on ski masks, armed themselves, and ditched their bags. Issa, who would serve as the cell's negotiator and therefore would be visible to German authorities and the public, did more: he smeared his face with black shoe polish, put on dark glasses, and pulled on a hat. The two groups, from different directions, then dashed toward the Israelis' lodgings. Or so they thought.

Despite Issa and Tony's earlier reconnaissance efforts, it seems the pair had made a mistake about the location of the Israeli delegation, the upshot being that the two sets of commandos rushed into the building only to find themselves face to face with a crew of athletes from Hong Kong. And other non–Israelis now glimpsed the terrorists as well. "Some postal workers saw one of the groups hurrying across the grounds and reported the sighting to security," writes Large, "but the police, assuming the men to be athletes, took no action."[25]

By 4:30 a.m., the terrorists had succeeded in pinning down the duplex apartments that housed the twenty-one members of the Israeli delegation, among them coaches, athletes, and judges. The two-story, townhouse-style apartments were situated on the ground and second floors of the four-story building.

As the members of Black September crowded into the ground-level foyer, one of them attempted to enter Apartment One, which housed seven Israeli coaches and judges. Because the commando was using a makeshift key, however, he was unable to unlock the door. He did, however, awaken a sleeping giant: wrestling judge Yossef Gutfreund, who weighed nearly three hundred pounds. The middle-aged Gutfreund had served in two wars, during one of which, the 1976 Arab-Israeli War, his altruism emerged on the battlefield when he provided medical care to a group of enemy soldiers, Egyptians, who had been severely burned and whose commander had left them for dead. Gutfreund was once again about to demonstrate his profound selflessness as he approached the door to investigate the clacking sound at the lock.

As the door opened a few inches, the massive Israeli caught sight of masked men with AK-47s. Straightaway, he threw his weight against the door at the same moment that a terrorist wedged his rifle between the door and its frame and began crowbarring his way into the room. Gutfreund shouted a warning to his colleagues who were asleep in the apartment, while planting his six-foot, three-inch body against the door. "Hava Tistalku!" he called out, an English translation being, "Take cover, boys!"[26]

As Gutfreund fended off the intruders, weightlifting coach and Holocaust survivor Tuvia Sokolovsky, hearing Gutfreund's cries, sounded his own warning to his fellow Israelis. Barreling into the flat, the commandos now began firing at Sokolovsky, who tore across the room, shattered a window with his fists, and leapt onto the sidewalk, shards of glass slicing his flesh as he jumped. Seconds later, he was crouching behind a cement flowerbed in a garden situated in the building's courtyard. Barefoot and pajama-clad, he was bleeding, yet he was free. And then he took off again, not thinking in terms of a destination, until he collapsed, crying, in the arms of a policeman a considerable distance away. Sokolovsky would be the only Israeli from Apartment One to escape the mayhem.

In the same apartment, the terrorists, who were holding Gutfreund at gunpoint, set about rounding up those who had been unable to flee. In one of the bedrooms, Issa found Moshe Weinberg, a thirty-three-year-old wrestling coach, who grabbed a paring knife from the nightstand and took a swipe at the terrorist's chest. As the blade pierced Issa's jacket, but not his skin, another commando materialized and shot Weinberg in the mouth, the bullet exiting through the right side of his face. Severely injured but still standing, the wrestling coach grabbed Issa in an effort to seize his assault rifle, prompting a third commando to appear and shoot Weinberg again. Still, the stalwart Israeli did not surrender or succumb, although he did collapse onto the floor.

It was at this point that the cell herded the apartment's captives, clad only in their underwear, into a bedroom and tied their hands and feet with nylon cords. Having been asleep only moments before, the Israelis were stupefied. As for the remaining members of the Israeli delegation who were still sleeping elsewhere in the building, Tony and a small band of commandos pulled Moshe Weinberg to his feet, shoved an AK-47 into his back, and forced the maimed coach to lead them to his comrades. During this phase of the operation, Issa remained in Apartment One, keeping his weapon trained on the five uninjured, but bound, hostages.

In a snap decision by Weinberg, a shrewd one, he maneuvered Tony and the other guerrillas past Apartment Two, which housed Israel's comparatively lean track and field athletes. Instead, he deposited them at Apartment Three, a flat on the second floor where six wrestlers and thickset weightlifters were lodged.

Storming into the apartment, the Black Septembrists seized a pair of Israelis in one of the bedrooms, while in a nearby room another athlete, awakened by the commotion, decided to investigate. Pulling on a pair of pants, the light-flyweight wrestler Gad Tsabari suddenly found himself confronted by a terrorist in a yellow sweater and a ski mask. Moments later, Tsabari's roommate, David Berger, entered the room as well. Originally from Cleveland, Ohio, the twenty-eight-year-old Berger, an honors student who had earned a degree in psychology at Tulane University and another in jurisprudence at Columbia Law School, had relocated to Israel so he could compete on its Olympic team. As soon as he glimpsed the danger, Berger, in Hebrew, pressed his companions to overtake the terrorists. "We have nothing to lose!" he yelled.²⁷ And although his compatriots did not follow his advice, they also did not dismiss it entirely.

Lining up the captives from Apartment Three, the commandos ordered them to place their hands behind their heads, then trooped them down a staircase and onto an outdoor walkway that led to the foyer of Apartment One. The strategy was to transfer the men to that flat and combine them with its captives. In this way, the entire group of Israelis would be in one spot, with the apartment henceforth serving as the cell's base. As the Israelis were being forced into the foyer, however, the captive at the head of the line glimpsed an opportunity. Pushing aside an AK-47 that a terrorist was pointing at him, he broke into a sprint. This man was the flyweight wrestler Gad Tsabari, who, he later said, had echoing in his mind David Berger's exhortation that they had "nothing to lose." Tsabari added that he believed God's hand had guided him during the escape.²⁸

Tsabari ran down a flight of stairs and into an underground parking garage that was situated beneath the dormitory. As he was fleeing, a terrorist began firing at him, prompting Moshe Weinberg to hurl himself onto a nearby commando and attempt to grab the man's assault rifle. It was at this moment that the guerrilla firing at Tsabari spun around and pumped several rounds into Weinberg's chest, killing him. Dragging his body out of the foyer and heaving it onto the exterior walkway, the terrorists shoved the remaining captives into Apartment One. In all, ten living Israelis were now in the BSO's possession, all of them trapped in the same quarters.

As these events were unfolding in the dormitory, Gad Tsabari was running through the expansive parking lot, taking refuge behind its support pillars as commandos fired at him. Covering a distance of a half-mile during which he scaled the ten-foot fence around the Village's perimeter, the dazed athlete came to a stop when he reached the Olympics media center. Inside, he found a relaxed, cheerful press corps that was wholly unaware of the horror at 31 Connollystrasse. Catching the attention of a knot of journalists, the athlete told them what was happening to the Israelis, after which a security officer set about calming him and providing him with a shirt. Tsabari, who was five-feet, four-inches tall and weighed slightly over a hundred pounds, later said the shirt was "as big as a dress on me."²⁹ The authorities next placed him under police protection, and, in due course, took him to join some of the other Israelis who had not been seized. Huddled together in large room in a building located a safe distance from their dormitory, the members of the delegation, having fled their beds in panic, sat stunned as they awaited news of their friends and colleagues. Joining them in their vigil was Tuvia Sokolovsky, the traumatized coach who had escaped the gunfire in Apartment One.³⁰

As for the ten hostages who were being held in that same apartment, one of them refused to stand down. Yossef Romano, a weightlifter and interior decorator who was using crutches because of a damaged tendon, decided to confront the guerrillas. Having witnessed a Black Septembrist kill his colleague Moshe Weinberg only minutes before, he must have known the outcome would be grim. All the same, Romano dove at one of the commandos and tried to seize the man's weapon, but another commando took aim and shot the weightlifter to death. The terrorists left his blood-soaked body in the middle of the room where the captives would have to look at it during the ensuing hours. It would be unavoidable. As in psychologist Georg Sieber's hypothetical scenario, Situation 21, the corpse would serve as a warning to the remaining nine hostages.

In the short time since the commandos had scaled the fence into the Olympic Village, seized the Israelis, murdered two of them, and tethered the rest in Apartment One, Dr. Shaul Ladany's roommates in Apartment Two had awakened him to the crisis. "We've been attack by Arabs," one of them shouted to him.[31] An Israeli racewalker and teacher at Tel Aviv University, Ladany, as a boy, had been imprisoned in the Bergen-Belsen concentration camp where he had honed his survival skills. Now he was ready to act on them once again.

Stealing a look out of the window, he spied four figures speaking heatedly in a huddle outside of Apartment One. "From the window above my head, someone signals me to get back inside," Ladany writes in his memoir. "I climb the spiral staircase to the second floor, where I find the five other occupants of my unit in the front room."[32] He continues,

> When I ask what happened, they point to a dark stain on the ground in front of the door to the stairwell, telling me it is [Moshe's] blood. The body has already been taken away. Everyone appears calm and rational and shows no signs of fear or panic. Everyone, that is, except for Henry Hershkowitz, who looks as white as a ghost and seems to be shaking in terror.[33]

A competitor in the marksman events, Hershkowitz, like his colleagues, was a remarkable athlete. He was also the team member who had led the Israeli delegation in the Parade of Nations during the opening ceremony at the Olympic Stadium.

Hurrying out of the building to search for help, Ladany ran to the adjacent dormitory in which the American team was quartered and pounded on Bill Bowerman's door. Although he would later become famous as the creator of the waffle-sole running shoe and the cofounder of Nike, Inc., Bowerman, at this time, was a well-regarded, if opinionated, track coach. When the befuddled American, who was still emerging from a deep sleep, opened the door, the Israeli blurted out that Arabs had entered his delegation's quarters. "Well, tell them to get out," said Bowerman.[34] But Ladany explained that they were terrorists and were murdering the Israelis. "That," says the coach, "changed the whole complexion."³⁵ His senses clearing, the coach leapt into action, pulling Ladany to safety inside the apartment and phoning the United States Consulate in Munich. Advising the consulate staff that there were Jewish athletes on the U.S. team, most notably the javelin-thrower Bill Schmidt and swimmer Mark Spitz, he insisted on extra protection for the team. And sure enough, a brace of Marines arrived soon thereafter and secured the entrance to the Americans' building. In addition, Spitz, who had earned seven gold medals thereby making him the Games' most prominent Jewish athlete, was assigned a Marine guard of his own. Before the day was over, three German bodyguards would hustle the swimmer out of the Olympic Village altogether and put him on a jet to the United States. The fast-thinking Bowerman, on the other hand, would have a wholly different destination.

It seems the dignitaries on the International Olympic Committee (IOC) were infuriated by the coach's deed—that is, initiating a U.S. military presence in the Olympic Village—and ordered him to stand before them that same morning to account for his actions. Bowerman, however, was unbowed. "If it's trouble to secure a building where people might be killed," he said, "then I guess I'm in trouble."³⁶ A couple of hours later, the outspoken coach arrived for the IOC meeting, and he did not turn up alone. At his side stood Olympic icon Jesse Owens, the African-American runner who had earned four gold medals at the 1936 Games in Nazi Germany. In so doing, Owens had helped put the lie to Hitler's doctrine about the supremacy of the Caucasian race. If anyone were to be deferential during the IOC meeting, it would be the committee members themselves.

As it happened, Bowerman had not been the only person to notify the authorities about the attack. A German housekeeper, having heard gunshots in the vicinity of the Israelis' dormitory, alerted the Olympic security office. Also phoning for help was Shmuel Lalkin, the leader of the Israeli Olympic delegation. Having heard the same worrisome sounds, Lalkin looked out his window and spotted Weinberg's corpse. "He was naked," Lalkin said, "blood was all around him."³⁷ Lalkin, it will be recalled, was the man whose worries about the safety of the Israeli team had been brushed off by those whose job it was to protect the group, the man whom Arie Shumar had told to leave security to the professionals and who had been prohibited from carrying a handgun by the Israeli embassy. It was now Shmuel Lalkin who dialed the Sheraton Hotel in Munich where Israeli representatives and reporters were staying, shouting into the phone that Arab terrorists were attacking his nation's team and to "Call Israel!"³⁸

At 4:50 a.m., help, of a sort, began to arrive when a lone figure jogged to the Israelis' dormitory, an unarmed Olympic security officer carrying a two-way radio. Having been instructed to assess the situation, he approached the building, whereupon a masked commando stepped outside the door of Apartment One and cast an eye over the surroundings. When the security officer, from a distance, began questioning him, the terrorist ignored the man and walked back inside. Radioing his superiors, the security officer was soon joined by two cohorts, both of them also unarmed. The fact is, it would not be until a Munich policeman showed up at the building at 5:10 a.m. that a Black Septembrist would toss a two-page, typewritten list of demands from the apartment's balcony. Snatching up the document, the law enforcement officer raced back to his superiors with it.

As the clock ticked, dozens of German policemen began showing up at the Israelis' dormitory. Also arriving at this time—it was now between 5:30 a.m. and 5:45 a.m.—was the police president, Manfred Schreiber. Many years later, it would be revealed that Schreiber was, at the time, under investigation on suspicion of negligent homicide in an unrelated case.[39] Walther Tröger, the ceremonial mayor of the Olympic Village, arrived as well, as did an ambulance from which sprang two Red Cross paramedics. Disregarding the Black September commandos posted outside of Apartment One, the pair rushed to Moshe Weinberg, checked the Israeli for signs of life, and, finding none, withdrew from the scene.

As this was occurring, a news blackout was ordered and the Olympic Village was placed in lockdown, meaning civilians would not be allowed to enter or leave it. By all accounts, confusion reigned. "None of the officials," writes Large, "had any clear idea of who the attackers were, much less how many of them were involved or how many hostages they might have taken."[40]

The lockdown notwithstanding, armed officers were permitted into the Village, and scores of them now surged onto the concourse and walkways near the hostages' dormitory. Their attention fixed on Apartment One, they included "marksmen with bulletproof vests, submachine guns, and rifles with telescopic sights," writes Reeve.[41]

In Israel, meanwhile, all eyes were fixed on Prime Minister Golda Meir, who was fielding calls from Munich. Reminding her administration that the nation in which an assault takes place has precedence in managing it, she ruled out the prospect of an Israeli military unit mounting a rescue operation on German soil. She did offer to send a military team to Germany to assist, however, although the authorities in that country declined her proposal. Meir also told her administration that the Mossad was not to be directly involved because the attack was not considered to be within the province of the intelligence agency. Yet she dispatched the chief of the Mossad, Zwicka "Zvi" Zamir, to Munich on the assumption that the Germans might wish to consult with him. And the prime minister made a request of the International Olympic Committee itself, namely, that the Games be suspended until the terrorist situation was resolved. It was, however, an appeal that IOC President Avery Brundage, an eighty-four-year-old American, rejected outright.[42] It also was a decision that was consistent with his past ones.

In 1936, when many American organizations were calling for a boycott of the Olympic Games because they were to be held in Nazi Germany, Brundage, a former Olympian and an unabashed admirer of Hitler's efforts to rehabilitate the German nation, fought vigorously for the United States to participate in them.[43] Brundage had long argued that sports should not intersect with politics. Yet there was a curious underside to his position. "Although the Iron Chancellor of amateur sport regarded himself as the last true defender of the strict separation of sport and politics," writes Carolyn Marvin in the *Journal of American Studies*, "he also frequently insisted that more than the future of amateur sport was at stake in shielding sport from political manipulation."[44] More to the point, he believed amateur athletics, by their nature, promoted the Western values of individualism and industriousness; this, at a time when he was preoccupied with the threat of Communism.[45] Thus, Brundage fought for the Games' continuation in large part because he believed they promoted the democratic ideals he cherished.

In response to Golda Meir's request, the IOC president offered two reasons, or pretexts perhaps, for not halting the Games during the Black September attack. First, he claimed that doing so would interfere with the management of the hostage crisis, although he did not elaborate on how this might be the case. And second, in Brundage's words, "German television does not have any alternative programming."[46] So the Games rolled on.

Back at 31 Connollystrasse, Manfried Schreiber and Walther Tröger read the list of Black September demands. It consisted of the names of two hundred thirty-six inmates whom the BSO characterized as political prisoners, and it insisted they be released. While the vast majority were Palestinians being held in Israeli penitentiaries, one was a Japanese extremist who had been involved in a terrorist operation at Israel's Lod Airport. Also on the list were two members of a German urban guerrilla group, the infamous Baader-Meinhof Gang, who were confined in West Germany. The document called for the authorities to hand over these figures to a receptive Arab nation, and it spelled out the consequences of a failure to do so. "[I]f their demands were not met by nine o'clock that morning," writes Paul Taylor, "they threatened executions by the hour."[47]

Of course, it was unrealistic for Black September to believe its demands could be forwarded to, and processed by, the State of Israel in such a short period of time. With fewer than four hours until the deadline, neither the German nor Israeli authorities could give serious consideration to the cell's terms, let alone fulfill them. It was for this reason, then, that a negotiator was dispatched at the designated hour to speak with Issa, the cell's spokesman, in an attempt to stall for time.

Annaliese Graes was the mediator's name. A forty-two-year-old German policewoman, she was selected for the unnerving task because of her maturity and assertiveness. Certainly these were qualities that were on display the moment she came face to face with Issa at his post, the front door of the apartment.

"What kind of rubbish is this?" she asked him, point-blank.[48] Issa, attempting to remain cool-headed, reiterated Black September's ultimatum that its list of prisoners be freed. When Graes asked if he would be willing to discuss the demands with a small group of German and Olympic officials, among them the Egyptian member of the IOC, the terrorist leader agreed. Thus began several hours of start-and-stop talks even as German police and Olympic representatives, behind the scenes, brainstormed ways to liberate the hostages.

One idea was to release a gas into Apartment One's ventilation system, a chemical that would render the terrorists unconscious. Knowing that the police in Chicago had used this method in the 1920s, authorities set about trying to track down American police departments that might be able to explain the procedure. The notion was abandoned, however, when it became apparent that there would not be sufficient time to locate such knowledgeable people, let alone plan and carry out the measure itself.

Another imaginative strategy involved sending police officers disguised as chefs into Apartment One to deliver food to the commandos and hostages. Once inside, one of the faux chefs would trigger a device that was concealed on him, an apparatus that would emit a searing light, temporarily blinding the terrorists and making possible their capture. The idea seemed so promising, in fact, that German officials proceeded with it a few hours later, disguising a handful of policemen as chefs and sending them to 31 Connollystrasse lugging baskets of food. The astute Issa, however, refused to permit the men to enter, ordering them to leave the baskets outside and thus scotching the light-device approach.

Besides rescue tactics of this sort, officials also sought to barter with the cell's spokesman. Germany, they told Issa, would give the BSO an unlimited amount of cash if the terrorists would release the Israelis. Issa turned down the offer, however, declaring that the commandos' mission was not about money; it was about the Palestinian situation and those who had been incarcerated because of it. So the negotiators suggested a different type of exchange: five German officials would serve as substitutes for the Israeli hostages. But again, Issa refused. Black September did not want German hostages, just as, it was later concluded, it had no interest in the Jewish-American luminary Mark Spitz. The BSO wanted Israeli citizens in its clutches since the organization's quarrel was with the State of Israel.

As it stood, Golda Meir, in the past, had made it clear that it was the Jewish state's policy not to negotiate with terrorists. To do so, she insisted, would mean opening the door to future threats, since extremists would have proof that Israel was, in fact, amenable to bargaining.[49] And she declared her position once again on the morning of the Munich attack, a stance that now became known not only to the Black Septembrists but to the world at large, since the media blackout had been lifted and the crisis was being beamed around the world. Yet owing to the prime minister's position on the matter, she was criticized in certain quarters, even by Olympic participants themselves.

"Golda Meir, holding the fucking world to ransom again," railed an athlete from Ireland.[50] It was nearly noon when the frustrated Irishman made this remark. What he had no way of knowing is that discussions were taking place at that moment between Meir and Willy Brandt, the Chancellor of Germany, and they centered on a secret Israeli proposal to the terrorist organization. "Golda Meir's offer of a deal to the Black September," writes David Korn, "was not known until several years later."[51] Presumably, this was because Israel wished to continue being perceived by the world at large as non-cooperative with extremist groups.

Regarding the Jewish state's offer, "Israel suggested that her hostages be exchanged for German volunteers, who would then be flown with the kidnappers to an Arab country," write Bar-Zohar and Haber. "After two or three months, with no visible connection with the kidnapping, Israel would free about fifty hostages from her prisons."[52] Relieved by the offer since it might bring the crisis to an end, Brandt rushed the proposal to Issa, who was receptive to exploring it further. He therefore phoned a contact in Tunis to discuss the matter, since this was the procedure he had been instructed to follow in the event of such a development. "But his contact was not there," says Korn, "so the momentary prospect for a deal vanished."[53] As a result, the afternoon hours would be marked by tension and mounting desperation, as a billion people watched the ordeal on television and seventy thousand spectators at the Olympic Village jockeyed to get near the building on 31 Connollystrasse.[54] It was at this point that the International Olympic Committee decided to suspend the Games for the remainder of the day.

By 4:30 p.m. Black September, having observed no progress in the negotiations, concluded that the German and Olympic officials were not bargaining in good faith. Accordingly, Issa insisted that the commandos and their hostages be flown out of the country, preferably to Egypt, where he expected President Anwar Sadat to be sympathetic to their actions. German officials, in response, explained that they first needed to look in on the nine captives to make sure they were still alive and well, otherwise Egypt might reject the BSO's proposal.

So it was that Issa and Tony permitted two German intermediaries to enter Apartment One and speak to the fraught athletes, coaches, and judges. "The picture of the room will stay with me as long as I live," said one of the two visitors. "I will never forget those faces, full with fear, and yet full of hope."[55] The other gentleman, likewise shaken by the experience, described the hostages as "very depressed and fearful."[56] The captives explained that they were not only afraid Black September might execute them, but they also worried that they might be killed unintentionally if a strike force tried to rescue them. It was the opinion of the two Germans that the hostages were painfully aware of the impossibility of their dilemma. Inside the apartment, bullet holes and bloodstains marred the walls, garbage and food cluttered the floor, the deceased Romano lay face-down in his own blood, and the stench in the room was unbearable.[57] Reviving an earlier proposal, the pair of intermediaries offered themselves in exchange for the Israelis, but, as before, Issa refused.

As it happened, the Germans had misled Issa when they claimed that they wished to come into the apartment to confirm the hostages' well-being. Their real purpose was to count the number of terrorists and scrutinize the rooms for explosives and other weapons the Black Septembrists might use for self-defense. The reason was because the police were putting the final touches on a rescue mission and needed to know what they could expect to encounter in the apartment.

And indeed, dozens of German officers had already scrambled onto the buildings surrounding 31 Connollystrasse by this point, while on the roof and sides of the Israeli dormitory itself crouched thirteen policemen dressed in tracksuits and bulletproof vests and armed with revolvers and machine guns. None of the thirteen had been trained in special operations tactics, although they did have backgrounds in hand-to-hand combat. Removing the screws from the grate that covered the apartment's ventilation shaft, the men prepared for the decisive stage of the mission, which would commence when they heard the code word *sonnenschein*, or "sunshine," on their two-way radios.[58] They would then drop down through the ventilation shaft and into Apartment One, where they would capture or kill the terrorists.

The rescue, however, was not to be. Police officials shelved it when they realized that the Black Septembrists may have been watching live television coverage of the operation unfold on the dormitory's roof. And it is true that television cameras had been mounted high on the Olympic Tower, most notably those of the sports division of ABC, the American Broadcasting Company, thereby offering a birds-eye view of the rescue-in-progress. ABC Sports, in turn, shared portions of its material with smaller networks. But while today it is taken for granted that the commandos observed the forthcoming raid in this manner, a principal figure in the telecast has challenged this notion. Roone Arledge, who was the president of ABC Sports at the time and was in the control room in Munich, has stated that his network, during the would-be rescue operation, aired the disputed Olympic Tower footage only to audiences in the United States.[59] In regard to the commonly-held belief that the terrorist cell watched it on television, Arledge asserts that this is part of a mythos that has grown up around the Munich Massacre.[60] Whatever the case, German authorities, because they suspected the rescue strategy of having been compromised by the television coverage, called off the operation.

For Black September, the tipping point had now been reached. Repeating the organization's demand that the commandos and their captives be flown to Egypt, Issa threatened to begin executing the hostages if this did not happen. Visibly agitated, the terrorists were determined to get out of Germany. And seconding their wish was Avery Brundage, who longed for the crisis to move away from the Olympic Village so the Games could resume. One contingent that was staunchly opposed to Black September's demand, however, was made up of the nation's top administrators, precisely the ones who would make the final decision. And behind closed doors, their position was unequivocal: the German nation would not permit a group of terrorists to slip into the country, kidnap its guests, and abscond with them. Under no circumstances would the Palestinians be allowed to leave Germany with the Israelis. And although it was irrelevant, Egyptian President Anwar Sadat's position was that he would not permit the terrorists' plane to land in Egypt. Officials, however, did not share any of this information with Issa.

So it was that a handful of German strategists once again found themselves grasping for a viable means of bringing the ordeal to an end and in such a way as to spare the lives of the hostages. What they did not do, however, was confer with the Mossad's representative, Zvi Zamir. "The Bavarian officials were outspoken in their opposition to Israeli interference in the hostage crisis," writes Klein.[61] According to the Mossad chief, German authorities attempted to prevent him from entering the Olympic Village when he arrived in Munich, and even when he did gain access they refused to talk to him.[62] "He felt slighted and ignored," says Taylor.[63] Although it will never be known for certain, it is conceivable that the hostages may have paid a price for Zamir's marginalization, since the Mossad leader, being highly experienced and well-placed in military and intelligence circles, was in a position to deliver considerable help at this crucial moment. As he later explained to British journalist Dudley Doust, a small number of Israeli marksmen could have been put into place to ensure a successful rescue mission.[64] But alas, this was not to happen.

What did occur was that German strategists, with an eye on the clock, reviewed their options and found them lacking. Adding to the urgency of their situation, it was at this juncture that Black September announced a 9:00 p.m. deadline. To the German and Olympic authorities, it was evident their efforts to continue stalling were no longer feasible, even if this tactic did appear to have been effective in wearing down the intruders. But Issa, sensing the ruse, was adamant that the BSO cell leave the country without delay, the consequence being that German authorities had no choice but to act.

"Finally it was decided to appear to give in," says Christopher Dobson.[65] The Germans would thereafter attempt, one last time, to save the hostages.

Informing Issa that Egypt was willing to accept the commandos and their captives, negotiators claimed that a Lufthansa airliner was being fueled for the flight. They also agreed to Issa's requirement that he and his men, along with the nine Israelis, be transported by bus to a pair of waiting helicopters which would take them to the airport. The Germans had decided not to use the Munich-Riem airport, an expansive international facility, since conducting a military-style operation in such a congested setting would be far too dangerous to the traveling public. Instead, they picked a military airstrip at nearby Fürstenfeldbruck, an airbase for the German Air Force and an opportune setting for what promised to be a lethal assault.

As the deadline approached, officials assured Issa that everything was taking place on schedule. Suspicious but cooperative, the Black September cell, minutes later, hustled the hostages out of Apartment One and into a bus in the parking garage beneath the Israeli dormitory. As they led the captives to the waiting vehicle, David Hart, the Canadian water poloist who had unknowingly helped the Black Septembrists scale the fence at the outset of the attack, watched with dismay as the beleaguered Israelis were paraded at gunpoint. The terrorists had blindfolded and chained them together at waist-level. Repulsed by the scene, Hart recounted that the commandos manhandled the hostages, who appeared to be filled with fear, shoving them into the bus as if they were livestock.[66]

Minutes later at the Olympic helipad, the terrorists divided the hostages into two groups and forced each group onto a helicopter. It was at this late stage that the authorities realized there were eight terrorists. Until now, they thought there were only five of them, the upshot being that the impending rescue operation at Fürstenfeldbruck airfield would be grievously undermanned.

After the two helicopters took flight, a third one touched down at the Olympic helipad and key officials in the hostage-rescue mission climbed aboard; everyone, that is, except Zvi Zamir. German officials turned him away, claiming there was no room for him. Undeterred, the spirited Zamir elbowed his way onto the aircraft, which, moments later, was aloft.

As a side-note, it has since come to light that Moshe Dayan, the Israeli

Minister of Defense, arrived in Munich at 7:30 p.m. on the night of September 5. His presence was kept secret by both the Israeli and German governments. To date, there are still no public accounts of Dayan's actions in Munich on that evening.[67]

As to the helicopters carrying the terrorists and hostages, what should have been a ten-minute flight to the Fürstenfeldbruck airfield took over thirty minutes, a state of affairs causing the Black Septembrists to become suspicious because they knew the airstrip was only twelve miles from Munich. Their skepticism, moreover, was spot-on. It seems the helicopter pilots had secretly been ordered to delay their arrival at the airfield so that officials in the pursuing helicopter could be the first to land, the latter wishing to be on-site when the commandos touched down.

The strategy was devised and supervised by the Bavarian police, with no input from other agencies, not even the military. Anticipating five Black September terrorists to arrive at the airfield, five sharpshooters would be lying in wait atop the terminal and nearby structures. On the runway would be a Boeing 727, the Lufthansa airliner that Issa was expecting. Unbeknownst to him, however, seventeen police officers would be stationed inside the jet and disguised as the flight crew. As to the plan of action, when the terrorists' helicopters landed at Fürstenfeldbruck, Issa and Tony, officials assumed, would climb aboard the jet to inspect it. And once the pair was aboard, the police on the plane would capture them, while outside the airliner, the rooftop marksmen would kill the remaining terrorists who were expected to be standing on the tarmac. A dicey plan at best, it was riddled with problems and quickly fell apart.

As noted, the authorities miscalculated the number of terrorists, believing there were five, not eight of them; this, despite the fact that a pair of intermediaries had visited Apartment One earlier in the day purposely to count the commandos. Then, too, standard sniper operations assign two sharpshooters for each target, meaning that the number of marksmen in the Fürstenfeldbruck mission was markedly insufficient.[68] Worsening matters, not all of the snipers had two-way radios, meaning that their actions at this critical time could not be coordinated. And then there was the manner in which they were positioned: the marksmen could accidentally open fire on one another, a deadly twist that contributed to the slapdash nature of the plan.

A separate failure involved the Lufthansa airliner that sat idling on the airstrip. It seems the seventeen policemen stationed inside the plane developed a case of cold feet while the helicopters were en route to the airfield, and for this reason abandoned their posts. Since they were wearing Lufthansa jackets but not the matching pants and caps, they figured the terrorists would spot the subterfuge and execute them. Furthermore, the aircraft, being loaded with fuel, could explode if the terrorists were to deploy hand grenades. So the police bolted. "At the heart of the matter," writes Klein, "lay negligence and a glaring lack of professionalism."[69] Then again, supporters of the police point out that the squad realized it was on a suicide mission, and therefore the decision to scrap it was wholly justifiable.[70] It was a matter of self-preservation in the face of a poorly-conceived mission.

And then the moment arrived. At 10:30 p.m. the helicopters carrying the commandos and captives touched down at the Fürstenfeldbruck airfield, which, to Zamir's shock, had been darkened. His worry was that the snipers would have difficulty sighting their targets, being unable to distinguish among the terrorists, hostages, and helicopter pilots. Meanwhile, the snipers themselves braced for action. "The police sharpshooters were already positioned in the control tower and on the roofs of the nearby buildings," write Bar-Zohar and Haber, although their weapons consisted of "single bolt-action sniper's rifles, while the eight terrorists carried submachine-guns and hand grenades."[71]

As it turned out, the terrorists' movements at Fürstenfeldbruck, beginning at the moment their helicopters landed, were different from those on which the Germans had constructed their rickety rescue plan. Although Issa and Tony disembarked and hurried to the Lufthansa airliner as anticipated, not all of the commandos came onto the runway to wait for them; some remained in the helicopters with the hostages. The commandos also refused to allow the four German helicopter pilots to leave the airstrip, as previously agreed, but rather kept them as additional hostages.

Next, Issa and Tony boarded the Lufthansa airliner and, finding no flight crew, realized they had been tricked. Exiting the aircraft, they shouted a warning to their comrades. And it was now that all hell broke loose and continued for the ensuing ninety minutes. Finally, as sharpshooters fired at the terrorists on the tarmac, one of the terrorists, in turn, fired a machine gun into a helicopter, killing all of the Israelis who were tied together inside it. It was later discovered that the captives had chewed the ropes that bound them and had been nearing the point at which they could escape. At the same time, another commando tossed a grenade into the second helicopter, the explosion killing most of its hostages and causing the remaining one, David Berger, to succumb to smoke inhalation. As this was occurring, marksmen shot and killed Issa and three other terrorists. And then there was Tony, who, unlike his comrades, did not brave the gun battle but instead fled on foot, although he was subsequently apprehended in a parking lot and shot to death. Also losing his life in the mayhem was a young German police officer. In the end, three terrorists survived, although they were wounded, with the authorities promptly taking them into custody.

The following morning, a memorial service was held at the Olympic Stadium for the fallen Israelis and the German policeman, and it was attended by tens of thousands of the Games' participants as well as dignitaries from around the globe. Joining the American delegation was Jesse Owens, who wept unabashedly. Not present at all, on the other hand, were the Arab delegations, which boycotted the ceremony.

Adhering to protocol, Avery Brundage, as the IOC president, made a statement at the memorial service, standing before the vast audience and offering his condolences. Many Israelis, along with attendees from other nations, were offended by his remarks, however, complaining that he deliberately understated the significance of the slaughter of the Israeli athletes. "Brundage's defiant speech [did] not seem simply anti–Semitic," writes Kenny Moore. "The man was a genuinely tragic character, his flaw and strength inextricable."[72] It was during this same ceremony that Brundage made an announcement that was startling in its exuberance. "The Games must go on!" he intoned. "All events will be held twenty-four hours after originally scheduled!"[73] And with this, the Olympic competitions resumed.

"The next day an El Al flight carried ten of the dead sportsmen home to Israel along with the remaining fourteen members of the team, while the last of the dead, David Berger, was sent to Cleveland, Ohio, where his parents lived," writes Dobson. "Four days later the dead Black Septembrists were flown to Libya, where funeral prayers were said for them in Tripoli's main mosque."[74] Furthermore, throngs of Arab mourners took to the streets to pay tribute to the commandos who were now regarded as heroes; this, despite the fact that they had kidnapped and murdered eleven unarmed sportsmen, most of whom, being manacled at the time of death, were unable to defend themselves. But to those who championed the Black Septembrists, the commandos were admirable not because they had put to death eleven innocent men but because of their efforts, at the cost of their own lives, to plant the Palestinian dilemma squarely on the world stage and win the release of Palestinian prisoners incarcerated in Israel. It was for this same reason that the Palestinian Liberation Organization was jubilant about the attack, its grim denouement notwithstanding. "Operation Iqrit and Biri'm, declared a PLO spokesman, had been a '100 percent publicity success,' for it had drawn the world's attention to the Palestinian cause in truly spectacular fashion," writes Large.[75] That said, the publicity was negative in the extreme, and therefore failed to generate the desired compassion for the millions of Palestinians who had been relegated to lives of hardship in refugee camps strewn across the Middle East.

North American and Western European nations, for instance, sympathized with the departed Israeli athletes, whom they considered to be the real heroes. Among these figures were Yossef Gutfreund and Moshe Weinberg, who were remarkable for their courageous, self-sacrificial actions in the course of the ordeal. And the United States' principal nemesis of the era, the USSR, disapproved of the massacre as well. It did, however, offer a different, less condemnatory take on it, presumably because it did not wish to offend its client states in the region. The USSR's view was that the Black September Organization was somehow disconnected from the Middle East at large, that it was merely an aberration, a fluke. "Soviet criticism was mild and restrained," write Arhey Yodfat and Yuval Arnon-Ohanna, "suggesting that neither Arab countries and governments, nor Palestinian organisations, [had] any responsibility for what was done by a few extremists in Munich."[76]

After the three terrorists who survived the Fürstenfeldbruck shoot-out were taken into custody, there was no indication that the German government was remotely interested in making them account for their crimes. If anything, authorities seemed more concerned with pacifying the Black September Organization, along with the PLO and the Arab states in general. Documents have come to light which reveal that Germany was determined to avoid further Black September attacks on its soil, and, for this reason, steered clear of any actions that might provoke the terrorist organization.[77] Also high on Germany's list of priorities was the preservation of productive business relationships with the Arab states, its officials not wishing to strain the nation's Middle Eastern ties for fear that such a development might "jeopardize Germany's oil supply and export contracts."[78] All told, then, the government's overarching concern appears to have been the protection of the German nation and its economic interests. Given these values, it should come as no surprise that the government also may have played an instrumental role in the abrupt release of the incarcerated terrorists a few weeks later.[79]

It was on October 29, 1972, that a group of Arab extremists hijacked a Boeing 727 in Damascus, Syria, one that was scheduled to fly to Beirut, Lebanon, before continuing on to its final destination in Frankfurt, Germany. A German airliner, it was one of the Lufthansa fleet. The hijackers called for the release of the three Black September commandos who were behind bars in Germany. Within hours, the German government not only conceded to these demands, but also flew the terrorists to a location in Yugoslavia so they could meet up with their comrades. From there, the former prisoners traveled to Libya, where they enjoyed a hearty welcome.

Bolstering the notion of German complicity in the affair, it turns out that the Lufthansa jet, other than the flight crew, was unoccupied when it took off from the airport in the Syrian capital despite the fact that the plane could hold 150 passengers. To date, there has been no explanation as to why there were no passengers on the airliner upon departure. Then, when the plane made its stopover in Beirut, only eleven passengers got on board for the flight to Frankfurt, along with two additional hijackers. All of these passengers were men. Again, this was highly improbable. And compounding these dubious occurrences, Germany not only met the hijackers' demands, but it placed the prisoners in the extremists' hands in record time, at no point notifying Israel about the act of air piracy or the Palestinians' impending release. For these and other reasons, astute observers maintain that the operation was stage-managed by Palestinian extremists in connivance with the powers-that-be in Germany. Supporting this notion were the remarks of one of the surviving terrorists who, in a subsequent interview, confirmed the existence of the joint setup.[80] Whatever the truth of the matter, one thing is certain: Germany and the Palestinian extremists reaped immediate gains from the skyjacking. The former was rid of its BSO prisoners, whose presence in the nation's prison system carried the unspoken threat of further terrorist acts to bring about their release, while Black September once again had in its possession the commandos who had been left behind at the Fürstenfeldbruck airfield. Conversely, the losers in the deal were the State of Israel, the murdered Israeli sportsmen, and the concept of justice itself. Then, too, the public lost, since it would be vulnerable once again to the deeds of the three surviving guerrillas. As a concluding note, it is perhaps telling that the German government did not file extradition requests for the Black Septembrists who had committed heinous acts inside its borders. Clearly, the nation's leadership wished to wash its hands of the Black September affair.

As could be expected, the State of Israel felt differently. Within seventy-two hours of its athletes being murdered at the Fürstenfeldbruck airstrip, the Jewish state bombed twenty PLO bases and guerrilla camps in Syria and Lebanon. "The raids killed over two hundred people," writes Large, "many of them women and children."[81] But although the offensives also managed to eliminate scores of guerrillas-in-training from various groups, they did not reach their true targets. "[T]he dead and injured had no connection with Black September or the massacre in Munich," says Klein.[82]

A few days later, the Israeli military staged an even more sweeping operation, this one obliterating a swath of territory in Lebanon suspected of harboring members of the Palestinian Liberation Organization and possibly Black September. And while it is unclear if the latter was, in fact, affected, it is known that the political fallout, for Israel, was immediate and unforgiving. To the delight of the PLO, which was always eager to foment discord between the Arab countries and the Jewish state, the entire region became enraged by Israel's onslaughts. Infuriated, too, was President Richard Nixon, since the Israeli attacks threatened to trigger a war in the Middle East and pull the United States, Israel's principal ally, into the conflict. Inflaming Nixon further, the Israeli leadership, knowing he would object to its aggressive plans, did not notify him in advance. And joining these critics from outside the Jewish state were those who repudiated the attacks on humanitarian grounds, their complaint being that the Israeli airstrikes, far from being effective in eliminating Black Septembrists, were instead killing hundreds of civilians. Yet within the Jewish state itself, the citizenry supported the bombings. "The Israeli public, still thirsting for revenge, barely registered the carnage caused in the name of their dead athletes," writes Reeve.[83]

Zvi Zamir, the Mossad chief, was not among those cheering on the sorties. Disapproving of this spree of violence, he argued that Israel should fix its sights on those who were directly responsible for the Munich attack—the actual members of Black September who carried out the massacre—and those who had collaborated with them, such as by financing or helping set up the assault. And, in the end, Golda Meir concurred, due in no small part to the sweeping condemnation of Israel's foregoing strikes in Syria and Lebanon. Yet at the same time, Meir and her advisors added another objective to the plan, a more challenging one; namely, the destruction of the roots of Palestinian terrorism itself. A tall order, it would culminate in Operation Wrath of God.

6

Mission: Operation Wrath of God

In a well-furnished living room in a Jerusalem apartment in the middle of September 1972, a woman and four men gathered for a secret meeting. Black September had delivered its devastating attack in Munich only two weeks earlier, and now, in Prime Minister Golda Meir's home, she and her guests—they were top military and intelligence figures—were hashing out the Jewish state's response. Because Israel's recent sorties in Lebanon and Syria had met with scathing disapproval from Western and Middle Eastern nations, not in the least because the bombings had killed or wounded scores of innocent Palestinian families, the group had devised an alternate response. And its objective was ambitious: "to hunt down and eliminate not just those responsible for the Olympic massacre but the political and military leadership of the PLO."[1] It was at this meeting, moreover, that one of the men who would help lead this extraordinary mission would be offered the job.

His name was Juval Aviv, and here it will behoove us to briefly examine his credibility since a portion of this chapter is based on his account of events. As it stands, Aviv's recollection of the meeting at the prime minister's apartment, as well as the ensuing mission itself, was the basis for the 1984 nonfiction book *Vengeance*, written by investigative reporter and Canadian television producer George Jonas.[2] Prior to composing the text, Jonas and his publisher undertook the arduous task of vetting Aviv, who, they concluded after considerable footwork and expense, was a reliable source. All the same, the book met with controversy upon its release, since the State of Israel did not want it known that it employed assassins, let alone that Golda Meir had personally given the go-ahead for killings in foreign lands. Attempts were therefore made to discredit the text by demeaning its source of information—Juval Aviv—although such efforts were ultimately unsuccessful.

Two decades later, DreamWorks and Universal Pictures optioned the *Vengeance* book, with its content slated to become the primary material for Steven Spielberg's 2005 feature film, *Munich*.³ To assess yet again the reliability of its source, Spielberg approached former president Bill Clinton, along with an American diplomat in the Middle East and other experts, and asked that they look into Aviv and his claims.⁴ Even more productive, the director tasked his in-house staff with tracking down the mysterious Mossad agent and confirming his credentials, which they did. "Spielberg's brain trust discovered FBI files proving that [Aviv] and his team were not fictitious," writes Nicole LaPorte.⁵ Subsequent to this, the director invited Aviv to Los Angeles, where he interviewed the informant at length and established, to his own satisfaction, the legitimacy of the former operative and his depiction of the Mossad mission.

This was not, however, the sole verification of Aviv's credentials. It turns out that an unrelated legal case prompted the release of documents, obtained through the Freedom of Information Act, that confirmed not only that he had served with Israeli Intelligence but also that he had been under contract to the United States Department of Justice.⁶ Such findings, then, lend credence to the former agent's account of Operation Wrath of God, as the post–Munich mission was dubbed. For the reader interested in learning more about the debate surrounding Aviv's identity and background, the 2005 edition of *Vengeance* contains an insightful essay on the subject, titled *Notes on a Controversy*.⁷ As for Aviv's name, it was, for security reasons, changed to "Avner" in both the book and the film, but the present text will use his real name since it has become public knowledge.

In the gathering at Golda Meir's apartment, Aviv recalls that the other three men who were present consisted of Mossad chief Zvi Zamir, along with Aharon Yariv, the former chief of Military Intelligence, and the Ariel Sharon, the military leader who would eventually become the head of state. It was at this time and place that the twenty-five-year-old Aviv, a former captain in the reserves who had served in a commando unit and fought in the Six-Day War, was asked to help lead a secret mission unlike any Israel had heretofore undertaken. And he agreed to do it, even though its exact nature was so hush-hush that Meir and her trio of associates did not divulge its particulars to him at this time. Certainly such secrecy was understandable given that the proposed plan to send Israeli intelligence agents into other nations to carry out assassinations was a flagrant violation of international law. If the Israeli government's handprints were to be detected on the project, the political blowback would be tremendous.

In the ensuing days, Aviv was assigned a set of tasks, which he approached conscientiously since he was eager to please both the prime minister and the chief of the intelligence agency. The most important undertaking required him to fly to Geneva, Switzerland, where he would open two accounts at the Union de Banque Suisse. One would be for his personal use, an account into which the Mossad would transfer, through a circuitous route, his monthly salary. The other account would be used for the Wrath of God's operational expenses, an amount to be maintained at a quarter of a million dollars. As Aviv and his team spent this money, a Mossad operative, who would be kept in the dark as to the reason, would deposit additional funds into the account by means of foreign bank transfers so as to keep the amount at the quarter-million level.

Also at the Swiss bank, Aviv was to rent a lockbox. Containing two keys, it would serve as the exchange site for written communication between him and the Mossad. He was to only use it if he found it essential to make contact with his superiors.

Upon returning to Tel Aviv, Aviv was escorted to a secret location and introduced to an enigmatic figure by the name of Ephraim. This man, a high-level Mossad staffer, would be his case officer. And it was now that Ephraim unveiled to Aviv the full extent of the forthcoming mission and the rationale behind it.

The objective of Operation Wrath of God, the case officer informed him, was to eliminate the Black Septembrists who had perpetrated the Munich Massacre, and, equally important, to put to death certain members of the PLO itself. In all, roughly a dozen individuals would be targeted. Although this number was a drop in the bucket given the size of Black September and especially the Palestinian umbrella organization, the PLO, it was a matter of influence, not quantity. As Ephraim explained to Aviv, it was the removal of this small cadre of dominant figures that would lead to the gradual degradation of the Palestinians' extensive terrorist network.

"If you eliminate one top terrorist," Ephraim explained, "it may take a year or two for another to emerge." He continued,

> The old network has gone to pieces in the meantime; it may take the new guy another year to rebuild it. While he's doing it, he has to show his hand. We may be able to identify and eliminate him, too, before he can do much harm. Meanwhile, you have saved hundreds of innocent lives.[8]

Thus, Operation Wrath of God was designed to forever cripple the PLO and its factions, most of all Black September, the Fatah, and the PFLP, by extracting their most powerful and persuasive figures while ensuring that the groups never again reached their present levels of organization and potency. From a strategic standpoint, the idea made sense. And while the approach would not completely eradicate Palestinian terrorism, the prime minister and the Mossad believed it promised to reduce it considerably.

As things stood, Operation Wrath of God was arguably the most ambitious component of a larger, more pervasive Israeli response to the Munich Massacre and the ongoing PLO threat to the Jewish state. As Aaron Klein points out, the State of Israel was planning, alongside the assassination program, a bold new effort to prevent terrorist attacks that were known to be imminent, a program entailing the use of preemptive strikes to interrupt them.[9] As well, the Mossad, in company with the Meir administration, decided to employ psychological tactics to dissuade Palestinian youths who might aspire to become terrorists from proceeding with their ambitions. Together, these methods were expected to weaken the PLO and its factions in the short term, while, in the same stroke, serving notice about the nation's plans for addressing terrorism in the longer term. "The message to all terror operatives would be clear," says Klein: "[T]he state of Israel will settle its score with all who have harmed or intend to harm its citizens."[10]

The decision as to who would be murdered would adhere to an exacting procedure. The Mossad would draw up a list of candidates for assassination, with the list being extended as additional information became available about various terrorist groups and their members. When the intelligence agency determined that a person on the list should be liquidated, the individual's name would be sent to Committee X, as the secret group became known. Comprising this board would be the prime minister, select members of her cabinet, and Mike Harari, the head of a Mossad strike force known as Caesarea. Also called Kidon, Caesarea specialized in executions.

Committee X would hear the Mossad's rationale for proposing the assassination and rule on it, approving or disapproving the killing or deferring the decision until further information could be put forth warranting the death of the target. But there was a stipulation that would apply to all targeted assassinations: "The prime minister would authorize the plan only when certain that innocent civilians would not be harmed, and that the strategic interests of the state would not be harmed," writes Klein.[11] It was the same policy Ephraim had voiced in his initial meeting with Aviv. "Yours is the cleanest operation there is: one person, one homicidal criminal, and no one else," the case officer said. "If you're not one hundred percent sure it's him—you let him go."[12] No civilians, which included the target's friends and family members, were to be injured or killed.

And so it began.

The Assassinations

Rome: The Wael Zwaiter Affair

The Mossad's first hit was to be a "soft target," meaning the subject would be unprotected and comparatively easy to eliminate. His name was Wael Zwaiter (Zu'aytir), and he was a Palestinian intellectual, poet, and translator, as well as the PLO's envoy in Italy. Thirty-six years old and single, Zwaiter was the product of a family of scholars and was perhaps best known for his translation of the classic Arabian tale *One Thousand and One Nights*. He was also Yasser Arafat's cousin, although Zwaiter, in sharp contrast to his infamous family member, was an unassuming figure widely regarded as a pacifist. Indeed, he had once approached the Israeli government with a proposal for a Palestinian state in the West Bank and Jordan in an effort to facilitate a constructive solution to the Palestinian issue.[13] At the time of his scheduled killing, he was residing in a nondescript flat in the Italian capital, a city that had been his home for the past fourteen years and one in which he worked as a translator at the Libyan embassy.

Although Zwaiter was not one to publicly espouse violence against Israel, he firmly opposed the way in which the Jewish state, in his view, treated Palestinian Arabs, and he did not hesitate to speak out about the matter. Three weeks before his slated murder, he penned an essay for the newsmagazine *L'Espresso* which contained an explicit statement on what he regarded as the irony of Israel's behavior. The piece was later reprinted in a book of essays, titled *For a Palestinian*.[14]

"The tragedy here," Zwaiter writes, "is that a people who suffered at the hands of one group of people should now in their turn persecute another people, an innocent people with no such word in their language as 'anti-Semitism." He continues,

> It is tragic that the Jews, who understand ... the meaning of suffering and humiliation, do not protest against the racist movement that pretends to speak in their name. It is not only tragic, it is catastrophic.... The world is one unit and nobody in it comes from beyond this planet. The Palestinian people therefore belong to this world and it is up to the Jews in Palestine to accept living with them in a democratic state. That would mean a great saving in bloodshed and bring about justice.[15]

From such writings, it is evident that Zwaiter's passions ran high, but the question remains as to whether his deeds crossed the line into terrorism. The Mossad claimed they did. Among other circumstantial evidence, it pointed to the fact that Zwaiter had been in contact with the Fatah in the past, although the Palestinian's defenders insisted that he had rebuffed the group's use of violence. It was for this reason, they explained, that he had left the Middle East and settled in Italy.[16] Regardless, the Israelis remained convinced that Zwaiter's bookishness and pacifism were merely a facade, the intended manifestation of a well-designed masquerade.

The scholar's actions were uncertain. Some members of the Mossad suspected that Zwaiter may have been involved in the Munich attack, although there was no evidence to support such speculation. Many more believed he was a prominent figure, quite possibly the leader, of a Fatah-Black September unit in Italy. And still others insisted he was partly responsible for the July 1968 hijacking of an El Al flight from Rome to Tel Aviv. Because it occurred two years before the creation of the Black September Organization, the argument was that Zwaiter must have been working for the Fatah at the time. And further incriminating him in the eyes of the intelligence agency was the fact that, together with numerous Palestinians residing in Rome, he had recently been questioned as part of an investigation into the bombing of another El Al flight. The incident had occurred on August 16, 1972, just two months earlier.

In this cold-blooded affair, two young Englishwomen on holiday in Rome became acquainted with two Middle Eastern men. As the women were preparing to travel to Israel, which was to be the next stop on their vacation, one of the men asked that they take with them a small record player, a gift for his family in the West Bank. "The innocent English girls," write Bar-Zohar and Haber, "could not know that ... the record player had been thoroughly taken apart, stuffed with explosives and sophisticated devices, then reassembled and repacked in its brand-new box."[17] And sure enough, the bomb exploded when the plane reached cruising altitude, although the terrorists' desired outcome, the wholesale loss of life, was not forthcoming. Having gained experience in such matters, El Al Airlines had taken to fortifying its cargo holds in anticipation of such an event. Then, too, the pilot was superb. "The El Al captain, seeing the flash of a fire-warning light, pressed the SOS signal that alerted the Rome control tower," write David Tinnin and Dag Christensen.[18] A seasoned aviator who had served in the Israeli Air Force, he managed to bring down the airliner in under six minutes. Not only that, the passengers and flight crew were uninjured, while damage to the aircraft was minor and limited to the interior of the cargo hold. As for Zwaiter, nothing tied him to the bombing, so police officials in Rome released him shortly after interviewing him. All the same, the Mossad suspected him of having had a hand in the affair, which, combined the earlier El AL attack and other incidental events and indirect connections, rendered him a marked man.

On the evening of October 16, 1972, Wael Zwaiter enjoyed his last meal when he and his longtime Australian companion, Janet Venn-Brown, dined together before he began walking back to his apartment in an unpretentious neighborhood of Rome. As always, he was unguarded, taking no precautions for his own safety since he either was, or pretended to be, a benign Palestinian intellectual who had no reason to expect to be assaulted. Having dropped by a grocery store on his way home, Zwaiter, dressed in a black trench coat over a gray sports jacket, was toting a bag of bread and a bottle of fig wine. As he neared his block at 10:30 p.m. several yards ahead of him a young couple stepped out of the shadows and began strolling along in front of him, walking in the same direction as Zwaiter. He had no way of knowing that the man and woman were working for the Mossad and that their arrival ahead of him was a signal to a second set of operatives in the vicinity, a signal that he was coming near. For that matter, the couple did not know much more about what was happening than did Zwaiter, certainly not that he was about to be murdered; the two were simply performing their assignment of stepping in front of him. Their "need to know" did not extend beyond this act.[19]

As the Palestinian came even nearer to his apartment building, a young woman on the opposite side of the street laughed and waved to the couple ahead of him, then ran to the pair and embraced them as if they were old friends. This, too, was a signal, one informing the hit squad that Zwaiter was about to arrive at his destination and they should get into position.

It was now that the unsuspecting Palestinian stopped at Bar Trieste, which was adjacent to his apartment building, to place a telephone call.[20] The Mossad had been surveilling him for the previous fortnight and knew this was his routine, his own phone service having been disconnected because he could not afford to pay the bill. A few minutes later, he walked into the darkened lobby of his building—to save energy, the lights automatically brightened and dimmed at two-minute intervals—and rummaged around in his coat pocket for a ten-lire coin to insert in the pay-elevator. As he was doing this, a voice from the shadows asked him, evenly, "Are you Wael Zwaiter?"[21]

At precisely this moment, the lights in the lobby brightened, causing Zwaiter to see the two Mossad agents standing a few feet from him. He had no idea they were his executioners. One of them, Juval Aviv, later described Zwaiter's reaction during these, the last seconds of his life. "His expression wasn't frightened," the Israeli said. "He wasn't even startled, only a little puzzled, perhaps."[22] Since the operatives could now see that it was indeed their target who stood before them, they did not wait for his answer. Instead, they pulled their .22-caliber Berettas from their coat pockets and shot him twelve times, then walked briskly out of the building, slid into an idling green Fiat, and vanished into the night. The pair never explained why they performed an overkill—a dozen shots into the target at close range—since two bullets would have been sufficient to bring about his death and would also have been in keeping with standard Mossad procedure. In any event, four hours later the four-man hit squad along with its seven collaborators were no longer in Italy. In the inquiry that followed, police confirmed that a dozen shots had hit Zwaiter in the head and the back, but the authorities were unable to identify the shooters.[23] It didn't matter; the Mossad was widely assumed to have pulled off the execution.

"Looking back, his assassination was a mistake," writes Aaron Klein, a conclusion based on the Mossad's dearth of meaningful evidence that Zwaiter was associated with Black September, the Munich Massacre, or the two El Al incidents.[24] Others have cast doubt on Zwaiter's guilt as well. His dinner companion on the night he was killed, Janet Venn-Brown, later compiled a book of writings in his honor, one in which a contributor, the Italian scholar Romano Ledda, insisted that Zwaiter was philosophically opposed to political violence. "He had a very clear idea of what political and armed struggle meant," Ledda writes, "and terrorism played no part of it."[25] Ledda added that one reason Zwaiter did not carry a gun was because he had never learned how to use one.[26]

That said, there are others who continue to argue that the Palestinian's murder was justified, and they point to the lack of direct evidence against him as indicative of just how effectively he and the Fatah/Black September had managed to cover his tracks over the years. Of course, this line of reasoning is flawed, since it interprets the absence of incriminating evidence as supporting Zwaiter's guilt in the same way it would interpret the presence of such evidence as supporting his guilt. It creates a no-win situation for the accused in that it leaves no means for establishing his innocence.

In the end, it may never be known if Zwaiter was, in fact, a terrorist or merely a renowned scholar who, through no fault of his own, happened to be a cousin of Yasser Arafat. All that is known for certain is that his expensive slaying in the lobby of a Rome apartment building—the project cost the State of Israel $350,000—was the opening shot of the Wrath of God mission, and that it was very effective in serving notice to the PLO and its factions that the time of reckoning was at hand.[27]

Paris: The Mahmoud Hamshari Affair

For Dr. Mahmoud Hamshari, a Palestinian historian and the PLO's envoy in France, the day of reckoning would be December 8, 1972, the last day of Hanukkah. During the two weeks leading up to this fateful day, a Mossad team had methodically tracked Hamshari's every move, along with those of his wife Marie-Claude and daughter Amina, in the course of which the operatives learned a great deal about their target's daily routine. In the process, they also learned about those areas of his life about which the Mossad had suspicions.

The agency was aware that Parisians considered Hamshari to be a cultivated, diplomatic gentleman who shunned violence as a political instrument. It was aware, too, that he published a reputable bulletin called *Faht-Information* and was a liaison between the PLO and the Arab contingent of UNESCO, the United Nations agency for educational, scientific, and cultural affairs.[28] None of this information was secret or controversial, and was, in fact, the way in which the thirty-eight-year-old Hamshari wished to be perceived. Certainly it is how he had studiously presented himself during his years in the French capital.

But the Mossad believed it knew more about the genteel Palestinian than did the Parisians. The agency was convinced, for instance, that he was a seasoned coordinator of terrorist activities as well as being the leader or second-in-command of the Black September Organization in France. The Mossad was also confident that Hamshari, before taking on the BSO role, had helped hatch a 1969 plot to kill then-prime minister David Ben-Gurion during a state visit to Denmark. In addition, it suspected Hamshari of having played a role in the 1970 bombing of Swissair Flight 330 en route from Zurich to Tel Aviv.

In this vile episode, a Convair CV-990 *Coronado* jet caught fire due to an explosive device extremists had been planted in its cargo hold. Nine minutes into the flight, the pilot, after struggling to land the plane, contacted the control tower and explained that there was smoke in the cockpit, that he no longer could see the instrument panel, and that the plane was going down. "Good-bye everybody, goodbye everybody," the pilot radioed.[29] Moments later, the airliner crashed into a forest near Zurich, killing all forty-seven of its passengers and crew.

The horrendous mass murder, combined with the attempt on Ben-Gurion's life and Hamshari's presumed involvement with Black September in France, prompted the Mossad to judge the Palestinian guilty of lethal acts against the people of Israel. Accordingly, he earned the next spot on the Wrath of God's roster of assassinations.

For his execution, the Mossad sought a dramatic method, one that would make it plain, although not provable or prosecutable, that the murder had been the work of professionals. Coming on the heels of the death of the PLO envoy in Rome, the death of Mahmoud Hamshari, the PLO's man in Paris, would drive home the point that the Israelis were homing in on the organization's leaders in Europe. It was imperative, however, that he be neutralized in such a way as to spare his wife and daughter, meaning that special precautions would need to be taken. So it was that the operatives began mulling over the prospects of isolating and liquidating their prey.

"What about a hand coming out of the shower and shooting him?" Aviv asked his accomplices.[30] An offbeat proposal, the team was not surprised by it since Aviv was known to be "much preoccupied with showers."[31] When the idea was duly nixed, a fellow agent suggested a twist on Aviv's *salle de bain* approach. He recommended that Hamshari be murdered while sitting on the toilet, a moment when the Palestinian would surely be alone. "Please, don't be disgusting," replied another operative.[32]

In due course, the team decided to pursue a method that would befit the reputedly talkative militant. As it stood, the Mossad was fairly certain that Hamshari was directing Black September's French operation from his fashionable apartment at 175 rue d'Alésia on the Left Bank. In part, this was because the agency had observed young Arab men frequenting it, as well as the fact that the Hamsharis' maid was barred from certain rooms of the residence during the day. The Mossad suspected the apartment of being an "advanced base, arms depot and communications centre for Black September commandos in Europe" write Bar-Zohar and Haber.[33] In keeping with this theory, it was known that Hamshari spent an inordinate amount of time on the telephone in his apartment, this being the way in which Palestinian terrorists orchestrated their missions in the early 1970s—at home, on the phone. With these particulars in mind, the team decided it would be an act of poetic justice to kill Hamshari with a telephone bomb.

At Mossad headquarters in Tel Aviv, Zvi Zamir, having learned that the team had settled on a technique that would involve breaking into Hamshari's home to plant an incendiary device, insisted that one of the agency's specialty units be dispatched to Paris to help with the preparations. Known as the Keshet ("Rainbow"), it was headed by Zvi Malkin, the covert agent who had helped abduct Nazi war criminal Adolf Eichmann in Buenos Aires a decade earlier. His unit's expertise included burglary.

Touching down in Paris shortly thereafter, the Keshet agents disguised themselves as telephone repairmen and set about insinuating themselves into the Hamsharis' lodgings. Once inside, the squad photographed the rooms from all angles and noted the specifications of the phone equipment. Subsequent to this, they handed over their findings to the core Mossad team, while a member of the latter (pseudonym: "Robert") hurried to Belgium to begin assembling a plastique bomb. A material favored by terrorists, plastic explosives were, and remain today, difficult to detect.

In the meantime, other members of the team began double-checking the particulars they had collected about Hamshari, first and foremost his telephone number. They knew, however, that they needed more than this piece of information, that it would be necessary for one of them to be able to identify his voice on the phone. This was because the Mossad would be calling his apartment immediately before triggering the bomb and needed to be able to confirm that it was Hamshari who had answered the phone. This meant an agent would need to talk to the Palestinian beforehand in order to hear his voice. So this became the next order of business.

Posing as an Italian journalist, "Carl," a Mossad agent in his forties, scheduled an interview with Hamshari at a small café on the Left Bank.[34] The envoy had readily agreed, of course, since one aspect of his cover as a PLO representative was to speak to the press about Middle Eastern affairs. So it was that the operative and the extremist met for coffee, with the ensuing discussion lasting such a long time that Carl suggested they continue it at a later date. After Hamshari agreed to the request, the interview came to a close, with Carl now knowing the sound of the target's voice.

On December 7, while the Hamshari family was away from the apartment, the Keshet squad returned to the flat and affixed the bomb to the base of the telephone. To ensure that Marie-Claude and Amina would not be accidentally killed, Robert had refrained from building one with a mechanical trigger. Such a device could be set off by anyone who happened to pick up the telephone receiver. Instead, he crafted one that could only be detonated by an operative deliberately transmitting a radio signal once it had been determined that Mahmoud Hamshari had been the person who had answered the phone. Although the bomb would be armed when anyone lifted the receiver, it would not be set off until the Mossad heard Hamshari's voice on the other end of the line and delivered the fateful signal. As to the magnitude of the explosion, Robert was careful to use a minuscule amount of plastique so as to avoid reducing the entire building to rubble.

The next day, a cold Friday in Paris, the Hamsharis did not stick to their usual routine, a problematical turn of events considering this was to be the day of the assassination. Whereas the Mossad's surveillance operation had revealed that the family's schedule never varied on weekdays—Marie-Claude and Amina left the apartment each morning at 8:00 a.m. and Mahmoud left exactly one hour later—Mme Hamshari and her daughter, on this particular day, did not appear to be going anywhere. Eight o'clock came and went with no sign of the pair. And this break in routine rattled the Israelis who were positioned around the ornate building waiting to perform the kill. Among them was Zvi Zamir, who had flown to Paris to be on hand during the execution.

Two of the operatives were posted in a van across the street from the apartment, while another pair was in a sedan close to the building's front entrance. "The latter were acting as guards," says Jonas, "and it was also their job to make sure Madame Hamshari or the child did not return to the apartment at the wrong moment."[35] A fifth agent, Carl, the "Italian journalist," bided his time at a payphone in a nearby bistro, a nondescript establishment from which he could observe the apartment's windows as well as his accomplices in the van.

For reasons unknown, Marie-Claude and Amina were thirty minutes late leaving the apartment, the upshot being that the team had under a half-hour to pull off the bombing once they spotted the pair's departure. And so the Israelis sped into action.

As the mother and daughter walked to a bus stop, Carl dialed Mahmoud Hamshari's phone number. When the Palestinian picked up the receiver, Carl asked if he was speaking to Mr. Hamshari, and, satisfied it was the right man, gestured to the two operatives in the van. Seconds later, an agent in the vehicle flipped a switch, sending an electrical impulse to the device concealed in Hamshari's telephone.

In the telephone receiver at this moment, Hamshari would have heard an ear-piercing sound, a high-pitched whistle, and it would have been followed by a burst of light and a pulse of searing heat. Because Robert had made sure not to over-stuff the bomb with plastique, however, the explosion was not devastating. In fact, it did not kill Hamshari instantly. The only way the Mossad team could tell the device had detonated was because the apartment's windows suddenly cracked, taking on the appearance of spiderwebs. All the same, the attack, which had cost the Mossad two hundred thousand dollars, would eventually prove fatal.[36]

Forty-eight hours later, the hit team and its supporting players vanished from the City of Light. Hamshari, meanwhile, clung to life for the next three weeks, during which time he futilely described to authorities an Italian journalist who had interviewed him at a café and called him on the phone that ill-fated morning. Since the murder had been exquisitely planned, there was nothing concretely linking it to the Israeli intelligence agency. That said, there was little doubt about the source of the assassination, and this is precisely as the Mossad had hoped. "PLO leaders in Europe began to fear for their lives," says Klein. "The deterrent effect was taking hold: Palestinian operatives, rather than planning their next high-profile attack, began to concentrate on their own survival."[37]

Although Black September did proceed with a planned attack on the Israeli Embassy in Bangkok, Thailand, on December 28, 1972—the operation turned out to be a fiasco—the leaders of the Palestinian Liberation Organization and the BSO now became less visible for fear they might be the Mossad's next target. With the death of Mahmoud Hamshari, who, as it happened, had traveled to Rome a few weeks earlier to oversee funeral arrangements for his colleague Wael Zwaiter, Palestinian activists in Europe decided it was a wise moment to drop off the radar screen. Naturally, the Mossad had anticipated such a response, so it ramped up its efforts to detect and eliminate its prey.

At this point, Operation Wrath of God began to increase in manpower, eventually boasting three dozen members who, due to the extreme secrecy of the project, were kept isolated from the larger Mossad membership. And side by side with this growth in the operation's workforce were refinements to its configuration. Besides the hit squad composed of Aviv and his accomplices— the men who carried out the Rome and Paris assassinations—two more teams were added to the Wrath of God mission. Like the one headed by Aviv, they would function autonomously, having limited interaction with Mossad headquarters in Tel Aviv or, for that matter, with the Jewish state itself. It was imperative that the political murders not be traceable to the Israeli government.

Each team was made up of three components: a surveillance unit, a logistics unit, and an assassination unit. The first of these, the surveillance squad, occasionally included a female operative serving alongside a male agent whose assignment was to keep watch on the target.[38] The rationale was a sensible one: a man conducting surveillance was less likely to attract suspicion if he was accompanied by a woman. Then, too, the female operative could conduct surveillance along with the man, thereby enhancing the comprehensiveness of the process.

The second component, the logistics unit, was charged with securing supplies and coordinating the team's attack. Once a modus operandi had been selected, it would be this unit that would make the arrangements to ensure the assassination could take place without a hitch.

The third component, the assassination unit, typically consisted of two young men who had served in the Israeli military, usually as commandos, and who were considered the *crème de la crème* in their specialty areas. Each pair worked in tandem. This was the manner in which the murder of Wael Zwaiter in Rome was carried out, when former commando Juval Aviv and his accomplice liquidated the Operation Wrath of God's first mark in the lobby of an apartment building. And the same setup would apply in the upcoming execution, which would take place in an unusual location so as to convey to the Palestinian extremists that there was no longer anywhere on earth they could feel safe.

Nicosia, Cyprus: The Hussein Abad al-Chir Affair

After the Rome and Paris executions, the Mossad broadened the criteria of its hit list. No longer was it necessary for a prospective target to be a Black Septembrist or a PLO leader; any influential Palestinian who encouraged violence against the Israelis was now fair game. And one man whose stature in the Palestinian movement fit the bill was Hussein Abad al-Chir, alternately known as Hussain Abu-Khair and Hussein Abd el Hir.

6. Mission: Operation Wrath of God

At thirty-six years of age, al-Chir's day job was that of an instructor of Eastern languages, although he spent the greater share of his time helping orchestrate terrorist attacks. Unlike the culpability of Wael Zwaiter and, to a lesser extent, Mahmoud Hamshari, there was no doubt about al-Chir's involvement in extremist plots. At this time, the early 1970s, he was serving as the PLO's envoy to the Republic of Cyprus, the Mediterranean island known for being, among other things, an intelligence hub where operatives from an array of nations chose to rendezvous. Even more significant, he was the principal point of contact between the Fatah and the KGB, the Soviet Union's intelligence agency. In his capacity as a go-between, he procured Soviet arms and arranged for Soviet training of Palestinian guerrillas while drumming up support in the Middle East for the USSR and its political ambitions in the region. For these reasons, the Mossad placed his name on its list. And there was another reason as well.

For several weeks, the agency had been receiving reports that al-Chir was crafting a plot in Cyprus, one that would involve a handful of terrorists smuggling a cache of weapons aboard a ship bound for Haifa, Israel. Upon the vessel's arrival in the port city, a group of Palestinian commandos masquerading as passengers would seize the weapons and launch an attack on the ocean liner and the port itself. Accordingly, the Mossad wanted al-Chir dead not only because he was a PLO heavyweight who was liaising with the KBG, but also because it hoped to thwart the forthcoming attack in Haifa.

So it was that a Mossad team, on the evening of January 22, 1973, landed in the beguiling city of Nicosia, the capital of Cyprus. It was in response to a telephone call that the team's leader had received from an Israeli surveillance operative who had been keeping an eye on the Palestinian. It seems the target was due to arrive in Nicosia within a matter of hours and would be residing at his usual spot, the Olympic Hotel. Like Zwaiter and Hamshari, al-Chir eschewed bodyguards and other precautions presumably because he felt safe in the outlying nation. The Mossad classified him as a "hard target," however, because he spent a considerable amount of time outside of its sphere of operations, most notably in Syria. Because so much remained unknown about him, then, the agency felt its risk was enhanced.

The team now set to work planning al-Chir's execution, the method having already been selected by one of its members and endorsed by the others. "Six little bombs under his bed," the operative, an expert in demolitions, told his accomplices, "[t]o make sure we get him without getting anyone else."[39] In contrast to the comparatively weak explosion that led to Hamshari's demise in Paris, the Mossad agents were determined that this next device would be powerful enough to destroy the target on the spot. It was imperative that al-Chir not linger for weeks before succumbing, since such a situation presented the possibility that he might furnish damning evidence against the Mossad before his death. And yet, the intensity of the new incendiary device notwithstanding, the prime minister's overarching rule still applied: No innocents were to be placed at risk.

Because the team members did not know how long al-Chir would be staying in Nicosia—he was always in motion despite the fact that the Cypriot capital was his home base—they quickly arranged for plastique to be smuggled to them in the island city, where an operative set to work constructing the casing that would contain it. The device's design would be similar to the one used in Paris. The Nicosia apparatus, which would contain a half-dozen small explosives, would be couched in a wooden crate the size of a shoebox with springs wedged between the explosives and the shell. When pressure was applied to it, such as by squeezing it, the bomb would become armed. An operative could then transmit a radio signal to detonate it. The reason the team chose this design, which was essentially a modified "pressure bomb," the type sometimes placed under car seats in car bombings, was because the agents had decided to assassinate al-Chir in his hotel room and needed a weapon they could conceal in his mattress. If everything proceeded according to plan, al-Chir's weight, when he lay on the bed, would compress the incendiary device, priming it for the radio signal.

The signal, as it happened, would be transmitted to the target's hotel room on January 24, 1973, merely six weeks after the assassination of Mahmoud Hamshari. It was on a brisk Monday morning that the marked man walked out of the Olympic Hotel and climbed into a vehicle awaiting him, a chauffeured KGB sedan. A Mossad surveillance unit tailed the car to a safe house known to be that of the Soviet intelligence agency, and parked nearby. The unit's job was to alert the other members of the Mossad team when al-Chir left the safe house to return to his hotel.

In the interim, a separate Mossad unit—the Keshet, once again—monitored al-Chir's quarters at the hotel, lingering in the corridor as a housekeeper cleaned the Palestinian's room. After she left, the Keshet members slipped inside, slid the bomb under the mattress, and disconnected the wiring in the ceiling light fixture. Their aim was to ensure that the room had only one source of illumination and that it was located beside the bed. This way, the team would know when al-Chir stretched out on the mattress, since the last thing he would do before going to sleep would be to turn off the lamp on the nightstand.

While the Keshet was planting the incendiary device, a top-tier Mossad official registered at the hotel. He wanted to be on-site when the blast occurred. At the same time, an operative scanned the guest registry and floor plan on which al-Chir's room was situated, and discovered, to his dismay, that a Jewish man and woman, newlyweds, were staying in the room adjacent to that of the target. Of course, there would be no way the Mossad could justify its actions to Golda Meir if it injured or killed the honeymooners. Yet the demolitions expert was confident his bomb would not hurt anyone other than the intended Palestinian, and therefore the mission went forward.

Once the set-up was completed, a handful of operatives assumed their positions in and around the hotel. Among them were two agents installed in a car across the street from al-Chir's room with an unimpeded view of his window. One of them clutched the electronic device that would transmit the radio signal to activate the bomb. Now it was simply a matter of waiting.

The decisive moment would not come quickly, however. Indeed, it was only after lengthy delay—the hour was nearly midnight—that the Mossad unit posted in the car was alerted to the Palestinian's arrival at his hotel. Watching his window, the agents noticed his room go dark a few minutes after he entered it, meaning that al-Chir had turned in for the night. And so one of the operatives, adhering to the plan, flipped the switch on the electronic device, causing an explosion to rip through the target's hotel room, sending glass and mortar raining onto the street below. As intended, the blast was far more intense than the one in Paris and therefore the death of al-Chir was instantaneous, the force having "launched him and his mattress into the ceiling," according to Tinnin and Christensen.[40] As for the honeymooners in the next room, they "dived under the bed, fearing a terrorist attack," write Bar-Zohar and Haber. "Chunks of plaster showered all around them."[41] Thus, the agency had eliminated its third mark in a spectacular fashion and with no civilians being wounded or killed in the incident. But there were repercussions. In the face of this latest instance of the Mossad's mounting aggression, Black September decided to jump-start its pursuit of vulnerable Israelis, with the first murder in its new string of attacks occurring on January 26, 1973, merely forty-eight hours after al-Chir's assassination.

Black September, Spring 1973

It was at a café in Madrid. A thirty-six-year-old Israeli, Baruch Cohen, had a rendezvous with a young Palestinian by the name of Samir. Cohen, whose family had lived in Haifa for several generations, was a *katsa*, a Mossad case officer or "gathering officer," and Samir was a university student and member of the Fatah.[42] From time to time, the two got together for chats, in the course of which Samir would share inside information about Palestinian political activities. And so it was on this day, with the pair conversing once again. It was when they prepared to take their leave, however, that it happened: two men strode up to Cohen while Samir suddenly vanished from the scene. Given Cohen's past association with the Shin Bet and, currently, the Mossad, he no doubt realized that Samir had double-crossed him, that the young man was actually a double agent for Black September and had set him up. And he was right. "Three quick rounds slammed into his chest," writes Klein. "Cohen collapsed on the sidewalk, in a pool of his own blood, his internal organs ruptured."[43] He died in surgery shortly thereafter, prompting Black September to release a boastful statement that evening taking credit for the kill. As could be expected, the murder was widely interpreted as the organization's response to the recent Wrath of God assassinations, but some insiders believed the attack had been planned months in advance.[44]

Similarly unclear was a dreadful attack five weeks later, on March 1, 1973, at the Saudi Arabian embassy in Khartoum, Sudan. It was the strike that was recounted in Chapter Five, the one in which a Black September cell stormed into an embassy party and machine-gunned three American and Belgian officials. Although the attack may have been a retaliatory strike against the State of Israel for its recent assault on a Palestinian refugee camp, it may also have been an attempt by Black September to reconfirm its presence, and its venom, during a period when the international intelligence community was watching the Israelis bludgeon the guerrilla organization. Whatever the reason, the BSO abruptly increased its run of murders at this time.

"In quick succession, Palestinian gunmen carried out three operations in Cyprus in which they killed an innocent Israeli businessman, attacked the home of the Israeli ambassador, and unsuccessfully attempted to hijack an Israeli plane," write Tinnin and Christensen. "In Rome, Black Septembrists shot down an Italian guard who was employed at the El Al ticket office."[45] Yet the Mossad remained active as well, albeit more focused and purposeful than Black September, with the Israeli agency continuing to select for assassination the most persuasive voices in the Palestine Liberation Organization and other terrorist groups.

The Quickening of Operation Wrath of God

The next of these figures to enter the Mossad's crosshairs would be Dr. Basil Paoud al-Kubaisi, a specialist in international law, a professor of jurisprudence at the American University in Beirut, and an Iraqi living in the Lebanese capital. April 6, 1973, however, would find him in Paris, and it was here that the Mossad prepared to execute him.

Al-Kubaisi had always loved Paris, a city he visited whenever he had the opportunity. Not only was it beautiful to behold, but its food was superb and sex readily available. And the latter was a plus in the eyes of the forty-year-old Iraqi, who was not averse to paying for it.[46]

6. Mission: Operation Wrath of God

Like the other extremists the Wrath of God operatives put out of commission, al-Kubaisi's veneer was that of a man who was at once erudite and eloquent, a gentleman who longed for a thoughtful resolution to the Palestinian conflict. Behind the facade, however, he was the antithesis of diplomatic. According to the Mossad's research, al-Kubaisi had collaborated for seventeen years with the Popular Front for the Liberation of Palestine. Throughout the PFLP's span, al-Kubaisi had been significantly involved in its violent operations, having been a participant in its plot to assassinate Iraq's King Faisal and two schemes to eliminate Golda Meir. The Iraqi law professor was also thought to have had a hand in the mass murder at Israel's Lod Airport in the spring of 1972. And, adept at logistics, he was known to have helped the PFLP smuggle arms into various nations. Now, however, the tables were turned; a plot was in place to murder al-Kubaisi himself.

Preparing itself for his execution, the Mossad had begun shadowing him several months earlier, in October, 1972. Although he was a soft target who traveled without security, he was shrewd enough to avoid placing himself in vulnerable circumstances. It was for this reason that it took the Mossad such a long time to finalize his elimination. What made it possible, moreover, was the work of "Kathy," the pseudonym of a clever Canadian-American woman affiliated with the Mossad.[47]

Tailing the Iraqi professor during his excursions on the Right Bank, Kathy became adept at anticipating his movements with uncanny accuracy. Among other consistencies, she noticed that he tended to walk in heavily trafficked areas presumably because he could obtain a degree of invisibility by blending into the crowds. Another advantage of this tactic: if the Mossad were to spot him, there would be far too many witnesses for the team to abduct or assassinate him. Kathy also noticed that if a conspicuous, congested street were not close at hand, al-Kubaisi would favor embassy districts and other areas that maintained security forces and purposely kept them in plain sight. Rarely did she find him alone at an isolated location. But now, owing to her sharp observational skills, it would at last be possible for the Mossad to bump off the slippery terrorist. And like the Wael Zwaiter murder in Rome, it would happen after dinner.

At 9:00 p.m. al-Kubaisi had his last meal, and it was at the Café de la Paix, a colloquial translation being "Coffee in Peace." A feature of the renowned Le Grand Hôtel, the establishment was near a small pension that he had selected for his lodgings. In the neighborhood was the magnificent *L'église de la Madeleine* ("Madeleine Church"), as well as prostitutes who strolled the boulevards. And it was to be with one such woman that al-Kubaisi shared the concluding hour of his life, having procured her services after finishing his dinner.

At 10:00 p.m. the Iraqi left the prostitute's quarters and resumed his walk to the pension. Cautiously, two Mossad agents stepped out of the shadows and began following him, while a third walked along the other side of the street. The latter's task was to keep the area clear of potential witnesses while the pair that was trailing al-Kubaisi moved in for the kill. Besides these agents who were on foot, operatives in two cars, which were traveling in opposite directions, monitored al-Kubaisi's steps as well. One of them would later serve as the escape vehicle for the gunmen and their lookout.

Not surprisingly in light of his past experience, it did not take long for al-Kubaisi to realize he was being pursued, with the Palestinian looking repeatedly over his shoulder and quickening his pace. Inexplicably, though, he came to a halt at a crosswalk when the light turned red, standing stock-still near a corner drugstore. At this moment, the two agents stepped in front of him, with the Iraqi seeming to sense what this portended. "La! La!" he cried out in Arabic, meaning "No! No!"[48] But it was too late. The hitmen fired their Berettas at point-blank range as their quarry stepped backward onto the curb, then tumbled to the ground. The men continued firing on him, riddling his body with nine bullets even as he lay stricken on the pavement. Moments later, recalled one of the assassins, al-Kubaisi let loose with "a series of short, sharp, rasping sounds as if he were clearing his throat."[49] And then the Iraqi expired.

The gunmen and their lookout hurried to a side street, where the escape vehicle was waiting for them. By morning, all members of the team had scattered throughout Europe and the Middle East. As for al-Kubaisi's connection to the shadowy world of international terrorism, French investigators, upon searching his hotel room, discovered that he had been traveling with six passports. The Popular Front for the Liberation of Palestine, meanwhile, issued a statement announcing the death of its devoted member and collaborator and calling for his memory to be honored. To be sure, al-Kubaisi had been far more than a lawyer. He would not be the only attorney-terrorist to die at the hands of Israeli intelligence, however, with another one being knocked off within days, accompanied by a pair of his comrades.

The Spring of Youth

Merely seventy-two hours after the assassination in Paris, Israel launched another covert operation knowing the PLO would not expect one so soon after al-Kubaisi's execution. Unlike the previous Wrath of God missions, this one was not orchestrated by the Mossad, although its top officials and some of its agent-assassins would take part in it. Instead, two military organizations would lead what was dubbed Operation Spring of Youth. The two groups consisted of the *Sayeret Matkal*—the Israeli Defense Forces' commando unit—and *Shayetet 13*, which was the commando unit of the Israeli Navy. Like the U.S. Navy Seals, the *Shayetet 13* was an elite unit noted for, among other specialties, its topnotch sea-to-land campaigns. As for the targets, they included Abu Yussuf (a.k.a. Mahmoud Yussuf Najjer), an attorney and top-tier leader of the Fatah; Dr. Kamal Butros Nasser, a journalist, poet, and official spokesman of the Palestine Liberation Organization; and Kemal Adwan (a.k.a. Kamal Adwan), an engineer, cofounder of the Fatah-Kuwait, and chief of the Fatah's covert operations inside Israel. Two of these men, Abu-Yussef and Adwan, were further suspected of having provided support to Black September during the Munich Massacre.[50]

The Mossad's strategy was put into motion on April 9, 1973, when missile cutters transported the assassins into Lebanese waters. As the boats neared the shoreline a few minutes after midnight, the operatives transferred to dinghies, then came ashore in the suburban district of Ramlet-el-Beida. Here, eight cars sat waiting, as did scores of accomplices. All told, there were nearly forty operatives on the scene who now packed into the vehicles and sped into Beirut.[51]

Arriving at the apartment towers, the operatives broke into three groups, each of which had been assigned one target. The plan was to carry out the killings simultaneously. Furthermore, the agents, to make sure bystanders would not be able to identify them, donned disguises, with the smaller men dressing as women and wearing blonde or brunette wigs and the larger commandos remaining dressed in their usual clothing. The two "genders" then walked arm in arm to the towers.

The killings themselves were swift and efficient, the culmination of weeks of planning and outstanding teamwork. As intended, they also were conducted at essentially the same moment.

In the first one, the team placed a small explosive device near the front door of Abu Yussef's fourth-floor apartment, blowing it off the hinges. When the Palestinian tried to shield himself behind the dislodged door, operatives peppered it with bullets, killing not only Abu-Yussef but his wife as well. Unfortunately, they were not the only casualties: a neighbor perished in the melee as she peeked out her door at the commotion.

At the same moment these events were unfolding, the second team burst into the apartment of Kamal Nasser and shot him to death as he sat at his desk. The gunfire ignited the sofa next to him because the bullets contained phosphorus.[52]

In a parallel action, the third team stormed into Kemal Adwan's apartment, who, like Nasser, was sitting at his desk. But unlike his comrade, Adwan had the presence of mind to grab an AK-47 and fire at his Israeli assailants, one of whom was struck by gunfire and wounded. Still, Adwan was no match for the band of assassins, their rain of bullets bringing his life to an end within seconds.

The body count was higher than anticipated. Although the operatives liquidated their three marks, they had also murdered a spouse and a neighbor. Then, too, the agents, prior to firing on these individuals, had killed a number of security guards posted at the buildings' entrances. In order to silence them so they would not alert the three targets, the agents eliminated the guards as quietly as possible using knives and pistols. It was for such reasons that the total number of casualties was larger than the number of intended targets.

Despite the civilian deaths, the Israelis regarded Spring of Youth as a grand achievement because it removed from the equation three figures known to have been instrumental to the PLO, the Fatah, and quite possibly Black September. Their absence was expected to weaken the Palestinian Liberation Organization's factions and thus help avert its attacks on Israel. Yet the mission proved to have an impact well beyond the Jewish state's expectations.

"Spring of Youth made a searing impression in the Arab world, a combination of anger, embarrassment, and awe," said David Elazar, Chief of Staff of the Israeli Defense Forces. "In Lebanon, the government collapsed in the aftermath of the attack."[53] By this point, Operation Wrath of God, together with the Spring of Youth project, had executed seven high-level PLO figures. But Israeli Intelligence did not wind down the assassination program at this juncture; rather, it ramped it up.

In rapid succession, three key Palestinians were annihilated. On April 11, 1973, Ziad Mokhsi (a.k.a. Zaid Muchassi), the PLO envoy who replaced the murdered Hussein Abad al-Chir in Cyprus, was blown up in his bed at the Hotel Aristides in Athens, Greece. Although some maintain that Mokhsi was not a terrorist himself, that he was only eradicated because he was an easy target who was closely associated with the PLO, others insist that he was, in fact, a "senior Black September commander."[54] In any event, the Mossad, in short order, liquidated him. "The Wrath of God Squads could scratch another Black September leader off their list," write Fred Burton and John Bruning.[55]

Next on the roster were Abdel Hadi Nakaa (Abed Al-Hadi Naka'a) and Abdel Hamid Shibi (Abdel Al-Hamid Shibi), two Palestinians the Israelis annihilated in Rome. The date was June 13, 1973, and the pair, under the watchful eye of the Mossad, were in a Mercedes headed to Leonardo Da Vinci Airport where they were expected to park near the El Al terminal. The car, the Israelis had discovered, was rigged to explode when it received a signal by remote control, and it would be at the terminal that this would happen. It was for this reason that Mossad operatives secretly rewired the vehicle to explode at the time and place of their own choosing—to wit, far removed from the El Al building and with the Palestinians still sitting in it. And, sure enough, the plan was a success, the Mercedes lighting up the sky as its passengers, the two guerrillas, sustained wounds that eventually proved fatal. In this case, Operation Wrath of God not only erased another pair of extremists, but it also foiled what would have been a bloody attack on Israel's national airline.

Countless more strikes would be prevented, or at least handicapped, by the elimination two weeks later of the Mossad's next mark, one of the world's top terrorists. To gauge his significance, one has only to note that, after his assassination, he was replaced by the diabolical Ilich Ramirez Sanchez—Carlos the Jackal. Such was the prominence of Mohammed Boudia, a forty-one-year-old Algerian intellectual and actor, as well as a beguiling man whom women found irresistible. As could be expected, he often used his charisma to lure them into his furtive schemes.

The Mossad considered the Boudia execution a priority. By liquidating him, it would be removing a pivotal player from the realm of global terrorism. Certainly Boudia's criminal record speaks for itself, the cunning Algerian having served a three-year prison sentence in France for sabotage and, at the time of the Wrath of God mission, being under pursuit by Italian authorities for his central role in an attack on an oil refinery that had cost a petroleum company billions of dollars. In addition, the Dutch and Swiss governments were on his trail for reasons of their own. Boudia, to be sure, kept Interpol busy.

Intimate with the KGB, the Irish Republican Army (IRA), and the Baader-Meinhof Gang, he was also connected to the PFLP and the Fatah and was presently believed to be overseeing Black September operations in France. Yet his role was much larger than that of managing the Palestinian group. "His assignment was to knit the various terrorist groups in Europe into a coherent organization," write Tinnen and Christensen. "Eventually he hoped to create a global network in which the wide spectrum of terrorists—from Basque separatists to Italian fascists to the Japanese Red Army to Black September—could stage joint operations, exchange intelligence, provide weapons and logistic support for one another, and undertake attacks simultaneously in different parts of the world."[56]

Equally disconcerting, Boudia, who was regarded as "Black September's foreign minister for terror," was a close friend of Ali Hassan Salameh, the BSO leader who helped orchestrate the Munich Massacre.[57] The Mossad had recently obtained evidence, moreover, indicating that the pair was preparing a major attack somewhere on the European continent. Not surprisingly given his rap sheet and current plans, Boudia, after Salameh, presented the greatest threat to the State of Israel owing to his international reach.

As it stood, the Israeli agency had been stalking the Algerian for quite some time, but to no avail. Operatives would have him in their sights, then he would simply vanish. He would enter the apartment of one of his many lovers, for instance, but never be observed leaving it. And this, in turn, left the Mossad stumped. Over the course of time, however, the Israelis solved the riddle of his comings and goings. "After his amorous encounters," write Burton and Bruning, "he would dress in drag and slip away every morning with none of the Mossad operatives the wiser."[58] As a trained thespian and currently the manager of a small Parisian playhouse, *Le théâtre de l'Ouest* ("Theater West"), Boudia was adept at refashioning his appearance. But even as he succeeded in concealing his physical features, he failed to take rudimentary precautions in another area.

Bafflingly, Boudia, who owned a gray Renault, registered the vehicle in his own name with the French government. Not only that, he refused to part with the car. Whereas it was common practice for terrorists to borrow, steal, or rent vehicles for brief periods and under assumed names, Boudia drove his own beloved Renault around Paris on a regular basis. "This habit was a colossal security oversight," says Klein.[59] And the result was predictable: the Algerian's lapse in judgment allowed the Mossad to track him down.

After identifying Boudia's car, the Wrath of God operatives set to work formulating his murder. Shooting him at close range, as had been the method in the al-Kubaisi execution a few weeks earlier, was one option, although it carried a risk of harm to the assassins. By necessity, they would be face to face with Boudia, who could be expected to fight for his life. Then, too, there was the possibility that bystanders might witness the operatives' deed, which would not bode well for Israel and its relations with France. Alternately, the team could use a remote-controlled bomb, which was far less likely to endanger the agents and would also reduce the chance of eyewitnesses. If the explosion were too intense, though, it might harm bystanders, with this being its principal drawback. Still, the team, upon giving the matter considerable thought, adopted the latter method because, compared to the former, it offered a higher probability of success coupled with a lower probability of incidental deaths.

The strike plan was sound: the operatives, in the evening, would follow Boudia to one of his lovers' apartments and, while he was engaged with her during the night, wedge a bomb beneath the driver's seat of his car. When he came out of the apartment the next morning wearing one of his disguises, it would not be imperative that the Mossad recognize him at once; whoever unlocked and climbed into the Renault would almost certainly be Boudia.

As to the device, the bomb to be employed was akin to the others used in Operation Wrath of God in that it would be a modified pressure bomb designed to become armed when Boudia sat down in the driver's seat. The weight of his body would prime it. Further along the street, an operative would be waiting in a parked car to send the signal detonating the incendiary device, but only when the operative had determined that it was indeed Boudia who was behind the wheel and that no pedestrians or bystanders were in the vicinity.

And, sure enough, this was precisely how it unfolded at 11:00 a.m. on June 28, 1973. The assassination took place on the Left Bank, near Boulevard Saint-Germain, and, as planned, injured no one except Muhammad Boudia. And he was an instant fatality. "[T]he force of the blast splattered his body parts over the cars parked nearby," says Klein.[60] His was a murder that would not go unanswered, however.

A comparable scenario played out forty-eight hours later in suburban Washington, D.C., when Black September retaliated. The victim was Colonel Yosef Alon, an attaché at the Israeli embassy and a former pilot, a decorated one, in the Israeli Air Force. As Alon returned home at the end of the workday, he was gunned down as he emerged from his car. "The Mossad," report Tinnen and Christensen, "believes that he was shot by Black Power gunmen on a twenty-thousand-dollar contract placed by a Black September representative in the United States."[61] On this subject, a BSO spokesman in Beirut subsequently acknowledged that his organization had indeed been behind the killing, although he would not confirm that Black September had paid a militant African American organization to pull the trigger.[62]

Notwithstanding what had become for the Israelis and the Palestinians a deadly dance of tit-for-tat killings, the Mossad took pride in its triumph, namely, the remarkable speed and efficiency with which it was striking off the names on its hit list. Over and again, its teams had demonstrated their aptitude for materializing in diverse cities and annihilating those the agency had fingered as threats to the Jewish state. In fact, the majority of extremists who made up the Mossad's roster had now been killed, eight of them, and Operation Wrath of God had only been in place for eight months. And it was this impressive feat that led to a new development: because the teams had been so effective in their tasks, routinely working around the clock in high-risk conditions, the agency's leadership decided the time had come to provide them with a much-needed respite. But while this was no doubt a wise and humane decision, the ones that followed were far from sensible.

The Mossad decided, for instance, that a newly-assembled team would carry out the next execution, a team composed of fifteen men and women, some of whom had never before participated in a covert operation. Of course, this was a staggering error in judgment given the significance of the Wrath of God project. It was certainly no place for greenhorns. Bewildering as well, the Mossad ordered the team to kill the number-one terrorist on the agency's list, the elusive engineer of the Olympic bloodbath himself. And compounding the Mossad's folly, it would be sending the team into novel territory, Scandinavia, where the agency had never before conducted an operation. The operatives could therefore expect to be hampered by their unfamiliarity with the setting. As a result of such off-kilter decisions, the likely product of the agency's growing overconfidence, the Mossad created a perfect storm composed of a second-rate team, a slippery target, and an unstudied venue; a veritable textbook example of how not to construct a clandestine mission. Not surprisingly, it would prove to be the undoing of Operation Wrath of God, at least for the time being.

The Norwegian Affair

It started with an intriguing piece of intelligence. On July 14, 1973, the Mossad received word that a meeting had been set up between Kamal Benaman, a twenty-eight-year-old Algerian living in Geneva, Switzerland, and Black Septembrist Ali Hassan Salameh. The purpose of the get-together, it was suspected, was to lay the groundwork for a terrorist attack to take place in Scandinavia.

Benaman was no stranger to the Mossad. He originally came to its attention because of his network of associations, with the agency concluding that he was probably a BSO courier. The fact that he was always on the go, cavorting with powerful Middle Eastern figures in palatial estates and, just as often, with former "hippies" and other countercultural and revolutionary figures in low-rent digs, supported the Mossad's theory that he was a messenger for the PLO. Of course, the other man, Salameh, was already known to have been a key engineer of the Munich Massacre. As for Scandinavia, it would be fresh territory for Palestinian extremism, a largely unguarded region where the Israelis would not anticipate a terrorist strike. With the recent tip-off about the upcoming Benaman-Salameh rendezvous, however, the Mossad was now expecting such an attack and, to avert it, set about assembling a team to shadow Benaman in the hope he would lead it to Salameh, whom the agents would then murder.

Among the operatives would be a twenty-five-year-old woman by the name of Marianne Gladnikoff, a Swede who had moved to Israel and taken a position as a data processor for the intelligence agency. "Marianne had just started the Mossad evening course that would qualify her in a year's time to apply for full-time intelligence training," write Tinnen and Christensen.[63] Even though she was not yet suitable as a covert operative, the agency tapped her for the project because she had a Swedish passport, was fluent in the Swedish language, and could therefore legitimately present herself as a Scandinavian.

Another operative would be Dan Aerbel, whose selection seems to have been based on the same thin criteria as those of Gladnikoff. A Dane who had relocated to Israel, Aerbel was the holder of a Danish passport and was thus an authenticated Scandinavian. The agency had also used him in the past in some of its other endeavors.

The remaining agents, by and large, were seasoned professionals who had been itching to join the impressive Wrath of God operation and looked upon the Scandinavian hit as a unique opportunity to do so. Their motives varied, however. Some of the participants were banking on their involvement in the mission to help them ascend within the organization, advancement being at the heart of their involvement. To them, the Scandinavian venture was a career move. Others were dedicated to thwarting the PLO and its Black September faction and believed that eliminating one of the Palestinians' top figures would be an effective means of kneecapping the organizations. Still others were intent upon exacting revenge on the guerrilla unit that had slaughtered their nation's Olympic athletes.

The result, then, was a curious collection of male and female operatives, some of them amateurs, others practiced and proficient, and many of them driven by ambition or anger. And there was another distinguishing characteristic: most of these people, being new to Operation Wrath of God, had been kept in the dark about its previous assassinations and were thus unaware of the lessons that had been learned. As well, they lacked the special skills their predecessors had developed and refined thus far during the mission. It would be this dubious team, then, that would soon set off for Scandinavia.

The Mossad had come to believe that the Israeli embassy in Stockholm, Sweden, was to be the site of an impending attack, since the agency had been intercepting messages that hinted at an upcoming covert meeting in the Scandinavian city. More recently, observations by agents and *sayanim* in Western Europe revealed that Salameh was traveling from his provisional home in Ulm, Germany, northward to Hamburg, with the Mossad taking this to mean he was on his way to the Swedish capital. Concurrent surveillance of Kamal Benaman in Geneva revealed that a limousine from the Saudi consulate had driven him to the city's airport, where he had booked a flight to Copenhagen, Denmark. Connecting the dots, the Mossad concluded that the latter was also en route to Stockholm, the purpose being to establish contact with Salameh. Thus the Mossad dispatched three of the new team members to the Swedish city with instructions to be on the lookout for the extremists.

As it came to pass, the Stockholm assignment proved to be exasperating for the trio because Salameh never surfaced, just as Benaman, upon landing in Copenhagen, did not continue on to the Swedish capital. Instead, agents in Denmark watched as Benaman flew to Oslo. This turn of events prompted the Mossad to quickly send the entire fifteen-member team to the Norwegian city to tail the Algerian in the hope his path might lead to Salameh.

Within twenty-four hours of arriving in Oslo, however, Benaman was on the move again, checking out of his hotel and boarding a train for Lillehammer. A summer resort town situated an hour to the north, the Mossad likewise descended on it by rail and by car the next day—it was now July 18—in what was clearly a careless course of action. It was unwise because the sudden presence of over a dozen Israelis in the small Norwegian town was bound to attract attention owing to the contrast between the operatives' outward appearances and those of the Nordic people indigenous to the region. Not only that, Lillehammer was, and remains today, a rather staid town. "Because almost nothing ever happens in Lillehammer, the inhabitants take an intense interest in anything unusual," write Tinnen and Christensen.[64] By all accounts, it was not standard practice for the Mossad to deposit a sizable number of conspicuous operatives at the site of a mission. More the opposite: the customary procedure was to send as few agents as possible to such a locale and ensure that this nominal presence was unnoticeable or at least forgettable.

Be that as it may, the team, upon arriving in Lillehammer, began trying to ferret out Salameh but was unable to detect any trace of him. Two operatives did manage to find Benaman, however, a task they accomplished by making inquiries at the town's tourist bureau. It seems he was staying at the Hotel Scotte, a tourist-class inn near the train station.

Convinced that Benaman was in the faraway Nordic town to meet up with Salameh, the team monitored the Algerian's every movement, from his strolls through the streets of Lillehammer to his dips in the municipality's swimming pool. Two days later, its vigilance paid off when he popped into the Karoline Café situated next to a public plaza. After he was shown to a table on the balcony, a pair of Mossad agents seated themselves nearby to keep tabs on him. And soon there came a startling development.

Two men in the café soon joined Benaman and commenced chatting with him. One of them appeared to be a Middle Easterner and the other, a European. For the single-minded operatives who, since leaving Tel Aviv, had been straining at the leash, this was the break they needed. Electrified, they hurried out of the establishment and rejoined their accomplices.

"We found him!" exclaimed one of the agents, confident the olive-skinned man was the cagey Salameh.[65] And so it was that the team, fired up by this breakthrough, wasted no time fanning out around the café in order to get a better look at their target. For Marianne Gladnikoff and Raoul Cousin, the latter being a veteran agent operating under a pseudonym, this entailed sitting on a bench facing the café balcony and keeping their eyes glued to the gentleman suspected of being Salameh. Gladnikoff also scrutinized a photograph of Salameh during this time, a photo she kept in her pocket, comparing its image to that of the man on the balcony. But her conclusion was a letdown: she was doubtful the team had the right person. The others remained adamant that it was the guileful Palestinian, however, and soon set off to plan his execution even as the gentleman himself, after an hour-long conversation with Benaman, departed from the café and peddled away on a bicycle.

Next morning, the Mossad principals fine-tuned their strategy while Gladnikoff took a swim in the pool where Kamal Benaman was once again talking to the man from the Karoline Café. Swimming near to them, she heard the two conversing in French, which was one of the languages in which Salameh was known to be fluent. It was an observation that the team latched onto as further proof it was on the right track.

Continuing to surveil both men, the Israelis watched as Benaman climbed out of the pool, checked out his hotel, and boarded a train to Oslo. The agents figured he was returning to his home in Geneva, having concluded his discussions with Salameh. While these events were unfolding, a second set of agents observed the other man likewise leave the pool, the one thought to be Salameh, after which he dropped by a coffee shop and exited a few moments later with a pregnant woman, a blonde Norwegian. Given that Salameh had a wife and children in Germany, the presence of the Scandinavian woman should have raised a red flag. Yet the agents brushed aside this inconvenient incongruity just as they discounted the fact that the same slender man with the dark complexion had been spotted using a bicycle for transportation. Instead, they proceeded to follow the couple to an apartment building in a residential district of Lillehammer, where the operatives parked their four vehicles at the building's exits and waited for their target to re-emerge.

After a few hours, the Mossad got its wish when the man believed to be Salameh, accompanied by the blonde woman, walked to a nearby bus stop. Because the pregnant woman was wearing a cheerful yellow coat, the agents found it easy to follow the pair. It turned out that the couple was going to the cinema to watch *Where Eagles Dare*, a popular movie of the day.[66] Set in World War II, covert intelligence operations were a feature of its storyline, thereby making the film oddly appropriate in light of the real-life situation that was unfolding on this summer evening.

When the movie ended at 10:35 p.m. the man and woman left the theatre, caught a bus back to their neighborhood, and walked casually along the street leading to their apartment, talking and laughing. Ahead on them, a white Mazda sedan carrying four passengers, three men and a woman, sped directly toward the couple and stopped a few yards in front of them. Because it was late at night, the pair would have seen only the headlights. Suddenly, two men leapt from the backseat and began firing their Berettas at the man for a total of fourteen rounds.

Among other parts of his body, the bullets pierced his vital organs, including his stomach, causing him to grip his abdomen and fall to the ground, bleeding profusely.[67] Hovering over him, the shooters kept firing, then jumped back into the car and sped away.

The woman, screaming uncontrollably, dropped to her knees beside the writhing man. She was uninjured but hysterical. Minutes later, an ambulance arrived and paramedics tried to save the victim's life, but, having been sprayed by bullets, he was beyond their help. Shortly thereafter, a physician at a Lillehammer hospital pronounced him dead.

In point of fact, the man's name was Achmed Bouchiki and he was a thirty-year-old Moroccan waiter. Ambitious, he also worked part-time at the town's swimming pool, where his father-in-law was the manager. A handsome, well-liked man, Bouchiki "smiled often," it was said, and was "irrepressibly friendly and engaging."[68] Four years earlier, he had relocated to Norway from his North African homeland to pursue a better life, and he had made a fine start. He and his wife, Torill, were both employed and eagerly awaiting the birth of their first child in a couple of months. By all accounts, the Moroccan's dream was coming true. Concerning his encounter with Kamal Benaman, it is assumed that Bouchiki noticed him in the Karoline Café and proceeded to visit with him because Benaman was from Algeria, another North Africa nation.

Within hours, the report of the late-night homicide hit the newsstands, the ruthless murder being the first in Lillehammer in forty years. Initially, the Mossad suspected that the name Achmed Bouchiki was simply a pseudonym and that the team had indeed taken out Ali Hassan Salameh. It soon became obvious, however, that the agency was wrong, that its operatives had slain an innocent man. Devastating as well, it appears that Salameh and Black September may have choreographed the whole affair, artfully leading the Mossad into a trap that would bring about the Israeli agency's humiliation before the world.[69] Hastening the Mossad's undoing, moreover, would be its operatives' actions immediately after killing the Moroccan waiter.

The team, following the shooting, tooled around Lillehammer in the white Mazda as well as a green Mercedes and a white Peugeot, with the police noticing the latter and contacting headquarters for the details of the car's registration. In short order, authorities tracked down the Peugeot and arrested one of its passengers who had taken refuge in the home of an Israeli diplomat. As could be expected, this did not bode well for the Jewish state. Golda Meir could hardly deny Israel's involvement in the incident since her own emissary had been added to the mix.[70]

In Oslo, meanwhile, newbie agents Marianne Gladnikoff and Dan Aerbel attempted to return their rental car and fly out of the country. Instead, they found themselves handcuffed and driven back to Lillehammer. It seems the authorities had been on the lookout for the couple's car, which had been seen speeding out of Lillehammer after the murder. Reporting the pair to the police was the clerk at the car rental office in Oslo.

Within forty-eight hours of the killing, then, four members of the team had been apprehended, and two more would soon be arrested thanks to Gladnikoff and Aerbel divulging under interrogation virtually everything they knew about the Mossad. Not being trained or experienced in the field, the two were unskilled in withholding information or misleading interrogators. And what the agents revealed proved to be substantial.

"They not only provided details of the Lillehammer operation but also supplied vast amounts of information related to how Mossad functioned in Europe," write Burton and Bruning. "Their revelations forced the Israelis to withdraw agents, abandon safe houses, extract informants, and change phone numbers all over the continent."[71] The incident also damaged Israel's reputation and its relationships with other nations, above all Norway, which had no prior knowledge of the covert operation. "This was a violation of Norwegian sovereignty," states *The Guardian*.[72] Much to Israel's annoyance, the Norwegian government not only refused to cover up the events that had transpired, but it also publicly rebuked the Jewish state for its violent and illicit undertaking. Aghast that an extrajudicial execution had been carried out on its soil, the peaceable Scandinavian nation wanted the world to know that neither the Norwegian government nor its intelligence service had been complicit in the plot. To demonstrate its adherence to the law, moreover, Norway issued an arrest warrant for presumed the leader of the Mossad team, Mike Harari, despite knowing that it was highly improbable he would ever be arrested, tried, and convicted. In fact, it cancelled the warrant a year later, considering it to be futile. As for the six operatives who were jailed, one was freed and the others served prison sentences in Norway, including Marianne Gladnikoff and Dan Aerbel.

To date, the Israeli government, speaking for the Mossad, has never publicly accepted responsibility for the homicide. It did, however, pay Achmed Bouchiki's family an unspecified amount of money in 1996, twenty-two years after his murder.[73]

Lastly, the fiasco forced Golda Meir to suspend Operation Wrath of God.[74] Whereas the mission had heretofore met with remarkable success in striking back at Black September and the PLO, in the longer term the operation had failed to stop or significantly reduce terrorist acts in the region. The lesson seemed to be that violence actions are not stopped by violent reactions. Then, too, the debacle in Norway gave Israel, the Mossad, and the mission itself a black eye. Even the

Mossad's agents, most of all the seasoned professionals who had conducted the earlier Wrath of God executions, were mortified by the staggering incompetence of the mission in Norway. A few even left the agency because of it, no longer wishing to be associated with the organization for fear it was losing its edge. Clearly, the time had come for the powers-that-be in Israel to reassess Operation Wrath of God and, at the very least, put a leash on it, which is precisely what happened.

Just as the assassination project started to wind down in 1973, Black September also began closing up shop. As noted, Yasser Arafat was repositioning the Palestinian Liberation Organization toward a more cooperative approach to regional affairs in a bid for acceptance by the United Nations and other bodies. So it was that Operation Wrath of God and the Black September Organization ground to a halt as the year came to a close. Yet there was at least one more prominent assassination to come, and it would take place long after the controversy had subsided, and the world, like the target, was no longer expecting it.

Attaining Closure: The Salameh Project

Five years after the Lillehammer fiasco, the Mossad once again decided to pursue the mastermind of the Munich attack. For authorization, it approached Israel's new prime minister, the former guerrilla leader Menachem Begin, who gave his blessing to the renewed effort to track down Ali Hassan Salameh and execute him.

Salameh's life since the Olympic murders had continued to be eventful. During this period, the Palestinian lived in Beirut and collaborated with the Central Intelligence Agency, which had been the case, albeit sporadically, since 1969.[75] It seems the United States government needed a well-placed source who would notify Washington of impending strikes on American citizens in the Middle East and Europe, and Salameh fit the bill because of his connections to the numerous PLO factions. His value, moreover, had increased after the Olympic attack due to his mounting influence within the Palestinian Liberation Organization itself. So it was that in 1973, a few months after the Mossad's botched operation in Norway, Salameh and CIA case officer Bob Ames came together to forge a deal.

"Starting at the end of 1973, Salameh and Ames negotiated an understanding that the PLO would not attack Americans," writes Tim Weiner in *Legacy of Ashes: The History of the CIA*.[76] It was an arrangement that would yield enormous dividends for the United States, not the least being a last-minute tip that saved the life of Secretary of State Henry Kissinger. "For four years, they shared intelligence on their mutual enemies in the Arab world," says Weiner. "During that time, the CIA's reporting on terrorism in the Middle East was better than it ever had been, or ever would be again."[77]

Although the American intelligence agency offered to pay the extremist handsomely for his services, a six-figure sum per month, he refused the money. Salameh insisted he was helping the Americans in order to enhance their understanding of, and sensitivity to, the needs of the Palestinians, as well as to acquire information from the CIA that would help protect his own interests. He did, however, permit the American government to pick up the tab when he and his Hungarian-Lebanese bride, Georgina Rizak, honeymooned in New Orleans, Disney World, and the Hawaiian islands while on a business trip to the United States. The complimentary honeymoon was a recruitment tactic, the informer having been brought to Washington, D.C., to discuss once again his formal employment by the CIA. As before, though, he rejected the offer.

During this period, neither the Mossad nor the Israeli leadership knew Salameh was a CIA collaborator, the United States having gone to considerable lengths to ensure that the Jewish state, along with the rest of the world, remained in the dark about its covenant with the terrorist. White House policy, at the time, was unequivocal: it refused to recognize the PLO, let alone communicate or cooperate with the organization. But it was a deceit that was bound to be challenged, and this is precisely what happened in 1978 when the Mossad decided to jumpstart its pursuit of Salameh. To get to the bottom of the rumors about the link between its Palestinian target and the CIA, Israeli operatives met with their American counterparts. To the Mossad's relief—and to Salameh's detriment—the Central Intelligence Agency, hoping to avoid being caught in a lie, denied any association with the extremist, the upshot being that the Israeli organization proceeded with its plan for his execution.

Into the picture comes Erika Chambers at this point. A seasoned Mossad combatant, Chambers moved to Beirut in November, 1978, ostensibly to take a job at a charitable Palestinian agency that provided care for children. In reality, her arrival signified the beginning of the end for Ali Hassan Salameh. Before long, she was joined by additional operatives who fanned out across the Lebanese capital in a concerted effort to track down the terrorist leader's whereabouts, and, remarkably, they managed to do so within a matter of days. His security measures, it seems, had become more relaxed with the progression of the years.

"As the Mossad team observed him, they quickly discovered he had sunk into a routine," write Fred Burton and John Bruning. "They soon figured out when and where Salameh would go during his days and mapped out the streets he frequented the most."[78] With this information in hand, they began closing in on him.

Presenting herself as a middle-aged, single woman from England who loved stray cats and enjoyed painting as a pastime, Chambers rented a posh eighth-floor apartment in Beirut's Anis Assaf Building on January 10, 1979.[79] Among other plusses, the apartment had a balcony that offered a panoramic view of the surrounding streets, including Beka Street, which was a narrow course that connected two larger thoroughfares. It was from this balcony, moreover, that Chambers subsequently spent a substantial amount of time at an easel painting the skyline of the exotic city. What her inquisitive neighbors did not know is that the long hours the dowdy Englishwoman spent on her balcony did not reflect a love of art; rather, she was scrutinizing the activity on the streets surrounding the building, most of all Beka Street, down which Salameh's entourage was known to travel when he visited his mother. Chambers' assignment was to determine precisely when the extremist did so, Beka Street having been selected as the spot where the Mossad would murder him. As it happened, an earlier plan to blow up Salameh in the sauna of his health club had been ruled out because it would be too risky to the other patrons. This new idea, that of a bomb planted in a blue Volkswagen and parked on Beka Street, had supplanted it. The Mossad would detonate the incendiary device as the Palestinian's motorcade drove past the Volkswagen.

The assassination was scheduled for Monday, January 22, 1979. The Israelis knew that Salameh spent each afternoon at his fashionable apartment in the Snoubra neighborhood with his pregnant wife Georgina, a Christian and a former Miss Universe. The agency also knew that he was slated to visit his mother in the old quarter of Beirut on this day, where she was hosting a birthday party for his three-year-old niece. And the Mossad was ready.

Having recently procured eleven pounds of a plastic explosive in the middle of the night—Israeli frogmen delivered it to a Mossad agent at an isolated beach near Beirut—the operatives planted the material in the Volkswagen. The amount of plastique was equivalent to seventy pounds of dynamite, explains Simon Reeve, and therefore promised an intense blast.[80] Next, the operatives parked the car on Beka Street and waited, while Erika Chambers and an accomplice watched from the balcony.

At 3:45 p.m. the agents at ground level received a signal from Chambers indicating that Salameh's beige Chevrolet was approaching Beka Street. In the car were the terrorist leader, his driver, and two bodyguards, and tailing it was a Land Rover carrying two additional bodyguards. When the vehicles turned onto Beka Street, a Mossad agent standing several yards from the Volkswagen radioed the operative who was posted in Chambers' apartment. Looking down on the

6. Mission: Operation Wrath of God

Chevrolet, the latter flipped a switch as Salameh's car drove alongside the Volkswagen. Instantly, an explosion shook the entire block. It could be heard for miles. Recalls an eyewitness,

> It was like hell. There was a flash, then a big bang. It was incredible. I'd never seen anything like it before, not even in Beirut. It was as if the whole of the city was on fire. So many dead people, burnt cars and young bodies littering the street. Then I saw [Ali] Hassan Salameh getting out of a car and falling on the ground. The people told me who he was.[81]

Nine people perished in the inferno. Salameh survived, but only briefly. Shards of metal embedded in his brain, he was rushed into emergency surgery at the American University Hospital where he died on the operating table a few minutes later. The Mossad, by killing him, had finally closed the book on a principal engineer of the horrific attack at the 1972 Summer Olympics.

Most of the remaining targets met with violent deaths at the hands of the Mossad or other organizations. Of the three terrorists that the German government freed in the weeks following the Munich Massacre, the Mossad eventually killed one of them, with another having expired either as a result of heart failure or murder by the Mossad as well. The third is thought to still be alive and hiding in an African nation, the guerrilla having done so for four decades owing to his fear that the Israelis will eliminate him if he ever surfaces.

In addition, Abu Iyad, a top PLO leader and an organizer of the Olympic attack, met his fate in 1991 in Tunisia when a disloyal bodyguard brandishing an AK-47 assault rifle put a fast end to him. The assassin, a member of a competing PLO faction, was alleged to have received backing from the Israelis, according to the *Los Angeles Times*.[82] In a similar vein, Atef Bseiso, the PLO's chief of intelligence and security, was shot to death on the steps of the Meridien Hotel in Paris during an official visit to the city, where he had secretly been scheduled to meet with representatives of the French intelligence service.[83] His executioner was either a rival Palestinian organization—the bloodthirsty Abu Nidal group—or, as the PLO claims, the Mossad. The latter is certainly a possibility, since the Israeli agency had chanced upon information suggesting that Bseiso had been a collaborator in the Munich Massacre. His assassination took place in June, 1992.

Lastly, Abu Daoud, the remaining planner of the Olympic attack, succumbed to kidney failure in 2010 in Damascus, Syria. Perhaps the only Wrath of God target to die of natural causes, Daoud remained unrepentant to the end, insisting that the bloodstained strike at the Olympic Games had been justified and had succeeded in awakening the world to the plight of the Palestinians.

So it was that Operation Wrath of God came to an end, with the mission having achieved its fundamental objective. "The Munich athletes had been avenged," says Reeve.[84] Despite the fact that the covert operation did not permanently avert Palestinian attacks on Israel's citizens and interests, it did convey to the world the seriousness with which the Jewish state viewed politically-motivated assaults on its people and properties, and its willingness, even at the risk of occasional failure, to pursue, for years on end if necessary, those it was intent upon rebuking.

Part Three

Operation Entebbe

Introduction

During the 1970s, the Mossad's original mandate, that of intelligence-gathering to help secure the Jewish state, expanded to include collaboration with other Israeli military and intelligence organizations in a concerted effort to intervene in attacks against the nation and its people. Whereas the agency had, on occasion, shared intelligence with such bodies in the past, it was during this decade that the Mossad's presence in integrated, multi-organizational missions became a more critical and lasting feature, with some of the ventures proving to be both high profile and precedential.

Among such missions was Operation Entebbe, perhaps the most daring of the lot. A renowned undertaking, it centered on commandos of the Israeli Defense Forces storming a hijacked Air France airliner in Entebbe, Uganda, in an effort to liberate the passengers while subduing the terrorists. By turns known as Operation Thunderball, Thunderbolt, and Thunder, the mission has also been termed Operation Yonatan in honor of one of the soldiers killed during the mission, Yonatan Netanyahu, brother of Prime Minister Benjamin Netanyahu. Because the Israeli Defense Forces, as well as Israel's parliament, the Knesset, identify the mission as Operation Entebbe, however, this is the title used in the present text.

One subject on which virtually everyone agrees, on the other hand, has to do with the quality of the mission. Operation Entebbe demonstrated the brilliance of the Mossad, the Israeli Defense Forces, and associated components of the Jewish state's defense community in tackling one of the prevailing forms of global terrorism of the era, air piracy or "skyjacking." Even today, the mission continues to stand as a sterling example of the success that may be achieved when first-rate organizations work together harmoniously to attain what they hold to be a noble objective.

7

The Emergence of Skyjacking as a Tool of Palestinian Terrorism

It was Palestinian extremists who first used international air piracy as a political truncheon and it was the State of Israel that was the target. "The advent of what is considered modern, international terrorism occurred on July 22, 1968," says Bruce Hoffman, Director of the Center for Security Studies at Georgetown University.[1] It was on this day, at the height of the turbulent Sixties, that three terrorists representing the Popular Front for the Liberation of Palestine steeled themselves to commandeer an El Al airliner en route from Rome to Tel Aviv. What made the hijacking historic—the dawn of "modern, international terrorism"—is the fact that it had nothing to do with transportation and everything to do with intimidation, and thus constituted a sharp break from such acts of the past. "This hijacking was a bold political statement," writes Hoffman.[2] And it was more: it was a powerful, high-stakes offensive that the world could not afford to ignore. For this reason, the practice quickly gained currency among extremists in the Middle East and beyond, this new and chilling exploitation of commercial air travel.

In the four decades preceding the incident, aviation records reveal that aerial hijackings were not, in themselves, used for political manipulation, although criminal acts involving aircrafts did occur within political contexts. In such circumstances, captured planes were used for purely practical purposes, as was the case in the first documented instance of air piracy on February 22, 1931. It was during a period of acute political upheaval in South America that it happened.

On this date, an American pilot, the twenty-two-year-old Byron Rickards, landed a small Pan-American airliner in Arequipa, a city ensconced high in the Peruvian Andes.[3] To his consternation, upon touching down he found himself in a nation that was in the throes of a revolution. Worse still, a band of rebel soldiers was determined that he would play a part in it. "The soldiers had been hiding behind the hangar," Rickards said. "They surrounded the plane and told me to cut the engines."[4] The armed rebels now informed him, with surprising politeness, according to Rickards' account, that he would henceforth use his aircraft to drop political pamphlets for the uprising. But the American aviator had other ideas: making it clear he had no intention of participating in Peru's domestic conflict, he set about staging a stand-off that would last until the insurgency came to an end.

As it happened, this would be ten days later. And it was as the conflict was winding down that the rebel soldiers, realizing they no longer needed to hold Rickard against his will, released him and his copilot, along with the handful of passengers who had also been on the plane. At this juncture, one of the soldiers, in a spirit of bonhomie, asked if Rickards would give him a lift to Lima, although it is not known if the put-upon pilot accommodated him. What is known is that Pan-American Airways, impressed with Rickards' mettle, presented him with a check in the amount of one hundred dollars, which was, of course, a considerable sum in the midst of the Great Depression. And with this act of corporate generosity, the world's first confirmed episode of air piracy came to an end, with the Andean affair thereafter assuming a treasured spot in aviation lore. "The bumbling, almost charming amateurishness of the first recorded aircraft hijacking persisted for several decades," writes Oliver Burkeman in *The Guardian*.[5] Unfortunately, airplane hijackings, or "skyjackings," would not be nearly so benign in the years that lay ahead.

In his book *Flights of Terror*, a compendium of aerial sabotage and commercial aircraft seizures, author David Gero chronologizes such incidents from their inception through the September 11 attack on the New York World Trade Center. In the latter, Saudi terrorists, as is well-known, used airliners as missiles in the first large-scale strike of its kind. As such, the event was consistent with the pattern demonstrated in Gero's chronicle, namely, that of the mounting use of violence in aerial crimes.

In 1933, for instance, merely two years after Byron Rickards' curious experience in the Andes, comes the first documented report of an airliner being the target of sabotage. A United Airlines Boeing 247, it was *en route* from Newark to Chicago when a nitroglycerine-based bomb blasted it out of the sky. All seven passengers and crew perished in the incident, in which neither a culprit nor a motive was ever identified.

A smattering of bombings using comparable makeshift devices occurred in the ensuing years, although the perpetrators and their intentions became easier to detect now that authorities were aware of the possibility of such devious deeds. In more than one case, the motive centered on the collection of life insurance benefits, a fact that became apparent through an inspection of suspects' recent legal and financial dealings—or through a last-minute confession, as was the case for John Grant.

In this shady affair in the spring of 1950, Grant, a Los Angeles laboratory technician, took out $25,000 in life insurance on his wife and two children. "Reportedly, he was heavily in debt and infatuated with an airline stewardess," writes Gero.[6] As his family was boarding a United Airlines DC-3 for a flight to San Diego, Grant, having hidden an incendiary device in an overnight bag, handed the lethal piece of luggage to a baggage clerk. As the would-be murderer prepared to leave the airport, however, something happened within him: pondering the horror his actions were about to inflict, he rediscovered his conscience. So it was that Grant shouted frantically to the baggage handlers that they were loading onto the plane a valise containing an explosive device, a change of heart that no doubt saved lives.[7] As for Grant's life, it would never be the same again.

As international air travel routes proliferated in the ensuing years, skyjacking overtook sabotage as the top aerial crime, particularly during the late 1940s and 1950s when the latter came to be used as a method of escape from the Iron Curtain countries. In the wake of World War II, desperate citizens of the Soviet Union and Eastern Bloc nations, prohibited from emigrating, turned to commandeering airliners as a means of fleeing communist oppression. Their aim was to obtain political asylum in Western nations. Among their points of departure were Bulgaria, Czechoslovakia, Hungary, Poland, and Romania, with destinations that included Austria, Denmark, Germany, Greece, Italy, Switzerland, and Turkey. In some instances, the defectors sought continuance to, and refuge in, the United States. As to the characteristics of those committing the hijackings, they consisted not only of individual passengers but pilots and aircrews as well. Among the most fascinating cases, in fact, were those in which virtually everyone aboard a commercial airliner—pilot, crew, and the majority of passengers—orchestrated the takeover, a dramatic development that occurred on flights touching down in Munich, Germany, and on the Danish island of Bornholm in the Baltic Sea. Such was the single-minded determination to break free of Soviet subjugation.

Through the 1950s, hijackings by Iron Curtain defectors gradually decreased although air piracy itself persisted, with Cuban citizens now picking up the baton. Starting in 1958 and cresting in 1960, a period during which Fidel Castro's forces overthrew the self-serving, pro–American regime of Fulgencio Batista, a wave of hijackings occurred. Many were committed by law-abiding citizens fleeing a homeland in crisis, but others were perpetrated by Batista's henchmen and moneyed cronies who commandeered Cubana de Aviación airliners and demanded they be re-routed to Miami. Upon their arrival, the United States government routinely granted sanctuary to both categories of defectors, and, in several cases, lionized them for their boldness. But furnishing the escaping Cubans with refuge was not necessarily as it was portrayed to the public; that is, as an act of compassion by a sympathetic administration. The fact is, the U.S. government publicized the defectors' tales of distress in its hardline anti–Castro campaign, while the American businessman, Erwin Harris, took possession of, and sold, several of the costly Cuban airliners on the grounds that the former Batista regime was indebted to him because of an abandoned business deal.[8] Such incidents would be eclipsed in 1961, however, by a startling turn of events that would send shockwaves through Washington, D.C.

It was at this time that a number of disaffected Americans began storming into cockpits and ordering pilots to fly to Cuba, a reversal of the previous procedure and one that persisted throughout the course of the decade. Most of the hijackers were criminals on the lam, such as William Lee Brent, a one-time Black Panther member who shot two San Francisco policemen, then hijacked a plane to Cuba to avoid incarceration.[9] The remainder were political dissidents who had become disenchanted with the American Dream and enamored with Castro's revolutionary vision. Despite Cuba's totalitarian government, they yearned to be a part of the island nation's socialist experiment, a brush-off to Western democracy that dictator Fidel Castro not only savored but exploited in his ongoing campaign against his neighbor to the north. The United States was taken aback by the spate of skyjackings committed by its citizens. "[N]o one imagined that Americans eager to join Castro's revolutionary experiment might resort to desperate measures," writes journalist Brendan Koerner.[10] But resort to such measures they did, and, like the Iron Curtain defectors before them, their reason for seizing the planes centered solely on transportation. It would not be until 1968 that the hijacking of commercial airliners would acquire a new and deeply troubling dimension as Palestinian extremists repurposed the practice, in effect transforming it into a formidable political weapon in and of itself.

The Skyjacking of Flight 426

On July 22 of that year, a summer afternoon in Rome, El Al Flight 426 was scheduled to depart from Leonardo da Vinci International Airport for a nonstop flight to Tel Aviv. Due to a mechanical malfunction on the aircraft, however—some claim it was a bomb threat—it became necessary to bring in a replacement plane from Israel, thereby delaying the original flight until shortly after midnight.[11] Authorities were unaware that among its thirty-eight passengers and crew of ten were three terrorists who were members of a PLO faction and were preparing to take control the plane. And, indeed, it was while the Boeing 707 was soaring over the island of Capri twenty minutes after take-off that they made their move. Flashing guns and grenades to daunt and demoralize the passengers, the hijackers rushed to the cockpit to overtake those at the controls. "They pistol-whipped the navigator, and then fired a shot in the cockpit," says Edward Mickolus, a former CIA intelligence analyst. "Captain Oded Abarbanel, the pilot, did not offer further resistance."[12] Notifying ground control of the situation, Abarbanel informed air traffic controllers of his revised destination. "I am being forced to head for Algiers," he radioed.[13] Investigators later determined that the hijackers were convinced, wrongly, that Ariel Sharon was onboard, Sharon being the future prime minister of Israel and, at this earlier date, a revered commander who had led Israeli forces during the Six-Day War.[14] The terrorists' destination: Algeria.

The North African nation's complicity in the affair has been debated. Some insist the Algerian government had no advance knowledge that the El Al flight was headed to its capital city, Algiers, while others argue that such denials are disingenuous. They point to the fact that television crews, before the flight touched down at Algiers' Dar al-Bayda Airport, were already on hand and awaiting the plane's arrival. Also worth noting, Algerian president Houari Boumédiène made no attempt to discourage, let alone block, the commandeered airliner from landing in his country. No friend of the Jewish state, it was widely known that he harbored hostile feelings toward Israel, an animosity that had intensified after the Six-Day War thirteen months earlier. Then, too, Boumédiène had been "a top commander for the military wing of the National Liberation Front, the party that had led the independence fight against France," writes Koerner. "His wartime experiences had turned him into a fierce anticolonialist, committed to supporting revolutions the world over."[15] By all accounts, Boumédiène's sympathies extended to the Palestinian people and their enduring struggle to possess a homeland.

Once the airliner was on the tarmac in Algiers, the hijackers, who had realized by this time that Ariel Sharon was not among the passengers, changed their plans. Holding hostage the passengers and crew, they insisted that the State of Israel release from its prisons an unspecified number of Arab inmates. An impetuous, fuzzy demand, it would also be the terrorists' last act of any significance since the Algerian authorities would step in at this moment and take charge of the situation. From this point forward, the three PLO members were essentially *personae non gratae*.

Refusing to issue exit visas to the hijackers because their passports were forged, officials confined them to a nearby military camp where the three would stay until the hostage problem was resolved. In the same stroke, authorities placed the flight's twenty-two Israeli passengers and crew in a military camp as well, although they released the women and children a few days later. As to the non–Israeli passengers, officials freed them at once, offering them an escorted tour of the capital city while arranging their transport to Paris. In the end, then, the remaining hostages consisted exclusively of Israeli men, a dozen of them.

It was at this juncture that the situation became muddled. "The PLO and Fatah sent a six-man delegation to Algiers to request that the [Israeli] hostages be held until the release of twelve hundred Arab prisoners from Israeli jails," says Mickolus, "arguing that because Israel had claimed that one Israeli life was worth one hundred Arabs, the trade was fair."[16] And there was more. "Arab nations began making their own demands," writes Mickolus.

> Iraq demanded the return of an MiG21 stolen by an Iraqi pilot who flew it to Israel in 1965. Egypt wanted Israel to withdraw from the occupied Sinai. Jordan wanted the old city of Jerusalem. Syria demanded the Golan Heights.[17]

Meanwhile, on the other side of the fence, the International Federation of Air Line Pilots' Associations called for a boycott of Algeria. Specific airline companies did likewise, with commercial carriers in Switzerland, France, and Italy refusing to fly to the North African nation. As for the State of Israel, hurled into the crisis as it was, it refused to negotiate with the PLO on the grounds that doing so would only embolden the hijackers and encourage further acts of air piracy.

The predictable result was an impasse that dragged on for thirty-nine days, in the course of which Algerian officials relocated the hostages to a comfortable estate even as Israel secretly considered launching a military assault to liberate its hapless countrymen. Discussions about a rescue plan were shelved, however, when Algerian and Israeli leaders achieved a resolution to the crisis, one that infuriated the PLO because the terrorist organization had been shut out of the discussions. Although the terms of the agreement were not made public, the results were immediate.

On September 1, the twelve Israeli hostages were freed, with an Italian airliner flying them to Rome. On September 2, Israel released sixteen Arab inmates from its prisons, while taking pains to portray the handover not as a surrender to the PLO's demands but as a humanitarian act. The Israeli government claimed it had chosen to liberate the prisoners on the recommendation of Italian advisors. Such denials notwithstanding, it was evident that the Jewish state had yielded to the Palestinians' demands, and that it had done so out of a concern for the hostages who had been held captive for over a month. But there may have been another reason as well. "The [Israeli] government was apparently also motivated to act by an incident at the Suez Canal on August 29, in which Palestinian guerrillas attacked an Israeli patrol, killing two soldiers and taking prisoner a third," writes David Green in the Tel Aviv-based newspaper *Haaretz*.[18] Clearly, Palestinian violence against the people of Israel promised to escalate if the latter nation did not acquiesce.

All told, the skyjacking had been effective. The PLO's audacious stunt had transfixed the world, drawn attention to the Palestinian cause, and forced the release of several Arab prisoners. And if, as David Gero has suggested, the PLO had a secondary reason for seizing an El Al plane—"to humiliate the government of Israel"—it had accomplished this objective, too.[19] The PLO would not do so again, however, since El Al Airlines promptly put into place an array of uncompromising security measures that would lead to the air carrier's enduring reputation as the most fiercely protected in the world. "Armed security guards known as 'air marshals' were now routinely carried on flights," writes Simon Dunstan, "while all luggage was hand searched and the aircraft flight decks protected by armored doors."[20] Unfortunately, other forms of aerial terrorism would not be prevented as effectively. Although El Al skyjackings would cease, the airline would still fall victim to onboard incendiary devices at times.

Most consequential of all, the El AL hijacking signaled the birth of modern, international terrorism, as Bruce Hoffman has stated, with terrorist cells henceforth using airliners for political leverage and with passengers and crew as bargaining chips. And this adverse development was due, in large measure, to the ill-considered actions of the nation that had opted to accommodate the hijackers of Flight 426. "Algeria," says Mickolus, "wound up aiding a group of skyjackers in their demands, setting a precedent for future incidents."[21] Certainly the figures speak for themselves.

Documents released by the Central Intelligence Agency reveal that the number of air hijackings quadrupled the following year, 1969, and then doubled in 1970.[22] This figure fell sharply starting in 1971, however, as nations around the world set about implementing stringent measures to prevent air piracy. But as skyjackings became more difficult to execute, alternate methods of inflicting fear gained favor among extremists, most notably "barricade and hostage" situations, abductions, assaults, assassinations, and bombings. In some cases, terrorists introduced even more extreme methods into the picture.

In January, 1976, for instance, a PLO faction, the Popular Front for the Liberation of Palestine, concocted a scheme to obliterate a plane-load of passengers by conventional military means. Providing support would be Germany's formidable Baader-Meinhof Gang. The target was to be an El Al airliner, the location was to be the Embakasi International Airport in Nairobi, Kenya, and the principal weapon was to be a surface-to-air missile (SAM). The plan called for the terrorists to launch the missile as the plane, which would be traveling from Johannesburg, South Africa, to Tel Aviv, came in for a landing in Nairobi for a scheduled stopover. Along with Soviet-made rocket launchers, the commandos had an assortment of other weapons, the source of which remains unknown. This should not be taken to mean, however, there were no suspects. "Some reports claim that the machine guns, grenades, pistols, and SAM-7s were provided by Idi Amin of neighboring Uganda," writes Mickolus.[23] If true, it would reflect the stormy relationship that had existed between the Ugandan strongman and the Israeli leadership since 1972, when Amin expelled all Israelis from Uganda in order to curry favor with Muammar Gaddafi, the Libyan dictator.

Three terrorists, two of whom were believed to have to been involved in a plot to blow up an El Al airliner at Paris' Orly Airport the previous year, were to carry out the plot. The scheme did not succeed, though, just as the Nairobi attack would fail. The reason: the Mossad "had ears" in Kenya, in the jargon of the intelligence community. "Together with Zaire in Central Africa and Nigeria to the west, Kenya became one of the three strategic centers of Israeli intelligence activity in Africa," write Dan Raviv and Yossi Melman.[24] The Mossad, then, was well aware of its adversaries' covert goings-on in the East African nation.

The PFLP's plot was set to occur on January 25, 1976. On this day, the Mossad alerted Kenyan authorities to an intelligence dispatch it had just received, one warning that Palestinian terrorists were about to launch a missile at the Nairobi airport. At once, Kenyan officers rushed to the scene, located the commandos, and arrested them less than an hour before the El Al plane, which was carrying over a hundred people, was due to land.[25] Certainly the evidence was highly incriminating: the Palestinians were discovered at the edge of the airport, just outside the perimeter fence, with rocket launchers and heat-seeking Strela missiles in hand. This meant, of course, that prosecuting them would likely be a breeze. Then, too, it would also be a secret. Because the Kenyan government worried that the PFLP might unleash an attack on Kenyan civilians as a form of retaliation, the nation's leadership decided to withhold news of the attempted mass murder while the Mossad brainstormed ways of smuggling the commandos to Israel to face criminal charges. In the meantime, a Mossad unit in Nairobi geared up to ensnare two more terrorists, this time from the Baader-Meinhof Gang.

This latter action occurred a few days later when a pair of German extremists landed in the Kenyan capital. Their task was to track down and retrieve the missing Palestinians whose missile launch had failed to materialize and who had disappeared so abruptly. Although it has never been confirmed, it is believed that a Mossad operative, posing as an anti–Israel extremist, fed information to the Baader-Meinhof Gang about the capture of the commandos in the hope that the organization would send some of its members to rescue them. And sure enough, the German group took the bait and dispatched a couple, a man and a woman, with the Mossad making off with them shortly after their arrival in Nairobi.

From Kenya, the agency spirited the three Palestinian and two German terrorists to Israel, with some accounts claiming the Mossad tranquillized them in their sleep and concealed them in coffins on an El Al flight to Tel Aviv. Whether or not this version is accurate, it has been confirmed that an Israeli court subsequently tried, convicted, and sentenced the terrorists in secret legal proceedings. Their true identities were also held in secrecy, with the Israelis assigning them false names, even in prison records.

Among the incarcerated was Brigitte Schulz, a twenty-three-year-old Baader-Meinhof member who, upon arrest, was found to have a message penned in invisible ink on her abdomen. It was a set of instructions for the Palestinian commandos if she succeeded in locating them. But now it was Schulz who needed locating, which is precisely what her family in Germany set out to do.

Alarmed by her sudden disappearance, Schulz' loved ones publicized the matter ceaselessly in the hope it would encourage witnesses to come forward with information about her. Equally important, they were banking on the publicity to keep pressure on the police to continue their search. Two organizations that did not require such prodding, however, were the Baader-Meinhof Gang and the PFLP, both of which were convinced the Mossad had arrested, or possibly assassinated, Schulz and the other terrorists. This was despite the fact that their names did not appear in the arrest logs or prison records of the State of Israel or the Republic of Kenya. Thus, the two organizations, their hands tied at the moment, had little recourse but to bide their time until they could make a meaningful attempt to reclaim their five members. And this, it turned out, would come about a few months later in Entebbe, Uganda, as part of a more extensive Palestinian-German terrorist action. Unfolding before an international audience, it was one that would be undone by the Israeli hostage-rescue mission, Operation Entebbe, with consequences that would include the virtual cessation of Palestinian skyjackings for the next ten years.

8

Mission: Operation Entebbe

"A few moments after taking off I suddenly hear a terrible scream," recalls a passenger on Air France Flight 139 en route from Athens to Paris. "I see two persons rush forward. One is a long-haired youth wearing a red shirt, gray trousers, and a beige pullover. The other has a thick mustache, wears long trousers and yellow shirt. They are running toward the first-class compartment."[1]

Within seconds, the two young men, both of them Palestinians, are joined by a pair of Germans in their twenties, a man and a woman. The man's name is Wilfried Böse. Tall, stocky, blond-haired, and blue-eyed, his appearance suggests refinement, in part because he is dressed in a fashionable suit. The passengers and crew have no way of knowing that he is a former member of the Baader-Meinhof Gang, co-founder of an urban guerrilla organization known as Revolutionäre Zellen, and, at the moment, a commando with the Popular Front for the Liberation of Palestine (PFLP). The passengers are also unaware that he is a longtime comrade of Carlos the Jackal, the infamous terrorist who occupies the top spot on the international community's "most wanted" list. But most importantly, they are oblivious to the fact that Böse, on this day, is the leader of a hostage scheme dubbed Operation Uganda, although they are about to come face to face with this awful truth. As for his female collaborator, her name is Brigitte Kuhlmann and she is his wife. Like him, she is a former Baader-Meinhof member and a co-founder of Revolutionäre Zellen. Together, the couple, along with their two Palestinian accomplices, are kicking off one of the PFLP's most audacious skyjackings, with their prey being the two hundred fifty-eight passengers and crew packed aboard the Airbus A300.

Preparations for the takeover began a few months earlier, with the operation itself having been set in motion the previous night in Bahrain, the island nation situated in the Persian Gulf. At the Bahrain International Airport, the four commandos arranged for a sympathetic baggage handler to smuggle a cache of weapons onto a Singapore Airlines plane, after which they boarded it for an overnight flight to Athens. Here, the terrorists planned to transfer onto an Air France jet. As to why they had selected the Greek airport, it was the logical choice because of its proximity to the Middle East and its dreadful standing insofar as security measures were concerned. "[T]he conditions were ideal for terrorists: two hours of flying time from the Arab countries and Israel, and the terminal was crowded around the clock," says Yeshayahu Ben-Porat. "The slow-moving Greeks were well known for their apathy, and their security provisions were no exception."[2] Compared to other international airports that had introduced an array of safeguards to protect the traveling public from terrorist attacks, Athens' Ellinikon International Airport lagged far behind. "Few security officers circulated in the terminal, and even fewer outside," writes Ben-Porat.[3] On this stifling summer weekend, moreover, conditions were worse than usual owing to a workers' strike that had left the facility with an insufficient number of staff, thereby galling those who had shown up for work only to be told that they would be shouldering extra duties. It was in this unregulated, understaffed setting that the terrorist scheme commenced.

Day One: Sunday, June 27, 1976

At 6:45 a.m., Singapore Airlines Flight 763, the plane carrying the four commandos, touched down in Athens. The sky was cloudless and the temperature already rising. After disembarking, the German couple walked together to their connecting Air France flight, where they took seats in different parts of the first-class cabin after having been waved through by airport security. Had the officers performed routine body searches or required the couple to pass through the facility's metal detectors, they would have found pistols and hand grenades concealed on them.

The man, Wilfried Böse, polite if somewhat aloof, was dressed in a green shirt and brown suit, while his wife was clad in a blue denim skirt, blue blouse, and flat-heeled shoes. Fellow passengers described her as pale, with mottled skin, a ponytail, and wire-rimmed glasses.[4] They added that she was wearing a blonde wig which she kept adjusting, and said that her demeanor was conspicuously belligerent.[5]

Also disembarking from the Singapore airliner were the two young Palestinians, who side by side approached security personnel for scrutiny before being allowed onto the Air France jet. As with the German pair, safety was not a priority. "The metal detector was unmanned," says Simon Dunstan, "and the official working the hand luggage X-ray machine was paying little heed to his duties."[6] Boarding the French airliner, the Palestinians took their seats in the economy section but, unlike their German comrades, remained together.

As the planeload of passengers settled in for the three-hour flight to Paris—the aircraft was still on the tarmac—one of the Palestinians placed a metal container on his lap. Given the airport's reputation for lax security, it was a sight that worried a couple seated nearby. "I'm telling you, that one is a terrorist," the woman whispered to her husband.[7] In turn, the husband shared their concern with a flight attendant, who relayed it to her superiors. But, alas, it was to no effect. The flight was given the go-ahead, the consequence being that it would become the first Air France hijacking in the airline's forty-three-year history.

At 12:25 p.m. the Airbus took off for Orly Airport, the plane being in the capable hands of a handsome, fifty-two-year-old Frenchman by the name of Michel Bacos.[8] Married with two children, he had been a pilot for twenty-one years and had racked up over seventeen thousand hours of flight time.[9]

A few minutes later when it reached an altitude of two thousand feet, Bacos switched the airliner to automatic pilot and programmed it to ascend to thirty-one thousand feet. And it was at this moment that chaos erupted. "Seven minutes after departing from Athens we heard screams on board," says Bacos. "We thought there was a fire in the cabin."[10] As he scanned the controls to pinpoint the source, someone began kicking the cockpit door from the outside. Still suspecting an onboard fire, Jacques Le Moine, the flight engineer, opened the door only to be knocked aside by Wilfried Böse who was clutching a hand grenade in one hand and a pistol in the other. Planting himself directly behind Bacos, the German took control of the flight and would remain in charge throughout it. "The terrorist had his gun pointed continuously at my head and occasionally he would poke my neck not to look at him," says Bacos. "We could only obey the orders of the terrorists."[11] And one of the first commands was to re-route the plane to Benghazi, Libya. Another was to cut off all communication with ground control.

Meanwhile, the pandemonium in the passenger compartment intensified. After the initial outburst—the scream in the economy-class cabin that had alarmed the passengers—the two Palestinians raced to the first-class cabin, where they joined Brigitte Kuhlmann. While Böse remained in the cockpit monitoring the aircrew, Kuhlmann, her two accomplices at her side, announced over the intercom that the aircraft was being seized by the Che Guevara Group and Gaza Unit of the Popular Front for the Liberation of Palestine.[12]

Kuhlmann then commenced berating, and in some cases striking, those who voiced their resistance to the takeover. Some of the passengers later commented that she seemed to be making an effort to appear more unfeeling and brutal than her male counterparts, perhaps to prove that her gender did not diminish her ruthlessness.¹³ Among her victims was a Frenchman, whom she and a Palestinian accomplice thrashed until he collapsed in the aisle.

Kuhlmann next set about examining each passenger for items that might be used as weapons while also confiscating their documents, first and foremost their passports. The two Palestinians, in the meantime, hurried to the emergency exits, where they attached packages to the doors, packages they claimed contained explosive devices. Of course, the threat was evident. If the passengers tried to escape, they risked blowing up the airliner and killing everyone onboard. Along the same lines, if an attempt was made by an outside rescue team to enter the plane, the same tragedy would ensue. Certainly the possibility of such an attempt would, in due course, come to mind as Israeli officials learned about the large number of their fellow citizens who were passengers on the aircraft. And it would be at 12:59 p.m. that these officials would be notified about this situation.

In the regional Air France bureau in Tel Aviv at this moment, the telecommunications room came alive with the sound of a teletype machine. "RADIO CONTACT LOST WITH FLIGHT 139," the message stated. "AIRCRAFT VANISHED FROM RADAR SCREENS. SEEN SOUTH OF SUDA CRETE."¹⁴

In Jerusalem at 1:32 p.m. Prime Minister Yitzhak Rabin and his nineteen ministers were in session, this being the scheduled time of a weekly cabinet meeting. Their conference was interrupted, however, when Rabin's senior military advisor slipped a note to the head of state informing him about the French airliner carrying Israeli passengers. At once, Rabin placed Lod Airport in Tel Aviv on alert in case the errant plane were to be re-routed to the Israeli airfield. He also alerted the Sayeret Matkal, the Israeli Defenses Forces' elite counterterrorism unit. Besides performing reconnaissance missions and targeted assassinations, the Sayeret Matkal also conducted rescue operations on occasion. Given the nature of the Air France drama, Rabin suspected the unit might end up playing a role in it.

As the prime minister next set about assembling an emergency task force to monitor the situation, conditions on the airliner itself began to stabilize, with travelers lining up to use the restrooms and parents reassuring their children and one another. "Though forbidden to talk, the passengers whispered to each other, usually speculating about where they would be taken," writes Peck. "Indeed, it appeared to the passengers that the most nervous people on the plane were the hijackers."¹⁵

Using the pilot's microphone on the flight deck, Wilfried Böse now laid out for the bewildered travelers the rationale for Operation Uganda. "This hijacking is being carried out because of the Zionist crimes in Palestine and throughout the world," he said. "Israel has taken it upon herself to usurp territories and suppress peoples who are only fighting for their freedom, and she has had the vicious support of hostile nations such as Germany, France and the United States."[16] Like Kuhlmann's earlier announcement, he declared the operation to be the work of the Popular Front for the Liberation of Palestine's Che Gueverra Brigade.[17] Afterward, Böse ordered Michel Bacos to radio the control tower at Benina International Airport in Benghazi and inform its controllers that the Airbus would be landing shortly. Bacos was to further request that Libya supply the plane with at least four hours' worth of fuel. And it was while he was transmitting these messages that a shriek came from the economy-class cabin where the hijackers had corralled the entirety of passengers, the scream breaking the calm that had finally begun to settle.

It seems that a woman in possession of a British passport, Patricia Martel, had begun bleeding. Turning to terrorist Brigette Kuhlmann for help, Martel said she was two months pregnant and in dreadful pain, her symptoms presumably indicating the onset of a miscarriage. So it was that Kuhlmann, her mask of mercilessness slipping momentarily, set about comforting the panicked passenger, moving her to a seat in a vacant cabin and hurrying off to find a doctor. And sure enough, an American gastroenterologist soon appeared and began examining the distressed Englishwoman. Her first words to the doctor, however, caught him off-guard. "I'm bluffing," she whispered.[18] A nurse, Martel had intentionally cut herself to produce a small amount of blood so as to convince the terrorists of her predicament.[19] In truth, her mother had died a few days earlier and Martel was *en route* to the funeral services in Manchester, England. She was unable to finish explaining her unfortunate situation to the physician, though, because hubbub broke out anew in the cabin with the announcement that the Airbus was preparing to land in Libya.

And indeed, shortly after 2:00 p.m. the airliner put down at the Benina International Airport. The Libyan government, for its part, had no advance knowledge of the air piracy and did not appreciate the fact that the PFLP had selected the North African nation as a refueling stop. Appearances suggested the two were in league in the skyjacking, a misunderstanding that could invite adverse repercussions for Libya.

On this summer afternoon, the heat was scorching in Benghazi, where the temperature had reached one-hundred six degrees Fahrenheit a few days earlier. And it was here that the distraught passengers were forced to sit in the plane while the terrorists worked out refueling arrangements with the Libyans—that is, all of the passengers except one. It seems that the fast-thinking Patricia Martel had managed to convince yet another doctor, a Libyan physician this time, that her pregnancy was in jeopardy. The doctor, in response, persuaded Brigette

Kuhlmann to let her leave. So it was that Libyan representatives promptly escorted the British woman to the airport clinic, then furnished her with five-star lodgings at the Geneira Palace Hotel where she would remain until morning.[20] Those acting on behalf of the reluctant host country were determined that no harm should come to their stricken guest lest their nation be held responsible. Then, too, they appeared to be genuinely concerned about her. "The Libyans behaved marvelously," says Ben-Porat. "They brought her drinks and cigarettes, and smiled all the time as though their expressions might soothe her jangled nerves."[21]

The next day, Martel flew to Tel Aviv and then London, where intelligence officials debriefed her at Heathrow Airport. Because she was able to provide incisive information about the terrorists, including their appearances and relationships, officials not only concluded that the skyjacking was a PFLP operation, as the terrorists had claimed, but were also able to identify the two German team members.

The passengers who had remained on the plane in Benghazi endured another seven hours of waiting and worrying in the sweltering heat before finding themselves airborne once again. By this time, late Sunday evening, the airliner had taken on forty-two tons of fuel and was headed for Entebbe, Uganda. Situated near Lake Victoria in eastern Africa, the city had been the hijackers' destination all along.

The flight itself was ghastly. "Throughout the five-hour journey," says Dunstan, "the passengers had to endure a constant torrent of abuse from Brigitte Kuhlmann, much of it anti–Semitic in nature."[22] The German terrorist had obviously reverted to her previous persona.

Day Two: Monday, June 28, 1976

It was a few minutes after 3:00 a.m. on Monday, June 28, that Air France 139 arrived in Entebbe. However, it was not until noon, nine hours later, that the weary passengers and crew were allowed to deplane, and even then they were only permitted to move a short distance away, and at gunpoint. Rather than confining them in the Entebbe International Airport's main terminal, the terrorists locked up the captives in the airport's old, defunct terminal, which was situated a mile away. The building—"dusty, dirty, and dilapidated"—would keep them isolated as well as inaccessible in the unlikely event of an attempted rescue operation.[23]

As the captives adjusted to their decrepit surroundings, the Ugandan president, Idi Amin, paid them a visit. His theatrical entrance notwithstanding—

he arrived waving and shouting "Shalom!"—Amin was no friend to the Jewish men, women, and children who were present.[24] His past remarks about the Black September attack in Munich, for instance, revealed his animosity toward the Jewish people.

"On 11 September 1972," says former Israeli ambassador Arye Oded, "Amin sent a telegram to UN secretary-general Kurt Waldheim in which he applauded the massacre of the Israeli Olympic athletes in Munich and said Germany was the most appropriate locale for this because it was where Hitler burned more than six million Jews."[25] And if this document were not sufficient evidence of Amin's naked anti–Semitism, he had also expelled all Israelis from Uganda while forging a political bond with Libya. Then, too, he procured many of his bodyguards from the PLO. These actions, combined with his renowned megalomania—he became enraged at a hostage when she failed to address him as His Excellency Field Marshal Doctor Idi Amin Dada—and his delusional thinking (e.g., he had little formal education, let alone a doctorate), meant the captives, especially the Jewish ones, could not look to him for help.[26] Supporting this assertion, Amin told them that the State of Israel, not the PFLP, was ultimately the responsible party in the Entebbe affair due to its ill-treatment of the Palestinian people, with whom his sympathies lay.[27] Obviously, the organization had chosen wisely when it designated Uganda as the site for its ground operation; it could count on the country's erratic leader to offer his full and enthusiastic support.

Idi Amin's advocacy of the skyjacking was at once evident by the conduct of the Ugandan troops that were surrounding the terminal, their weapons trained on its entrances and exits. "To the hostages, it appeared that there was complete cooperation between the terrorists and the soldiers," writes Peck. "They took orders from the hijackers, and there was no question at any point that they were collaborating with them."[28]

The terrorists exchanged the pistols they had flaunted on the Air France plane for AK-47 assault rifles that were waiting for them at the Entebbe airport. Waiting there, too, were additional terrorists. While the original four hijackers rested, their principal contribution—the seizure of the aircraft—being behind them, three men now arrived to take charge of the mission. Gliding onto the tarmac in a gleaming white Mercedes-Benz was Antonio Dega Bouviet, the operation's new leader and a man who had once held a high-level position in Carlos the Jackal's guerrilla network. By Bouviet's side was Faiz Abdul Rahim Jaaber, his second-in-command, whose reputation was likewise well-known in the realm of international terrorism. The identity of the seventh extremist was Jaïl el Arja, and this was his first mission.[29]

As the day progressed, the PFLP cell paraded the captives before newspaper photographers and Ugandan television cameras. "Everyone tried to push in towards the radius of the lenses in the hope that the film would be shown on television screens in their home countries and their families there would be reassured of their welfare," writes Ofer. "The air-pirates, too, posed in front of the cameras, exuding an air of over-weening triumph."[30] And it was through these Ugandan media reports that the French government learned the Air France plane was in Entebbe, with the Israeli government obtaining the same information, at roughly the same time, from a BBC report. The perpetrators, at this point, offered no reason for their illicit actions.

For answers, France's president, Valéry Giscard d'Estaing, dispatched a pair of representatives from his nation's embassy in Kampala, the capital of Uganda, to Entebbe International Airport. After repeated attempts to discuss the situation with the extremists, however, the French ambassador and foreign minister came away empty-handed. "We still don't know what the hijackers want," said a spokesman, "and until we do, there is little that can be done."[31]

In the afternoon, troops hauled urns of rice and curry to the captives. But although they now had food, they still had no explanation as to why their plane had been commandeered nor were they aware of any demands that would be made of their home nations. Instead, the captives remained in an unnerving, indeterminate state, with some of them, most notably the Holocaust survivors in the group, fearing execution at any moment.[32]

In Israel on this same afternoon, Defense Minister Shimon Peres persuaded a retired colonel, a man who had been on constructive terms with Idi Amin in the past, to telephone the Ugandan leader and attempt to secure his help in liberating the hostages. Such back-channel contact was necessary since there was no longer a formal relationship between Israel and Uganda. Elsewhere in the Jewish state, figures in the military establishment took it upon themselves to hold impromptu discussions about the prospects of armed intervention; this, despite the fact that it was an Air France plane that had been commandeered and therefore the French government was more or less in charge of the crisis.

One of these figures was Lieutenant Colonel Joshua Shani, commander of the "Yellow Bird" squadron of Hercules C-130 transport planes. The forward-thinking Air Force officer decided it would be a good idea for his staff to envisage the problems that might arise in conducting an air rescue mission over two thousand miles away in East Africa. "We looked at range, fuel, payload, navigation, weather problems, things that take time to cover," says Shani."[33]

Exploring the same possibility was Colonel Ehud Barak, a specialist in military intelligence who eventually would become Israel's prime minister. In talks with counter-terrorism experts, Barak learned that Amin's army was renowned for its apathy as well as for its reluctance to take on a fight except during the daytime. It was, to be sure, information that could prove useful in planning a hostage-rescue mission.[34]

As the day came to a close, Rabin and Peres reviewed the predicament once again. Until the terrorists came forth with information, however, the pair could do little to help the scores of passengers stranded in Entebbe. And the evening for these emotionally and physically depleted pawns promised to be a miserable one. Although Ugandan troops brought them baskets of bananas, meat, and potatoes for dinner, the abandoned terminal did little to awaken the captives' appetites, what with its soiled floors and makeshift chairs created from stacks of dusty newspapers. And although Amin's minions dragged in secondhand mattresses, most of them remained unused because the makeshift beds were infested with bugs. Of course, the swarms of mosquitos from Lake Victoria that descended on the captives at sundown did not help matters, with the group finding little comfort in the anti-malaria pills handed out by a local doctor. Such conditions were certain to ensure another sleepless night for the beleaguered Air France passengers.

Day Three: Tuesday, June 29, 1976

The following morning would be uneventful for the captives, who still had no news about their fates. In fact, it was not until mid-afternoon, at 3:30 p.m. to be precise, that the PFLP announced its demands on Uganda Radio. France's Ministry of Foreign Affairs relayed them immediately to the Israeli Embassy, and from there they made their way to Prime Minister Rabin and his administration in Jerusalem.

The PFLP's ultimatum called for the release of fifty-three prisoners, virtually all of whom were convicted terrorists. Forty of them were incarcerated in Israel, with the remainder being held in West Germany, Switzerland, France, and Kenya. It seems the PFLP believed the latter nation was incarcerating the five commandos who had tried to use a surface-to-air missile to shoot down an El Al airliner in Nairobi in January, 1976, this being the incident recounted earlier in Chapter 7. The imprisoned figures consisted of three Palestinian guerrillas, along with two German extremists, a male and a female, who had traveled to Africa to retrieve them. In actuality, all five were still locked up in Israel.

The PFLP further laid out the communication structure that would henceforth be used. It would consist of two figures, one of whom would be a representative of the terrorist organization and the other, an envoy of the French government. The PFLP's representative would be the Somalian ambassador to Uganda, Hashi Abdallah, with Giscard d'Estaing's administration being responsible for appointing Abdallah's counterpart. The cutoff time for agreeing to the PFLP's demands would be 2:00 p.m. on Thursday, July 1 (Israel Standard Time). The PFLP would blow up the terminal with the hostages still inside of it if the cell's requirements had not been accepted by the deadline.

Lastly, the Popular Front for the Liberation of Palestine insisted that the forty prisoners being held in Israel be flown to Entebbe on an Air France jet, which would, in turn, be used to fly both the hostages and the hijackers to freedom in a yet-to-be-disclosed Middle Eastern country. As for the original Air France plane, the one that had been hijacked and was presently on the ground in Entebbe, the PFLP insisted that the French government pay five million dollars for its return. Of course, this demand, like those pertaining to the release of the hostages, was excessive, and France, for one, would have none of it. "The French Foreign Minister," writes Yehuda Ofer, "informed reporters that France 'definitely rejected the unreasonable demands of the hijackers.'"[35]

The Israeli government was not as quick to dismiss them, however. When the PFLP released the names of the prisoners to be included in the exchange, the fact that the large majority were incarcerated in Israel meant the Jewish state would become a principal player in the affair. It was unavoidable. And the sizable number of Israelis who were being held hostage—at least eighty-three of the captives were citizens of the Jewish state—would draw Israel further into the mix.[36] Yitzhak Rabin called a cabinet meeting to discuss the crisis, during which it became apparent that most of those present believed Israel should accede to the PFLP's ultimatum. It was the same position the hostages' families would adopt, and quite vocally, in the ensuing days. The reason for considering such compliance, which ran counter to the Jewish state's policy of non-negotiation, centered on the assumption that Uganda was too far away for Israel to launch an attack against the PFLP cell and its Ugandan military support forces. For this particular operation, then, the terrorist organization had been smart to select the East African nation, since its distance from the Middle East, coupled with the military backup provided by Uganda, did indeed convince the Israeli government, at least initially, of the futility of an attempted armed response.

Be that as it may, Rabin was not ruling out such an intervention. To the same cabinet meeting, he invited General Mordechai "Motta" Gur, head of the Israeli Defense Forces, and asked this respected military man for his thoughts on a hostage-rescue mission. Gur's reply was not encouraging, however, mainly because of the dearth of actionable intelligence, including a lack of information about the exact location of the hostages and the amount of force being used to confine them.[37] The result is that the meeting came to an end without a decision being made. Before the evening was over, though, Rabin would call back the forty-six-year-old general to his office and instruct him to commence planning a rescue mission in case it was decided that it should proceed. The requisite intelligence, it was decided, would come from the Mossad.

In contrast to the hostages' families and those conciliatory elements within the Israeli government, Yitzhak Hofi, the chief of the Mossad, was adamant that the nation could, and should, liberate the captives rather than surrender to the PFLP's over-the-top conditions. For this reason, he promptly called in a host of covert agents upon learning that the government was considering a rescue mission and laid out a series of emergency assignments for them. A rescue operation, including the cabinet's final decision as to whether or not to conduct one, would depend in part on their findings.

Hofi's first act was to direct a handful of his Nairobi-based Israeli operatives to meet with their local counterparts and devise a safe house. It would serve as the headquarters for the prospective mission. Because the African city already contained a well-organized Mossad presence, Hofi considered it the logical choice for such a base, along with the fact that Kenya adjoined Uganda, with Nairobi being only three hundred miles from Entebbe. "There could be no question," says Stewart Steven, "of Nairobi's being used as a jumping-off point to attack Entebbe."[38]

Subsequent to this, it came to light—it was while the Mossad was constructing the safe house—that a Kenyan agent assisting with the preparations had an in-law, a Ugandan soldier, who was stationed at the Entebbe airport. Through this serendipitous connection, the Mossad was able to fulfill a second objective of its fact-finding venture, that of determining the conditions on the ground in Entebbe.

To his Kenyan relative, the Ugandan soldier divulged the number of PFLP guerrillas at the facility, as well as describing the health and well-being of the captives. The obliging insider also offered his observations of the military setup on the scene. "He reported that the terrorists were obviously nervous, but that, at least while he was there, only a half a dozen or so Ugandan troops were anywhere in the vicinity," says Stewart Steven.[39] To be sure, this was indispensable information that would not only help the Israeli military calculate the size and composition of its commando unit, the one it would dispatch to free the hostages, but it also signaled the likelihood that the mission would be a successful one. Since the PFLP and Idi Amin did not appear to believe the Israeli military, situated such a great distance away, could converge upon the Entebbe airport undetected, the number of troops at the facility had been markedly reduced. Only a quarter of the original two hundred soldiers remained at the airport. Clearly, the PFLP's overconfidence, as well as that of the Ugandan president, had compromised their judgment.

As crucial as it was to gauge the degree of armed resistance a rescue operation could expect to confront, it was also imperative that those planning the mission be familiar with the layout of the facility itself. In this regard, the Israelis were remarkably lucky. It seems that a prominent Israeli construction company, Solel Boneh, had built the Entebbe airport at a time when Uganda and the Jewish state were on still friendly terms, the upshot being that its blueprints were readily available to strategists in Jerusalem and Tel Aviv.[40]

To supplement this information, Mossad operatives contacted a former member of MI-5 who agreed to fly a private plane over Lake Victoria ostensibly to snap photographs for a tourist brochure. In reality, the plane also carried a Mossad agent who took pictures of the airstrip, terminals, and adjacent structures. To pull this off, the British pilot veered the Cessna off-course, then established radio contact with the control tower and claimed that one of his aircraft's engines was malfunctioning, hence his stray into Entebbe airspace. And the air traffic controller, falling prey to the deception, did not pass it on to the PFLP or the Ugandan military.

To further assess the resistance that a rescue mission could expect to encounter, the Mossad dispatched another unit to inspect a residence known to have been the PLO's headquarters in Entebbe. The agency was familiar with it because the estate had served as the Israeli ambassador's private home until Amin expelled all Israelis from the African nation. As a deliberate affront to the Jewish state, Amin subsequently awarded the sprawling estate to the Palestinian Liberation Organization. Now the Mossad needed to know if the PLO still occupied it, and, if so, the number of members it held.

To this end, a Mossad unit, under cover of darkness, sped across Lake Victoria to Entebbe in a Kenyan police boat, then hurried to the former ambassador's residence. To the operatives' relief, they discovered that the PLO had vacated the premises apparently when the organization's base of operations relocated to Angola. Thus, like most of the information the Mossad was obtaining, the finding was encouraging in that it suggested comparatively little resistance to an Israeli raid.

In the intervening time, Mossad operatives in Nairobi secured the consent of the Kenyan government for the city's airport to be used in the mission. The plan was for a special plane, a Boeing 727 that would serve as a field hospital, to be stationed at the Kenyan airfield where it would receive and treat the operation's casualties. Kenyan officials knew they could portray their cooperation, if discovered, as a humanitarian act.

In a matter of days, then, the resourceful intelligence agency had verified that the hostages were in satisfactory condition, that a small group of terrorists and soldiers were confining them, and that the PFLP's parent organization, the PLO, no longer maintained a sizable presence in the city of Entebbe. The Mossad also had secured aerial photographs of the Entebbe airport, established a base of operations in nearby Nairobi, and obtained permission to use the Kenyan city's airport to deliver emergency medical care. And lastly, the Mossad had secured information about recent Ugandan troop movements and concluded that there were roughly ten thousand soldiers posted between Entebbe and Kampala—a reason for concern, but not for alarm. The result: the Israeli military could be fairly confident in mounting an operation that would succeed in extracting the hostages from Uganda and spiriting them safely to Israel. And so it was that the Mossad's role, upon furnishing this vital intelligence to the Israeli Defense Forces over the course of a few days, was more or less complete, with the facts it provided helping the military reassure the powers-that-be that an effective rescue operation was possible and should therefore proceed.

Adding a sense of urgency to the notion of an Israeli-led mission was a disturbing turn of events that occurred later in the day on Tuesday, June 29. According to hostage testimony, it was at this time that the PFLP cell set about examining the captives' passports and separating the Israelis in the crowd—citizens of Israel and those holding dual nationalities—from the hostages of other countries.[41] Here it bears mentioning that there does exist a different, and a persistent, account of this process.

The predominant narrative since the Entebbe incident has been one in which the terrorists segregated the Jewish hostages, Israeli or otherwise, from those who were gentile. In this depiction of events, the PFLP's actions recalled the selection process the Nazis used in the death camps during the Holocaust, that of deciding, on the spot, who would live and who would be exterminated. This rendering of the Entebbe procedure has been disputed, however, most recently in 2008 by Ilan Hartuv. A retired member of the Israeli Foreign Ministry and a surviving Jewish hostage from the Entebbe affair, Hartuv insists religion was not a factor. "There was no selection applied to Jews," he states in a *Haaretz* interview. "Entebbe was not Auschwitz."[42] To illustrate his point, Hartuv draws attention to the fact that the terrorists released a pair of teenage Yeshiva students because the two were citizens of Brazil, not Israel. Then, too, the German leader of the hijack team, Wilfried Böse, was said to have become deeply shaken when a hostage referred to him as a Nazi, adamantly denying the charge of anti–Semitism and explaining that he had performed terrorist acts against West Germany in part because its ruling elite had absorbed former Nazis into its ranks.[43] The PFLP's argument centered on the mistreatment of the displaced Palestinian population, Böse maintained, not on age-old religious precepts. The assertion was identical to the one voiced four years earlier by the Black Septembrists during the Munich Massacre, namely, that the athlete-hostages were targeted because they were Israeli, not because they Jewish. That said, many Israeli captives at the Entebbe airport, especially the Holocaust survivors among them, experienced the sequestration as targeting them because of their Jewish faith. Certainly their wariness was understandable.

Day Four: Wednesday, June 30, 1976

For many of the non–Israeli captives, their fear would dissolve on the fourth day of the crisis when the terrorists prepared forty-seven of them for release. Composed of mothers with children, this first batch also included the elderly and those with physical limitations and infirmities. After being escorted to the French embassy in the morning, the group boarded a jetliner for the nine-hour flight to Paris. The plane would not, however, be piloted by Captain Bacos.

Although the PFLP released him at this time, Bacos, along with his crew, refused to depart, instead staying behind to help the remaining hostages. "Michel Bacos went through each day with an expression of relaxed composure on his face," writes Ben-Porat. "He separated passengers who argued among themselves, placed himself between terrorists and hostages who were about to challenge them, and—with ever-present good humor—he tried to create the atmosphere of a holiday camp."[44] And he did more. "According to the hostages," writes Peck, "Bacos attended the sick, dispensed medicine, made beds, and even swept the floor."[45] For such unwavering support throughout the Entebbe crisis, the captives later showered Bacos with praise.

In Jerusalem this same morning, Prime Minister Rabin, along with his cabinet and advisors, reassessed the situation, while other Israeli officials spread disinformation suggesting that the Jewish state believed it had no choice but to give in the PFLP's demands. Stealthily, these officials planted stories for a handful of duplicitous figures known to be in contact with Wadia Hadad (AKA Wadi'a Haddad), the forty-six-year-old physician and leader of the PFLP and its offshoot, the Revolutionary Front for the Liberation of Palestine.[46] By all accounts, the Palestinian extremist was a daunting figure. "Dr. Hadad commanded an international army of fanatics armed with weapons of terror," writes Stevenson, the Entebbe mission being only one of his exploits.[47] Evidently, Hadad quickly became emboldened by the Israeli disinformation, little knowing he was being misled and that his operation in Uganda would prove to be among his last.

As intelligence from the Mossad continued pouring in to the Rabin administration, military leaders accelerated their efforts to come up with a workable plan of attack. Since a land-based raid was not considered viable, a foray by water or air remained the options. With this in mind, the Israelis decided to find out if inflatable boats could be dropped from an aircraft onto Lake Victoria as a means of gaining access to the nearby Entebbe airport. To test the idea, a plane dropped rubber vessels onto the surface of the Mediterranean Sea from the same height it would be necessary to use over Lake Victoria. The boats exploded on impact, however, thus ruling out the air-drop method. Of course, it was probably just as well that the approach was being ruled out, since, as one seasoned military officer pointed out, Lake Victoria was home to some of the largest, fiercest crocodiles on the planet, reptiles that could be expected to make a meal out of rubber boats packed with commandos.

The process of elimination, then, left a rescue by air. And while military strategists brainstormed an array of plausible aerial scenarios, the one that gained the most traction centered on a team of commandos arriving in Uganda in the middle of the night in a small fleet of Hercules C-130 transport planes and liberating the hostages. This, then, became the foundation of the mission.

Several hours later—it was Wednesday night in Paris—the former hostages landed at Orly Airport, where officials from the Israeli Defense Forces, the Israeli embassy, and the French Secret Service debriefed them. The objective was to obtain further information about conditions at the Entebbe airport that could be used to help plan the raid. And although the ex-hostages made a valiant effort to recall the details of their Entebbe ordeal, the observations of one French gentleman in particular, a former military officer, were exceptionally precise.

"Realizing immediately that the Israelis were planning a rescue mission, his prodigious memory provided a wealth of intelligence that had been completely lacking to date," says Dunstan.[48] Among other pieces of valuable information, he was able to describe the exact location of the hostages inside the old terminal, as well as pinpointing where the terrorists congregated, ate, and slept. He also revealed that the PFLP cell was convinced that the Israeli government was preparing to concede and therefore had let down its guard.

In such ways, the recollections of the ex-hostages were instrumental in helping to finalize Operation Entebbe. Still needed, however, was supplementary intelligence and, of course, more time. As to the former, the Mossad was on top of the situation. "[O]n June 30, 1976," writes Ben-Porat, "the head of the *Mossad* was issuing instructions to get him every piece of the vital information on what was happening at Entebbe Airport."[49] Regarding the latter—additional time—it was more problematical in that the deadline was only hours away.

Day Five: Thursday, July 1, 1976

The PFLP released the remaining non–Israeli hostages, approximately one hundred of them, in the early morning hours. The cell then turned its attention to the 2:00 p.m. cut-off time when Israel, West Germany, France, Kenya, and Switzerland would indicate whether or not they agreed to release the fifty-three prisoners being held within their borders. But as the hour approached, Prime Minister Rabin, for one, found himself torn. Although he still favored a rescue operation, the military, according to his advisor, General Gur, was not ready for such a complex task in a faraway land. To date, the military had only been able to establish that a rescue mission would need to be conducted by air; it had not yet devised a strategy for incapacitating the terrorists and removing the hostages. More time would be needed to assemble this part of the project, which was, in effect, its heart. In the interim, Rabin was facing a tough choice: stand by while the PFLP executed the hostages or comply with the organization's demands. The moment for a decision was fast approaching.

A few hours before the deadline Rabin scheduled a cabinet meeting in which he reiterated that the hostages would be executed if Israel did not meet the terrorists' terms, and reminded the cabinet members that the hostages' families were insisting that the government negotiate with the PFLP. Afterward, he called for a vote. As expected given the tenor of its previous discussions, the cabinet agreed to fulfill the terrorists' demands, and it did so unanimously.

Without delay, Rabin notified France's foreign minister of the decision in order that the official could convey it to the Somalian ambassador representing the PFLP. A last-minute notification, it took place merely ninety minutes before the deadline. And so it was that Idi Amin, at the actual moment of the deadline, took to the airwaves and announced triumphantly that preparations for the prisoner-hostage exchange were under way and that the PFLP's new deadline—the date when the exchange itself would take place—would be 2:00 p.m. on Sunday, July 4. This would allow time for the five target nations to arrange for the transfer of the inmates.

For the remainder of the day, Israel pursued a dual course. While Rabin's administration made arrangements for the release of the fifty-three prisoners it was holding in the nation's penitentiaries, the military readied itself for a rescue operation. If the covert mission was not ready by the Sunday deadline, the State of Israel, the government had decided, would hand over the prisoners to the Palestinian organization. The Jewish state would not allow its people to be murdered.

Day Six: Friday, July 2, 1976

For the Israeli intelligence and military communities, what followed in the wake of the deadline's extension was a hectic day brimming with discussions, debates, and fleeting turf wars. It was a natural commotion that arose from the best of intentions, namely, saving the lives of the nation's citizens.

As the Mossad and other intelligence entities continued collecting and sharing material, including critical information pertaining to the Entebbe airport's radar protocol and its intermittent shutdown of runway lights, the Sayaret Matkal, which would be leading the commando raid, wrapped up its ground plan in conjunction with other segments of the IDF. During this same period, the Israeli Air Force readied the aircraft to be used in the mission, while the man who would serve as the lead pilot practiced "blind landings." If a night operation were to take place, the latter might become necessary since the airfield at Entebbe sometimes turned off its runway lights after sundown.

Also during this period, the Mossad assigned a specialty unit to modify a Mercedes-Benz so that it would appear identical to the one in which Idi Amin was known to travel. The car would be transported by air to Uganda and used in the operation. It was to be part of a charade.

For the Sayaret Matkal team that would be at the vanguard of the rescue, the day would be spent performing drills. While some members rehearsed the maneuvers that would take place as soon as the Hercules C-130s touched down in Entebbe, such as unfettering the Mercedes and other vehicles, another group practiced subduing the terrorists and Ugandan troops as well as liberating the hostages.

To prepare for this latter aspect of the raid, an IDF crew had labored overnight building a wood and canvas replica of the old terminal such that, come morning, the Sayaret Matkal commandos would have at their disposal a site identical to the one in which they would be conducting the mission. Because the strategists behind Operation Entebbe had been fortunate enough to have access to the airport's blueprints, along with precise descriptions of the captives' location from former hostages and Mossad informants, the Sayaret Matkal was in a position to know precisely where to find and extract them. And with each drill, the commandos gained speed and precision.

At the Entebbe Airport on this same day, the terrorists released a Jewish woman, a dual citizen of Israel and Britain, so she could receive medical attention. Her name was Dora Bloch and she had been *en route* to New York to attend her son's wedding when she instead found herself being held against her will in Uganda. Here, the seventy-five-year-old Bloch, a feisty woman who debated the hijackers vigorously throughout the Entebbe ordeal, choked on a piece of food and was taken to Mulago Hospital in Kampala. By all accounts, she was in satisfactory condition following the obstruction, although she still felt somewhat ill.

As it turned out, Dora Bloch would be the last captive to leave the old terminal before Operation Entebbe was launched. And it would be the next day that the mission would commence.

Operation Entebbe

On Saturday morning, July 3, 1976, General Gur appeared at an emergency cabinet session to lay out the military's plan. Everyone present was painfully aware that the operation would be politically risky, and that failure, or even success, could result in an international incident. Part of the concern centered on the United States, with the cabinet members expressing reservations about their nation's use of arms supplied by its number-one ally. This is because there was a proviso that such weaponry could be used only for Israel's self-defense. Also a worry: the cabinet, like the military strategists, expected heavy casualties among the hostages, with some sources suggesting that the death toll could reach twenty-five percent. For these and other reasons, the government did not greenlight the rescue plan at once but deliberated several more hours on this, the Jewish Sabbath or *Shabbat*, while the IDF and Sayeret Matkal anxiously bided their time. But then came a rather unexpected directive.

At 1:20 p.m. the powers-that-be, rightly perceiving the situation to be a countdown to a crucial deadline, ordered Operation Entebbe to begin despite the fact that the cabinet had not yet sanctioned it. The clock was ticking and the flight time to Entebbe was nearly eight hours; military strategists knew the IDF could not remain idle much longer if it hoped to conduct a late-night raid in Uganda. Fortunately, the decision to start the operation before it had been okayed did not present a problem, since it could be aborted before the squadron reached Uganda if the plan did not receive the necessary nod from the cabinet.

So it was that five planes took off at five-minute intervals from Lod Airport in Tel Aviv, initially flying in different directions so as to avoid the appearance of being in military formation. Four of them were Hercules C-130 heavy transport planes, manufactured by Lockheed Martin and a component of Israel's fleet since 1971. They carried the Sayeret Matkal commando unit and IDF support troops that would land at the Entebbe airport. The fifth aircraft was a Boeing 727, and it would serve a command and control function. Remaining airborne over Entebbe throughout the operation, the overarching task of those onboard would be to relay information to and from the Israeli forces on the ground and military headquarters in Tel Aviv.

In addition to these five planes designated for action in Uganda, two others were also dispatched at this time, but to Kenya. One would be positioned at the Nairobi airport and provide medical treatment to the casualties after the rescue had taken place. The plane contained two surgical suites and carried twenty-three physicians.[50] The other aircraft, author Stan Dunstan has convincingly proposed, was a C-130 tanker plane that would be stationed in Kenya's Chalbi Desert.[51] Its purpose: to refuel all of the other aircraft before their journey back to Israel. Interestingly, this aspect of the mission has remained secret, with the Israeli government declining to acknowledge its occurrence even today. Presumably, the political aftermath would be too damaging to Kenya. Whereas the Kenyan government could claim that it was for charitable, non-political reasons that it permitted the Boeing 727 field hospital to be stationed within its borders, it could not offer the same justification for the tanker aircraft idling in its desert. The latter could only be regarded as what it was, namely, an act of complicity in an Israeli military action in Uganda, with the consequences promising to be considerable for Kenya if this feature of Operation Entebbe ever became known.

Returning to the actions of the squadron, the planes traveled southwest to Sharm el–Sheikh on the Sinai Peninsula's southern tip. An Egyptian city, it was under Israeli control at the time, the Jewish state having seized it in 1967 during the final hours of the Six-Day War. As the opening leg of the journey, the stretch from Tel Aviv to Sharm el–Sheikh proved to be stomach-churning; so dreadful, in fact, that at least one soldier was unable to carry on with the mission. The discomfort was attributable to the weather, an aspect of the operation over which General Dan Shomron, its leader, and Lieutenant Colonel Yonatan ("Yoni" or "Yonni") Netanyahu, commander of the Sayeret Matkal, had no control. And compounding the problem were the adverse conditions under which the aircraft were forced to travel.

"The pilots flew at a very low altitude to elude Jordanian radar," says Iddo Netanyahu, Yonatan's younger brother. "Flying so low, along with the summer heat, caused tremendous turbulence, and the troops suffered severe nausea."[52] Aboard the lead plane, Hercules One, was Colonel Muki Betser, deputy commander of the mission's assault unit. "Around me, troopers vomited into air sickness bags, turning the closed hold into a reeking den of unhappiness," he recalls. "If it went on like this all the way to Uganda, I worried to myself, we wouldn't be fit for the job."[53]

While a physician dispensed anti-nausea pills during the stopover at the Sharm el–Sheikh airfield, the various IDF divisions rehashed their upcoming assignments in Uganda. These components included the mission's command unit, along with the Sayeret Matkal team, a contingent of the Sayeret Golani of the Golani Infantry Brigade, a paratrooper unit, and a medical unit. On top of that, a team would travel with the squadron and provide fuel at the Entebbe airport so that the planes, after the hostages were liberated, could continue on to the tanker aircraft in the Kenyan desert, where they could refuel completely.

Altogether, the Hercules C-130s were carrying twenty-nine Sayeret Matkal commandos, fifty members of the Golani Brigade, seventeen paratroopers, a ten-person medical crew, and a ten-person refueling crew. Onboard, too, were four armored personnel carriers, or APCs, with a total crew of sixteen men. The transport planes also carried nine additional vehicles, among them Jeeps, Peugeot trucks, Land Rovers, and the refashioned Mercedes. By any standard, such military force was immense for a hostage-rescue operation, but it was necessary since the mission was set to unfold a great distance from Israel and would entail confronting not only a terrorist cell but another country's armed forces as well. Accordingly, the principal planners of Operation Entebbe—Motta Gur, Dan Shomron, and Yonatan Netanyahu, with further input from Muki Betser—had formulated what would be an overpowering assault, one spearheaded by a superb commando unit and buttressed by more conventional military forces.

An hour later, at 3:30 p.m. in Sharm el-Sheikh, the squadron took to the air once again, still without a formal go-ahead from the cabinet. Those conducting the mission, however, were determined to stick to the IDF's timetable.

Initially, the squadron traveled westward across the tip of the Sinai Peninsula. "After a while the planes stabilized and made the turn southward towards Africa without mishap," writes Iddo Netanyahu. "They flew the length of the Red Sea only about 200 feet above the waves, to avoid Saudi radar on the east and Egyptian radar on the west."[54] Fortunately for those onboard, the weather was calmer during this main stretch of the journey, with conditions on the planes, although cramped, being such that the IDF contingent could get some rest before the raid. According to the lead pilot, Lieutenant Colonel Joshua Shani, it was during this leg of the trip that the Israeli government, in a roundabout way, finally relayed its consent for the mission. "Somewhere over Ethiopia," Shani recalls, "we received a cryptic message—'Efrez. Mazel tov. Authorized. Good Luck.'"[55] It would have been far too dicey for the approval to be stated in more explicit language, since the message might be intercepted and the rescue operation, exposed.

It was over Ethiopia, too, that the squadron was able to fly at a more reasonable altitude for the first time since leaving Tel Aviv. "Ethiopia had no radar that could effectively track combat aircraft at night," writes Netanyahu.[56] This meant the planes could ascend to twenty thousand feet, an altitude, he adds, that burned less fuel.[57]

Toward the end of the flight, when the squadron reached northwestern Kenya—the aircraft were an hour away from Lake Victoria and Entebbe— it confronted a massive storm. "As the aircraft pounded on, horribly buffeted, the dreadful, debilitating scourge of airsickness returned to many of the assault force," says Dunstan.[58] In one respect, though, the foul weather was a godsend in that it disrupted the region's radar systems.

One minute after midnight (East Africa Time Zone), Hercules One, the

8. Mission: Operation Entebbe

lead plane carrying the Sayeret Matkal commando team, came in for a landing at the Entebbe airport. Due to the torrential rainstorm, the pilot, the one who had practiced blind landings a day earlier, was unable to see the runway lights until the very last moment. Even so, he landed the plane safely, and he did it unobtrusively by using the brakes but no reverse thrusters. The team then leapt into action.

"From the moment the wheels of the first 'Hercules' carrying Yoni [Netanyahu] and his assault force kissed the tarmac only a few seconds elapsed before they were on their way to the terminal," writes Ofer. "Dan Shomron stayed behind to await the arrival of his auxiliary forces which would later fan out in other parts of the airport."[59]

After unshackling the Land Rovers and the Mercedes, the commando unit armed itself. "We all carried lightweight gear," says Betser, "mostly Kalashnikov AK-47s and some Galils, an Israel Military Industry assault rifle still in experimental form at the time."[60]

Climbing into the Mercedes and escorted by the Land Rovers, the commandos sped toward the old terminal. Since their vehicles appeared identical to those used by Idi Amin, the unit was hoping the Ugandan troops at the airport would assume the dictator was making an unannounced visit to the hostage site. And sure enough, the motorcade passed several soldiers, none of whom attempted to stop it. Except one. Near the old terminal, a sentry aimed his rifle directly at the vehicles—in the Ugandan military, it was a benign, customary response to an approaching motorcade—prompting two of the Israelis to panic and fire at him with their silenced Berettas. The soldier fell to the ground, but then managed to get back on his feet and shoot at the Israelis, with the sound of his gunfire alerting everyone at the airport that a firefight was under way. Meanwhile, the remaining C-130s continued landing in sequence.

"Fire came at us from the darkness around the tarmac," says Betser.[61] And the situation deteriorated further. "The Ugandans switched off the electric power," writes Ofer, "and the last of the trio of 'Hercules' aircraft was compelled to land by moonlight, as the verge beacons on the runway were darkened."[62]

While the commando unit split into three groups, stormed into the old terminal through separate entrances, and gathered in the room where the hostages were bunched, the other IDF detachments rushed to their assigned locations elsewhere at the airport and set about carrying out their duties. The plan called for the infantry and associated divisions to take control of the overall facility, blocking all entrances and securing the runway, while the Sayeret Matkal liquidated the terrorists and evacuated the hostages.

Charging into the old terminal, the commandos held an advantage in that their brash arrival bewildered the terrorists. According to one of the Israelis present at the scene, the PFLP members appeared to mistake the Sayeret Matkal for the Ugandan military and seemed unable to understand why their comrades-in-arms were attacking them.[63] It was a confusion that briefly immobilized the PFLP cell. In the same moment, the three Sayeret Matkal groups, knowing it was imperative that the hostages, for their own safety, *not* misunderstand what was transpiring, told them precisely what to do.

"The fighters who had burst into the hall shouted warnings in Hebrew to the captives to lie on the ground and they then wiped out the Palestinian Arab terrorists in the hall within a few seconds with crackling volleys of automatic fire," says Ofer. "The terrorists had not had time to hurl grenades at the soldiers or the hostages."[64] This should not be taken to mean that there were no casualties other than the two young Palestinian extremists, however. There were, and they included both terrorists and hostages.

With his AK-47, a Sayeret Matkal commando gunned down the German extremists, Wilfried Böse and Brigette Kuhlmann, while his Israeli comrades shot and killed the three remaining PFLP terrorists. All were dead within forty-five seconds of the commandos entering the old terminal.[65] Also killed were hostages Pasco Cohen and Ida Borochovitch, both in their fifties, and nineteen-year-old Jean-Jacques Maimoni, whom the commandos mistook for a terrorist when he jumped to his feet during the raid. They also shot, again accidentally, a fellow hostage who rushed over to help the fallen French youth. The man, an Auschwitz survivor by the name of Yitzhak David, took a bullet to the lung, but survived. And then there was the aged Dora Bloch, who was left behind in a Ugandan hospital bed and thus was at the mercy of the Amin government.

With the terrorist threat having been eliminated and the Ugandan military held at bay, the hostages dashed to the airplanes that sat idling in the summer night. On one of the aircraft was Yonatan Netanyahu, who had been shot in the chest and arm, and was being treated by medics. His wounds were life-threatening.

Once all of the liberated hostages had boarded the rescue planes, an Israeli commander, Omer Bar-Lev, decided to destroy a sizable portion of the Ugandan Air Force's fleet of Libyan MiG fighter jets that were parked nearby so they could not be used to pursue the Israeli squadron. Although he had sought authorization to do so, he had not yet received it and time was of the essence. For this reason, Bar-Lev proceeded without it, with he and his men, traveling in an armored personnel carrier, using grenade launchers to obliterate nearly a dozen MiGs. It was a parting shot that cost Idi Amin's military a quarter of its MiG force, as well as bringing to a close, in a spectacular fashion, a successful mission. The entire operation on the ground was completed in under an hour.

As the Israeli aircraft took off, the hostages were jubilant, although the same could not be said for the commandos traveling in Hercules Four. "No joy broke out in the fourth plane as we lifted off from Entebbe," says Betser. "We all knew that Yonni was seriously wounded."[66] Shortly thereafter, the thirty-year-old patriot succumbed after uttering a few unintelligible words to a medic who was attending to him. As it turned out, Netanyahu, the commander of the Sayeret Matkal, would be the IDF's only casualty in the course of Operation Entebbe.

By comparison, over forty-five Ugandan soldiers perished, although Dustan has suggested that at least half of them may have been killed by their fellow soldiers after Operation Entebbe wrapped up.[67] Certainly it is true that there was a sense of rage in Uganda owing to its military's trouncing at the airport, a rage that would soon find Idi Amin murdering anyone he suspected might have contributed to it.

Celebration and Scorn

It was on July 4, 1976, that the hostages were liberated, a date that happened to coincide with the heavily-promoted bicentennial of the United States. So it was that the eyes of the world were not only on America but also on the Jewish state because of its incredible accomplishment in liberating its citizens. And in Israel, more than any other nation, the euphoria was beyond compare.

"The wave of national joy touched off by the hostages' homecoming was unlike anything Israel had experienced since its victory in the Six-Day War," writes Peck. "Even the loss of four hostages and one soldier could not alter the dominant mood of jubilation and pride."[68]

Citing the organizations responsible for Operation Entebbe's triumph, Prime Minister Yitzhak Rabin made sure to honor those comprising the Israeli intelligence network. Not only that, he placed them high on the roster of contributors. "It was no slip of the pen that the intelligence community headed that list," notes Stewart Steven.[69] Undeniably, the mission had relied on information furnished by the Mossad, along with the arrangements the agency had devised with the Kenyan government. Accordingly, the praise was merited.

It should be noted, too, that the hostage-rescue operation had importance for the Jewish state beyond that of saving of its citizens' lives. It had immense symbolic value. The nation's morale, it seems, had waned as a result of the Yom Kippur War in 1973, when Egyptian and Syrian troops launched surprise attacks on Israeli-occupied territories, most notably the Sinai Peninsula and Golan Heights. Having come to believe that its military could forestall any such offensives, Israel's population was stunned by the onslaughts on the Jewish holy day. This was one more reason, then, for such exhilaration over Operation Entebbe; it renewed the citizenry's pride in its country's military. Yet even as the nation basked in the glory of the breathtaking rescue mission, many other countries were dismayed by the endeavor.

Within days, the UN Security Council received two draft resolutions contending that Operation Entebbe had violated the rule of non-aggression between nations. One was prepared by Britain and the United States, and the other by Libya, Benin, and Tanzania. Both resolutions echoed the sentiments of UN Secretary-General Kurt Waldheim, who had already weighed in on the matter. "I have not got all the details," he declared, "but it seems to be clear that Israeli aircraft have landed in Entebbe and this constitutes a serious violation of the sovereignty of a State Member of the United Nations."[70] Waldheim did not mention that the African nation had not been a neutral bystander in the affair, that Idi Amin's troops were observed to have cooperated with the PFLP in holding the hostages at gunpoint at the Entebbe airport. This meant, of course, that Uganda had willfully aided the terrorist operation. (No friend to the Jewish people, Kurt Waldheim would later be exposed as having been an intelligence officer in Germany's *Wehrmacht* during the Holocaust. "His initials are to be seen on reports about mass deportations of Jews from Greece to death camps, the bloody suppression of partisans, the use of Italian troops as forced labour after Italy's surrender and the 'special treatment' [summary execution] ordered for captured British commandos," *The Guardian* reports.[71])

As the UN debate over Operation Entebbe blazed, Western nations attempted to use the ordeal to shift the global body's attention to the grave problem posed by international terrorism and the need to address it, even as they condemned the Israeli raid in Uganda. The United States representative did, however, point out the uniqueness of the Entebbe episode while alluding to Israel's right to protect its citizens. The African coalition, on the other hand, focused exclusively on Israel's violation of Uganda's autonomy. In the end, neither resolution passed, nor did a motion by the Amin administration that would have required the Jewish state, the principal target of the mass kidnapping, to pay financial compensation to Uganda for damages the African nation purportedly sustained.

Not surprisingly in light of his mental instability and infamous temper, Amin did not rely solely on the United Nations for action. In the weeks following Operation Entebbe, his henchmen dragged Dora Bloch, the elderly hostage who had been hospitalized after on a choking piece of food, out of her bed and to a waiting sedan. Although she shouted and fought against her abductors, Bloch was unable to save herself, being shot to death and dumped in the trunk of the car. Years later, her body was found buried at a sugar plantation twenty miles from the city of Kampala, and with severe burns on it. Not stopping there, Amin's minions also murdered the police officers who had been assigned to guard her while she was in the hospital. Appalled, the British government recalled its High Commissioner and broke off ties with Uganda.[72]

And there was more: Amin's soldiers hammered nails into the head of an air traffic controller at the Entebbe airport, then crushed his body. The deranged dictator also ordered the assassination of a British official and former intelligence agent, a murder that was performed rather ingeniously by means of a rigged hunting trophy; to wit, an exploding antelope head that was presented to the diplomat as a gift.[73] And if this were not enough, Ugandan troops slaughtered thousands of tribesmen in Kenya on Amin's assumption that the neighboring country had cooperated with Israel in pulling off the hostage rescue.[74]

All of these events disturbed the Israeli government, as could be expected. But the Rabin administration was also upset by the fact that disapproval of the mission was not limited to Idi Amin or the delegates at the United Nations. In several countries, opinion on the street was against Operation Entebbe. Particularly grating to the Israelis was the fact that the British government did not publicly support the Jewish state even though the mission had brought about the freeing of British hostages. On this point, Israeli officials were piqued because the British prime minister did not send his congratulations to his counterpart, Yitzhak Rabin, according to a British government memo retained in the National Archives and released in 2007 in response to a Freedom of Information request.

Curiously, this document also reveals that, in the midst of the crisis, an assertion was made to a British official that an Israeli intelligence organization, Shin Bet, had played a central role in setting up the skyjacking. "According to the file released by the National Archives," reports *Yedioth Ahronot* (*Israel News*), "an unnamed contact told a British diplomat in Paris that the Shin Bet and the PFLP collaborated to seize the plane."[75] Referring to the same memo, a BBC report adds that the contact asserted that "the [skyjacking] operation was designed to torpedo the PLO's standing in France and to prevent what they [the Israelis] see as a growing rapprochement between the PLO and the Americans."[76] Yet beyond this single report filed on June 30, 1976—after the skyjacking but before Operation Entebbe—there are no further allegations of Israel having had advance knowledge of the terrorist plot, let alone having worked with the PFLP to plan and implement it. In the fog of war, or terrorism as the case may be, government officials often receive such claims and pass them on to their superiors. This in no way means the claims are sound, although further investigation may be merited if several similar ones are received, especially from divergent and dependable sources. This was not the case with the Shin Bet allegation, however. Accordingly, it continues to appear that the State of Israel had no involvement in the skyjacking, a notion that is consistent with the behavior of its government officials and particularly its military and intelligence organizations in the course of the crisis itself.

Political complications notwithstanding, experts the world over concurred that Operation Entebbe, from an intelligence and military standpoint, had been a brilliant piece of work. Not only had the intricate project taken place without a hitch, but it also demonstrated that the various components of Israel's intelligence and military communities, which were known to be rather territorial and competitive at times, could unite and produce outstanding results—and in a remarkably brief period of time. For the Mossad, in particular, the agency's important contribution to the operation led, among other things, to its inclusion in future military endeavors outside of the Jewish state.

Regarding the impact of Operation Entebbe itself—specifically, its long-term effect on air piracy against the Jewish state—it was powerful and permanent. "No plane flying to or from Israel has been hijacked since then," write Black and Morris.[77]

That said, the cessation of anti–Israeli air piracy may have been hastened by the termination of Wadia Hadad himself, the PFLP leader who had masterminded the harrowing Air France affair. In the wake of Operation Entebbe, the Mossad regarded Hadad as a continuing threat to Israel and therefore stepped up its efforts to monitor him. And what the agency learned, moreover, stirred it to action. "Haddad seemed certain to be planning more attacks on Israelis," write Raviv and Melman, "and [the Mossad] intended to erase him first."[78] Recruiting one of the Palestinian leader's associates, the Mossad positioned this accomplice to deliver the fatal blow, all the while being careful not to leave behind any evidence that could be traced to the Jewish state.

"A year after the Entebbe rescue," write Bar-Zohar and Mishal, "the Mossad agents found out that Haddad adored chocolate, especially fine, Belgian chocolate."[79] Exploiting this fondness, the Israeli agency instructed its PFLP collaborator to deliver a box of Godiva chocolates to the extremist, who, as expected, did not waste any time devouring the sweets.[80] And what happened afterward baffled doctors in Iraq, where Hadad was living at the time, as well as in East Germany, where he subsequently sought treatment. "[T]he plump Haddad started losing his appetite and losing weight," write Bar-Zohar and Mishal. "Nobody ... understood what was happening to the leader of the Popular Front."[81]

A month later, Wadia Hadad was laid to rest, with the PFLP weakening as a consequence of his demise. In the end, then, the State of Israel had prevailed over the organization that had abducted its citizens and held them hostage, and, equally important, it had ensured that such an offense would not recur. And in no small measure it had succeeded because of the supreme proficiency of the Mossad and its affiliates in the larger Israeli intelligence community and their laudable teamwork with the Jewish state's military establishment.

Part Four

Operation Opera

Introduction

As the Mossad evolved, it not only expanded its role in protecting Israeli interests but it also became increasingly provocative in carrying out its functions. As noted, its principal missions in the 1960s and 1970s, despite being denounced at times, were designed to ensure that no harm came to those who were innocent. Operation Eichmann and Operation Wrath of God, for instance, were crafted in such a way that only the targets themselves would be impacted; the Mossad teams were to suspend their missions if extraneous individuals were found to be at risk of injury or death. Likewise, Operation Entebbe was designed to safely liberate as many hostages as possible and fly them to freedom.

As the years rolled by, however, the agency dispensed with such imperatives and adopted an attitude marked by greater expediency, the mindset being that the Mossad would achieve its ends even if it meant endangering or killing those who were innocent. Whereas the organization had, in special instances, exercised such license in the past—the 1962 kidnapping and letter-bombing of German scientists suspected of contributing to Egypt's military program comes to mind—such actions now became more commonplace.

The Mossad's actions in the late 1970s and early 1980s are illustrative. As many nations rushed to acquire nuclear energy, a development that was partly in response to the worldwide energy crisis, the Israeli government worried that its foes in the Middle East would be among those acquiring such capabilities and might proceed to build nuclear weapons. At the time, the Jewish state was one of only seven countries in the world that possessed such weapons and the only Middle Eastern nation to have them, with the Israeli leadership being determined that this state of affairs would remain unchanged. For this reason, the Israeli leadership panicked in 1976 when Iraq, its adversary, purchased a nuclear reactor from France and began constructing a nuclear facility near

Baghdad. Ostensibly, the device was to be used for peaceful purposes—research and domestic applications—with Iraq agreeing that the reactor's operation would be overseen by the International Atomic Energy Agency. What would not be peaceful were the Mossad's ensuing efforts, in concert with those of other Israeli intelligence and military organizations, to terminate the "suspect" Iraqi project, with strategies that would include state-sponsored assassinations and sabotage in France and presumably Italy, cresting with an unprecedented military offensive in Iraq itself. The mission would come to be known as Operation Opera.

9

Saddam Hussein and the Nuclear Program of Iraq

In the 1950s, Iraq, a monarchy at the time, was on friendly terms with the West, a state of affairs that Britain and the United States fostered because it was to their advantage in two important respects. First, the kingdom deferred to both Western powers on fundamental matters, not the least being the content of a considerable share of its political and economic policies. And second, Iraq, due partly to its location, was a useful ally in the Cold War, being yet another country the British and American governments could add to the roster of nations that stood in opposition to the Soviet Union.

Of course, the Middle Eastern nation, in return, derived substantial benefits from its association with the West. Among other plusses, the United States brought it into the Atomic Age, furnishing the Iraqi scientific community with research findings from the U.S. Atomic Energy Commission, training its scientists and technicians, and providing basic equipment. Not only that, the United States, in 1956, played a principal role in establishing the Iraqi Atomic Energy Commission. The aim was to encourage the Iraqis to make productive use of nuclear energy, including its potential applications in medicine, agriculture, and other areas. But such contributions were not to last. Soon, the political landscape in the Middle Eastern kingdom would undergo a seismic shift and Western support would diminish.

Although the monarchy's twenty-three-year-old ruler, King Faisal II, expressed few qualms about the profound influence that Britain and the United States wielded in his nation's affairs, a segment of the Iraqi population did have misgivings about it, enraged by what it considered to be political domination by foreign powers. And it was this grievance, alongside other objections, that culminated in the 14 July Revolution, a coup d'état in which King Faisal II was assassinated and the British and American presence, jettisoned.

Promptly crafting a relationship with the Soviet Union, Iraq's new leadership—President Muhammad Najib ar-Ruba'i and Prime Minister Abd al-Karim Qassim—were eager to make use of this new partnership to advance the nascent republic. Among the domestic conditions they sought to preserve and hopefully enhance, moreover, was Iraq's access to nuclear research and technology. So it was that Iraq, on August 17, 1959, signed an agreement with the USSR, titled, "Co-operation in the Peaceful Uses of Atomic Energy."[1] The Soviet Union, according to the pact, would share with the Middle Eastern country advances pertaining to the constructive uses of nuclear energy. The USSR would also take up the reins in training Iraqi scientists and technicians in these applications. And, in due course, it would do even more.

In 1968, the Soviet Union supplied Iraq with its first nuclear reactor. A small, two-megawatt research reactor (as opposed to a large, high-megawatt "power" reactor), it was located at the Nuclear Research Center in al-Tuwaitha, twenty miles southeast of Baghdad. Besides the reactor, the site housed the Iraqi Atomic Energy Commission, and it also accommodated a handful of Soviet-made support facilities. The entire operation was nestled near a twist in the Tigris River.

It was at this time that the Republic of Iraq became a signatory to the Treaty on the Non-Proliferation of Nuclear Weapons, meaning the country was not in possession of, nor did it intend to acquire, nuclear arms. But although this may have been true at the time, matters began to change in the 1970s as a function of the mounting political power of Iraqi Vice President Saddam Hussein, who was also the head of the Iraqi Atomic Energy Commission. Even though Hussein favored biological and chemical weapons because of their relatively low cost and viable methods of production, he also voiced an interest in someday creating a nuclear arsenal.[2] On this point, his rationale was unambiguous: Iraq needed to acquire nuclear arms because its adversary, Israel, was already in possession of them despite the fact that it claimed otherwise.[3] At issue was the balance of power in the region.

Hussein's stance had been forecast a decade earlier by President John F. Kennedy. The year was 1961 and Israel, under the leadership of Prime Minister David Ben-Gurion, set out to achieve its nuclear ambitions. It would be a quest that would meet with intense domestic and foreign opposition, however. At this pivotal moment, Kennedy, foremost among Israel's critics on the subject, decried the Jewish state's decision to embark on an atomic research program on the grounds that it threatened to destabilize the already volatile region.[4] He warned that it could trigger a nuclear arms race in the region. Hussein's nuclear aspirations a decade later, then, appear to have been a fulfillment of the American president's prediction. As for further reasons the Iraqi vice president may have wished to create a nuclear arsenal, Shahram Chubin of the Carnegie Nuclear Policy Program has suggested that they included protecting the country from attack by Western nations and neighboring Iran, while, in the same stroke, impressing other Middle Eastern states.[5] "Nuclear weapons would emphatically affirm Iraq's leadership in the Arab world," says Chubin.[6]

Further spurring Hussein's desire for additional weaponry, both conventional and purportedly nuclear, was a turn of events three years later when Iraq found itself in a vulnerable position militarily. It happened in 1974 during a border war with Iran over the Kurdish issue. After months of fighting, the Iraqi military began running low on arms and ammunition and, for renewal, contacted the USSR, its chief supplier of military materials. But Hussein did not receive the response he anticipated. To his consternation, the Soviet leadership, which was opposed to a war against the Kurds, not only refused to furnish the supplies, but it refused to even discuss the matter. In the end, Iraq lost the war.

"The Soviet attitude was debilitating to Saddam, morally and military," says Timmerman. "Ever since they had replaced Great Britain as Iraq's principal arms supplier in 1958, the Soviets had very carefully, like drug pushers, built up Iraq's dependence."[7] Because the USSR would only dispense arms and ammunition if it was in ideological agreement with the reason for their purchase, Iraq's pact with the Soviet Union was, in effect, meaningless.

To correct this problem, Hussein resolved to diversify the sources from which the Middle Eastern nation purchased its materials. It was a case of not placing all of his eggs in the same basket. Whether it be conventional weapons for use in war or nuclear technology designed for constructive purposes, selecting vendors from an array of nations meant that a delay or suspension by a single supplier would be unlikely to create a crisis for Iraq's security or scientific communities.

Then, too, Hussein had come to realize that agreeing to spend his nation's wealth in several different countries would serve to enhance Iraq's status in those nations, while also cultivating their deference and support. "If [Hussein] couldn't create loyalty through ideology," says Timmerman, "then he would buy it."[8] And one country that was eager to sell to the oil-rich nation was France.

As it stood, France enjoyed a robust defense industry, being among the world's leading arms exporters for several years. Its Mirage aircraft, in particular, was superbly designed and a profitable product. In addition, the nation had a well-developed nuclear program, boasting some of the world's most advanced technology, including, of course, nuclear reactors. But France also had a problem: like many countries during the 1970s, it was feeling the effects of the energy crisis and, for this reason, found itself in need of a dependable source from which to purchase oil at a reasonable price.

Iraq, for its part, possessed vast energy reserves and could, quite literally, name its price for its oil; countries around the world were lining up at its door. At the same time, the government was casting about for new suppliers of conventional weapons and sources of nuclear expertise and equipment. Accordingly, Vice President Hussein, who was more or less in charge of the Iraqi administration, made deals with a handful of nations, as well as signing nuclear-cooperation agreements with Italy, Brazil, and India. Most consequential, though, was the arrangement he crafted with France.

Beginning in early 1974 and concluding in September, 1975, Hussein and Prime Minister Jacques Chirac of France held a series of meetings to discuss their countries' needs and assets. Resoundingly productive, their talks culminated in a far-reaching deal that promised to be of tremendous value to both nations. Iraqi and French representatives signed a bilateral civilian agreement on November 18, 1975, titled, "Co-operation in Peaceful Uses of Nuclear Technology."[9] The document stipulated that France would share its nuclear expertise with the Middle Eastern country. The two countries also agreed that France would furnish Iraq with a state-of-the-art research reactor. An illuminating document, the Franco-Iraqi contract reveals just how important it was to Saddam Hussein to obtain the device, detailing the financial lengths to which he was willing to go in order to secure it.

France, to its economic benefit, would sell Iraq billions of dollars' worth of military equipment, including tanks, helicopters, surface-to-air missiles, radar paraphernalia, and nearly three dozen Mirage fighter jets. It was a far-sighted move by the French. "Arms sales to Iraq would create jobs, improve the balance of payments, and could even reduce development costs on new weapons programs," notes Timmerman.[10]

And there was more. French automobile manufacturers would sell Iraq one hundred thousand cars, specifically Peugeots and Renaults, while French architects and contractors would fashion a sprawling luxury resort in the Iraqi town of Habbaniyah. The latter project was predicted to bring hundreds of millions of dollars to those associated with it.[11]

Besides making a stunning amount of money from these endeavors, France would be allowed to import seventy million barrels of Iraqi oil a year "at present market prices for ten years."[12] To be sure, the entire package was a coup for the French.

In return, France, for a staggering three hundred million dollars, would sell Iraq a forty-megawatt, Osiris-model nuclear device. "[T]he Osiris," says Claire, was a "huge, aluminum-domed, top-of-the line research reactor."[13] The apparatus held remarkable potential for the Middle Eastern country, being devised for "research into the behavior of materials in a radioactive environment, for production of radioisotopes for research and medical purposes, and similar uses."[14] The particulars of the deal included that France would construct and transport the reactor to Iraq, as well as train hundreds of Iraqi physicists, technicians, and support crew in its operation. It would also provide a small research reactor, a one-megawatt Isis-type model, to be situated near the Osiris reactor and used, among other things, for training purposes. Promising to place Iraq's nuclear research program on a par with those of a handful of other technologically-advanced nations, Osiris would become operative in 1981, five years later.

To ensure that it would be used for benign purposes, the reactor was to be under the close supervision of the International Atomic Energy Agency (IAEA), the UN-sponsored organization, based in Vienna, that keeps tabs on nuclear programs to make sure they do not cross the line into military applications. As with other participating nations, this meant the Iraqi operation would be subject to ongoing inspections by the international agency. Then, too, Iraq, as noted, was a signatory to the Treaty on the Non-Proliferation of Nuclear Weapons, and Hussein was no doubt aware that the world would be watching to see if he abided by it.

And there were other safeguards as well. "According to the terms of the agreement, Iraq was required to return all of the waste uranium to France," says Yair Evron, founder of the Security Studies Program at Tel Aviv University and Senior Research Fellow at the Institute for National Security Studies. If it failed to do so, "such an act would most certainly [lead] to the termination of the supply of enriched uranium."[15] The waste, it seems, could be used to create a bomb, which is why Iraq would not be permitted to keep it. Evron adds that the fuel itself would also possess a formidable deterrent of its own. "France," he writes, "announced her intention to apply radiation to the uranium prior to its transfer to Iraq. This treatment makes the uranium dangerous to handle, and would have effectively prevented its use for production of a bomb."[16] Equally important, the device's configuration narrowed its uses, explains Harvard nuclear physicist Richard Wilson, with the Osiris reactor being "explicitly designed by the French engineer Yves Girard to be unsuitable for making bombs."[17] To be sure, the French were intent upon guaranteeing that the Osiris reactor would be used strictly for nonmilitary functions, while the Iraqis, who may have hoped to pursue a nuclear weapons program sometime in the future, were, at the moment, adhering to the agreement for the reactor's peaceful applications. Certainly France did not seem unduly concerned about the situation. Describing the deal that had been struck, the French president assured the world of the arrangement's integrity. "During my visit to Iraq," Chirac reported, "I laid the foundation for nuclear cooperation—and I stress—*for peaceful purposes.*"[18]

Although the French leadership was comfortable with the notion of Iraq possessing a research reactor under tight IAEA supervision, Israeli Prime Minister Yitzhak Rabin and his administration were aghast at the thought and hoped to stop the project from moving forward. Contending that Hussein meant to use the apparatus to construct a bomb, one he would use against the Jewish state, members of the Israeli government set about contacting officials in allied nations and influential figures in private organizations and imploring them to discourage the Franco-Iraqi arrangement. At the same time, the Mossad, along with Israel's Military Intelligence Directorate, began monitoring developments in both France and Iraq.

After a short while, it became apparent that Israel's allies were unwilling or unable to intervene to a meaningful degree. Some did not consider it problematic that a signatory to the Nuclear Non-Proliferation Treaty had purchased a research reactor. It was Iraq's legal right to do so. Others were hesitant to interfere with what was clearly a positive development for the West during the Cold War: Iraq loosening its ties to the Soviet Union and replacing them with European business partners. The result, then, is that the project proceeded, while in Israel, five hundred miles to the west, a new prime minister was installed, the hard-nosed Menachem Begin.

Continuing to appraise events in France and Iraq into 1978, the Mossad, under the direction of Yitzhak Hofi, and Military Intelligence, overseen by Shlomo Gazit, came across nothing that alarmed them. All the same, Begin was intensely concerned about the Osiris project and placed it high on his list of priorities as the country's new leader. Unlike his predecessor, he also floated a radical idea to high-level figures in his administration, that of a military strike on the al-Tuwaitha site. It was a proposal that was met with considerable opposition, including that of both Hofi and Gazit.[19]

The view of the Mossad and Military Intelligence was that France had not completed construction of the nuclear reactor and would not do so for another three years. There was no immediate danger. "At present, they stressed, the reactor contained no radioactive material at all," writes Nakdimon.[20] Voicing the concern that an attack inside of Iraq could trigger a military retaliation against Israel, Hofi and Gazit pushed for more time to be given to the behind-the-scene maneuverings, which were still in progress.[21] And the prime minister, in the end, reluctantly deferred to their position, biding his time while the two intelligence organizations continued their watch on the situation. With the arrival of 1979, however, Begin could hold off no longer.

It was at this juncture that the substructure for Osiris was completed at

9. Saddam Hussein and the Nuclear Program of Iraq

the al-Tuwaitha Nuclear Research Center. It had taken three years to build the complex infrastructure in anticipation of the arrival of the reactor core from France. And thus far, the project was on-schedule. "The huge reinforced concrete reactor pool, dug deep into the rocky earth, had been completed on time by the French contractors," writes Timmerman. "The crane that was to hoist the reactors into place and manipulate spent fuel rods had been tested and greased to perfection."[22] Truckloads of testing equipment had arrived at al-Tuwaitha too, ranging from Hewlett-Packard computers to radiation sensors from Oak Ridge, Tennessee.[23]

With the Osiris project looming on the horizon, then, Menachem Begin decided to take definitive action. Concluding that Israel's attempts to persuade its friends to pressure France into annulling the deal had been ineffective, he decided that the Jewish state, by whatever means necessary, would itself prevent the Osiris reactor from becoming operative. And with this objective in mind, the Israeli leader contacted the Mossad.

10

Mission: Operation Opera

In the early days of 1979, Prime Minister Menachem Begin met with Mossad chief Yitzhak Hofi and made it known that Israel must halt Saddam Hussein's nuclear project. In twenty-nine months, the Osiris reactor was scheduled to become operative—"go hot" in the vernacular—and the Israeli leader's position was that the Jewish state could remain on the sidelines no longer. Accordingly, Begin, Hofi, and a handful of Mossad strategists concocted a scheme to disable a crucial component of the Osiris device, the core, while it was still under construction in France. The Mossad's operatives, this group reasoned, could expect to encounter a less formidable security presence in France than in Iraq itself.

At a nuclear plant in Sarcelles, a northern suburb of Paris, work on the core was being completed at this time. The Mossad's scheme was to sabotage this vital component while it was *en route* to the South of France for shipment to Iraq. What the agency needed to determine, then, was when the core was scheduled to be exported to the Middle Eastern nation.

To acquire this information, it called on one of its *sayanim* who worked at the Sarcelles plant and asked him to compose a list of Iraqi nationals employed at the facility.[1] Devoted to the Jewish state, the man, whose office was located in the company's personnel unit and who therefore had access to such materials, agreed to help. As recounted by former operative Victor Ostrovsky, the Mossad next instructed the *sayanim* to travel to a particular spot in Paris near the Eiffel Tower and be on the lookout for a red Peugeot.[2] Upon detecting the car, he was to park his own vehicle and walk away, after which an operative would step in and retrieve the document that would be concealed in the trunk of the man's car. And sure enough, the handover came off without a hitch: the agency got hold of the list and from it the name of a plant worker who, for a price, would surrender the timetable for the core's transfer to Iraq.

10. Mission: Operation Opera

From this latter source, the Mossad learned it would be during the first week of April 1979 that both the Osiris and the smaller Isis core would be arriving on France's southern seaboard. The devices now carried different names, however. As the Franco-Iraqi undertaking progressed, France, as a courtesy, had renamed the Osiris device "Osirak" (also spelled "Osiraq") in order to combine the words Osiris and Iraq. Unmoved by the gesture, Saddam Hussein planned to rename the devices yet again, this time to "Tammuz I" and "Tammuz II." Little did he know that such name changes would be pointless owing to a string of events heralded by a startling act in the French town of La Seyne-sur-Mer on the Mediterranean coast.

Operation Big Lift

It was here, at the Constructions industrielles de la Meditérranée, that technicians were to preparing the cores for the two-thousand-mile journey to Iraq.[3] "The plan was to load the reactor cores onto the Iraqi ship before dawn on the morning of April 9, 1979, before the day shift arrived," writes Kenneth Timmerman.[4] It was here, too, that Operation Big Lift, as the Mossad referred to it, was set to unfold.

It got under way on April 5, when two large trucks, under escort by a fleet of armored vehicles, approached the coastal town. Inside the trucks were the Osirak and Isis cores. While the convoy was traveling to the facility, however, it was stealthily joined by a third truck carrying a physicist and five commandos with expertise in sabotage. A Mossad team, the group's task was to blast the cores before the components could leave the continent.

"On the expert advice of the physicist," explains Ostrovsky, "the Israeli team [would plant] five charges of plastic explosives, strategically positioned on the reactor cores."[5] Although it carried certain risks, the plan was nevertheless feasible, mainly because no one at the La Seyne-sur-Mer site would be expecting it. First, though, the Mossad team would need to infiltrate the plant itself, which, as it turned out, was remarkably easy to do. As their truck pulled up to the gate along with the other vehicles in the convoy, the watchmen simply waved it through, the guards' cavalier attitude thus allowing the Israelis to fulfill their assignment.

At sunrise the next morning, a commotion erupted outside the facility. It seems that a woman on a side street began shouting that she had been grazed by a passing car. A feature of the Mossad's strategy, her role was to lure the facility's security guards away from the complex so they would not be harmed. And the ruse worked. As the night watchmen and other personnel rushed onto the street to help the woman, the commandos, who were stationed nearby, prepared to act.

"First checking the crowd to verify that all the French guards were out of harm's way, one of [the saboteurs] calmly and surreptitiously detonated a sophisticated fuse with a hand-held device," writes Ostrovsky.[6] A finely-pitched operation, the team applied just the right amount of plastique to do the job yet not so much as to demolish the entire plant. Despite the confined nature of the explosion, however, the incident soon became a magnet for the media, especially when it was determined that the cause was almost certainly sabotage.

By turns, the French press accused the culprits of being Palestinian militants working for Libya, radical French leftists, the French secret service, the FBI, and the Soviets, piqued at Iraq for having rejected further nuclear deals with them. "Others accused the Mossad," says Ostrovsky, "but an Israeli government official dismissed the accusation as 'anti-Semitism.'"[7] Shrewdly, a Mossad agent, posing as an anti-nuclear activist, phoned the newspaper *Le Monde* at this juncture and reported that the explosions had been the work of a new environmental organization, the *Groupe des Ecologistes Français*.[8] Since, as Rodger Claire notes, the Three Mile Island nuclear accident in the United States had happened only twelve days earlier, this claim, on the face of it, carried a degree of credibility.[9] Before long, though, experts concluded, if unofficially, that the bombing had been the work of the Mossad, not only because Israel had the most to gain from the cores' destruction but also because the residue of a hard-to-obtain plastic explosive, a Mossad favorite, was discovered at the crime scene. While the French were dismayed at what appeared to be an Israeli sabotage mission, however, there was little they could do considering that they lacked tangible evidence, only that which was circumstantial. Thus, the French company would simply have to swallow the cost of the damage.

An inspection revealed that the two cores sustained a number of hairline fractures, a finding that was deeply disconcerting. Given that nuclear fission takes place inside the reactor core, such fine cracks would be sufficient to produce a catastrophic meltdown once the device was operative.

As could be expected, Iraq insisted that the French company replace both reactors, since the sabotage had taken place while they were in the latter's custody, but company officials were reluctant to submit to the demand due to the exorbitant costs involved. Instead, they played to Saddam Hussein's impatient nature; they were well aware of his near-obsession with his country's nuclear program and his desire to keep it moving forward. So it was that the French explained it would take up to two years to manufacture a pair of new cores, and therefore they offered to mend the damaged ones. It was, to be sure, an option that would serve the interests of both parties: it would save the French a considerable amount of money, while, for the Iraqis, significantly reducing the delay to their project. And, as expected, Hussein, determined to keep Iraq's nuclear research program on schedule, agreed to the proposal. The refurbishments cost the French firm twenty-three million dollars, with the patched cores arriving at the Nuclear Research Center in al-Tuwaitha a few months later.[10] It was a moment that elated Hussein as much as it dismayed Menachem Begin, with the Israeli prime minister's worries intensifying the following year when Iraq rebuffed France's offer of a modified reactor fuel.

Because the Israeli government had, from the start, opposed the Franco-Iraqi deal and urged its allies to challenge it, French scientists, in 1976, had begun experimenting with a new type of fuel for the Osirak device, one they hoped would put to rest the Israelis' concerns. The alternate fuel would also have the advantage of placing France on firmer footing in the event that Iraq decided to pursue a nuclear weapons program at some future point. In such a case, the new French-supplied fuel could not be pointed to as a contributing factor. In terms of the nature of the modified substance, it had to do with uranium-fortification levels.

"The Osiraq reactor uses 93 percent enriched uranium, which France was committed to supply," says Yair Evron, Senior Research Fellow at the Institute for National Security Studies in Tel Aviv. In 1980, however, French officials asked Iraq to accept "a different type of fuel, known as the 'Caramel' type which operates on only 7–8 percent enriched uranium."[11] While the latter substance, which was relatively inexpensive and safe, would serve Iraq's declared purposes for the reactor—research and domestic applications—it would do nothing more. "It was sufficient to power up the Osirak reactor," writes Timmerman, "but totally useless for weapons production."[12]

Iraq, for its part, was wary of the altered fuel. Having paid hundreds of millions of dollars for the Osirak and Isis reactors, the project's scientists did not wish to rely on a recently-created substance whose quality, in their opinion, had not been fully established. Of course, the new product was also quite different from the one stipulated in the original agreement, meaning the substitution was unacceptable from a purely contractual standpoint. That said, the Iraqis did consider trying the novel substance with the proviso that the French allow them to purchase it in small amounts in case it proved unsatisfactory, although this possibility evaporated in the early weeks of 1980 when the Middle Eastern nation announced its final decision at a nonproliferation conference in Vienna.

"France plans to ship weapons-grade enriched uranium to Iraq following the failure of a three-year effort by Paris to persuade the Iraqis to buy a substitute low-enrichment fuel," reported *The Washington Post* on February 28, 1980.[13] It was a turn of events that perturbed Israel. Although the Osirak device would be unable to use the weapons-grade fuel to concoct a bomb because the reactor's configuration precluded such applications, the Begin administration pointed to Iraq's decision to eschew the "caramel" substitute as proof that Hussein was intent upon somehow creating weapons of mass destruction. And so, once again, the prime minister picked up the phone.

Conferring with the Mossad's Yitkhak Hofi, the Israeli leader and his intelligence chief decided the time had come to recruit or, if necessary, intimidate those scientists who were associated with the Osirak project. And by intimidate, they meant assassinating some of them in order to end these experts' contributions to the program while, in the same stroke, striking fear in the ones who remained. The expectation was that such shocking measures would delay the project or, better yet, lead to its termination.

The Assassination Option

On the staff of the Iraqi project was a highly-regarded Egyptian nuclear engineer, Yahya al-Meshad. A faculty member at the University of Alexandria, al-Meshad was a middle-aged, married man with three children. His role in the Osirak program was twofold: he was to monitor Iraq's compliance with its nuclear agreement with France and keep an eye on the latter's fabrication of the reactor. It was, by any measure, a position of immense importance and one that made al-Meshad a potentially valuable asset to Israeli Intelligence. Because he was well-versed in the details of the Osirak program and might also be privy to Hussein's plans, if any, to build a nuclear weapon, the Mossad decided the nuclear engineer's collaboration would be indispensable. Accordingly, it moved in on him in the spring of 1980.

At first, the agency tried to recruit him, approaching him through a fellow scientist who worked at the French nuclear plant in Sarcelles, but al-Meshad would not betray his loyalty to his Iraqi employer and colleagues. He was consistent in his refusals, moreover, if anything becoming increasingly indignant each time the Mossad attempted to lure him to its side. The last time the agency approached him, in fact, al-Meshad became openly hostile, ejecting a covert operative who offered to pay him "a lot of money" to hand over Iraqi nuclear information to an unnamed source.[14]

As it turned out, the Egyptian's refusal on this occasion would be one of his final acts. "Mossad decided that if Meshad could not be recruited, *other* arrangements would have to be made," writes Claire. "[T]hey might even have to show him a 'better world'—the *katsa* euphemism for an assassination."[15] And sure enough, it was to this "better world" that the Mossad soon delivered the eminent scientist.

On June 13, 1980, a rainy evening in Paris, al-Meshad returned to his room at the Hotel Le Méridien. He had just wrapped up a week of meetings and was set to return to Iraq shortly. Lingering in his hotel on this night was a woman by the name of Marie-Claude Magalle, a prostitute, who had trailed al-Meshad to his room on the ninth floor and propositioned him along the way.[16] When he turned down her offer, she waited in the hallway in case he had a change of heart, and it was during this time that she heard men's voices coming from inside his room. Although she had no way of knowing it, they were the voices of the Mossad. And so Magalle, realizing that a sexual encounter was not in the cards, left the hotel.

Late the next morning, a maid removed the *Ne pas déranger* sign and unlocked the door to al-Meshad's room. Stretched out on the floor in a lake of blood was the scientist, his throat slashed.

"The murder made big headlines in the Paris press," write Khidir Hamza and Jeff Stein.[17] Because he was a top nuclear engineer, al-Meshad's execution at the upscale hotel became the talk of the town. It was a shocker for the Iraqis, too, especially those at the Nuclear Research Center in al-Tuwaitha and the presidential estate—the Republican Palace—in Baghdad. "Saddam dispatched two Iraqi intelligence officers to look into the case," report Hamza and Stein, the head of state realizing it had not been a random slaying.[18] And other nations weighed in as well, with a British report speculating that Iraqi assassins had executed the scientist. "Another hypothesis argued that Meshad's interests included a covert link with Soviet curiosity about the French reactor under construction at [al–Tuwaitha], and that it was this involvement which led to his killing," says Nakdimon.[19]

But while those who were not at the crime scene believed they may have figured out the perpetrators' motives, the Paris police, the ones actually investigating the murder, were stumped. Other than the victim's body, al-Meshad's hotel room was shipshape and his money and other valuables, still present. And this feature of the scene, at least, seemed to rule out robbery. Searching for other reasons for the killing, investigators were optimistic when a witness stepped forward, this being Marie-Claude Magalle.

"Partly to protect herself, and partly because she was suspicious, she went to the police," write Ostrovsky and Hoy.[20] Explaining that she had propositioned al-Meshad, Magalle went on to describe the voices she had heard coming from his room shortly before she left the hotel; voices, she added, that were not loud, suggesting that the men were not arguing. Perhaps it was because of this claim that investigators now turned their attention to the prospect of a gay murder.

Le Méridien, an elegant hotel catering to foreign businessman and businesswomen, was known to attract sex workers, among them male prostitutes hoping to service its well-heeled guests.[21] Investigators wondered, then, if this might explain the men's voices emanating from al-Meshad's quarters. Soon enough, however, they ruled out a sex-related killing mainly because the murder simply did not possess the characteristics of an impulsive crime of passion. More the opposite: it looked premeditated. Based on Magalle's account, it appeared that awaiting al-Meshad in his hotel room had been one or more men. When the scientist entered, they did not raise their voices, which might have alerted the security staff, nor did they shoot him, since gunfire would have attracted attention as well. Instead, they cut his throat, severing his vocal cords and thus preventing him from crying out. For these and other reasons, the available facts seemed to point to a professional execution, a precision hit.

This was more or less confirmed a short time later when police officials decided to speak once again to Magalle on the chance she might have remembered something else since her previous interview. When they tried to contact her, they discovered that she had been killed, and rather mercilessly. Like the police, the Mossad had also wondered if she might have recalled further details, namely a piece of information that might expose its hand in the slaying, and therefore the agency had decided to silence her.

It happened on a Saturday night on the Boulevard Saint-Germain. Magalle was working the busy Left Bank venue when a black Mercedes stopped across the street from her, its driver motioning for her to approach his car. As she crossed the street toward it, another black Mercedes, one that had been parked further down the boulevard, raced forward and slammed into her. Both cars then fled the scene as Magalle lay dying on the pavement. As in the al-Meshad homicide, her murder on a Paris street was eventually consigned to the cold case files.

And the violence persisted. A month later, the Mossad killed a "bright, energetic young electrical engineer," writes Claire.[22] Educated in Britain and a member of the Osirak team, the victim, Salman Rashid, was embarking on a two-month academic fellowship in Switzerland when the Mossad slipped him a deadly poison. "Rashid was having trouble swallowing, and soon he began to bloat, his neck and jowls becoming alarmingly swollen."[23] Although American and Iraqi doctors in Geneva labored to save him from his puzzling malady, the cause of which they could not pinpoint, Rashid was dead within a week.

Next up was Abdul-Rahman Abdul Rasool, an Iraqi nuclear engineer. While on a business trip to Paris, the Mossad exposed him to a toxin at a dinner party, with the poisonous agent leading to a diagnosis of food poisoning.[24] It was a medical opinion that was abandoned a few days later, however, when

Rasool's health spiraled downward and he perished. As with the Mossad's previous assassinations of Osirak scientists, the message was unmistakable.

"These killings shook me to the core," said Mahdi Obeidi, the former director of Iraq's Ministry of Industry and Military Industrialization and a man who had been on friendly terms with the three casualties. "I realized I was now involved in an endeavor that someone was determined to stop at any cost."[25]

Among those scientists working at the al-Tuwaitha nuclear research center was Khidhir Hamza, whom, as a result of the murders, Iraqi security forces now trained in self-protection measures so he would not fall victim to such sinister acts when traveling outside the country. "To avoid poisoning we were instructed not to eat in the same place twice, to locate cafeterias where we could choose our own food, and to decline impromptu invitations from strangers to restaurants or private homes," he says. "Never leave food in your room, we were told, or drink any hotel water."[26] They were instructions Hamza took to heart given what had befallen his colleagues. "I followed the rules to the letter."[27] Accounts such as Hamza's reveal that the Mossad was successful in frightening the project's scientific staff, although, on balance, the assassinations accomplished little else.

The fact is, the Israeli intimidation campaign did not stop the Osirak program from proceeding, nor did it slow it significantly. Iraq's nuclear research program had progressed too far, and was far too important, to be brought down by a handful of murders; killings that, despite their technical sophistication, constituted a rather crude approach to the problematic situation that existed between the two nations and revealed the Israelis' mounting desperation. All the same, Yitzhak Hofi and the Mossad kept up the pressure, with many assuming it was the Israeli intelligence agency that next terrorized an Italian company, one that was cooperating with Iraq on the latter's nuclear program.[28]

The Italian target was SNIA Technit, a Rome-based firm that was constructing four laboratories at the Nuclear Research Center in al-Tuwaitha. The company's manager, Mario Fiorelli, lived in an opulent apartment in a picturesque neighborhood of Rome, Via della Lungaretta, and it was here on a summer evening in August of 1980 that a bomb shook his residence, without inflicting any injuries.[29] It was a warning whose gravity was underscored by another series of explosions at the same moment elsewhere in the city, specifically, at the headquarters of CNIA Technit itself. In this simultaneous attack, perpetrators detonated incendiary devices at the company's offices, severely damaging the edifice.

Reminiscent of Operation Big Lift at La Seyne-sur-Mer, France, an unheard-of organization claimed responsibility for the Rome strikes. Ingeniously depicting the unseen malefactor as a Middle Eastern group—the "Committee to Safeguard the Islamic Revolution"—the attack's true source had come up with a disguise that would deflect attention away from itself, while, at the same time, heightening tensions among Iraq and Iran's religious and political factions.[30]

As could be predicted, the ersatz organization was never heard from again. Equally predictable, the Mossad at no time acknowledged it was behind the bombings, even though the method was in line with its other Iraq-related campaigns during this period.

The motive was obvious. "[L]ike the attack on the Iraqi reactor cores in April 1979 and the murder of [al]-Meshad in June 1980, it was surely intended as a warning to the Iraqis," write political scientist Amos Perlmutter and his colleagues. "But this time the warning had a dual purpose."[31] This additional function centered on expanding the threat: not only could Iraqi, Egyptian, and French scientists and facilities expect to face continued attacks, but those in other nations, such as Italy, could now anticipate them as well if they collaborated on the Osirak program. And yet, as before, the Israelis' efforts to intimidate those involved in the Iraqi program were insufficient to hinder it, with the nuclear project progressing unabated as Prime Minister Begin continued watching from Jerusalem. The Israeli leader was not one to stand by indefinitely, however, as would soon become apparent when he made the fateful decision to eliminate the Osirak reactor altogether. A risky decision, it was consistent with his character, values, and personal history.

Menachem Begin, as noted in a previous chapter, had once headed up an extremist organization, the Irgun, during the period when the British Mandate was still in force in Palestine. And it was while he was the Irgun's leader that the group bombed the King David Hotel in Jerusalem, among other lethal acts. Like his comrades, he believed the time was long overdue for the British to depart from the region and he intended to make sure they did so, the defiant Zionist having no qualms about taking on what he regarded as a redoubtable adversary. "He fought with every weapon available against the British, who branded him as the preeminent terrorist in the region," writes President Jimmy Carter. "A man of personal courage and single-minded devotion to his goals, he took pride in being a 'fighting Jew.'"[32] But it was partly because of this same confrontational disposition that Begin's critics, decades later, considered him a risky head of state. They disparaged him for being, in their view, a driven, obstinate, and occasionally impetuous man.

This view was mitigated in 1979, when he and Anwar Sadat, the president of Egypt, signed the Camp David Accords, thereby formally ending hostilities between their nations. A historic event that brought the Nobel Peace Prize to both men, it also brought Israel a bonus, one that Begin would now put to use in his plot to annihilate the Osirak reactor.

In the spring of 1979, President Carter, in recognition of Israel's peace accord with Egypt, granted the Jewish state partial access to the United States' newest spy satellite, a technical marvel capable of producing richly-detailed earth images from hundreds of miles above the planet. Known as KH-11, it was the "supersecret, supersophisticated reconnaissance satellite" of the National Security Agency (NSA), writes Claire.[33] Circumnavigating the globe every hour and a half, it transmitted "high-resolution, digitally enhanced, real-time photographs so clear one could make out parked cars on the ground."[34] It was, by all accounts, the most advanced long-distance imagery in existence.

The arrangement with Israel called for the United States to send KH-11 photos to the Jewish state, but only those of the countries that bordered it— Lebanon, Egypt, Jordan, and Syria. Even then, not all images were to be sent. The United States would share those that Israel might need for its own protection; images, for instance, of an Arab neighbor's troop movements that implied an impending attack. A responsible procedure, one that did not imperil any Arab states, it was followed to the letter during Carter's remaining days in office.

In 1981, however, the United States began to flout the practice when Ronald Reagan became president and his former campaign manager, William Casey, the new director of the Central Intelligence Agency. "Mossad and the IDF had many friends deep within the agency," writes Claire, a situation that, coupled with the pro–Israel tenor of the Reagan administration, meant the CIA would soon be furnishing Israel with all manner of Middle Eastern surveillance data despite the official prohibitions against it.[35] Since Israel was surrounded by adversaries, the Reagan administration evidently considered it justifiable to hand over such highly classified materials. And there may have been another reason for the administration's ostensible generosity as well. "There was also the conviction that if Israel were refused intelligence, it would simply turn around and lobby supporters in Congress for the money to build its own satellite," writes Claire.[36] And so it was that the Mossad, along with the IDF and Menachem Begin himself, became privy to classified, state-of-the-art satellite imagery, most importantly high-resolution photographs of the Nuclear Research Center in al-Tuwaitha, Iraq.

The proscribed KH-11 images, which began arriving in Israel in 1981, supplemented the conventional intelligence the Mossad had been gathering and forwarding to Begin since his election four years earlier. The latter included "human intelligence" picked up from workers in France and Iraq, along with land-based photographs, meeting summaries, travel itineraries, shipping records, and so forth.

It was information that was actionable, and it became even more so when crowned by the new satellite imagery. Accordingly, the Mossad, by early 1981, was able to furnish Begin with the date that France was scheduled to deliver uranium to Iraq, as well as the point in time when the Osirak reactor was slated to go hot—July 1 of that year. And it was these two pieces of information that prompted the Israeli leader to set the date for the demolition of the nuclear reactor at al-Tuwaitha.

Regarding the timing, Begin insisted that the operation be conducted before the Osirak device became operational. His concern was that the reactor, if the Israeli military shelled it after it was already functioning, might contaminate the region. However, French experts subsequently reported that, given the nature of the Iraqi device, there would not have been such widespread radiation. The French report aside, Begin's argument ultimately led to an Israeli attack on the Osirak reactor merely three weeks before it was scheduled to be activated.

Certainly the road to obtaining official consent had not been an easy one for the strong-willed prime minister. Although he had long believed that Israel should destroy the device and, as noted earlier, had begun exploring strategies for a raid in 1979, his position had been met with equally strong resistance from within the Israeli government. It was in 1979, for instance, that Moshe Dayan, the influential Foreign Minister at the time, voiced his disapproval of a military strike in Iraq, and it was during the summer of 1980 that Defense Minister Ezer Weizman went even further: he expressed his opposition by tendering his resignation.

By the autumn of that year, Begin knew he lacked the support of key figures within his government. Standing against an airstrike on the Iraqi reactor was Yitzhak Hofi (Director of the Mossad), Yehoshua Saguy (Director of Military Intelligence), and Yigael Yadin, the Deputy Prime Minister, who threatened to relinquish his position over the issue. Among those outside the Begin administration who likewise opposed an attack were Shimon Peres (Labor Party leader) and Mordechai Gur, the former Chief of Staff of the Israeli Defense Forces and the man who had helped organize and execute Operation Entebbe a few years earlier. Their political and public repute was formidable and Begin did not discount their voices.

In terms of the small number of military and political figures who backed military action, they included Rafael ("Raful" or "Rafi") Eitan, who had replaced Gur as the head of the IDF and who was a former Mossad operative who had played a principal role in Operation Eichmann. Also siding with the prime minister was the new Foreign Minister, Yitzhak Shamir, along with Begin's longtime ally, Ariel Sharon, who was serving as Minister of Agriculture.

The arguments against the Osirak attack were numerous. Some opponents noted that an assault in Iraq, a sovereign nation, could be considered a violation of international law, as well as being an act of aggression that could pull Israel into an all-out confrontation with Iraq. Others were concerned that unilateral military action would alienate the United States, which supplied the Jewish state with weapons to be used exclusively for self-defense. It was a near certainty that the White House would not consider a preemptive strike on Iraqi property a justifiable use of U.S.-supplied weapons, but rather a straight-out defiance of this elemental feature of the two nations' contract. And the cabinet members were well aware of the potential consequences if Israel provoked its top ally in this way, especially in such a highly visible manner on the world stage. "If the United States were sufficiently angered by the attack to cut its political support and its billions of dollars per year in foreign aid to Israel," reads a RAND report, "the effects would be devastating, leaving Israel without any significant ally."[37] Along these same lines, Cabinet members warned that an assault could alienate European nations as well, France foremost among them, leaving the State of Israel even further cut off from the international community.

And there were additional concerns, such as the secondary fallout a military strike could have on the recently-signed Camp David Accords. Egypt and other Arab nations, for instance, might align in solidarity against the Jewish state. Even more chilling was the possibility that an unprovoked strike in Iraq would invite a retaliatory strike from nuclear-armed, non–Arab countries. "[Opponents] suggested that it might establish a norm that could encourage the Soviet Union to consider launching an attack against Israel's nuclear capabilities," says the RAND report, an attack aimed at Israel's own secret nuclear installation in the Negev Desert.[38] A nightmare scenario, it was one in which the Jewish state would be irradiated. Yet Prime Minister Begin, in the end, remained impervious to such arguments and proceeded with his plan, ordering the armed forces to begin preparing attack plans while he, still attempting to influence the raid's opponents, prepared to bring the matter to a vote.

Throughout the debate, Begin's position had been that Saddam Hussein was a scheming, headstrong leader who detested the concept of the Jewish state and would stop at nothing to obliterate it. Certainly it is true that Hussein, from Israel's inception, had adamantly refused to recognize its right to exist. Also illustrative, Iraq had never officially made peace with the Jewish state, unlike Israel's other adversaries in the region that had signed an armistice with it in 1949, the one that had brought to an end the First Arab-Israeli War. At least on paper, then, the two nations continued to exist in a condition of war, a state of affairs that Israel hoped might afford it a degree of legal protection from charges of violating the law by attacking the Iraqi reactor; arguably, the two countries were not in the peaceful state in which such a charge would apply. Now, however, the prime minister was not only pointing to Hussein as a longtime foe; he was stating *as fact* that the Iraqi leader was plotting to manufacture a nuclear weapon, and not in the ten years or so predicted by nuclear experts. "Begin went with the worst-case estimate of a bomb within one to two years," writes Joseph Cirincione of the Carnegie Endowment for International Peace.[39] Whether or not the Israeli leader truly believed a nuclear attack on Israel was imminent or was merely using such a horrific specter to scare the cabinet into voting for a military strike, his prediction was effective in instilling the fear of a second holocaust in a handful of cabinet members.

Yet there was more to Begin's argument than protecting the nation at the immediate moment. Dan McKinnon summarizes what were expected to be additional plusses for Israel. "Three things: (1) they would gain time by setting the Iraqi nuclear program back at least three years; (2) they would send a clear message to their enemies that Israel's military capability is undiminished; and (3) they would send an indirect warning to foreign sources of nuclear technology such as France and Italy to stop supplying the Arabs."[40]

More fundamentally, the obliteration of the Osirak reactor would serve notice to all Middle Eastern nations to refrain from pursuing nuclear technology in general. In this way, Israel would remain the only country in the region that could, like Western nations, conduct nuclear research and benefit from the domestic uses of nuclear energy. This interpretation of Israel's motives is one that several commentators have forwarded, since it was largely known at the time that the Osirak and Isis devices were incapable of producing weapons. "The only logical inducement for Israel to bomb [the] reactors," writes physicist Imad Khadduri, "would have been to prevent Iraq from obtaining scientific and technological nuclear expertise, but not nuclear weapons."[41] That said, destroying Iraq's non-military nuclear research program would also help to ensure that Hussein and his scientists would not be in a position to someday upgrade their program so that it would, in fact, be capable of producing weapons of mass destruction. Thus, by making sure no other countries in the Middle East, including Iraq, had access to nuclear technology of any sort, Israel would remain the most technologically-advanced nation in the region. As well, it could take comfort in its ability to continue defending itself, while preserving its status as one of the most powerful nations in the world.

Lastly, domestic politics may have been at play in Begin's decision to stage an attack. It seems that he was up for re-election in less than a year and was performing poorly in the polls; the lion's share of observers was convinced that he and his party would not receive the votes necessary to remain in power. Ostensibly, it was partly because of the prime minister's concern over his shaky political future that he sought to launch an offensive in Iraq. "A successful strike could sway voters to view Begin as a decisive man of action," writes Peter Ford, "willing to buck world opinion to protect Israel."[42] It was surely a gamble, but the Israeli leader seems to have carefully weighed the consequences, both for his nation and for his own political life, before making his decision. "The domestic political payoffs for Begin offered significant rewards compared to the risks."[43]

With even greater certainty it is known that the prime minister was aware that if he did, in fact, lose the election, it would be to Shimon Peres. And this troubled Begin because Peres was expected to continue pursuing a non-military approach to the Osirak issue, working closely with his contacts in the French government to alter that nation's uranium agreement with Iraq. Accordingly, Begin evidently felt it imperative that the assault be carried out before the next election in the event that he lost to Peres.[44]

In due course, and after a considerable struggle, the tenacious prime minister did receive the cabinet's authorization for the destruction of the Iraqi device. But whereas he initially vowed that Israel would not carry out the offensive without the unanimous support of the cabinet, he settled for the 10–6 vote the measure managed to receive during a special session in October, 1980. The actual date remains unknown because it was held secretly. What is known is that the military now went into high gear.

Operation Opera

"Immediately following the secret October 1980 cabinet meeting," writes McKinnon, "Israeli Defense Forces Commander Raphael ('Raful') Eitan quickly ordered the air force to begin preparations and training for the maximum range low-level bombing attack against Iraq."[45] At Eitan's side was his colleague Yitzhak Hofi, whose agency, the Mossad, was still gathering information, including blueprints of the structures comprising the al-Tuwaitha facility. These documents, along with related materials, would help the planning team orchestrate the attack.

When devising the bomb impact plot—in effect, the target zone—the team decided to restrict the airstrike to the domed containment building of the Osirak reactor rather than shelling the entire al-Tuwaitha complex. Since the containment structure housed the reactor, which was the crux of the matter, the strategists thought it advisable to concentrate the entire payload on this one edifice. Furthermore, because the building was three stories tall and made of concrete, they tentatively decided to use explosives that each weighed two thousand pounds. The planners assumed the American-made, unguided weapons, known as Mark-84 (M-84) bombs, would be sufficient to breach the domed structure. Also an advantage, this particular weapon, which is classified as a "dumb" bomb, does not contain complex guidance components like a "smart" bomb. Instead, it is released above the target—gravity does the rest—

the result being that it would make the demanding mission a little easier for the pilots.[46]

But assumptions about the M-84s' effectiveness, regardless of how well-founded they might have been, were not enough; the operation was far too important to rely on speculation. To ensure that the bombs would indeed be up to the task, the Israelis decided to approach the most knowledgeable source on the subject, the U.S. military. Unfortunately for the Jewish state, however, the American administration, as of December, 1980, still had a very different assessment of the Osirak device. "[W]hereas Israel affirmed outright that Iraq planned to manufacture nuclear weapons, the Americans denied that the evidence was irrefutable," says Shlomo Nakdimon.[47] Because the White House would undoubtedly oppose the airstrike, Israeli planners decided to trick their Western ally into furnishing it with the information they desired.

With this aim in mind, Israeli Intelligence, in conjunction with the IDF, recruited a pair of nuclear experts from the Israeli Institute of Technology and dispatched them to the Nuclear Regulatory Commission (NRC) in Washington, D.C. According to Rodger Claire, the Israeli scientists, pretending to speak for the Israel Electric Corporation, claimed that their firm was considering the purchase of an American-made reactor and they needed to know, among other things, whether it could withstand a terrorist attack; specifically, whether it could survive the impact of an M-84 bomb.[48] In response, the Americans disclosed that although a nuclear research reactor with a concrete containment structure was durable, it was not invincible and could not, in fact, bear a direct hit by such an explosive. And with this information in hand, the two Israelis returned home, reassured that their military's plan was feasible and could therefore proceed. Regarding its designation, the mission was now given its name—Operation Opera—although it has come to be known by other terms as well, among them Operation Babylon, Operation Sphinx, and Operation Hatakh Moshem.

In Israel, Begin, upon receiving the heartening information from the hoodwinked Americans, hoped to launch the offensive the following month—November 1980—but, as the moment neared, it was scrapped because of unfavorable weather conditions in Iraq. Another factor centered on the Israeli Air Force, which had not had sufficient time to fully conceptualize and organize Operation Opera, an audacious undertaking that would mark the military's farthermost airstrike outside of the State of Israel. The fact is, the distance from the Israeli airbase to the Iraqi nuclear complex was six hundred miles and would entail a three-hour roundtrip flight. Considering that the Israeli Air Force normally conducted its training exercises within its own borders—the Jewish state is approximately two hundred nautical miles in length and forty-five nautical miles in width, or the size of Massachusetts—neither the airmen nor their planes were equipped to conduct a bombing mission as far away as Iraq.[49] The airmen would need further training to increase their airtime endurance, essentially tripling it, while a method of refueling the F-16s would need to be assessed and approved. Thus, more preparation would be necessary.

"Decisions now had to be made," explains McKinnon, determinations that would include "how to plan the attack, the types of weapons to be used, procedures, implementation of intelligence, navigation courses to avoid detection, time of day, best angles of attack to destroy the reactor, how many planes to use to ensure destruction and hundreds of other details."[50] Much of this was accomplished in record time by Military Intelligence. "The air force's own intelligence unit focused on the best route to fly," write Raviv and Melman, "what load of munitions would be required for maximum effective destruction, how best to avoid detection by friendly or enemy radars along the way, and what resistance the pilots might meet from Iraqi air defenses."[51]

Because the operation was not a matter of releasing M-84s across the sprawling al-Tuwaitha compound but rather zeroing in on the containment structure itself, strategists turned to the blueprints the Mossad had pinched. "Physicists and other scientists studied them to determine precisely the best location to drop the bombs to render the reactor useless," writes McKinnon, a former fighter pilot.[52] By establishing the point of impact that would obliterate the Osirak device, the air force could better train its pilots in the maneuvers needed to accomplish the task. And this is precisely what transpired during the countless hours the airmen now spent priming for the offensive.

"They practiced 30- to 45-degree dive angles and artfully reduced required tracking time from five to three seconds," says McKinnon.[53] These exercises took place at a non-nuclear installation in the Negev Desert, one that contained a radome—a radar enclosure—that resembled the Osirak containment structure. "It realistically portrayed the reactor dome," the one-time airman adds.[54] Because military leaders were concerned that the pilots might figure out that the mission would involve targeting the Iraqi nuclear device—the shape of the radome threatened to give away the secret—officials led them into believing they would be shelling a different type of site. It was imperative that Operation Opera remain secret, even from those executing it, until the last moment.

As could be expected, the airmen also spent considerable time practicing defensive maneuvers, since an Iraqi counterattack was a distinct possibility and one that would be especially thorny for them. "[O]ver Osirak, the pilots would not have enough fuel to engage in a dogfight and then expect to make the return trip home," writes Claire. "A quick evasion was their only hope of completing the mission and returning to base."[55] Thus, the airmen, to increase their odds, took turns playing Israeli fighter pilots in F16s and Iraqi fighter pilots in F15s, the latter aircraft "standing in for the Iraqi MiGs," in order to hone their evasion skills.[56] Unfortunately, the exercises turned out to be nearly as hazardous as the mission itself. "While in training, two of the twelve pilots collided in mid-air and died," writes Gary Solis. "A third pilot died in another training mishap."[57]

While the air drills proceeded, the operation's planners pored over images of Jordanian, Saudi, and Iraqi terrain, their aim being to anticipate any problems that might arise over the regions the pilots would be traversing at low altitudes. Like other elements of Operation Opera, this was partly the responsibility of tacticians from the intelligence community. And, as usual, they were successful. "Israeli intelligence located and charted electricity and communication cables in several enemy countries," write Raviv and Melman, "and that mission alone involved putting spies at risk, in every sense behind the lines."[58]

With the Israeli Air Force, Military Intelligence, and the Mossad continuing to make preparations for Operation Opera, Menachem Begin and his advisors set about selecting dates for the attack, then changed them. As had been the case in November, 1980, such switches were most often because of weather conditions, which were variable across the four nations to be traversed in the course of the raid. It would not be until the spring of 1981, in fact, that Begin and his closest associates would arrive at a firm start-date for the operation: May 10, the date of the presidential election in France.

As it stood, the election promised to be historic, one in which François Mitterrand, the socialist candidate who was antagonistic toward Saddam Hussein and his nuclear program, was expected to be victorious. And perhaps Prime Minister Begin sought to green-light the airstrike at precisely this moment due to a concern that the Israeli cabinet might be less inclined to continue supporting Operation Opera once Mitterrand won the election. Certainly it was widely anticipated that the environmentally-conscious Mitterrand, if he became the new French leader, would demand firmer assurances from Iraq about the uses of the Osirak reactor; furthermore, that he would prohibit French companies from supplying weapons-grade uranium to Iraq but rather insist on exporting the "caramel" substitute. Whatever the case, it is known that Mitterrand did become his nation's next president but that Begin did not proceed with the attack because he was thrown off balance by a development within Israel itself.

It seems that a nuclear scientist who had once worked at Israel's secret nuclear weapons installation in the Negev Desert leaked the upcoming date of the Osirak assault to Shimon Peres. In turn, Peres penned an urgent letter to Begin on May 9, the day before the scheduled attack and the French election. In it, he implored the prime minister to wait until after the election results had been announced before ultimately deciding to proceed, since Mitterrand was expected to be a moderating factor in the Iraqi situation. And Begin acquiesced. But to ensure that no one, including Peres himself, would be tipped off in such a way again, the prime minister now restricted those who would determine the timing of the attack to himself and a trio of like-minded colleagues, specifically Agriculture Minister Sharon, Foreign Minister Shamir, and IDF Chief of Staff Eitan. These four men, all of whom had been in favor of an attack from the start, would select the new date of the airstrike, with no other person in the government or the intelligence community contributing to the process or being privy to the date. They decided, moreover, that Operation Opera would transpire a month later, on June 7, 1981.

"A Sunday was the selected day for the attack, the assumption being that the European experts would not be working then," says McKinnon.[59] Evidently, it was such a basic assumption that no one thought to confirm it—"a goof by Israeli intelligence."[60] The fact is, everyone, including the Europeans at the plant, worked Sundays; it was Fridays, the Muslim Sabbath, that employees were granted a day of rest. To be sure, it was a slip-up that could cost lives at the al-Tuwaitha complex. But whereas the day of the week held genuine importance since it was directly related to the number of endangered personnel at the compound, the overall timing of the assault itself had little relevance for Israel's safety. Despite the way in which Prime Minister Begin portrayed the situation, today it is generally agreed that the raid was not, in fact, an urgent matter.

"[T]he attack was not made with Israel's back against the wall, at the eleventh hour," writes Joshua Kirschenbaum in the *Journal of Strategic Security*. "It is more accurate to say that Israeli decision-makers chose the strategic time and opportunity that they believed ideal, for reasons that have yet to be fully clarified."[61] Most other experts have drawn the same conclusion over the years.

Be that as it may, top military and intelligence officials, still in the dark about the scheduled date of the attack, periodically updated the prime minister on the status of the preparations, and by early June all of the elements were in place. The Israelis now possessed comprehensive information about the al-Tuwaitha nuclear facility. They knew the details of its seventy-odd structures, including the buildings that housed its researchers in the fields of geology, chemistry, physics, and agriculture. They were also knowledgeable about its isotope production laboratories and administrative offices, as well as the quarters of the Iraqi Atomic Energy Commission. And they were aware of the specifications of its energy substations, cooling towers, training facilities, machine shops, and, of course, the Osiris and Isis research reactors and their containment structures.

The pilots were likewise ready. Primed for the three-hour mission, they had extended their airtime endurance, fine-tuned their shelling of the mock reactor, and perfected their evasion skills. They were also prepared to make their way back to Israel in case they were forced to touch down in hostile territory. It was a strategy that Hofi's intelligence agency had helped to concoct, one that involved large sums of cash. "The pilots had, in their gear, Iraqi money provided by the Mossad," write Raviv and Melman, "just in case they had to bail out and somehow buy their way to freedom."[62]

Then, too, the planes were ready. Due to the distance involved, ground crews had fitted them with external fuel tanks, thereby solving the refueling problem. As to the composition of the squadron, it would consist of eight F-16 fighter-bombers and a half-dozen F-15s. The scheme was for the F-16s to carry out the airstrike, accompanied by four of the F-15s. The latter's job would be to intercept any enemy aircraft that might be encountered. The remaining two F-15s would travel to other areas near the target, but for other purposes.

The Osirak Attack. It was on Friday, June 5, 1981, that Begin ordered those who were to serve in Operation Opera to assemble at the Etzion Air Base in the Israeli-occupied Sinai Desert. To guard the mission's secrecy, authorities maximized security measures, even going so far as to block nearly all incoming and outgoing communications. "Telephone lines from the base, except for a few for official use, were cut off," writes John Correll.[63] As per orders from the top, the pilots would remain at this location for the ensuing forty-eight hours, as would Rafi Eitan and David Ivri. Although the latter two high-ranking officials would not be heading to Iraq themselves, they wanted to be on hand as a show of support for the men who would be carrying out the assault. The pair had hand-picked all of the pilots for the unprecedented operation, which, as noted earlier, would be the most distant airstrike Israeli had ever conducted. It was also expected to be among the most treacherous. "No-one thought that all eight F-16s would return, no-one," says the mission's commander, Colonel Zeev Raz.[64]

By the time Sunday, June 7, rolled around, the pilots, officials, and ground crews at Etzion Air Base were becoming restless. They yearned for the operation to commence. But it would not begin in the early morning hours, as many expected, but rather in the afternoon, the plan being for the aircraft to arrive at the al-Tuwaitha complex near sunset. This is because the planes would be less visible with the sunlight directly behind them. Then, too, the Mossad had informed Israeli planners of the Iraqi facility's dinner hours, so they could schedule the attack for a time of day when few non–European workers would be present; the European staff, as noted, was not expected to be on-site at all on a Sunday. And so, at midday, the pilots were fully briefed, learning the nature and details of the mission as well as the contingency plans for unforeseen developments. "After the brief," says Peter Ford, "the pilots stepped to their aircraft."[65]

It was from the desert airbase that the planes left the runway at approximately three o'clock in the afternoon. Some of the pilots worried that their air-

10. Mission: Operation Opera

craft might have difficulty becoming airborne owing to the weight of the extra fuel tanks and heavy munitions, but no problems were incurred. Within minutes the fighter-bombers were speeding eastward toward the Red Sea, while the mission's status was being relayed to Jerusalem.

"Immediately, Begin had his secretary contact all Cabinet members and request them to come to his home at 4 p.m.," writes McKinnon. "Each member thought he was going to have an exclusive session with the prime minister."[66] They had no way of knowing the entire body would be gathering at Begin's residence to monitor a military strike in real-time.

Moments later, the squadron flew over the Red Sea, then entered Jordanian airspace over the Gulf of Aqaba, where, as it happened, King Hussein was unwinding on his yacht. Catching sight of the tight formation of fighter jets, the monarch suspected what was occurring and contacted Iraqi officials, although a subsequent breakdown in communication among the Iraqis meant that his warning would never be received at the Republican Palace in Baghdad.

The squadron next changed direction, heading northeastward across Jordan and Saudi Arabia at a speed of approximately four hundred miles an hour and an altitude of one hundred feet. The planes, in effect, were hugging the ground to avoid radar detection. Ninety minutes later, as the squadron approached the Iraqi border, the F-16s broke into two formations. Above each formation soared a pair of F-15s, the interceptors, while the remaining pair separated from the group and traveled to areas near al-Tuwaitha to check for Iraqi radar. In case of a counterattack on the F-16 formations, these remaining two jets would cease scanning for radar and set about serving as interceptors as well.

Throughout the flight, silence was the rule. "No radio calls or radar emissions, which could tip enemy outposts to the coming attack, came from the formation of F-15s and 5–16s," writes Ford.[67] The only time the silence was broken occurred when the lead pilot came to a pre-determined coordinate—the 38 longitude—where he uttered a single word into his transmitter.[68] So short that Arab forces would be unable to identify and track it, the utterance—the word *Charlie*—was a signal to the Israeli Air Force that the squadron was nearing Iraq's western border.[69] This meant the mission was on track and the airstrike, imminent, information that was promptly conveyed to Prime Minister Begin and the cabinet members waiting anxiously at his home.

As the formations crossed into Iraq, radio silence resumed and continued as the fighter-bombers continued moving eastward over the desert. At this juncture, some of the pilots jettisoned the supplemental fuel tanks that had been affixed to the wings of their aircraft since the containers were no longer needed. By decreasing the weight of the jets, this action increased their maneuverability.

Forty-five minutes later, the airmen spotted the al-Tuwaitha nuclear facility. As they approached the domed containment structure of the Osirak reactor, they aligned their F-16s and dropped sixteen Mark–84 bombs on it. The weapons' mass, according to Ford, exceeded fourteen metric tons.[70] And nearly all of the bombs were direct hits. "The accuracy of the bombing, considering the fact the IAF used no smart bombs, was astonishing," write Perlmutter and his colleagues.[71]

The Iraqis had little time and military personnel for a significant counterattack, with comparatively few gunners on the ground. Those who did fire failed to strike any of the Israeli aircraft.

"The surprise of the raid was total," says McKinnon. "In two minutes over Baghdad, Israeli warplanes in the surgical strike had reduced Iraq's technological centerpiece to rubble."[72] As the Israelis had hoped, the building in which the uranium was stored, which was near the target, remained unscathed, while casualties on the ground were relatively low given that it was a workday. In all, eleven people perished, among them ten Iraqi soldiers and a French civilian, Damien Chaussepied, a technician in his mid-twenties who worked for France's atomic energy agency.[73] As for the Israeli airmen, they were in fine spirits, not in the least because they had accomplished their objective. "The dome of the Osirak plant looked like a giant broken egg shell."[74]

Ninety minutes later, all fourteen Israeli aircraft touched down at the Etzion Air Base on the Sinai Peninsula, the mission having been completed with no loss of life or injury to the fighter pilots who had conducted it. It was, by any standard, a dazzling triumph. The air campaign was so remarkable, in fact, that military strategists around the world, since that day, have held up Operation Opera as a masterpiece of planning and execution. A combined effort of Military Intelligence, the Mossad, the Israeli Air Force, and more broadly the Israeli Defense Forces and Menachem Begin and his small coterie of like-minded officials, it demonstrated, like Operation Entebbe five years earlier, what may be achieved when a country's intelligence and military communities work hand in hand to tackle a perceived threat to their nation and its people. But while the mission, from a strictly military perspective, was a spectacular triumph, Operation Opera, from political, legal, and ethical perspectives, proved to be deeply problematic for Israel.

Repercussions

The Israeli cabinet decided that news of the attack should not be released by Israel but should come from another country, preferably the United States, since this might buffer criticism of the Jewish state. President Reagan and his administration, however, blindsided by the airstrike as well as infuriated by it, refused to cooperate. For several months, the United States had worked hard to improve relations with Baghdad and the Israeli offensive threatened to upend the progress that had been made in these efforts.

Of course, the Americans' refusal to grant Begin's wish made matters a bit more difficult for the prime minister, who was proud of the attack and hoped to bask in its glory even if he thought it prudent that another source leak the news. "Begin was anxious to get the word out," writes McKinnon. "It's believed that ... he now wanted to make political hay out of the success."[75] For this reason, the Israeli leader was delighted the next day when a Jordanian official made a broad public statement about Iraq, one that presented an opportunity for Begin to step forward on Tuesday, June 9, and take credit for the assault.

During his triumphant address to the press and the public, the prime minister declared that the Israeli military had performed an unparalleled act of self-defense. According to the *Los Angeles Times*, Begin was adamant that the airstrike was justified because, he claimed, the Iraqis were preparing to use the Osirak reactor to produce three to five bombs similar to those dropped over Hiroshima, bombs they planned to release over Israel and kill an estimated six hundred thousand citizens.[76]

"We shall not allow any enemy to develop weapons of mass destruction against us," Begin proclaimed, scoffing at assertions that the Osirak reactor was neither designed nor intended to manufacture nuclear weapons.[77] He was, in effect, claiming that Israel had engaged in an act of anticipatory self-defense, meaning an attack on the State of Israel was real and forthcoming, as opposed to preemptive self-defense, which refers to a less concrete danger. "Preemptive self-defense has to do with a hypothetical, future threat while anticipatory self-defense has to do with an imminent threat," says Elli Louka. "States that wish to launch a unilateral attack, under the blessing of international law, in an open fashion have no other option but to couch such an attack in terms of self-defense," she adds.[78]

Begin's media statement represented his attempt to convince both the Jewish state and the international community that Israel's choice had been clear-cut: either demolish the Iraqi reactor or face certain annihilation. But it was also an informal policy statement and a warning to the region itself. "Publishing the doctrine was intended to dissuade Iraq, as well as other Arab countries that might consider emulating Baghdad, from attempting to develop a nuclear weapons capability," writes Shai Feldman, director of the Project on Security and Arms Control in the Middle East.[79]

Not surprisingly, Begin's speech was well-received in Israel. But while most of the nation's citizens embraced the prime minister's words—the population seemed to accept his claim that Iraq had been counting down the minutes until it nuked the Jewish state—other Israelis were skeptical of his assertions, along with the timing of the military operation itself. Begin's principal opponent in the upcoming election, for one, stated forthrightly his view of the airstrike's basis. "Shimon Peres, the [Labor Party's] candidate for prime minister, called the attack an 'election operation,'" writes Norman Kempster, one designed to give a boost to Begin's image as the protector of the Jewish people.[80] (If Peres was correct and it had been an "election operation," an allegation that is subject to debate given that Begin is known to have been determined to stop the Osirak project since 1979, then the mission produced the political payoff the prime minister had sought: Begin and his Likud Party won the election three weeks later, albeit by a one-seat margin.) But it was not only prominent Israelis, such as Shimon Peres, who were critical of the prime minister and the airstrike; official reaction to Operation Opera was uniformly negative outside of Israel as well. It was a rare moment of global consensus, with the outrage, excepting that of Iraq, erupting most intensely from Western governments.

"Israel took a verbal beating internationally," says McKinnon, the diminutive Middle Eastern nation being "blistered by world opinion."[81] France was the first to condemn the attack, followed by Great Britain, where Prime Minister Margaret Thatcher decried the raid as illegal, and the Soviet Union, which labeled it an "act of gangsterism."[82] As for the United States, it rejected outright Israel's justification for the offensive. "State Department spokesman Dean Fisher," reports the *Los Angeles Times*, "said the United States disagrees with Israel's claim that the facility posed a potential security threat."[83]

As could be expected, the raid's possible impact in the volatile Middle East was a major concern. It was for this reason that U.S. Secretary of State Alexander Haig branded the assault "reckless," while Jeanne Kirkpatrick, the American ambassador to the United Nations and previously a champion of the Jewish state, deemed it counterproductive.[84] "The means Israel chose to quiet its fears about the purposes of Iraq's nuclear program have hurt, not helped, the peace and security of the area," the ambassador stated.[85]

Among a host of concerns, the White House worried that those Arab states that had signed arms agreements with the United States—deals, like the one with Israel, that stipulated that American-supplied weapons could only be used for self-defense—might now cast aside their promises and launch unprovoked, unilateral attacks of their own. For this reason, the Reagan administration decided to take firm action against the Jewish state lest the United States be seen as indulging Israel in what amounted to an unabashed violation of the U.S. Arms Export Control Act.

For starters, the State Department released a formal statement castigating Israel for violating the weapons agreement. Second, the White House suspended arms shipments to Israel, most significantly the remaining F-16s that were part of an existent deal. Third, the CIA stopped supplying the Jewish state with KH-11 satellite photographs of those nations, like Iraq, that did not flank it, since the Mossad and Israeli Military Intelligence had misused such images in planning the assault. And fourth, the United States joined other members of the United Nations in collectively denouncing the attack.

The UN Security Council voted 15–0 to condemn what it termed "armed Israeli aggression," with the General Assembly following suit several weeks later.[86] To provide background and structure to the organization's judgment, designated Resolution 487, the UN began by pointing out that Israel, like Iraq, possessed nuclear facilities, but that Israel, unlike Iraq, refused to permit international teams to inspect them. After spotlighting the disparity between the two nations' cooperation with the IAEA's safeguards, the resolution stated that the global body "[s]trongly condemns Israel for its premeditated and unprecedented act of aggression in violation of the Charter of the United Nations and the norms of international conduct, which constitutes a new and dangerous escalation in the threat to international peace and security."[87] The punitive action that the UN recommended, however, that Israel compensate Iraq for the destruction of the Osirak reactor and the loss of human life, did not win approval because the United States blocked the measure. Thus, the U.S. ensured that its Middle Eastern ally would not have to pay hundreds of millions of dollars in reparations.

Like the United Nations, the International Atomic Energy Agency also castigated Israel. "Israel's attack on a nuclear reactor was the first such attack and was widely viewed as setting a dangerous precedent," writes Elli Louka, alluding to the IAEA's concerns.[88] Sigvard Eklund, head of the IAEA, stated that the Jewish state, by attacking the Osirak reactor, had essentially attacked the IAEA's global system of nuclear safeguards, thereby weakening them. As one of the features of its response, the organization suspended the provision of further technical assistance to Israel.[89] As had been the case throughout the progression of the Osirak program, the bureau of nuclear scientists also reiterated that the reactor could not have been used to produce nuclear weapons, that its uses would have been confined to scientific and domestic functions.

To look into this oft-repeated assertion, investigators were dispatched to al-Tuwaitha to study the aftermath of the airstrike, among them the eminent nuclear physicist Richard Wilson, chairman of the Department of Physics at Harvard University. At the facility, Wilson examined the various structures, including a hall the Israelis had suspected of being intended for nefarious purposes.

"As far as one can understand the garbled 'justification' for the air raid provided by the Israeli Government," the physicist writes in the scientific journal *Nature*, "it was believed that this hall was for plutonium production."[90] Wilson then proceeds to explain why the structure could not have been used in such a manner. As well, he confirms that nothing was uncovered at the al-Tuwaitha site suggesting that the Iraqis were using, or preparing to use, the Osirak device to manufacture a bomb. "The reactor was irrelevant to any ambition Iraq might have for making nuclear weapons," the physicist concluded based on his examination of the physical evidence at the Iraqi compound.[91] While it appears that the nuclear facility was indeed innocuous at the time of the Israeli raid, however, Iraq's ensuing nuclear program would be anything but benign.

"The raid on Osirak did not work out as Begin anticipated," writes Bennett Ramberg, a foreign policy analyst and former State Department official.[92] The airstrike did nothing to quell any interest Saddam Hussein may have had in producing a nuclear weapon. If anything, it had the opposite effect. "There is reason to believe that the attack may have actually increased Saddam's commitment to acquiring nuclear weapons, perhaps because it could have raised Saddam's estimation of the importance of acquiring nuclear weapons," writes political scientist Dan Reiter.[93] That is to say, the Israeli bombing may have convinced Hussein of the need to obtain nuclear arms in order to better protect his nation from a foreign military that had just demonstrated its willingness to launch an unprovoked assault on it. Alluding to this process is the American linguist and political commentator Noam Chomsky in his book, *Failed States*.[94] "Israel's bombing of Iraq's Osirak reactor in 1981, which appears to have initiated Saddam's nuclear weapons programs," Chomsky writes, is "another demonstration that violence tends to elicit violence."[95]

Certainly it is true that Saddam Hussein's nuclear ambitions redoubled following the Osirak attack. "[T]he program became secret, Saddam's personal and material commitment to the program grew, and the non-proliferation tools available to the international community became ineffective," says Reiter.[96] If Hussein had always harbored a desire to possess a nuclear arms program, as most analysts assume, he was now more determined than ever to turn his desire into a reality.

"[I]n September 1981, Saddam—smarting from the Osirak incident and reminded of Iraq's vulnerability to foreign attack—established a fast-paced, well-funded and clandestine nuclear weapons programme outside of the IAEA's purview," writes British journalist Mehdi Hasan.[97] Whereas the Iraqi nuclear program prior to the Osirak attack consisted of four hundred experts, this number now rocketed to seven thousand, just as the four hundred million dollars Iraq had earmarked for its nuclear project before the Israeli assault soared to ten billion dollars after it.[98]

Also at this pivotal moment as Iraq's nascent nuclear weapons program was coming into existence, Hussein and his associates set out to ensure that their nation's new nuclear facilities would not be exposed to foreign aggressors, the Israeli attack having taught them an important lesson in this regard. Receiving guidance from the Soviet Union's KGB, the Iraqis now learned how to conceal their nuclear sites as well as scatter them across the country to make it less likely an enemy could locate and destroy all of them. They also learned how to build structures that, if damaged, could be rapidly reconstructed.[99] And the result was a far more formidable nuclear program, one that would progress at an accelerated rate throughout the 1980s.

Yet while the net effect of Operation Opera was the unleashing of a far more fearsome threat to Israel, Prime Minister Begin and subsequent Israeli leaders have insisted that the 1981 airstrike was both necessary and effective. Rejecting the assertion that the Osirak reactor was designed for research and domestic purposes, they continue to allege that Hussein was preparing to use the device to construct nuclear weapons and that Israel put a stop to it. It is a mantra that has been repeated in the twenty-first century by a handful of American officials, among them former Vice President Dick Cheney, whose declaration in 2003 that Iraq was constructing weapons of mass destruction helped launch the Iraq War. It was also an allegation that proved to be unfounded. That same year, Cheney, in a televised interview on *Meet the Press*, discussed Israel's previous attack in Iraq, with the politician erroneously stating that because Israel "took out the Osirak reactor," the Jewish state had terminated Hussein's nuclear arms program at that time.[100] Portrayed as a preventive measure, this policy of direct intervention in the face of a sensed threat has become known as the "Begin Doctrine," and continues to be presented as a valid approach by those who advocate eliminating other nations' nuclear programs, or alleged programs, as a form of self-defense.[101]

No doubt, the debate over the rationale and effectiveness of the Osirak bombing will persist, as has been the case for the past three decades. But one thing is certain: neither indirect nor direct measures managed to squelch Hussein's nuclear ambitions. As noted by Bennett Ramberg, a nuclear arms expert who served in the U.S. State Department under President George H. W. Bush, the murder of Iraqi and Egyptian nuclear scientists and the destruction of the Osirak reactor core on France's southern coast did nothing to hamper Iraq's nuclear program, just as the intelligence-supported Operation Opera proved to be counterproductive.[102]

As for the effectiveness of the Mossad's three-year involvement in the Osirak affair, the agency was successful in its circumscribed role, one that was defined by the highest level of the Israeli government and, as we have seen, entailed sabotage, assassination, and the acquisition of classified Iraqi, French, and American materials. The Mossad did what was required of it, and it did its job well; this, despite the fact that the agency's director, Yitzhak Hofi, disagreed with certain aspects of Israel's approach, most of all the military attack in Iraq. Likewise, the head of Military Intelligence, Yehoshua Saguy, made sure his organization performed its role diligently in helping prepare the Israeli Defense Forces for Operation Opera even as he registered his opposition to the bombing mission itself, his argument being that its consequences threatened to be detrimental to the Jewish state. And, of course, the intrepid pilots of the Israeli Air Force who conducted the airstrike, whatever their personal opinions about it may have been, achieved an objective that, against all odds, cost no Israeli lives. Thus, the Jewish state's multifaceted approach to the Osirak affair was carried out brilliantly by those whose role it was to implement its covert and overt components, their misgivings notwithstanding. The problem, in the final analysis, was the Israeli approach itself, one based on an interpretation, or misinterpretation, of Iraq's nuclear program by Menachem Begin and his administration, culminating in a choice of responses that ultimately fast-tracked Saddam Hussein's nuclear arms program. It was an approach that rightly remains the subject of considerable debate.

Part Five

Operation Plumbat and the Vanunu Affair

Introduction

During the latter half of the twentieth century, a clique at the top tier of the Israeli government decided that the diminutive nation should acquire nuclear weapons, a development that would render the country the most powerful military force in the region. There was, however, an obstacle. It seems the international community was striving to prevent the introduction of weapons of mass destruction into the Middle East, and the constituent nations, Israel among them, had pledged they would not be the first to bring such arms into the region. The question facing the Israeli leadership, then, was how to break its promise yet avoid the wrath of the global community. And the answer, the clique decided, was for the Jewish state to keep its planned multimillion-dollar nuclear weapons program under wraps, a far-reaching, long-term task that would require remarkable secrecy and subterfuge. As could be expected, it would also require the services of the Mossad in order to help ensure that the undeclared project made headway while remaining hidden from the world.

As it turned out, it was an obligation that would lead the intelligence agency to commit crimes at the international level, certainly not for the first time, with its offenses, more often than not, consisting of smuggling forbidden items into the State of Israel. In some cases, such as during a chancy mission on the high seas, it would entail re-routing yellowcake uranium from Belgium to Israel for use in the nation's principal nuclear reactor. In another case, it would involve seducing and seizing a fellow citizen who was traveling in England—a nuclear whistleblower—and spiriting him back to the Jewish state to face secret legal proceedings. During these and other covert operations related to Israel's nuclearization, the Mossad infringed the laws of European nations, yet it managed to avoid getting caught in the act. And although it suffered no negative fallout when its illegal deeds did eventually come to light, Israel itself sustained damage to its reputation on several fronts.

For our purposes—the exploration of the intelligence organization's evolution—the ensuing chapters will illustrate how the Mossad's deeds vis-à-vis Israel's nuclear arms program were the product of the agency's considerable ingenuity and a not inconsiderable degree of amorality.

11

Israel's Secret Nuclear Weapons Program

Shortly after the Jewish state was born, Prime Minister David Ben-Gurion set his sights on nuclear technology, an aim he hoped would eventually include the creation of nuclear weapons. Whereas many of his colleagues had become complacent after Israel's victory over its Arab foes in 1949, Ben-Gurion remained unconvinced of his nation's long-term security and looked fretfully toward the day when its enemies would return. As a sixty-two-year-old Zionist who had spent nearly a half-century in the Middle East, he did not trust the relative calm that prevailed after the First Arab-Israeli War. "His diaries, speeches, and extensive correspondence reflect his obsessive fear of the Arab world," writes Zaki Shalom in the book, *Israel's Nuclear Option*. "[T]he Arab world, he believed, would build on its experience, improve its abilities, force Israel to face greater threats, and perhaps even endanger its very existence."[1] By having a nuclear arsenal at its disposal, however, Ben-Gurion believed Israel would be in the optimal position to defend itself in case one or more of its Arab adversaries were to launch an attack against it.[2]

Another concern of the prime minister, and one that, like the security issue, dates back to the inception of the Jewish state, was the fact that only twenty percent of Israel's land was arable. To be suitable for farming, the bulk of the terrain, which encompassed vast stretches of the Negev Desert, would need a continuous supply of water. Such an immense irrigation system would, however, require a considerable amount of energy to operate, and this was a potential setback that caused Ben-Gurion to turn his attention once again to atomic energy. "A nuclear reactor, combined with a desalination plant, would be the source of a regular flow of water which could turn the sand of the Negev Desert into fields to feed Israel's rapidly growing population," write Tom Gilling and John McKnight.[3] Fortunately for the prime minister, two unforeseen developments would help bring his nuclear dreams into existence.

In the early 1950s, the Israeli government commissioned a series of studies of the Negev Desert in the course of which geologists uncovered extensive phosphate deposits. It was a heartening discovery, since uranium can be extracted from phosphate, converted into metal, and transformed into fuel components for use in a nuclear reactor. Uranium, then, would not comprise a barrier to Israel achieving its nuclear ambitions, at least not initially. Then, in 1953, another promising development came about when U.S. President Dwight D. Eisenhower delivered a speech titled "Atoms for Peace" before the UN General Assembly and again in 1955 at the Geneva Conference.

In his address, the American president acquainted world leaders with a forthcoming program, a U.S.–based initiative designed to reduce international fears of atomic energy and promote its peaceful uses. Through the Arms for Peace project, the United States would share its nuclear technology with research centers and medical facilities around the globe, while also furnishing educational materials to schools and other institutions. It was, to be sure, a potential boon for Ben-Gurion and his colleagues who yearned for Israel to possess nuclear energy, most notably scientist Ernst David Bergmann and Defense Minister Shimon Peres, the two men to whom the prime minister had entrusted the nation's nuclear future. Accordingly, the Jewish state became one of the first countries in the world to sign an Atoms for Peace agreement with the American government, the date being July 12, 1955.

The following year, construction began on a small, five-megawatt device in what would be Israel's first reactor. As mandated by its contract with the United States, Israel consented to the device's periodic inspection by teams from the U.S. and the International Atomic Energy Agency (IAEA). Regarding its location, Nahal Soreq was chosen as the site, a town nestled in the Judean Hills twenty-five miles west of Jerusalem. In the Old Testament narrative, it was in Nahal Soreq that Samson encountered Delilah, who proceeded to deceive him.

As it happened, deception would be a defining feature of the Israeli nuclear program as well. While working honorably with the American government on the Nahal Soreq endeavor and ensuring the reactor's use for peaceful purposes, including agricultural applications, Peres, behind closed doors, persuaded Ben-Gurion to fund a shadow site that would house a much grander reactor to be used for manufacturing nuclear weapons.[4] The scheme was for the low-wattage device at Nahal Soreq to serve as a decoy, diverting attention away from the more expansive compound to be located seventy miles away in Dimona, a remote settlement in the Negev Desert.

Establishing the secret nuclear arms operation would not be a slam dunk, however. "Most senior members of the ruling Mapai (Israel Workers') Party viewed an Israeli bomb as suicidal, too expensive, and too reminiscent of the horrors that had been inflicted on the Jews in World War II," writes Seymour Hersh, the Pulitzer Prize-winning investigative journalist.[5] And such high-level political figures were not alone in their opposition. "Prominent Israeli scientists ... argued that the cost of building the big Dimona reactor, in addition to the small Soreq reactor, was prohibitive for Israel," says Avner Cohen of the James Martin Center for Nonproliferation Studies. "Others worried about the difficulties of keeping the project secret for an extended period."[6] The result: Peres and his cohorts distanced these opponents from the clandestine venture, while hand-picking a crew of like-minded administrators and young scientists to implement the program and keep it hidden from the world. The quandary that remained was how to conceal the project's true purpose while, at the same time, acknowledging the reactor's existence so the operation could receive the outside support it needed. As things stood, the Jewish state was not in a position to craft a nuclear arsenal entirely on its own. And France, it turned out, would be the key.

Already the two nations enjoyed a healthy business relationship. A mutually beneficial arrangement, France supplied Israel with military products while Israel reciprocated with intelligence on Algeria, a nation with which France was warring as the North African sought to break free from colonial rule. Then, too, there was another, more personal reason for France's desire to work productively with Israel: among the French leadership were those who deeply regretted their country's actions toward its Jewish citizens during the Holocaust and hoped to make amends by helping the Jewish people acquire the ability to protect themselves from future assaults.[7]

Israel's purchases of weapons from France thus far had consisted of traditional arms; this, despite the fact that the latter was fast becoming recognized as a leader in nuclear technology. This meant that Shimon Peres, in his talks with the French, would have to shift the conversation from conventional arms sales to nuclear energy, a change of topic he would need to execute with the utmost finesse if he were to avoid raising suspicions about Israel's ultimate intentions. "He looked for the political opening that would allow the extension of the Franco-Israeli alliance in the nuclear field," explains Cohen.[8] It would be during the Suez crisis and the resultant Second Arab-Israeli War of 1956 that the defense minister would find such an entrée.

It was at this juncture that Egypt, left stranded by the United States and Britain when the two nations backed out of a deal to finance the erection of the Aswan Dam, nationalized the Suez Canal as a means of paying for the impending project. Egypt's bold deed, in turn, prompted Israel, France, and Britain to engage in battle with the Arab state over the vital waterway. The United States, meanwhile, not only refused to become enmeshed in the conflict but, along with its rival, the USSR, publicly castigated the warring nations. With the Cold War in full swing at the time, the two superpowers worried that the Middle Eastern conflict might escalate into an international showdown between East and West. And for Shimon Peres, the American response provided the pretext he had been seeking, his argument being that the United States had turned its back on the Jewish state during a critical period. Days later, the strident defense minister touched down in Paris to convene with French leaders, where he managed to convert the Middle Eastern quarrel and America's reaction to it into a coup for Israel: the French government agreed to help the Jewish state craft a nuclear program.

"He deftly manipulated the anti–Arab sentiment of the Suez era and the pro–Jewish sentiment of a decade after Vichy," writes journalist and former IDF paratrooper Ari Shavit. "The option Peres received was all-inclusive, providing engineers, technicians, know-how, and training."[9] Shavit continues,

> According to international publications, it comprised a nuclear reactor, a facility for separating plutonium, and missile capabilities. Ben-Gurion's vision, Peres's cunning, and the diligent work of a few other Israelis who joined Peres in Paris convinced France to place in Israel's hands the modern age's Prometheus' fire. For the first time in history, the Jews could have the ability to annihilate other peoples.[10]

Israel inked the deal with France in the autumn of 1957, with the arrangement including the construction of a G1 (graphite) nuclear reactor together with a plant for the extraction of plutonium. The twenty-four-megawatt reactor and separation facility would be a state secret, of course, as would Israel's illicit purchase of "heavy water" from Norway and France in the years that followed. The Israelis were particularly keen to keep the Dimona complex hidden from American eyes, its Western ally being fiercely opposed to the introduction of nuclear arms into the unstable Middle East. But the United States could not be deceived for very long owing to its on-the-ground spies—CIA operatives—coupled with the advent of the U-2 spy plane, the high-altitude reconnaissance aircraft that debuted in 1955 and was used by the Central Intelligence Agency and the U.S. Air Force to surreptitiously observe military activities around the globe.

Shortly after the U-2's inauguration, the United States began sending it on overflights of Israel, which proved to be an alarming development for the Jewish state once it realized the construction of its nuclear arms facility was under surveillance. Into the 1960s, American pilots continued monitoring Israel's progress on the Dimona compound, but they were able to detect only those features that were visible on the desert's surface. Even so, it was obvious that Israel was fabricating a nuclear installation in the Negev Desert, with the containment dome, if nothing else, being a dead giveaway. All the same, the Israelis insisted they were building a textile plant, not a reactor, with this fiction proving increasingly difficult to maintain when, a few months later, an anonymous source revealed the secret project.

During the winter of 1960 a leak to the press culminated in a series of exposés in the world media, incriminatory reports describing Israel's elaborate venture in the remote, arid region, and suggesting that it was to be a center for creating weapons of mass destruction. "Most estimates attributed the leak to American officials who wanted to create a negative and hostile international reaction to Israel's nuclear activity," writes Shalom. "An inimical atmosphere, the American administration believed, would assuredly intensify Israel's isolation in the international arena and prepare the way for massive pressure on Jerusalem to abolish its 'Dimona Project.'"[11] The immediate result of the disclosure was that Israel finally admitted to the United States that it was indeed building a nuclear complex in the desert, but it contended that it was for "research and development in industry, agriculture, and medicine" and that scientific teams from allied nations would be invited to visit the compound once it was completed.[12] Because Israel had placed what it claimed would be a benign research facility in such an isolated, barren region of the country, however, and because it had done so with inordinate secrecy, the United States did not accept the Jewish state's assertion of innocence. If the Dimona project were truly innocuous, there would have been no need for such highly-crafted measures to conceal its existence. Accordingly, the CIA upgraded its surveillance abilities in 1961 by assembling an advanced unit to analyze the U-2 spy plane's images, then ordered a fresh set of Dimona aerial photos. Yet revelations about the facility were still not forthcoming despite the transformed, state-of-the-art unit. "[T]he new set of photographs did little to move the basic issue," explains Hersh. "[T]here was no way to see underground in Dimona."[13] Exasperated, the White House decided that a face-to-face meeting was in order.

"Informed by the CIA that Israel was about to become a nuclear power, President Kennedy sent the U.S. Ambassador, Ogden Reid, to confront the Israeli Government over the issue," write Gilling and McKnight.[14] But the figures with whom Reid met, specifically David Ben-Gurion and Foreign Minister Golda Meir, were not obliging, the pair allowing a U.S.-imposed deadline to expire that would have required them to confirm that their nation was not on the path to nuclearization. They also refused to yield to Reid's call for a team of inspectors from the IAEA to examine the Dimona facility, this being the procedure with which other nuclear-energy nations were in compliance. It should be noted that France, a few years earlier, had likewise tried to persuade Israel to make public the Dimona project and permit external scrutiny of the compound's operations, but in the end shelved the matter because the Israeli administration would not seriously consider the recommendation. As for Reid's discussions with Ben-Gurion and Meir, he came away from them, like French officials before him, convinced that Israel had no intention of abiding by the standards established by the international community. Predictably, this state of affairs angered President Kennedy.

It would not be until 1962, one year before the Dimona reactor was scheduled to go online, that the Jewish state would at last consent to inspections.[15] Even this far along in its construction, however, Israel's leaders maintained that the device was to be used solely for peaceful purposes. As for the change of heart regarding inspections, the Jewish state, at this juncture, wished to purchase Hawk surface-to-air missiles from the United States and the Kennedy administration made it known that it would not proceed with the sale unless observers from the scientific community were allowed to visit the Dimona facility. Yet while Israel, to all appearances, agreed to inspections, it would not submit to those conducted by the IAEA's international teams but instead offered a compromise of sorts: an American group could scrutinize the Dimona site, but only under a set of conditions devised by the Israel government, conditions that were curiously restrictive in terms of the visits' timing. "[T]he American inspection team would have to schedule its visits well in advance, and with the full acquiescence of Israel," writes Hersh. "There would be no spot checks permitted."[16] It was a stipulation to which the Americans grudgingly agreed, and one that the Israelis subsequently undercut.

The strategy adopted by David Ben-Gurion, Shimon Peres, and their colleagues at Dimona began with postponements and progressed to chicanery. It would not be until after several delays that Israel permitted a pair of American scientists to view the Dimona compound, with the Jewish state, not the inspectors, deciding which features of the facility could be inspected.[17] This was, of course, a subversion of the evaluative process. And worsening matters, Israeli officials ushered the two scientists out of the nuclear complex only forty-five minutes after they arrived. Thus, the Israelis ensured that the reactor's maiden assessment would be a fiasco for the Americans, a calculated act that was not lost on the Kennedy administration or the U.S. Atomic Energy Commission and a development that, in essence, verified Israel's campaign of deception.

It was a duplicity that extended to the Knesset as well, which Ben-Gurion kept in the dark about the real reason for the Dimona project, thereby ensuring the legislative body would have virtually no voice in the project.[18] It was his belief that his colleagues in the Knesset, many of whom were opposed to a nuclear weapons program on financial, political, or moral grounds, did not fully grasp the existential threat faced by the Jewish state and the need for it to be able to defend itself using the most effective technology available. Accordingly, he considered his untruthfulness on the subject to be justified, his actions being a manifestation of his longstanding determination to make sure the Jewish people did not suffer a second Holocaust. And the prime minister continued misleading the Knesset well into the 1960s, just as he persisted in his attempts to hoodwink Kennedy and the U.S. Atomic Energy Commission. The reactions of the Israelis and the Americans to Ben-Gurion's deceit were quite different, however. The Knesset, as a whole, was not unduly upset with the prime minister's decision to keep the project away from it, just as the legislature welcomed his assurances that the reactor was intended exclusively for research and domestic applications. "The Knesset was only too eager to accept any government statement denying the intent to produce nuclear weapons," says Hersh.[19] The United States, on the other hand, was not at all eager to embrace the implausible cover story about the reactor's noble objectives, a story that the Mossad is suspected of having helped fabricate and disseminate.[20] And further chafing the Oval Office and the U.S. Atomic Energy Commission was the over-the-top pretense that awaited subsequent teams of American inspectors on their visits to Dimona in 1963 and 1964.

"Workers had been busy building false walls and bricking up the service elevators to underground floors where work was going ahead on the manufacture of nuclear weapons," write Gilling and McKnight.[21] And there was more. "[S]imulated control rooms were built, the entrances to underground levels were [sealed], and pigeon dropping were scattered around some buildings in which the forbidden installations were housed to give the impression that they were not in use," reports Ari Shavit.[22] It was a pattern of guile that would persist in the face of successive grievances registered by American inspectors, yet also a pattern that would ultimately prove effective in wearing down these visitors. "Six years later, complaining that harassment from Dimona staff made proper investigation impossible, the U.S. abandoned the inspections, allowing the Israeli scientists to carry on their military work undisturbed," write Gilling and McKnight.[23]

Questionable, too, would be the manner in which Israel went about obtaining uranium for its nuclear arms program, since the country did not possess sufficient quantities of the radioactive material to manufacture the large number of weapons it hoped to produce. With the reactor becoming operational in 1963, it now required an ongoing supply of fuel, and this would lead the Jewish state to commit a series of illegal acts. Some would be comparatively minor, such as its under-the-table purchase of uranium from Argentina, South Africa, and French-controlled mines located elsewhere on the African continent. Others would be more serious and would require the expertise of the Mossad. Among the latter: a uranium-diversion program carried out on the European continent, one in which "a specially created commando unit made four uranium hijackings in Europe, two with the co-operation of France and West Germany," according to Gilling and McKnight.[24] It was during this same period that the Mossad's efforts were supplemented by those of the LAKAM, a covert intelligence unit created by the Israeli government explicitly to help with its nuclear arms project.

In the chapter that follows, two of the more notorious episodes associated with Israel's unorthodox efforts to obtain uranium for the Dimona nuclear reactor are revisited. One is accepted as fact, even though the Israeli government neither confirms nor denies the undertaking, while the reality of the remaining case is still open to question. Also divergent, the first episode culminated in Operation Plumbat in 1968 and transpired in the Mediterranean Sea, while the second incident, the more debatable one, purportedly took place over the course of the 1960s and centered on a private uranium-processing plant located in the eastern United States. Together, the missions illustrate the ingenuity and bravado of the Mossad in acquiring restricted nuclear materials from disparate foreign sources.

12

The Quest for Uranium: Operation Plumbat and the NUMEC Affair

The year was 1967 and Israel had just struck the first blow in the Six-Day War. Disturbed by this and related developments in the Middle East, U.S. President Lyndon Johnson imposed an arms embargo on the Jewish state, a dramatic move that France promptly implemented as well. In fact, the latter was so opposed to Israel's offensive in the Middle East that it took the additional step of suspending its shipments of uranium for use in the Dimona program. Neither the United States nor France wished to encourage, let alone enable, Israel's controversial military endeavors in the region since, among other drawbacks, such perceived complicity could harm their relationships with the Arab states.

For Israel, concurrent embargoes by its two main arms suppliers meant it would no longer have access to significant sources of conventional weaponry—nor, due to the French embargo, to the uranium needed to fuel its principal reactor. But while Israeli leaders decided not to seek a new purveyor of traditional arms, especially since the likeliest supplier, the Soviet Union, had no interest in selling weapons in the region at this time, they did decide to pursue other methods of acquiring uranium. Their options, however, were few. They were so limited, in fact, that Prime Minister Levi Eshkol and his advisors decided it would be necessary for Israel to steal the radioactive material. Accordingly, the Mossad, under the direction of Meir Amit, embarked on a quest to purloin uranium, a breach of international law that would benefit from the handiwork of Dan Aerbel, the Danish gentleman described in Chapter Six who later played a role in Operation Wrath of God in Lillehammer, Norway.

According to the most comprehensive account of events, a work titled *The Plumbat Affair* by Elaine Davenport and her colleagues, it was in 1964 that the Mossad appears to have recruited Aerbel and dispatched him to the West German city of Wiesbaden in the guise of a furniture salesman.[1] Situated in the western part of the country near the Rhine River, Wiesbaden was home to a sizable American military community which conducted business with local merchants, and it was among these vendors that the new Mossad agent would now spend his days. "Part of Aerbel's job was, undoubtedly, to find likely friends for Israel," writes the Davenport team.[2] Among these collaborators would be Herbert Shulzen, a German textile expert who owned a chemical company that manufactured industrial soap and decontamination supplies. So it was that three years later, after the Six-Day War and stymied by the ensuing arms embargo, Israel and the Mossad, acting on the groundwork laid by Aerbel, brought into the fold Shulzen and his firm, Asmara Chemie. He and his company were to become the crux of the intelligence agency's mission to nick uranium for the Dimona reactor.

After purchasing three hundred decontamination kits from the chemist-entrepreneur, the Mossad, which had by now sized up Shulzen and found him trustworthy, asked if he could get his hands on two hundred tons of "yellowcake" uranium. A powder made of uranium oxide, yellowcake constitutes an early stage in the uranium-enrichment process, and, in itself, is a harmless mineral. At the time, it was also readily available in Europe. Not only that, the six countries that made up the European Common Market in 1967—West Germany, Italy, France, and the Benelux nations—were permitted to transport it to one another without significant restrictions. "This is because it was not unusual for uranium to be sent to specialized factories for enrichment or other refining processes," writes Dennis Eisenberg, adding that the existing protocols required the material to be returned to the sender once it had been processed.[3] And on this issue, the parameters were unequivocal: nuclear materials could not leave the Common Market countries. It was a regulation that was monitored, albeit in fits and starts, by the European Atomic Energy Community (Euratom), the organization responsible for ensuring the peaceful use of nuclear resources within the union of Western European nations. It was with these facts in mind that Shulzen and the Mossad put together a plan.

Their strategy involved two countries, both of them components of the European Common Market. Shulzen's firm, Asmara Chemie, would pay a company in one of the nations to ship yellowcake uranium to a company in the other nation. Once at sea, however, the vessel's cargo would be diverted to Israel by a third party, the Mossad. What remained to be determined, then, were the players: the two unwitting Common Market firms and the ship.

12. The Quest for Uranium

In the spring of 1968, Shulzen began shopping around for a company from which to purchase an immense amount of yellowcake without arousing suspicion, and soon he found it in a large, Brussels-based outfit by the name of Société Générale des Minerais (SGM). It was a cog in an august Belgian conglomerate that had its fingers in everything from public utilities to financial institutions to mining operations in Africa. For this company, such a massive order would not present a problem; the challenge would be in convincing its executives the deal was on the up-and-up. So, to eliminate this potential obstacle, Shulzen laid out a credible cover story to the effect that Asmara Chemie was preparing to expand its operations to include the large-scale production of petrochemicals and it planned to use the yellowcake "as a catalyst to begin, or to accelerate, the chemical reactions which this type of manufacturing calls for."[4] He further explained to Belgian executives that SGM would need to ship the powdery mineral to another firm for blending before his employees could manufacture petrochemicals with it. As regards SGM's response, its executives deemed Shulzen's proposal to be aboveboard, and upon confirming his firm's ability to pay for the product—the Mossad had set up a Swiss account to cover the nearly four-million-dollar payment—signed onto the deal. Satisfied with this element of their plan, Shulzen and the Mossad turned their attention to locating a receptive company to ostensibly blend the yellowcake uranium.

As it happened, finding such a firm was easy. Asmara Chemie had long conducted business with a Milan-based company known as SAICA, or Società Anonima Italiana Colori e Affini, which concerned itself with trading in such substances as paints, dyes, and varnishes. Its director, Francesco Sertorio, was a personal friend of Shulzen, the two men having known each other for over twenty years. On top of this, the Italian enterprise was falling on hard times and was in need of an influx of cash. It made sense, then, for Shulzen and the Mossad to bring the company into their scheme. Certainly Sertorio was delighted by the setup, not least because of the twelve thousand dollars he received upon signing the contract with Asmara Chemie, money that helped resuscitate his failing business. And this was no accident.

"The beauty of Operation Plumbat lay in the way it was designed to exploit weaknesses," writes Davenport and her co-authors.[5] While the Italian company needed an infusion of cash to stay afloat, the Belgian company, which was in sound financial condition, nevertheless stood to benefit handsomely from the multimillion-dollar sale of yellowcake partly because the product was not a hot commodity at the moment. "In 1968 there was little military demand because of the nuclear test-ban treaty passed five years before," says Davenport, "and little civil demand because peaceful nuclear programs were still in their infancy."[6] Most of all, though, the Israeli intelligence agency was exploiting Euratom's anemic reputation as a watchdog organization. "[The] Mossad was relying on the weakness of the European safeguards that were supposed to prevent uranium from falling into the wrong hands."[7]

The final element in the Mossad's scheme would require its getting hold of an ocean-going vessel to transport the yellowcake. To this end, it obtained the help of a mysterious figure, Burham Yarisal, who was rumored to have been involved in several questionable business endeavors around the world. Publicly, this is all that was known about him other than the fact that he was born near Istanbul, Turkey, and was fifty years old when the Mossad landed his services in acquiring a cargo ship.

In the summer of 1968, the Mossad asked Yarisal to establish a dummy corporation in Monrovia, Liberia—the Biscayne Traders Shipping Corporation—and to buy a cargo ship on the company's behalf. And sure enough, a few weeks later Yarisal tracked down a two-hundred-eight-foot vessel with a price tag of nearly four hundred thousand dollars. Although its owner, August Bolton, harbored suspicions about the transaction once it was in motion due to the uncommon ease and swiftness of the sale to Yarisal, a man virtually unknown in the shipping world, he closed the deal all the same. But Bolton remained unsettled by it. "It crossed his mind that the ship was perhaps going to be used for gunrunning or 'some other shady business.'"[8]

Once the vessel was in the Mossad's possession and re-christened the *Scheersberg A*, the agency decided the ship should sail from northern Europe to northwestern Africa in what would amount to a trial run. It would need to be done discreetly, though, so as not to attract attention. And this meant, among other things, limiting the size of the crew to only those who were essential; the fewer people involved in the covert mission, even if they were unaware of its true purpose, the fewer potential sources of its exposure. So as to reduce the number of seamen, the Mossad instructed Yarisal to exchange the ship's West German registration for Liberian, this being one of the reasons the Republic of Liberia had been selected as the home of the bogus Biscayne Traders Shipping Corporation. By switching to the West African nation's documentation system, the vessel would have the benefit of regulations that were far more relaxed, including permission to carry an unusually small crew. Once this business matter was finalized, the *Scheersberg A* put out to sea. The date was October 9, 1968. Carrying a meager number of Moroccan and Iberian seamen, the craft was commanded by an inscrutable captain, a man in his thirties claiming to be Welsh and going by the name Peter Barrow.

Weeks later, while the vessel was moored in Morocco, Euratom reviewed Herbert Shulzen's application for Asmara Chemie to transport yellowcake uranium from Belgium to Italy by sea route. As the Mossad expected, the nuclear watchdog group was lackadaisical in its response. "Nobody in Euratom saw any need to make any inquiries into Asmara's background or, indeed, into any other aspect of the deal," writes the Davenport group.[9] Accordingly, Euratom approved the firm's request, with the Mossad ordering the ship to head back to Europe at once and await its special consignment.

What was awaiting the crew members when they docked on November 15, however, was not cargo, but pink slips. Terminated on the spot, the bewildered seamen were told to clear off the ship, following which another crew boarded the worn craft a few hours later, none of whose members were Moroccan or Iberian. "Her new crew," writes Davenport, "was half the normal strength, and the seven deck hands were all Caucasian."[10] The chief engineer was Peter Körner, and the first officer, a man called Tilney. As with the trial run, the captain would be Peter Barrow, or at least this would be the moniker he would continue using at this point.

The next day, the yellowcake uranium, packed in drums, arrived by rail in Antwerp and was deposited by crane onto the *Scheersberg A*. On the barrels' sides the word "Plumbat" was stenciled, which is assumed to have been derived from the word "plumbate," a salt. After the freight had been loaded onto the ship, First Officer Tilney was asked to sign a form declaring that the chemicals had arrived in satisfactory condition. Because he was suspicious of the goings-on, however, he did not submit to this routine practice but instead scribbled on the form, "drums said to contain chemicals."[11] His use of the qualifier "said" was intended to protect him in case the containers did not, in fact, hold salt.

Setting sail shortly after midnight on November 17, the *Scheersberg A* traveled through the Western Sheldt, an estuary leading to North Sea, then headed southwesterly into the English Channel. In the ensuing days, it sailed around France, Portugal, and southern Spain, after which it navigated the Strait of Gibraltar. But now, rather than heading northeasterly toward Genoa, Italy, which was the plan Euratom had approved, the ship pursued an eastward course across the Mediterranean Sea. This is because the strategy of Operation Plumbat, as the Mossad had designated it, was for the craft to meet up with an Israeli contact in the eastern Mediterranean, a so-called daughter vessel, whereupon a ship-to-ship cargo transfer would take place. The *Scheersberg A* had been instructed not to sail the four thousand miles from Belgium directly to an Israeli port city, of course, since this would make it obvious that the Jewish state was behind the diversion.

It was during a pre-dawn morning, at the beginning of December, that the rendezvous transpired. An Israeli freighter, the daughter vessel, escorted by a brace of gunboats, traveled northward from the Jewish state until it spotted the *Scheersberg A* at the designated coordinates. Using side-to-side navigation, the freighter moored itself to the scuffed cargo ship. The crew of the *Scheersberg A* then set about hoisting the hundreds of drums of yellowcake uranium, one by one, onto the freighter, a chore that took several hours and throughout which the seamen remained silent on the orders of Peter Barrow. Subsequent to this, the freighter and its escorts, along with the four-million-dollar contraband, made haste for Haifa, Israel, while the *Scheersberg A* sailed northeastward to İskenderun, a Turkish port. The same day that the cargo ship docked in Turkey, the yellowcake, having reached the Jewish state and been placed on an overland transport, arrived at Negev Nuclear Research Center in Dimona. The Mossad's scheme had succeeded.

"Within weeks, the details of the uranium operation were known in every capital in the West," writes Eisenberg. "It was decided by mutual agreement to keep the matter a secret."[12] Not all of the details were known, however, most importantly that it had been a Mossad operation. As far as other governments were aware, the disappearance of the ship had nothing to do with Israel, since the only people known to have been associated with the missing vessel were German, Belgian, and Italian, along with its original Moroccan and Iberian crew. Thus, Israel was off the hook—that is, until five years later, when the Mossad, in the course of another mission, mistakenly gunned down a Moroccan waiter in Lillehammer, Norway, confusing him with the leader of the Black September Organization.

As noted in Chapter Six, the Norwegian police arrested one of the Mossad operatives involved in the Lillehammer fiasco, Dan Aerbel. And when Aerbel found himself imprisoned, he panicked. It seems he was claustrophobic owing to the fact that, as a Jewish child in Nazi-occupied Denmark, his elders had hidden him and other children in a cellar and sealed it with bricks. An extreme measure, it had saved his life, but it had also left him with an overpowering fear of confinement. And under such conditions in Norway, he cracked, revealing to his interrogators everything he knew about numerous Mossad missions. Among the treasure trove of information he provided: the entire story of Operation Plumbat, a mission in which he had not only secured the services of Herbert Shuzel and his West German firm, Asmara Chemie, but had also helped get rid of the *Scheersberg A* after the yellowcake heist had been completed so that the vessel could not be traced back to the Jewish state. Yet, for political reasons, Aerbel's staggering revelation to the Norwegian authorities was kept quiet at the time. "[A]nd so it remained for nine years," writes Eisenberg, "until Paul Leventhal, representing the United States at an antinuclear conference in Europe, revealed the disappearance of the *Scheersberg*'s cargo."[13] It was one more piece of evidence that the Jewish state was in possession of a large nuclear reactor and that the device required a considerable amount of uranium, far more than would be necessary if it were being used strictly for peaceful purposes. And Operation Plumbat would not be Israel's only attempt to illicitly procure from foreign sources radioactive material for the nation's nuclear arms program.

The NUMEC Controversy

At the same time Operation Plumbat was unfolding in Europe in the 1960s, there has also been a longstanding suspicion, albeit one having no confirmatory evidence, that another batch of uranium—not early-stage yellowcake, but fully processed, weapons-grade uranium—was being re-routed from a facility in the United States to the Dimona reactor site. Furthermore, it was occurring without the knowledge or consent of the American government. Israeli Intelligence was purportedly involved in this diversion, a deed that, had its American collaborator been tried and found guilty, could have resulted in a sentence of "imprisonment for not more than twenty years," under the Atomic Energy Act.[14]

The American at the center of the storm, Zalman Shapiro, was born in Ohio in 1920, the son of an Orthodox rabbi. Although Shapiro's childhood was largely without incident, his adolescence was marred by his relatives' deaths in Europe during the Holocaust. In his early adult years, the ambitious Midwesterner, who was lauded for his brilliance, attended Johns Hopkins University from which he earned a doctorate in chemistry in 1948. This was, of course, the same year that Israel attained its statehood, and Shapiro, like countless others who had lost relatives to the Final Solution, was convinced of the need for a Jewish homeland where Jews from around the world could enjoy a secure way of life. For this reason, he joined the Zionist Organization of America, as well as contributing to various initiatives, particularly those in the sciences, that promised to benefit the new State of Israel.

After completing his formal education, the young research scientist worked at Westinghouse's Bettis Atomic Power Laboratory, where he played an important role in the invention of the first nuclear-powered submarine, the *Nautilus*. Subsequent to this, he co-founded and served as president of the Nuclear Materials and Equipment Corporation, or NUMEC, in the small town of Apollo, near Pittsburgh, Pennsylvania. The year was 1957 and the company was a part of the Atoms for Peace program. In terms of its function, NUMEC was designed to process fuel for nuclear reactors and market the end product—highly-enriched uranium—to domestic entities, most notably the U.S. Navy. As part of the Atoms for Peace project, the government also granted the firm permission to sell uranium to allies of the United States. "It was an opportunity I felt was available to me and was the basis for the company I started," says Shapiro.[15]

A few years after launching NUMEC, which skeptical officials point out occurred at the same time that Israel kicked off its secret nuclear arms program at Dimona, Shapiro came under fire from the U.S. Atomic Energy Commission. Initially, the company's problems had to do with faulty record-keeping at its Apollo plant, along with the careless handling of uranium by its employees. But a more alarming matter came to light in 1965 when an AEC audit discovered that a sizable amount of weapons-grade uranium, two hundred pounds of it, appeared to be missing from the facility. Neither government inspectors nor the plant's staff could explain the loss. The former did believe, however, that the deficit was not attributable to the usual reasons that such materials seemingly disappear, for instance by minuscule amounts finding their way onto machinery or workers' uniforms. Using the methods that were available at the time, the inspectors had already explored these possibilities and ruled them out. To be sure, the NUMEC situation was a mystery, and a worrisome one, since the quantity of missing uranium was far more than that experienced by other such facilities, and also because it was a sufficient amount to build several atomic bombs. Accordingly, officials began to entertain more sinister possibilities.

In short order, organizations within the American government, among them the CIA, FBI, and NSA (National Security Agency), decided that Shapiro must have illegally diverted the highly-enriched uranium to Israel for its suspected nuclear weapons program. In a vehement defense of the scientist, however, Seymour Hersh, in his 1991 book, *The Samson Option*, challenged the government's conclusion and insisted it was rooted in prejudice.[16] In the eyes of American officials, Hersh asserted, Shapiro, the accomplished chemist, entrepreneur, and co-creator of the military's prized possession, the *Nautilus*, was also a Jew, a Zionist, and a businessman with access to uranium. And such characteristics were sufficient to brand him a man with a mission; a Jew with dual loyalties who could not be trusted. "Shapiro's emotional tie to Israel was enough of a motive for him to commit nuclear espionage," writes Hersh, referring to what he regards as the government's jaundiced viewpoint.[17]

Compounding the authorities' suspicions was a subsequent FBI surveillance operation that witnessed a supposedly clandestine meeting at a Pittsburgh airport between Shapiro and Jeruham Kafkafi, the latter being a science attaché and suspected Israeli operative. Kafkafi was known to work closely with Avraham Hermoni, whose cover was that of a science advisor at the Israeli embassy in Washington, D.C., but who was, in fact, the station chief of Israel's Office of Special Tasks, or LAKAM. A covert intelligence outfit, the LAKAM was associated with the Mossad and is the same organization that had previously orchestrated—and subverted—the United States' inspections at the Dimona nuclear facility.[18]

When congressional investigators confronted Shapiro about his airport encounter, he explained that he and Kafkafi had met to discuss a payment Israel owed NUMEC for anti-terrorist equipment the company had delivered to the Jewish state, a sizable payment that was long overdue.[19] While not dismissing Shapiro's explanation out of hand, investigators also did not embrace it.

According to Dan Raviv and Yossi Melman, Avraham Kafkafi was not the only figure from Israeli Intelligence to make the six-thousand-mile trek to Pennsylvania to meet with Shapiro. Traveling directly to the NUMEC facility itself was the LAKAM's Avraham Hermoni, as well as Avraham Shalom, who would eventually become the director of the Shin Bet, Israel's internal security agency. Another would be Rafi Eitan, the Mossad agent who had led Operation Eichmann in Argentina a few years earlier and now entered the United States posing as a research chemist. As to why Eitan showed up at Shapiro's door in Apollo, it may never be known for certain, but there is a prevailing theory. "There is no conceivable reason for Eitan to have gone (to the Apollo plant) but for the nuclear material," says Anthony Cordesman, a former Pentagon official, in a 1986 *Los Angeles Times* report.[20] It should be noted, however, that Shapiro insisted as recently as 2013 that he had never knowingly met with Israeli intelligence figures at his Pennsylvania plant, a statement that leaves open the possibility that he may have been misled by visitors with false credentials.[21]

That said, it seems that Shapiro was involved with the State of Israel in two important ways during the 1960s, one of which he concealed from American investigators and the other being a matter of public record. In the first case, the chemist-entrepreneur claims to have consulted with the Israeli government on a confidential project involving that nation's irrigation system, helping to determine why it was experiencing a considerable water loss and whether the water might be toxic. The study purportedly made use of radioactive tracers to monitor its flow, and was an undertaking the Israeli government wished to keep under wraps for security reasons. It was the same for Shapiro, who did not disclose his participation to U.S. congressional investigators because, as he later clarified, public exposure of the program might have given the Jewish state's enemies the idea of poisoning its water supply.

In the second case, Shapiro's company, NUMEC, partnered with the Israeli government in the 1966 to form ISORAD (Isotopes and Radiation Enterprises, Ltd), a company created ostensibly to conduct pasteurization, or food-preservation, research. Upon its establishment, there was no attempt by the Israeli government or Zalman Shapiro to hide the new business venture. As could be expected, though, U.S. government officials were skeptical of the arrangement, with some believing ISORAD was created to streamline Shapiro's access to Israel's nuclear arms program.

"Isotopes and Radiation Enterprises (ISORAD) was another dummy corporation in the United States," writes Ephraim Kahana, formerly of the National Security Program at the University of Haifa and currently an editor of the *International Journal for Intelligence and Counterintelligence*. "Officially ISORAD was engaged in developing technologies to preserve fruit through irradiation; in reality, it served as the pipeline for obtaining uranium from NUMEC for the Israeli nuclear weapons program."[22]

To date, it has not been proven that ISORAD was a conduit for American uranium. A large, diverse, and robust company, it is still in business today, and is based at the Soreq Nuclear Research Center, the site of Israel's first nuclear reactor designed for peaceful applications. Among the company's offerings are state-of-the-art products for medical, pharmaceutical, industrial, and defense use.

As highly-enriched uranium continued to vanish from the NUMEC plant—four hundred additional pounds of radioactive material would disappear during the 1960s even while the facility was under investigation—the company's reputation, tarnished by the rumor that it was illicitly helping a foreign nation devise weapons of mass destruction, prompted many businesses not to renew their contracts with it. The upshot: Shapiro, by 1967, had little choice but to merge his company with Atlantic-Richfield (ARCO). Not long after, he left NUMEC altogether.

In the ensuing years, federal officials, through various machinations, made sure the chemist-entrepreneur would never again be in a position to re-route uranium to Israel, if, in fact, he had done so in the first place. While Shapiro continued to obtain employment in his area of expertise, including a return to Westinghouse, it would always be in less sensitive capacities.

In 1971, a company by the name of Babcock and Wilcox took control of the former NUMEC plant from ARCO. And history repeated itself. A few years later, in the mid–1970s, the plant was again reported to have missing uranium, a considerable amount of it, with the disappearance taking place over a two-and-a-half-year period.[23] This time, however, the government body overseeing the matter, the Nuclear Regulatory Commission, successor to the Atomic Energy Commission, did not presume the uranium had been bundled off to Israel. Instead, an ensuing analysis brought to light previously unknown loss mechanisms at the facility coupled with errors in measurement. Taken together, these factors accounted for roughly half of the missing radioactive material.

Along the same lines, the Nuclear Regulatory Commission disclosed a startling discovery in 1990, one having to do with the continued clean-up efforts at the defunct NUMEC plant. "Nuclear Regulatory Commission officials subsequently admitted that more than one hundred kilograms of enriched uranium—

the amount allegedly diverted to Israel by Zalman Shapiro—was recovered from the decommissioned plant by 1982, with still more being recovered each year," writes Hersh. "[M]any sections of the plant, including its concrete floor, were so contaminated that they had to be dismantled, piece by piece, and buried at appropriate sites—after the valuable uranium was removed."[24]

It may or may not be relevant that a government-sponsored project to clean up a nuclear waste dump was launched in 2011 near Apollo, Pennsylvania, with officials reacting with shock to the findings of preliminary excavations at the site. "Digging was abruptly halted after just two months and the government classified documents on the project as secret, citing a security rule regarding 'special nuclear material'—typically uranium and plutonium isotopes usable in nuclear weapons," reads a November 2013 report.[25] Says another source, the Homeland Security News Wire, "security measures indicate that clean-up crews have discovered Category I special nuclear material, which can be used in nuclear weapons or dirty bombs."[26] During the 1960s, it should be noted, NUMEC routinely conducted disposal operations at the site, which a few smaller entities used as well.[27] It is estimated that the current clean-up project will cost ten times more than expected—up to half a billion dollars—due to the unforeseen content at the site, which the Department of Homeland Security has now placed under armed guard.[28]

In assessing the possibility that Shapiro and the NUMEC plant did indeed redirect nuclear materials to Israel, it is important to bear in mind that the man and his company were subjected to protracted inquiries and investigations by the CIA, NSA, FBI, NRC, AEC, and GAO (General Accounting Office), as well as by congressional bodies that included the House Subcommittee on Energy and the Environment along with the House Subcommittee on Oversight and Investigations. Fifty-one reports were compiled by the FBI alone, an organization that kept a file on Shapiro from 1949 to 1974.[29] In the course of these thoroughgoing procedures, investigators interviewed one hundred twenty employees of the NUMEC facility, with Shapiro himself being grilled on numerous occasions and placed under surveillance. At no point, however, did any of these measures yield tangible evidence linking the man or his company to the Israeli nuclear arms program. The entirety of evidence was circumstantial.

As of this writing, the federal government has not cleared Shapiro's name despite the fact that there is no "smoking gun" proving that he re-routed highly-enriched uranium from the United States to the Jewish state. In 2009, Pennsylvania Senator Arlen Spector requested that the Nuclear Regulatory Commission issue a statement absolving Shapiro of wrong-doing, but the organization declined to do so on the grounds that it lacked information which would allow it to confirm his innocence.[30] As recently as November 2013, the *Wall Street*

Journal noted that the former head of the Nuclear Regulatory Commission, Victor Gilinsky, is still voicing doubts about Shapiro's actions. "The 79-year-old Mr. Gilinsky says his research in the decades since has led him to conclude Israel probably did get bomb-grade uranium from Numec."[31]

It should be noted that there are currently two competing hypotheses as to the government's awareness of Shapiro's deeds, both of them claiming that officials do know, in fact, whether he did or did not divert uranium to Israel yet are withholding this information from the public. Certainly it is true that after nearly five decades the government still refuses to declassify all of its materials pertaining to the case.

In the first hypothesis, government officials are believed to have become aware of the illegal transfer of uranium while it was taking place but decided to let it proceed.[32] If released to the public, however, this information would not only point to Shapiro's guilt but could also be taken to mean that the American government had tacitly endorsed the illicit operation.

Related to this hypothesis is the notion that the American government did not know about the diversion as it was happening, but upon subsequently learning about it decided that it is would in the nation's best interests to keep the information close to the vest. The reason: the U.S. government would find itself in the awkward position of having to act on the incriminating material if the situation were to be made public.

On this subject, documentary filmmakers Andrew and Leslie Cockburn point to the recollections of Mort Halperin, a National Security Council staffer during the Nixon era who subsequently described closed-door meetings at the White House centering on Zalman Shapiro, NUMEC, and the Jewish state. "The concern was that if the diversion became public," says Halperin, "it could jeopardize our relationship with Israel."[33]

Halperin's statement indicates that the Nixon administration took as fact the diversion of NUMEC's uranium; furthermore, that if the unlawful transfer were to become publicly known, it would oblige the White House to punish the Jewish state for conspiring to remove radioactive material from the United States. In turn, such disciplinary action could further complicate an already complex situation in the Middle East. Of course, it should be kept in mind that the purported discussions to which Halperin refers occurred during the Nixon presidency, an administration that was basing its conclusions on the information that existed at the time, which was years before more advanced analyses at the NUMEC plant detected previously unknown methods of uranium loss at the facility.

At the other end of the spectrum is the second hypothesis which holds that the federal government knows that Shapiro is innocent but decided long ago to suppress the fact so as to avoid sparking a public discussion about the environmental damage that nuclear power plants may cause. Such damage was a passionate concern of many citizens' groups in the 1960s and 1970s, a concern that increased in the wake of the Three Mile Island incident in 1979. If the government's files were to have revealed that Shapiro was, in fact, not guilty of transferring uranium to Israel, questions would have arisen as to the whereabouts of the missing mineral. And this could have caused public attention to turn to the hot-button issue of the potential toxicity of domestic nuclear facilities and associated liability issues. In this scenario, then, the powers-that-be may have found it expedient to promote the foreign-diversion story.

In the end, the Shapiro controversy may never be resolved, at least until the government releases all of its files on the case. Even without such closure in the NUMEC affair, however, including whether or not the Mossad played a role in it, there is still sufficient evidence in the form of other covert activities, such as Operation Plumbat, to state with certainty that the Jewish state took extraordinary measures to illegally acquire foreign uranium for its nuclear weapons program. Yet even after reports of Israel's theft of uranium hit the international news wires, there were those who remained unconvinced that the Dimona facility was creating weapons of mass destruction, perhaps most disturbingly the Israeli people themselves. This is because the Israeli government's disinformation campaign, coupled with its suppression of public discussion of the topic, ensured that the citizenry's knowledge of the Dimona plant would remain both minimal and mistaken. In large part, then, it was to inform his fellow citizens of what lay within their borders that an Israeli technician by the name of Mordechai Vanunu decided to reveal to the news media the Jewish state's undeclared nuclear arsenal. Unfortunately for the whistleblower, it would be the Mossad who would respond to his efforts to expose the secret program.

13

Mordechai Vanunu: The Seduction of a Nuclear Whistleblower

The State of Israel, as noted, constructed a nuclear arsenal in the Negev Desert, a top-secret program that sidestepped recognized standards of global cooperation and accountability on nuclear issues. By design, the Jewish state hid the project from its allies, with the partial exception of France, as well as from oversight organizations, most notably the International Atomic Energy Agency and the U.S. Atomic Energy Commission. It also kept its own citizenry in the dark about their nation's nuclear capability, a circumstance that has yet to change. "Israeli state policy," writes Ari Shavit in his 2013 book, *My Promised Land*, "does not allow Israelis to discuss Dimona publicly."[1] As a part of this information embargo, military censors, before permitting the writings of Israeli journalists to be published, scrutinize the material to make sure it doesn't reveal that the Jewish state is nuclearized.

Yet what is perhaps most striking about the secrecy, as shown in Chapter 11, is that Israel's legislators in the Knesset were not informed that their nation was creating weapons of mass destruction (WMD), even when the cost of the project soared into the hundreds of millions of dollars. Instead, they were led to believe the Dimona nuclear reactor had been constructed for, and was being used for, peaceful purposes only. Thus, the customary method by which a representative democracy resolves to embark upon a program of profound militarization—discussion and debate, followed by decision-making—was not followed. In its place, a small coterie of men led by Prime Minister David Ben-Gurion and Minister of Defense Shimon Peres initiated and implemented the secret operation and made certain it bypassed virtually all domestic and foreign monitoring. Still reeling from the wholesale destruction of European Jewry during the Holocaust, Ben-Gurion was convinced that Israel needed WMDs and he took steps to ensure that it obtained them. Ari Shavit has depicted this notion of an Israeli nuclear arsenal as a dome of fortification encompassing the young nation.

"In order to create and uphold a Jewish state in the Middle East, a protective umbrella had to be unfurled above the fledgling endeavor, a structure that would protect the Jews from the animosity they provoked when they entered the land," says Shavit. "A bell jar had to be placed over them to shield them from the predators that lay in wait."[2]

It was the manner in which Ben-Gurion set out to achieve his nuclear bell jar, however, that was so unorthodox. "[N]othing [can] erase the historical truth that the reactor was built both without the full approval of the government and against the background of widespread public opposition to the bomb," writes Yoel Cohen, associate professor at the School of Mass Communication, Ariel University.[3]

Because the nuclear arms project was not approved by the Israeli legislature in accordance with established procedures, one may argue that the program's legitimacy is debatable, particularly its origin and development; and, by extension, that Israel's position on the public exposure of the project is therefore tenuous as well. As it stands, the law holds that an Israeli citizen who reveals information about the WMD program is committing treason.

In many respects, the situation is akin to the present-day controversy over the surveillance activities of the National Security Agency (NSA). For several years, the American organization has covertly collected vast amounts of data from governments and individuals around the globe, including millions of American citizens within the United States, but without the knowledge of the federal government. Because the NSA concealed its activities so effectively, the congressional body that was in place to oversee the organization was unable to effectively monitor it. And this is of the utmost concern given that the mass surveillance of the American population is widely considered to be a violation of the Fourth Amendment of the U.S. Constitution.

In the summer of 2013, a twenty-nine-year-old systems analyst associated with the NSA, Edward Snowden, exposed the unsanctioned surveillance operation. "I realized that they were building a system whose goal was the elimination of all privacy, globally," he says.[4] "My sole motive [was] to inform the public as to that which is done in their name and that which is done against them," the whistleblower adds.[5] Federal prosecutors promptly charged the analyst with espionage even though he had not revealed the NSA's wrongdoing in collaboration with a foreign government. As for reporting the agency's misdeeds to his superiors, it does appear that Snowden did express in writing his concerns to those in the organization's upper echelons, but without, in his view, a satisfactory response. Then, too, Snowden, as an NSA employee, was ineligible for protection from retaliation under the whistleblower legislation that applied to those working for other organizations within the federal government.[6] The reason: the NSA has its own version of the federal whistleblower act, one that excludes protection from reprisal. So it was that the systems analyst saw no option but to release his incriminating evidence outside of the borders of the United States.

No doubt, Edward Snowden was aware of the harsh consequences he could face if he were to expose the NSA's mass surveillance program, yet he proceeded all the same. In so doing, he placed himself in the company of previous whistleblowers who also knew their revelations would require great personal sacrifice and yet nevertheless chose to divulge the facts. Among these figures is the Israeli nuclear technician Mordechai Vanunu, who, in 1986, disclosed to a British newspaper the Jewish state's undeclared nuclear weapons program at the Dimona facility in the Negev Desert. Israel, in response, charged him with treason and espionage for exposing this program which it continued to claim did not exist. As would be the case for Snowden many years later, Vanunu believed his government's deeds did not reflect the knowledge or will of the public nor did they conform to international norms of conduct. Also like Snowden, he was aware that he would not receive legal protection in his homeland even though the program he exposed had been created on the sly, without ratification by the government at large.

It would be in terms of the two men's fates that differences would emerge. At the time of this writing, Snowden has not been seized, whereas Vanunu was apprehended and placed in the hands of the Israeli government. And it was the Mossad that tracked down and captured the Israeli whistleblower in a case that continues to inflame those who champion, as well as those who oppose, the disenchanted technician and his struggle to alert the world to the presence of a massive nuclear arsenal in the Middle East.

The Making of a Whistleblower

Those who expose state secrets may be driven to such a drastic measure for any number of reasons, including, but not limited to, ideological principles in conjunction with an element of altruism, the thirst for revenge, or the hunger for cash. Not uncommonly, a combinations of factors lead to the decision. In regard to patriotism, whistleblowers vary widely in the degree to which they are devoted to their homelands. In some cases, a longstanding commitment to one's country may exist as evidenced by the person's avowal of patriotism and, more tellingly, by their past actions—Edward Snowden falls into this category—while, in other cases, the individual may harbor a negative attitude toward his or her homeland, or, as with Mordechai Vanunu, adopted homeland.

It was in the city of Marrakech, Morocco, a highly-populated oasis resting on the edge of the Sahara Desert, that Vanunu was born on October 13, 1954. France, at the time, controlled Morocco, a state of affairs that changed two years later when the European nation relinquished its hold over the North African country, with Morocco returning to self-rule. While this development benefitted the nation's Arab population, however, it did not bode well for the Jewish citizenry. With France no longer in place to protect this religious minority, Moroccan Arabs now behaved more aggressively toward the their Jewish compatriots, an unnerving situation that touched the life of young Vanunu.

"Arab mobs stoned Jews on the streets and pillaged their businesses," writes journalist Louis Toscano. "Mordechai's twenty-minute walk to school every morning was increasingly fraught with danger."[7] Worried about the deteriorating conditions that were endangering his family, Solomon Vanunu, its patriarch, decided in 1963 to move his wife and eight children to Israel. And he was not alone in his decision; tens of thousands of Moroccan Jews had already migrated to the young nation by this time. It was an exodus in which the Mossad played a crucial role, moreover, since Moroccan officials, before long, set about preventing Jewish citizens from emigrating for fear that their growing number in Israel would strengthen the Jewish state. "The Mossad managed to slip out more than 80,000 ... Jews after Morocco gained independence," says Toscano.[8] It was one of the intelligence agency's largest missions in terms of the number of those who directly benefited from it.

Unfortunately, Israel would not prove, for the Vanunu family, to be a land flowing with milk and honey. One reason was because they were Sephardic Jews, a minority in Israel where Ashkenazi Jews comprised the majority and purportedly acted on their ascendancy. Another reason was the family's former nationality. "The Moroccans were held in lowest esteem," writes Cohen, "as primitives coming from beyond the Atlas Mountains."[9]

In short order, the Vanunus settled in a town in the undesirable and unforgiving Negev Desert—Be'er Sheva—and, worse still, in the sordid district in which the town's illicit drug trade was situated.[10] This was because they had no choice in the matter; Israeli officials decided where the family would live. Even when an exasperated Solomon took it upon himself to relocate his wife and children to a safer, more pleasant city, the police arrived on their doorstep and forced them back to their desert domicile. In such ways, the Vanunus watched their hope for a better life turn to dust, a turn of events that was especially difficult for Solomon, who accused himself of failing his wife and children and who became deeply demoralized as a result. Unfortunately, it was an anguish that spread beyond him.

"Solomon's travails had a profound effect on young Mordechai," says Toscano. "He was depressed and angered by his father's plight."[11] Certainly it was not the sort of early experience that fosters an indelible respect for a country and its leadership. More the opposite: it instilled in Mordechai a skepticism of the nation he felt had degraded his loved ones. And because he did not become blinded by an allegiance to the Jewish state, the stage, it seems, was being set for his future actions.

Contributing to Mordechai's growing disillusionment was the onset of doubts, during his teenage years, about the practice of Orthodox Judaism. Although Solomon was a devout Jew who had functioned as a lay rabbi in Marrakech and now sold religious artifacts in Be'er Sheva, Mordechai could not help but detect what he considered to be the disdainful manner in which Ashkenazi Jews treated his family of Sephardic Jews. And it dismayed him. Then, too, he was put off by what he regarded as Orthodox Judaism's fixation on rigid, antiquated dictates. "I didn't like to keep the old laws without caring about human beings," he says.[12] In due course, he relinquished the faith that had been a significant part of his upbringing, including an adolescence spent as a student at a religious school, the Yeshiva Ohel Shlomo in Be'er Sheva.

At the age of eighteen, Vanunu entered the Israeli army and served as First Sergeant of a unit of combat engineers in the Golan Heights. Upon receiving an honorable discharge three years later, he enrolled in Tel Aviv University but withdrew a few months afterward for financial reasons.[13] Then, in 1976, he chanced upon a newspaper advertisement placed by the Israel Atomic Energy Commission, one that described an entry-level job as a nuclear technician. His curiosity piqued, he applied for the position which was to be located at the Dimona complex twenty-five miles from his family's home in Be'er Sheva. In due time, he secured the post and began formal academic training at the government's expense.

For the next two years, Vanunu studied math, physics, chemistry, and the English language.[14] After completing the requisite coursework, he signed a security agreement—in essence, a confidentiality oath—and began working full-time at the Dimona compound in a minor capacity while pursuing advanced studies in nuclear chemistry and nuclear physics. Once he had mastered this additional subject matter, Israeli officials issued him a security pass and introduced him to the most sensitive part of the Dimona complex, a subterranean facility known as Machon 2. Here, plutonium was reprocessed for an unspecified purpose, although Vanunu assumed it involved weapons of mass destruction. As it turned out, he was correct, with Machon 2 producing plutonium not only for Israel's nuclear weapons but reportedly for those of South Africa as well.[15]

By the autumn of 1978, Vanunu was spending his workdays hidden away from the world, deep in the recesses of the Machon 2 facility. Along with its other employees, each day he was bussed to and from the high-security site where he enjoyed considerable freedom of movement, although not total.

It was also in 1978 that Vanunu, while working full-time at the Dimona compound, enrolled part-time at Ben-Gurion University of the Negev and earned baccalaureate degrees in both geography and philosophy. He then set about pursuing a master's degree in philosophy.

Vanunu's critics assert that it was at this juncture that he became radicalized, although his supporters prefer to characterize the change as his becoming more aware of the social and political conditions that surrounded him. However one chooses to portray his transformation, it was during his graduate years that Vanunu's opinions "began to swing towards the Palestinian cause," in the words of Gilling and McKnight.[16] Side by side with his concern over the plight of the Palestinians who were struggling in the Occupied Territories was his broader disapproval of the Israeli government itself, especially what he regarded as its excessive militarism. It was a topic about which Vanunu was truly passionate. And he put his views into action; for instance, by going out of his way to help his Arab classmates who had difficulty obtaining academic materials. And he did more, and quite publicly. Since Israel was a democracy, the nuclear technician and philosophy graduate student assumed it was his right as a citizen to express himself in public forums.

"Vanunu became increasingly politically active calling for the equal rights for Palestinians within the state and for the inclusion of Palestinians in negotiations for the establishment of an independent and separate state," says James Thompson. "He also advocated religious freedom and separation of religion from the state."[17] He joined in rallies, too, one of which took place in March, 1985, and may have had adverse consequences for him.

"Shortly after being photographed at an Arab rally, Vanunu was summoned to an interview with the Shin Bet, Israel's internal security organisation, and senior officials of the Israeli Atomic Energy Authority," write Gilling and McKnight. "As a result of that interview, Vanunu was forced to resign from Dimona in November 1985."[18] For the record, the official position was that the technician was merely one of nearly two hundred Dimona employees who were to be laid off for fiscal reasons, although some observers remained convinced that Vanunu's impending termination stemmed from the burgeoning dissident's political activities. Vanunu himself believed he was being singled out because he was a

Sephardic Jew.[19] Whatever the reason, Dimona officials allowed him to continue working at the Machon 2 facility for the remaining weeks until the layoff would take effect, a period during which Vanunu made a move he had been contemplating for quite some time. And it would be a game-changer.

As things stood, he was already planning to leave Israel, a decision that had been inspired in part by the departure of one of his similarly disenchanted brothers. Then, too, Mordechai's decision was bolstered by an alarming discovery he had made earlier in the year when he began tracking the movements of his colleagues in Machon 2. During his observations on the evening shift, he learned that the manager of the shift prior to his own, when returning home at the end of the day, deposited the keys to the elevator leading down to the most secret part of the facility—Level 5—in an unlocked cabinet. A stunning breach of security, it was a lapse that made way for Vanunu to inspect Level 5 while the evening crew took its meal break.

A sensible and perceptive man, Vanunu had already deduced that weapons of mass destruction were probably being developed at Dimona, specifically in the Machon 2 facility. But he was aghast when he walked onto Level 5 and saw what stretched out before him: a vast system designed to create scores of nuclear bombs, an extensive and sophisticated operation far beyond that which he had imagined.

"Vanunu was now convinced that Israel, not content with producing a few bombs for a last-ditch defense, was building a powerful offensive nuclear arsenal rivaled only by the superpowers," writes Toscano. "And the government was flatly lying about it, assuring the world that it would never be the first to introduce nuclear weapons into the Middle East."[20] It was a discovery he decided to document on film.

Two months before his scheduled November termination date, Vanunu slipped a 35mm camera into his kitbag, climbed off the afternoon bus at Dimona, and strolled past the same security officers who had greeted him for nearly a decade. Because they had no reason to be suspicious of such a familiar face, they did not inspect his bag. So it was that the resolute technician, once he was inside Machon 2, commenced with his customary tasks until later that night when his colleagues took their meal break. And now he seized the moment. Hurrying to the roof, he shot a series of photographs of the sprawling Dimona complex, then he returned to his post undetected.

Having succeeded thus far in his dodgy pursuit, Vanunu decided to press on the next evening. Snaking his way through the underground labyrinth of Machon 2, he snapped pictures of control rooms, laboratories, and equipment devised to extract plutonium. He also photographed the Golda Balcony, a gallery named for Golda Meir and commanding a view of the production hall on Level 2. Next on the list was Level 5, with Vanunu pocketing the key to its private ele-

13. Mordechai Vanunu: The Seduction of a Nuclear Whistleblower

vator and making his way down to this most sensitive area of the facility. Here he managed to acquire forty images in a matter of minutes. "He photographed the glove boxes where the plutonium discs were machined into spheres, and the instrument panels that controlled the process," writes Toscano. "There was even a full-scale model of a hydrogen bomb."[21] When they were eventually developed, the images, fifty-six in all, would leave no doubt about the mammoth arsenal that was being created at Israel's principal nuclear facility.

At the end of his shift, the technician caught the bus out of Dimona with two canisters of undeveloped film stashed in his kit bag. "Shortly afterwards, Vanunu sold his car and apartment in [Be'er Sheva] and left for Europe, Australia, and the Far East, telling his friends he would never return," write Gilling and McKnight.[22] But although he would be traveling alone, he would not be doing so empty-handed: concealed in his baggage was the incriminatory film, which he slipped past the security officers at the Port of Haifa as he set off on the first leg of his fateful trip.

Interrupted Journey

At sunset on Sunday, January 19, 1986, Vanunu boarded a ferry bound for Athens. During the two days it would take to complete the voyage to the Greek port of Pireaus, the former nuclear technician wrestled with whether he should make public the damning Dimona images or keep them to himself. It was a nagging ambivalence that soon got the better of him, with Vanunu sharing an account of his days at the secret nuclear facility with a fellow passenger, a Canadian writer, and soliciting his advice. Of course, the latter's response was predictable given his line of work. Urging Vanunu to act on the information, the writer specifically recommended that he offer the story to *Newsweek* magazine, along with the accompanying photographs. But while Vanunu gave serious consideration to his fellow traveler's counsel, in the end he decided not to follow it, still being unsure of the most constructive course of action.

A few weeks later while touring Thailand, Nepal, and the Himalayas, Vanunu recounted his tale once again, this time to a woman whose father was a reporter in London. Explaining that he was considering handing over the Dimona materials to a reputable journalist, he asked the woman to secure her father's collaboration in the matter. She declined, however, which prompted Vanunu to retreat to his earlier, safer stance of withholding the story from the media. Not only that, he vowed not to broach the subject with anyone else during his Asian sojourn.

During his stint in Asia he pursued another aim, an inner one. Although it often goes unmentioned in written accounts of the man and his deeds, he seems to have been on a spiritual quest during this period of his life. Just as he had washed his hands of Israel and was eager to create for himself a more fulfilling life on another continent, he had also struggled with Judaism and was seeking illumination through other religions.

To this end, he traveled to an ashram, a spiritual hermitage, while in Thailand, where he remained for a stretch of time, according to Toscano's account of the Vanunu saga.[23] He also visited a handful of Buddhist monasteries "trying to reconcile his doubts about Judaism," writes British journalist Peter Hounam.[24] And it didn't end there. In the ensuing months, the future whistleblower delved into Western belief systems in what would culminate in his conversion to Christianity at the age of thirty-three. Then, too, it would be a close-knit, public-spirited Christian community, one that stood in opposition to the proliferation of nuclear weapons, that would persuade him to finally release his revelatory photographs; that, and the fact that Vanunu's spiritual evolution was leading him to believe that he had a moral obligation to warn humanity about a potential nuclear holocaust. It was a personal and spiritual transformation that would reach its apex while he was living in Australia.

It was on May 20, 1986, that Vanunu's ship docked in Sydney, where he leased a flat in Kings Cross, a low-rent section of the city. Promptly landing jobs as a dishwasher in a hotel and a worker in a bar, he eventually earned a license to operate a taxicab, with this becoming his full-time occupation.

Because scores of transients regularly found their way to the King's Cross neighborhood in which he lived, social services were available to them at various spots. One such source was St. John's Anglican Church, which offered material and spiritual sustenance to those who were in short supply. And it was while Vanunu was strolling past the church one evening, as he had done so many times before, that he realized its lights always seemed to burn far into the night. It was as if St. John's were a beacon to those at sea. His inquisitive nature taking hold, he stepped inside the church, whereupon he met Reverend John McKnight and struck up what was to become a lasting friendship, one warmed by compassion and enlivened by discussions of theological subjects. Among the latter were the works of Danish philosopher and religious author Søren Kierkegaard, whose teachings had long resonated with Vanunu.

In a matter of weeks, the future whistleblower succeeded in befriending several congregants of St. John's, along with another of its clerics, David Smith. As Vanunu melded with this group of amiable, well-informed, and conscientious people, he came to appreciate the earnestness of their convictions. Being devoted to Christ's teachings, they felt obliged to act on their beliefs in order to foster in the world a greater humanity, even when this meant entering the political sphere to do so. And their principled approach to life had an impact on Vanunu, who still had the two rolls of undeveloped film in his apartment, a vital possession with which he had done nothing. As he confided to those closest to him, his paralysis on the matter was due, in no small measure, to his fear of endangering his family, his friends, and himself. Yet the moral pressure within him continued to mount. So it was that all of these threads came together in July of 1986, when Vanunu attended a discussion group held by his fellow congregants.

"By an extraordinary coincidence," writes Hounam, "they were debating whether the church should take an active stand against nuclear weapons."[25] The members' concern had been sparked by a controversy that recently had been revived, one involving Britain's use of Australia in the 1950s as a site for nuclear tests. The tests' aftereffects, it seems, were still playing havoc with the nation's environment. Equally influential was the Chernobyl disaster in the Soviet Union, which had occurred only three months earlier. "For Mordechai Vanunu, who had worked for seven years as a technician at the supersecret Israeli nuclear reactor," says Cohen, "Chernobyl was a confirmation of the dangers of excessive secrecy in the nuclear industry."[26] So it was that these developments and the congregation's reaction to them brought Vanunu face to face, yet again, with the subject of nuclear arms; an issue that, for him, was as personal as it was political. It was also a matter on which his political views were increasingly dovetailing with his Christian beliefs. "[H]e was already committed to peace and then became committed to Christ," says David Smith, "and the two were always going to be bound up very closely together."[27]

Facilitating Vanunu's contemplation of his duty as a Christian, especially the way in which it applied to his material evidence of Israel's nuclear arsenal, were the teachings of Kierkegaard. Of the Danish theologian's ideas, Vanunu was, in the opinion of a St. John's cleric, inspired most deeply by "the principle that the individual has to stand up and be counted, and act in the interests of humanity before God."[28]

As it came to pass, Mordechai Vanunu, during the summer months, formally converted to Christianity and, at the same time, notified the clerics of St. John's that he would be handing over the Dimona photographs to the media. Although he would perhaps be violating the security agreement he had signed at Dimona and even committing treason, he would, in his view, be fulfilling a higher principle, one transcending national boundaries and encompassing humanity as a whole; the principle of honoring the sanctity of life and protecting it from harm.

Meeting the Press

Whereas Vanunu, during his months in Australia, appears to have been a guileless man, even a naive one, the South American gentleman who now stepped forward to serve as the liaison between the whistleblower and the global media—Oscar Guerrero—was, by all accounts, the opposite number. Presenting himself as a freelance journalist from the Republic of Colombia, Guerrero was working in Australia when he heard about the photos of Israel's secret weapons program. Seizing the opportunity, he implored the future whistleblower to permit him to offer the images to *The Sydney Morning Herald*, and, in due course, Vanunu acquiesced. Before long, however, questions about Guerrero's motives began to arise when he introduced money into the equation.

As it stood, Vanunu had no interest in selling the Dimona pictures to the press. Self-enrichment had never been his goal. Although he knew from the start they could bring him a veritable fortune if he were to peddle them to one of Israel's enemies among the wealthy Arab states, he shunned such a transaction. Instead, he was content to settle in a downscale Sydney neighborhood and drive a taxicab for a living. And even when Guerrero, while shopping the Dimona story to the Australian press, started demanding an exorbitant sum for the photos, Vanunu made it clear he had no desire to become rich by trafficking in state secrets. In fact, he told John McKnight that he planned to donate any payment he might receive to St. John's Anglican Church.[29]

As it turned out, *The Sydney Morning Herald* had no interest in Guerrero's proposition. Undeterred, the ambitious operator traveled to Madrid hoping to sell Vanunu's tale to a Spanish newspaper, but instead, through a circuitous route, ended up at the London offices of the *Sunday Times*. Here he found a receptive audience, if a skeptical one, especially when he startled its editors with his asking price, a jaw-dropping $375,000.[30] Notwithstanding the over-the-top price tag, of which the newspaper provisionally agreed to pay only a fraction, its top tier thought it wise to look further into the story since, if true, it could prove to be a bombshell.

With this aim in mind, an editor of the *Sunday Times*, the aforementioned Peter Hounam, touched down in Sydney on August 30, 1986. He had come to acquaint himself with Mordechai Vanunu and see firsthand the Dimona materials. And indeed, for the next twelve days he appraised the Israeli's integrity while poring over the recently-developed photographs to determine if Vanunu's narrative held up to scrutiny. If factual, he would be bundled off to London, where an exposé would be readied for publication.

Oscar Guerrero, in the meantime, waited on the sidelines as Hounam sized up Vanunu, although the self-styled journalist did not completely remove himself from the scene. It seems he kept popping up to remind the editor that the story could be "as big as Watergate," with piles of cash to be made off the spectacular scoop.[31] Once again, Guerrero's behavior was at odds with that of Vanunu, who impressed Hounam with his refusal to capitalize on the situation. "He was fastidious about not profiting from his experience, even to the point of rejecting an occasional meal in an expensive restaurant," writes Toscano of Vanunu's meetings with Hounam.[32] The price of a dinner, however, was a trifling matter compared to something else that was taking place during the pair's meals, namely, the fact that they were being surveilled.

Unbeknownst to the Israeli whistleblower and his British editor, the Mossad was tailing them during their preliminary talks in Sydney.[33] Moreover, the agency, upon confirming that the two were preparing to bring to light the true nature of the Dimona facility, wasted no time scheduling a briefing with Prime Minister Shimon Peres in Jerusalem. It was at this juncture that the Israeli leadership began considering its options for dealing with the matter, options that included assassination, extradition, and calculated inaction.[34]

Assassinating the whistleblower, the first option, was doable, but it carried an unacceptable downside in that the British press was now familiar with Vanunu and recognized his political value. His sudden death would undoubtedly invite suspicion. Furthermore, if his murder were to become public knowledge, it promised to trigger a scandal in Israel since the government would have liquidated one of its own citizens without a trial. Yet the second option, extradition, had its drawbacks as well. Above all, it would essentially confirm that the Dimona materials were authentic and thus put the lie to Israel's longstanding insistence that it was not manufacturing weapons of mass destruction. And then there was the third option, calculated inaction, which was based on the notion that deliberately standing down and letting Vanunu release the Dimona images would show the Jewish state's enemies that, unlike them, it possessed a formidable nuclear arsenal and could handily defend itself against potential aggressors. Certainly a nuclearized Israel was no match for a non-nuclearized Arab state, a fact that, in and of itself, would serve as deterrent to the Jewish state's many adversaries in the region. The hitch: global pressure would thereafter be applied to Israel to sign the Non-Proliferation Treaty, permit international inspectors to monitor its nuclear facilities, and scale down its nuclear arsenal with the long-term aim of eventual disarmament. So this option was also unpalatable to the Israeli leader.

After a series of deliberations, Prime Minister Peres, in company with the Mossad, decided the intelligence agency should continue monitoring Vanunu while making plans for a fourth option. As in Operation Eichmann, it would entail kidnapping the target and smuggling him back to Israel to face legal proceedings. In Vanunu's case, however, it would be a private trial, not a public one. Not inadvertently, it would also be a way for Israel to silence him

While the Israelis were preparing to deal with this man whom they regarded as a traitor, Peter Hounam, still in Sydney, had concluded by September 11, 1986, that the whistleblower's narrative and photos of the Dimona facility were almost certainly authentic. Due to the gravity of the subject matter, however, he believed they still required a thorough vetting by a team of nuclear scientists. On this day, then, the pair boarded a flight to London. They had no way of knowing that Australian Intelligence was aware of their travel plans thanks to an off-the-cuff boast by Oscar Guerrero to a gentleman who happened be an Australian operative.[35] And what followed was foreseeable: Australian Intelligence contacted British Intelligence, which, in turn, alerted the Mossad that the whistleblower and his editor were *en route* to London. Hours later, a brace of British agents posted at Heathrow Airport watched, but did not act, as the two men deplaned.

Shortly thereafter, the *Sunday Times* booked Vanunu into a hotel near its offices and dispatched a man, and later a woman, to keep watch over him for security reasons. The bulk of his time would not to be spent lolling about in hotel rooms, however. During the ensuing days, the newspaper's staff, feverishly preparing the exposé, would interview him on numerous occasions as it fine-tuned and expanded the Dimona story and verified his observations with experts. For protective purposes, the *Sunday Times* would also shuttle him from hotels to guesthouses to reporters' apartments, keeping him on the move so as to elude detection by the Mossad. For the same reason, it would make sure he was never alone. That was the plan, at any rate.

Prime Minister Peres, as noted, had already ordered the Mossad to begin preparations to seize Vanunu and return him to the Jewish state, and now the agency, under the direction of Nahum Admoni, put the strategy into action. And it began by re-routing a small, battered Navy vessel in the Mediterranean Sea. Christened the *Noga*, it was bound for Haifa when its captain received word to turn around and head toward the town of Fiumicino on the west-central coast of Italy, where he was to drop anchor and await a handful of visitors. No explanation was given to him about the reason for the trip, just as he was not privy to the identity of the mysterious passengers. All the same, he steered the cargo ship northwesterly toward Italy.

In London on this day—it was September 23—the *Sunday Times*, having completed the final draft of its exposé, delivered an eight-page summary to the Israeli embassy and invited its reaction. Although this was done as a courtesy to the State of Israel, the newspaper nevertheless stood to benefit from that nation's review of the material. If the Israeli embassy were to convincingly dispute the whistleblower's claims, the *Sunday Times* could kill the story before it went to press and save itself from public humiliation. If, on the other hand, the Israelis confirmed the account, the editors would know their report was accurate and could more comfortably proceed with its publication. Vanunu, it should be noted, hoped the synopsis of the article would spur Israel to finally acknowledge the existence of its nuclear arsenal so that the Jewish state would not appear duplicitous on the world stage when the report hit the newsstands.[36]

As it came to pass, the embassy neither confirmed nor denied the newspaper's summary; rather, it panicked, dashed off an anemic "no comment," then went dark on the matter. Of course, it had reason for alarm. "Israel's nuclear capability was far greater than suspected," the *Sunday Times*' synopsis revealed, according to the Bertrand Russell Peace Foundation. It showed that "Israel probably has a stockpile of 100–200 nuclear weapons, [could] make thermonuclear devices of greater power than atomic bombs and that Israel also collaborated routinely with South Africa on nuclear matters."[37]

On this last point, Western countries during this period, due to South Africa's institutionalized racism, took a dim view of any democratic nation that collaborated with it. Specific to Israel, the UN General Assembly, in 1977, had passed a resolution insisting that it join with other nations in suspending commercial transactions with the South African government—in particular, that Israel terminate its business arrangements with that country's military establishment—so as to pressure South Africa into rescinding its apartheid policies.[38] But Israel ignored the United Nations' demand. And this rebuff, for a number of reasons, was not a wise political move. As it stood, the Jewish state's continued cooperation with South Africa was already a politically awkward matter, as well as one that the Israeli administration tried to sweep under the rug. It did not wish to be seen as cooperating with a racist foreign government when its own treatment of Palestinians living in the Occupied Territories was being interpreted by critics as itself a form of apartheid. This was another reason, then, that the Israeli government was so apprehensive about Vanunu's exposé; it promised to bare the nation's lucrative business alliance with the South African military, most disturbingly its heretofore secret collaboration in the realm of nuclear warfare.

The Israeli administration feared, too, that the whistleblower's presence in London might see the release of further classified material in the future. According to Seymour Hersh, officials were especially worried that Vanunu might reveal that the Jewish state had planted truly hideous weapons—nuclear landmines—in the Golan Heights in the early 1980s.[39] This revelation, more than any other, would not only shock, but horrify the international community and severely damage Israel's reputation. And this is where Oscar Guerrero re-enters the picture, with some accounts suggesting he unintentionally led the Mossad to its target in London and thus helped prevent Vanunu from making any such future disclosures.

It seems that Guerrero, who had stayed behind in Sydney, developed a worry of his own, the suspicion that the *Sunday Times* might try to cheat him out of his part of the financial agreement that had been reached; this, despite the fact that he had a document in his possession from Peter Hounam guaranteeing him payment upon publication of the exposé. For this reason, Guerrero flew to London with the aim of selling the Dimona story to the *Sunday Times'* lesser competitor, the *Sunday Mirror*. And sure enough, he handed over a small number of copies of the Dimona photos to the scandal sheet not realizing that doing so nullified his financial agreement with the former periodical. But then, he also did not receive the $5,000 that the *Sunday Times* had agreed to pay him even though it was a tiny sum for such a grand story. "The possibility someone else was paying him has therefore to be taken seriously," says Hounam darkly, suggesting the Mossad itself.[40]

But what was more important, at least from an intelligence perspective, is that Guerrero had placed a portion of Vanunu's materials in the hands of a publication owned by Robert Maxwell, who was a personal friend of Yitzhak Shamir, Israel's deputy prime minister.[41] Not surprisingly, the scuttlebutt was that Maxwell or one of his delegates at the *Sunday Mirror*, acting on Guerrero's information, wasted no time ensuring that Shamir, and, in turn, Shimon Peres and the Mossad learned even more about Vanunu's incriminating evidence, along with his location in London.[42] Purportedly, the latter made the Mossad's task easier, that of tracking down the whistleblower in the British capital.

As it turned out, the *Sunday Mirror* decided to run the story. As to why the tabloid chose to publish such an exposé—international political accounts were not the sort of minor-league, sensationalist chatter that normally packed its pages—the story's editor, Michael Molloy, explains the narrative did, in fact, possess the right stuff. "The Vanunu story had a spy element," says Molloy. "There was a James Bond feel to it—there was subterfuge, nuclear bombs, snatched photos."[43]

Yet others contend that Maxwell moved ahead with the story because he had agreed, on the sly, to help Israeli Intelligence discredit Vanunu's revelations and wreck his reputation.[44] Supposedly, the tabloid was instructed to take the position that the whistleblower's claims were bogus and his evidence, manufactured. Lending support to this version of events are the recollections of John C. Parker, a higher-up at the *Sunday Mirror*, who subsequently voiced his frustration that the British tabloid had knowingly abandoned the true story in favor of a political ruse. "The *Sunday Mirror* had the biggest story in the world at that time and it collapsed because of the line they took," he says. "It was a classic exercise by the Israelis in disinformation."[45]

Whatever it was that prompted the *Sunday Mirror* to publish the story and turn it against Vanunu, whether it was merely an act of competition with the *Sunday Times* or a nefarious scheme dreamed up by the Mossad to cast doubt on the Dimona evidence, the tabloid rushed its version into print on September 28, 1986. Under the disparaging headline, "The Strange Case of Israel and the Nuclear Conman," it painted Vanunu as a self-serving fraudster with little respect for the truth, the article being designed to leave readers persuaded that he had fashioned a colorful yarn for his own purposes.[46] Significantly, this was the same day the *Noga* dropped anchor off the Italian coast in anticipation of Vanunu's forthcoming arrival. The Mossad's plan was proceeding on schedule.

For the editors of the *Sunday Times*, on the other hand, their plans were unraveling. The fact that the *Sunday Mirror* had just printed a damning article about Vanunu, one supposedly based on a portion of the same material he had entrusted to the *Sunday Times*, triggered shockwaves at the latter newspaper, which was about to go to press with its accurate, comprehensive account of Israel's clandestine WMD program. Instead, its editors now decided to delay the article's publication until they could, once again, feel assured of its veracity. To this end, they sent a copy of the impending exposé, along with the Dimona images, to Theodore Taylor, who was a renowned nuclear physicist and weapon designer, a protégé of Robert Oppenheimer, and the chief of a nuclear test program at the Pentagon. They asked that he examine the materials and review the final draft of the article. And it was while they were awaiting the scientist's verdict in late September—Taylor would conclude that the whistleblower's account was factual—that Mordechai Vanunu vanished. To say that the staff of the *Sunday Times* was caught off-guard would not be entirely accurate, however, since its editors were already mildly suspicious of a romance that had recently blossomed between the whistleblower and a woman who seemed to come out of nowhere.

Dangerous Liaison: The Honeytrap

She said her name was Cindy Hanin and that she was an American tourist. The date was September 24, a Wednesday, and Vanunu was taking a stroll near the Mountbatten Hotel where he was lodging. Against the advice of the *Sunday Times* staff, he was alone, a circumstance that did not escape the attention of the Mossad team that had been shadowing him for the past two weeks. And it was during his afternoon jaunt that Vanunu spotted the blonde, plump, twenty-five-year-old woman, who, after making eye contact with him, walked away nonchalantly. Sensing a vibe, he followed her. Gradually gathering the courage to introduce himself—Vanunu was a socially awkward man with limited romantic experience—he invited her to join him for coffee. And when she pretended to be reluctant, thereby putting him in the position to continue encouraging her, he did so, with the two lounging in a coffee shop a few minutes later and chatting amiably about their experiences as visitors to the British capital.

In reality, Cindy's name was Cheryl Bentov, she was married, and although she had been reared in Orlando, Florida, she had since become an Israeli citizen, a staunch Zionist, and a willing instrument of the Mossad. To her advantage, she also possessed a background in intelligence work, having undergone formal training during a stretch with the Israeli military.[47] In the know, too, was her husband, who currently occupied a high-ranking position in Military Intelligence.

While Vanunu, of course, was unaware of the Mossad's presence in London, the agency was certainly aware of his whereabouts. It also knew he must be in a vulnerable state, feeling emotionally isolated in a foreign city and distraught over his impending public disclosure of Israel's nuclear secrets. And to the Mossad, this meant he must be in need of a friend. The agency further knew that sexual intimacy, even the prospect of it, can go a long way toward alleviating loneliness while also rendering a target more susceptible to emotional manipulation. On this autumn afternoon, then, Cindy's sudden materialization was no accident.

Enhancing the allure of the Mossad operative was the fact that she presented herself as an American citizen—Vanunu's goal, not coincidentally, was to settle in the United States—and she was fairly attractive, although not so dazzling as to intimidate a down-to-earth man like Vanunu. Rather, her appearance, like her personality, seemed both real and accessible. Presumably it was for this reason, as the Mossad had anticipated, that he felt comfortable approaching her while brushing aside the possibility that this new love interest might be a Mossad agent. "[S]he is an American," Vanunu explained to his editor the following day when cautioned about the woman and her motives. "I went up to her and asked her to go for coffee."[48] From the whistleblower's comments, it seems that Cindy's feigned coyness, especially her initial attempt to appear unsure about joining him at the coffee shop, was a stroke of brilliance on the part of the Mossad strategists who had prepped her—seasoned plotters who were renowned for their success in orchestrating so-called "honeytraps." The seductress' next task would be a shade trickier, however, that of convincing Vanunu to leave Britain with her.

On this subject, it is important to note that the Mossad, on strict orders from Prime Minister Shimon Peres, was to avoid involving British Intelligence in its mission to abduct the whistleblower. In fact, it was not to notify its British equivalent of the operation. This is because it was illegal for Israel to kidnap a citizen, even one of its own, on British soil, and British Intelligence would no

13. Mordechai Vanunu: The Seduction of a Nuclear Whistleblower

doubt refuse to permit the mission to proceed. In addition, Prime Minister Peres, during this period, was making every effort to remain on good terms with his British counterpart, the formidable Margaret Thatcher, and he knew she would not look kindly on the Mossad carrying out a political kidnapping in her nation. It was for such reasons that the agency, through the handiwork of Cindy and a unit of her fellow operatives, decided it would be wiser to create the conditions that would induce Vanunu to leave Britain of his own accord. Once Cindy had managed to coax him into escorting her to another country, preferably Italy, the Mossad could abduct him with less concern about the political fallout. Shimon Peres, it seems, was not nearly as worried about provoking Bettino Craxi, Italy's Socialist prime minister, as he was Britain's "Iron Lady."

As it happened, the Israeli *femme fatale* would find it surprisingly easy to lure her mark out of London. For the most part, this was because his anxiety was ratcheting up each day that the *Sunday Times* continued preparing its story; a delay, he was painfully aware, which increased the likelihood that the Mossad would find him. And although he had asked the newspaper not to identify him by name, even to the point of offering to give up any payment he might receive in exchange for anonymity, the periodical held firm to its position that the exposé must have his identity attached to it for the sake of credibility. Surely it is true that the story would be less convincing if Vanunu were not named in it; accusations of fabrication would undoubtedly erupt. But the account would be damaged even more seriously, if not irrevocably, were Vanunu not to be present, in person, to defend and discuss his assertions. And this is why the Mossad was determined to abduct him before the *Sunday Times* report appeared in print.

For Vanunu, the breaking point was reached on September 28 with the unexpected *Sunday Mirror* article about the Dimona project. Even though the piece was written in such a way as to discredit his disclosures about Israel's nuclear arsenal, what distressed him even more was the fact that it featured a photo of him from his days in Australia. This made it a near-certainty that the Mossad now knew his name, his face, and the substance of his materials, which further meant it was only a matter of time before the agency silenced him. And this unnerving realization sent the whistleblower to the verge of collapse, with his fitful state being on display when a staff member from the *Sunday Times* arrived at the Mountbatten Hotel that same morning and advised the normally reserved Israeli to relocate as a precaution. "Fuck off!" Vanunu shouted, being at wit's end over what he considered the newspaper's failure to protect him and his story.[49] And his distress intensified later that day when he found out that the *Sunday Times*, due to the doubts instilled in it by its competitor's article, had decided to postpone its own exposé by at least a week until Taylor, the American physicist, had vetted the content. Having come to see himself as a moving target,

Vanunu was sure the newspaper's delay would cost him dearly. Not unreasonably, he also wondered if it might abandon the story altogether, leaving him politically stranded with the Mossad on his tail.

"He spoke with great fear for his safety," recalls the cleric John McKnight, whom Vanunu phoned in Australia later that evening.[50] The whistleblower no longer believed the *Sunday Times* could guarantee his safety since it had been unable to guard his materials from the hands of the *Sunday Mirror* staff. He therefore was ready to listen when Cindy showed up at his hotel the next day waving a pair of airline tickets. Claiming her sister kept an apartment in Rome, the operative was emphatic that Vanunu travel with her to the Italian capital, where the Mossad, she explained, would not be hunting for him. And sweetening her offer, she implied they could spend their Roman holiday in bed together. Thus far, they had not made love, the couple having enjoyed little privacy in London and, additionally, Vanunu having been too preoccupied to pursue sex. But now his circumstances appeared to be brightening. Given all he had endured in recent weeks, the prospect of a tryst in Rome was one he couldn't refuse.

On Tuesday afternoon, the wearied whistleblower, with Cindy on his arm, hailed a taxi to Heathrow Airport. As they were climbing into it, Vanunu's arm brushed against something hard inside the sleeve of Cindy's jacket, an odd sensation that triggered in him a spark of suspicion. Unbeknownst to him, it was a remote listening device.[51] Also unbeknownst to him, the cab driver, like the seductress herself, was a Mossad agent.

Having misled the *Sunday Times* staff into believing he would be traveling to northern England for a brief stay, Vanunu, accompanied by Cindy, boarded British Airways Flight 504 for the trip to Italy. The flight would take less than three hours, which, he could not have foreseen, would be more time than he would spend on the ground in Rome.

Touching down in Fiumicino, a town thirty minutes southwest of the Italian capital, a man, purportedly a friend of Cindy's family, greeted them in the concourse, after which the trio traveled into Rome by car. Vanunu later recalled that Cindy seemed lost in thought during the drive and more than a little edgy, not at all like the warm and engaging woman with whom he had just spent the past six days.[52] Again, he experienced misgivings but tried to suppress them.

Coming to a stop in front of a small apartment building in a working class section of Rome, the three headed up a staircase to what was supposed to be the flat of Cindy's sister. When a dark-haired woman answered the door, Vanunu figured she must be this sibling. But as he stepped inside, two men dashed toward him from the shadows, pinned him face-down on the floor, and cuffed his hands behind his back while the dark-haired woman filled a syringe. His last memory was that of the needle jabbing his arm.[53]

13. Mordechai Vanunu: The Seduction of a Nuclear Whistleblower 265

Although the ensuing details are sketchy, it is known that the pair of male Mossad operatives lugged the whistleblower to a van and drove him back to Fiumicino. At the dock, they bound him to a stretcher and dispatched him by speedboat to the *Noga*, which sat waiting in the Tyrrhenian Sea. Once onboard, Vanunu regained consciousness, only to find himself in a windowless cabin with another Mossad agent filling another syringe. Then darkness overtook him again. Italy, by this point, was far behind him, the agency's operation having been both smooth and swift. "Vanunu was 'arrested' within two hours of landing on Italian soil," writes Hounam, "in violation of Italian and international law."[54]

Several hours later, Vanunu regained consciousness, but this time the Mossad operatives did not sedate him again. Instead, they drilled him mercilessly, demanding details of the material he had turned over to the *Sunday Times*. They were equally intent upon learning how he had come to possess the Dimona photographs, their concern being that he might have accomplices inside the high-security nuclear facility. During the days that followed, interrogation sessions like this one would become routine on the worn ship; that is, until October 7, when the *Noga* berthed in Tel Aviv and the operatives rushed Vanunu to Mossad headquarters.

Tossing him into a cell, a guard thrust a newspaper at him, the October 5 issue of the *Sunday Times*. "Revealed: The Secrets of Israel's Nuclear Arsenal" declared the banner headline, followed by the full Dimona exposé.[55] His present circumstances aside, Vanunu was elated by what he saw before him. The periodical had dared to proceed with his story despite his absence and its competitor's hatchet job a week earlier. Regardless of what his future might hold, then, he could take comfort in knowing he had succeeded in making public the facts about Israel's awesome nuclear arsenal.

And it was this awesomeness, more than anything else, that shocked the world. Although a few national leaders seemed genuinely surprised to learn that the Jewish state possessed weapons of mass destruction, all were astounded by the sheer magnitude of its arsenal, comprised, as it was, of both nuclear and thermonuclear devices. Even the CIA was taken aback by the enormity of the Dimona program, its size being disproportionate to any conceivable threat the Jewish state might ever face.

The second aspect of the story that grabbed the public's attention centered on Mordechai Vanunu himself. As could be expected, the Israeli government kept mum about the man and his whereabouts, even as the *Sunday Times* ran three more articles about the whistleblower's disclosures during the month of October. During this same month, it also launched an all-out effort to locate him. It seems the newspaper, most of all Vanunu's editor Peter Hounam, was concerned about the possibility, if not the high probability, of foul play. And such suspicions were not unfounded. The newspaper's staff, while Vanunu was still in London, had observed on several occasions what was presumed to be a Mossad unit posted outside its offices. To establish a record of the intrusion, the staff had snapped photos of the apparent intelligence agents who were attempting to pass themselves off as a camera crew.[56]

It was largely because of the successive articles in the *Sunday Times* and the pressure they applied to Israel—and because Hounam, as a potential defendant himself, risked arrest by traveling to the Jewish state to hunt for his missing source—that the Israeli government finally released a terse statement in November of 1968. It added nothing of value to the situation, however. True to form, it denied virtually everything pertaining to Mordechai Vanunu and the nation's WMD program. Yet within a few weeks, the world would come to know exactly what had become of the whistleblower despite the stonewalling by the administration of Yitzhak Shamir, Israel's newly-elected prime minister.

It was on the winter solstice—December 21, 1986—that Vanunu pierced the government's armor once again. On this day, a police van carrying the whistleblower arrived at the court complex in Jerusalem and was approached by a bevy of reporters and photographs, a standard duty for those assigned to the crime beat. But on this occasion they were in for a surprise. Vanunu, who was restrained inside the vehicle, managed to press his open palm against the window. On it, he had scribbled his name and a message. "It said that he had been kidnapped in Rome," reads an account from the Bertrand Russell Peace Foundation. "He had arrived there on September 30 with British Airways flight 504."[57] Based on this limited but crucial information, the *Sunday Times* was able to confirm that Vanunu had indeed been on Flight 504 to Rome and, moreover, that "Cindy" had been his seatmate. This was, of course, evidential that the Mossad's operation had begun in England and proceeded to Italy, meaning that both European nations had grounds for pursuing criminal charges against the Jewish state. Curiously, neither did, just as they showed little interest in Vanunu's extraordinary revelations.

Because the Israeli government could no longer deny the obvious, it now admitted that Vanunu was in prison for disclosing—"or pretending to" disclose—state secrets, as a former Israeli prime minister put it during an American television interview.[58] The belated announcement did not mention the way in which the whistleblower had come to end up in the Jewish state's custody, however.

The trial was set for the summer of the following year, with Vanunu to be held in isolation at Ashkelon Prison until the legal proceedings were completed. And it was during this period, with the court case on the horizon and Vanunu locked away and thus unable to defend his reputation, that the Israeli media unleashed a campaign to tarnish it. The strategy, which certainly is not unheard-of in such cases, was to smear his name in order to cast doubt on his disclosures and discourage potential whistleblowers from coming forward in the future for fear of defamation. Thus, in what was a cozy relationship between the Jewish state's media and government, including its intelligence services, there emerged a systematic and prolonged character assassination that proved to be remarkably effective in planting in the minds of the Israeli people a flawed picture of Vanunu.[59] The tactic did not convince the rest of the world, however, which had access to factual information about the man and his Dimona materials.

Among the distortions put forward by the Israeli press was the alleged opinion of a mental health worker, an unnamed one, suggesting that the whistleblower was gay. Since antigay prejudice was prevalent in Israel at the time, the assertion that Vanunu was drawn to other men was a devious but dependable means of ensuring that the public would question his moral integrity. The accusation was effective, too. "Three years later," writes Toscano, "people familiar with the case referred to Vanunu's alleged homosexuality as if it were a well-known fact."[60]

The media also made sure to mention that the whistleblower had modeled for art classes during his student days. Since academic courses in composition and the human form regularly make use of nude models, the media seized on this morsel of background information to further insinuate that he was morally corrupt.

Then, too, the Israeli press was relentless in its portrayal of Vanunu as a hater of Jews and a friend of the Palestinians. And time and again, it misreported that he had sold out his adopted homeland for money, sacrificing its security for his own personal enrichment.[61]

One of the few accurate facts that the press did put forward was that Vanunu had been a Sephardic Jew who became a Christian. It latched onto his religious conversion as yet another means of maligning him. Not surprisingly perhaps, the legal system followed suit, with prosecutors at his ensuing trial depicting his change of religion as tantamount to treason.

To be sure, the Israeli government, with the help of the domestic media, had no intention of allowing the whistleblower to be seen in a positive light—nor, for that matter, did it plan to permit the Mossad to be seen in a negative one for having seduced and ensnared him. Thus, while the press worked overtime to paint Vanunu as a self-serving anti–Semite, the Mossad implemented a disinformation campaign of its own, the aim being to conceal its unsavory deeds in Britain and Italy. Since it wished to bury the inconvenient fact that its covert operation had commenced in London with the intent to engage in kidnapping, the agency floated the colorful yarn that Vanunu, of his own volition, had boarded a yacht on the Mediterranean coast. His pleasure craft was then said to have encountered an Israeli ship in international waters, with the whistleblower suddenly finding himself under arrest and *en route* to Israel. A fiction that audiences outside of the Jewish state found rather implausible, the invention was dismissed altogether when the *Sunday Times* tracked down and exposed "Cindy" and her exploits in London and Rome.

Trial and Imprisonment

The legal proceedings commenced on August 30, 1987, and concluded on March 24, 1988. The charges consisted of espionage and treason, the trial was to be private, and three judges were to hear the case.

Vanunu selected his defense attorney, Avigdor Feldman, from a list of lawyers that the Israeli government considered acceptable to represent him. A noted advocate of civil rights, Feldman began by arguing that Israel's WMD program, which, from the outset, had been hidden from the Knesset and the population at large, was inherently improper. "The fact that the whole nuclear issue was declared top secret is not suitable to a democratic society," Feldman asserted, adding that Vanunu had performed a public service, and a legal one, by revealing the arsenal's existence to the people of Israel. "He was," said the lawyer, "practicing a freedom of expression, which is protected under Israeli law."[62]

It is true that Vanunu, on multiple occasions, had told the *Sunday Times* that the Israeli citizenry had the right to know about the weapons of mass destruction that lay ninety miles south of Jerusalem at Dimona. He further believed he had a moral responsibility to inform the population about them, since the government had no intention of doing so. And because Israel was a representative democracy, it was his understanding that it was up to the people, not the prime minister's office, to decide whether or not the nuclear arsenal should remain in their homeland, and, if so, under what conditions.

Continuing to press his case, Feldman advanced the notion that the whistleblower, by revealing a WMD program that was in violation of international law because it dealt in undeclared nuclear materials and technology, had not infringed the terms of the security agreement he had signed. Vanunu's Dimona agreement, strictly speaking, did not require him to remain silent about illicit activities. The court put aside all WMD-related arguments by Feldman, however, since any acknowledgement and discussion of Israel's nuclear arms program was forbidden during the proceedings.

Feldman next turned his attention to the charges that had been leveled against his client—treason and espionage—contending that Vanunu did not fit the definition of a traitor or a spy since he had not collaborated with a foreign government. Instead, he had made the Dimona materials available to an independent, non-governmental media outlet. There also was no indication that Vanunu had sought to damage the Jewish state's security, nor any evidence to suggest he had indeed harmed it. Since the court would not discuss Dimona or Israel's security apparatus, however, Feldman's argument carried little weight. In the end, the court's opinion was that a state secret is whatever the state says is a secret and that revealing it is treasonous.

Lastly, the defense attorney planned to submit that the Mossad's kidnapping of Vanunu violated several components of the United Nation's Universal Declaration of Human Rights. And this was significant in that Israel had assimilated the substance of this international standard into its legal system.[63]

It is true, of course, that the Jewish state, if it had intended to abide by the legal procedures established by the international community, would have sought Vanunu's extradition, just as the man himself would have had the opportunity to petition Britain for political asylum. But Israel did not follow the accepted legal protocol, even though it subsequently sought to use the legal system to judge the whistleblower himself. Put another way, the State of Israel broke the law so that it could put Vanunu on trial for breaking the law, a Kafkaesque state of affairs that was yet another cause for criticism. "The kidnapping called into question the legality of Vanunu's trial," writes Toscano, "as well as Israel's commitment to human rights."[64] The judges, however, refused to take into consideration how the State of Israel had managed to acquire custody of the defendant, his abduction remaining unacknowledged throughout the trial.

In such ways, the court restricted the scope of its deliberations, structuring the proceedings in such a way that the only matter to be determined, without the benefit of context or perspective, was whether or not Vanunu had breached the security agreement he had signed at Dimona. And given such limitations, the verdict was a foregone conclusion: guilty as charged.

Upon convicting the whistleblower of espionage and treason, the court handed down the maximum sentence of eighteen years, twelve of which were to be spent in solitary confinement. Officials explained that the latter stipulation was necessary to prevent him from revealing additional state secrets to the inmates he would otherwise encounter during his incarceration. Critics, on the other hand, insisted that the imposition of such protracted isolation was calculated to induce in Vanunu a psychotic state so as to undermine his future credibility. Whatever the court's reasoning, the sentence was opposed by scores of prominent men and women throughout the world, among them the American astronomer Carl Sagan, twelve recipients of the Nobel Peace Prize, and numerous scientists who proposed leniency for the whistleblower. The Israeli government rejected their appeals, though, with Vanunu spending the next eleven years alone in a six-by-nine-foot cell in Ashkelon Prison, in a unit reserved for the facility's most violent criminals.

In 1999, forensic psychiatrists determined that the former whistleblower's mental condition, due to his years of continuous isolation, had deteriorated to the point that it was imperative that he be removed from solitary confinement and permitted to interact with other inmates. And the Israeli government followed the psychiatrists' recommendation. All the same, Vanunu remained incarcerated, even if he no longer was in total isolation, with this state of affairs prompting thirty-five members of the U.S. House of Representatives to dispatch a letter to then-president Bill Clinton in support of the whistleblower's ethics and urging the American leader to request the Israeli's release on humanitarian grounds. Clinton did even more, however, adding his own voice to the matter by stressing his personal concern about the impact of prolonged imprisonment on Vanunu's well-being and calling for his discharge, as well as beseeching the Jewish state, yet again, to sign the Non-Proliferation Treaty and allow international inspections of the Dimona complex. The Israelis not only rejected all of the Americans' pleas, however, but criticized their ally for even making them.

It would not be until 2004 that Vanunu completed his sentence and was released from prison. But what happened next came as a blow to him. Above and beyond the conditions of his parole, the Israeli government placed on him the following restrictions: (1) he would not be permitted to leave Israel; (2) he would not be allowed to obtain a passport; (3) he would not be permitted to approach a foreign embassy in Israel; (4) he would not be allowed to talk to a foreign journalist without the government's prior consent; and (5) he would be required to notify the government twenty-four hours in advance if he planned to leave his home in East Jerusalem to travel within Israel itself. On top of these restrictions, Israeli intelligence would henceforth monitor his phone calls and movements. In effect, Vanunu would live out his remaining years as a captive of the state in a thinly disguised version of house arrest.

Not surprisingly in light of the severity of the constraints, human rights organizations, most notably Amnesty International, took the position that Israel's actions violated international law.[65] Today, the organization classifies Vanunu as a prisoner of conscience and continues to campaign for the renewal of his rights. Alongside it, scores of individuals have joined the call for the restoration of his liberties, figures ranging from former U.S. President Jimmy Carter to Desmond Tutu to Noam Chomsky.

As to the reason that Israel is unwilling to permit Vanunu to move ahead with his life without the government keeping a tight rein on his speech and movements, Israeli officials say they are concerned he may release additional state secrets. It is an explanation that is open to debate, however, since any scientific information Vanunu may still have in his possession would be three decades old by this point and therefore obsolete. Then, too, the former whistleblower has long maintained that the British press published the entirety of his Dimona materials by 1989. Accordingly, opponents of the government's restrictions have challenged its rationale.

Other plausible reasons include one hypothesis that Vanunu, if he were to speak freely to the international media, might share with it the specifics of how "Cindy" and her comrades in the Mossad first entrapped him, then kidnapped him. Amnesty International, among other organizations, has suggested this premise. "Israel's determination to curtail Vanunu's freedom and contact with the outside world would seem to be intended to prevent him from revealing details of his abduction by Israeli secret service agents 18 years ago in Rome in what was clearly an unlawful act," reads a press release from the organization.[66] Related to this, Vanunu could further disclose, to the humiliation of the Shin Bet, how Israel's internal security outfit knew about his anti-government sentiments yet permitted him to continue working at its secret nuclear facility and subsequently allowed him to leave Israel without first debriefing and searching him. To be sure, this was a major failing on the part of the Shin Bet.

Another hypothesis maintains that the Jewish state is worried that the former whistleblower might once again speak out about his nation's weapons of mass destruction, a formidable nuclear arsenal that the Israeli government still refuses to publicly acknowledge despite the published photos of the Machon 2 facility at Dimona. According to this premise, if Vanunu were to succeed in bringing the world's attention to the existence of Israel's WMD program, the consequences would be detrimental to Israel and its principal benefactor, the United States.

For one thing, revisiting the issue might reveal that the United States, for nearly half a century, has turned a blind eye to Israel's manufacture of weapons of mass destruction, thereby enabling the Jewish state to proceed with its nuclear arms program unencumbered. In this scenario, the United States' tacit support must continue being kept under wraps in order to protect its reputation, says Israeli author Uri Avnery. "The world must be prevented by all available means from hearing, from the lips of a credible witness, that the Americans are full partners in Israel's nuclear arms program, while pretending to be the world's sheriff for the prevention of nuclear proliferation," he writes.[67]

The American leadership might also be called upon to cut off aid to Israel if the latter's WMD program were to be successfully exposed. This is because the U.S. government is prohibited by its own Arms Export Control Act from providing funds to a nation known to be involved in undeclared nuclear activities.

And lastly, refocusing attention on the Jewish state's weapons of mass destruction could compel both the United States and Israel to justify their opposition to the efforts of other Middle Eastern nations to develop their own nuclear programs, countries that include Iran and Egypt. In the years since Vanunu's 1986 revelations, Israel has adopted a policy of "nuclear ambiguity," meaning it neither acknowledges nor denies that it has nuclear weapons. But, incongruously, it also continues to insist that it would not be the first Middle Eastern nation to introduce nuclear weapons into the region. Thus, if Vanunu were to effectively demonstrate that Israel has long been untruthful on this issue, the nation would lose all credibility in its attempts to block the nuclear ambitions of other Middle Eastern countries. And the result could have repercussions throughout the region. Such a situation, writes Yair Evron, "would make it virtually impossible for the United States to apply pressure on Arab states—even those friendly to America—to desist from producing their own capabilities."[68] Of course, this was President Kennedy's great worry when he so stridently opposed Ben-Gurion's entry into the nuclear sphere in the early 1960s, the American leader fearing it would, in due course, lead to nuclear proliferation in the Middle East and culminate in a nuclear inferno.

Whatever the rationale for muzzling the former whistleblower after his release from prison, Israel, by curtailing Vanunu's freedom of speech and movement, has given itself a black eye. "After the sentencing decision of the judges, and Vanunu's serving of his full sentence," writes Daniel Ellsberg, "the rule of law in a democracy is itself gravely compromised by what amounts to a retrospective, indefinite prolongation of punishment on false pretences."[69]

Daniel Ellsberg, of course, is the former RAND analyst and whistleblower known for the Pentagon Papers, a collection of classified documents exposing the falsehoods of Lyndon Johnson's presidential administration. The materials that Ellsberg photocopied and dispatched to the media revealed that the White House had lied to Congress and the American people about the nation's military involvement in Viet Nam; that, for example, the Oval Office had endorsed secret bombings campaigns in Cambodia and Laos, and had long been in possession of RAND data demonstrating that the U.S. could not possibly win the war. For bringing these and other disturbing facts to light, Ellsberg was charged with numerous crimes, among them espionage and conspiracy. The charges were dropped, however, after the ensuing administration of Richard Nixon was caught trying to steal psychiatric information about the whistleblower that it could use to smear his reputation.

A man of conscience, Ellsberg has repeatedly come to the defense of Mordechai Vanunu, and, more recently, to that of Edward Snowden, whose deeds were recapped at the outset of his chapter. For that matter, Vanunu himself, in early 2014, expressed his ideological kinship with the NSA whistleblower, describing Snowden as "the best example of what I did 25 years ago," and adding, "when the government breaks the law and tramples on human rights, people talk."[70] Recently, in the summer of 2014, the Israeli government barred Vanunu from attending a human rights conference in London that was designed to "promote the protection of whistleblowers including Edward Snowden and Chelsea Manning."[71] The Israeli administration also refused to permit Vanunu to address the British Parliament during what would have been the same three-day visit, notwithstanding the fact that fifty-four Members of Parliament had invited him to speak before the august body. It remains to be seen if the Jewish state will ever grant Vanunu his full liberties.

As noted at the outset of this book, the Mossad, in its early days, abducted a Nazi war criminal in Argentina, Adolf Eichmann, and smuggled him to Israel for a public trial. The objective was to bring to justice a man whose deeds had contributed to the liquidation of millions of European Jews. But it was also the Mossad, a quarter of a century later, that abducted a fellow Israeli citizen in Europe, Mordechai Vanunu, and smuggled him to Israel for a secret trial, the objective being to silence him for divulging the Jewish state's undeclared nuclear arsenal. To say the agency's mandate expanded and changed over the years would therefore be an understatement. Yet to judge the Mossad's missions in isolation would be a misstep, since its operations, including the two kidnappings noted above, came at the request, if not the orders, of the Israeli government itself. It appears to be the case, then, that the agency's transformation, for better or worse, was a response both to internal and external forces. One thing is certain, though: the Mossad, as it has evolved, has come to be perceived by many of its critics, including a number of its former operatives, as having moved beyond the acceptable bounds of a national intelligence organization, with some viewing it as too unrestrained and overly proactive. As Peter Hounam notes, the Mossad is frequently regarded as the "most interventionist" intelligence service in existence.[72] Surely it is undeniable that the agency has played a provocative role in global affairs on several occasions. And yet, regardless of how one chooses to characterize the organization, the Mossad was and remains today a creative, efficient, and audacious agency, one that is as courageous as it is controversial, and that occupies an unparalleled position in the realm of international intelligence.

Chapter Notes

Introduction

1. Black and Morris (1991).
2. Gilbert, M. (1998, 2008).
3. State of Israel (May 14, 1948).
4. Gilbert, M. (1998, 2008; p. 193).
5. Ibid.
6. Ibid.
7. Eisenberg, Uri, and Landau (1978, p. 10).
8. Thomas (1999, p. 26).
9. Ibid., p. 27.
10. Eisenberg, Uri, and Landau (1978, p. 10).
11. Thomas (1999, p. 30).
12. Malkin and Stein (1990, p. 79).
13. Eisenberg, Uri, and Landau (1978).
14. Black and Morris (1991, p. 503.)
15. Bascomb (2009, p. 101).
16. Geraghty (2010, 187).
17. Munich Officials (July 23, 2012a).
18. Steven (1980, p. 263).
19. Raviv and Melman (1990, p. 186).
20. Raviv and Melman (2012).
21. Thomas (1999).
22. Ostrovsky and Hoy (1990).
23. Thomas (1999, p. 145). 4 wds
24. Simons (1994, p. 286).
25. Thomas (1999).
26. Ibid.
27. Chant (2012, p. 121).
28. Ibid., p. 121.

Part I: Introduction

1. Malkin and Stein (1990, p. 121).
2. Harel (1975, p. 70).

Chapter 1

1. Aharoni and Dietl (1996).
2. Ibid.
3. Arendt (1963, 1964; p. 33).
4. Bascomb (2009, p. 35).
5. Cesarini (2004, p. 157).
6. Wiesenthal (1967, 1968; p. 97).
7. Ibid., pp. 97–98.
8. Aharoni and Dietl (1996, p. 40).
9. Bascomb (2009).
10. Sachs (2001, p.78).
11. Aharoni and Dietl (1996).
12. Segev (2010).
13. Bascomb (2009).
14. Cesarini (2004, p. 208).
15. Bascomb (2009, p. 69).
16. Aarons and Loftus (1991).
17. Cesarini (2004).
18. Ibid., p. 209.
19. Ibid.
20. Ibid.
21. Adolf Eichmann, in Walters (2009, p. 262).
22. Aharoni and Dietl (1996).
23. Walters (2009, p. 110).
24. Wiegrefe (April 1, 2011).
25. Goñi (2002).
26. Ibid., p. 302.
27. Ibid.
28. Cesarini (2004, p. 210).
29. Walters (2009).
30. Ibid., p. 264.
31. Aharoni and Dietl (1996, p. 68).
32. Klaus Eichmann, in Walters (2009, pp. 263–264).
33. Goñi (2002, p. 312).

275

34. Ibid.
35. Ibid.
36. Cesarini (2004, p. 222).
37. Harel (1975).
38. Cesarini (2004, p. 222).
39. Harel (1975).
40. Walters (2009, p. 271).
41. Cesarini (2004).
42. Ibid., p. 224.
43. Harel (1975).
44. Ibid., p. 10.
45. Aharoni, in Bascomb (2009, p. 138).
46. Cesarini (2004, p. 227).
47. Harel (1975).
48. Cesarini (2004, p. 221).
49. Aharoni and Dietl (1996, p. 107).
50. Ibid., p. 108.
51. Ibid.
52. Malkin and Stein (1990, p. 156).
53. Aharoni and Dietl (1996).
54. Ibid., p. 112.
55. Aharoni, in Bascomb (2009, p. 152).
56. Aharoni, in Harel (1975, p. 61).
57. Cesarini (2004, p. 225).
58. Ibid.
59. Ben-Gurion, in Bar-Zohar and Mishal (2012, p. 67).
60. Arendt (1963, 1964; p. 4).
61. Raviv and Melman (2012, p. 68).

Chapter 2

1. Thomas (1999, p. 64).
2. Bar-Zohar and Mishal (2012, p. 67).
3. Tavor, in Bascomb (2009, p. 167).
4. Aharoni and Dietl (1996, p. 131).
5. Bascomb (2009, pp. 163).
6. Bar-Zohar and Mishal (2012, p. 68).
7. Steven (1980, p. 113).
8. Harel (1975, p. 74).
9. Aharoni and Dietl (1996, p. 127).
10. Ibid.
11. Eisenberg, Uri, and Landau (1978, p. 28).
12. Malkin and Stein (1990, p. 127).
13. Ibid.
14. Ibid., p. 177.
15. Steven (1980, p. 113).
16. Bascomb (2009, p. 181).
17. Ibid., p. 182.
18. Malkin and Stein (1990, p. 177).
19. Harel (1975).
20. Ibid.
21. Ostrovsky and Hoy (1990, p. 35).
22. Malkin and Stein (1990, p. 128).

23. Ibid.
24. Ibid.
25. Steinbicker (1995, p. 88).
26. *Paris* (1993, 1995; p. 254–255).
27. Malkin and Stein (1990, p. 145).
28. Bascomb (2009).
29. Goñi (2002).
30. Malkin and Stein (1990).
31. Eisenberg, Uri, and Landau (1978); Raviv and Melman (2012).
32. Cesarini (2004, p. 229).
33. Walters (2009, p. 294).
34. Harel (1975).
35. Ibid.
36. Ibid., p. 145.
37. Bascomb (2009).
38. Ibid., p. 220.
39. Aharoni and Dietl (1996, p. 136).
40. Ibid.
41. Raviv and Melman (2012, p. 69).
42. Bar-Zohar and Mishal (2012, p. 71).
43. Raviv and Melman (2012, p. 69).
44. Malkin and Stein (1990, p. 182).
45. Bar-Zohar and Mishal (2012).
46. Segev (2010, p. 144).
47. Bascomb (2009, p. 219).
48. Malkin and Stein (1990, p. 183).
49. Bascomb (2009, p. 220).
50. Malkin and Stein (1990).
51. Aharoni and Dietl (1996).
52. Ibid., p. 137.
53. Bascomb (2009, p. viii).
54. Malkin and Stein (1990, p. 186).
55. Ibid.
56. Ibid., pp. 186–187.
57. Bascomb (2009, p. 227).
58. Aharoni and Dietl (1996, p. 138).
59. Bar-Zohar and Mishal (2012, p. 74).
60. Aharoni and Dietl (1996, p. 140).
61. Malkin and Stein (1990, p. 188).
62. Arendt (1963, 1964; p. 240).
63. Bascomb (2009).
64. Aharoni and Dietl (1996, p. 140).
65. Ibid., pp. 142–143.
66. Bascomb (209, p. 231).
67. Aharoni and Dietl (1996, pp. 142–143).
68. Ibid.
69. Gat, in Bascomb (2009, p. 233).
70. Harel (1975, p. 148).
71. Ibid.
72. Raviv and Melman (2012, p. 70).
73. Aharoni and Dietl (1996).
74. Malkin and Stein (1990).
75. Aharoni and Dietl (1996, p. 152).
76. Harel (1975).
77. Malkin and Stein (1990, p. 193).

78. Ibid.
79. Ibid., p. 197.
80. Raviv and Melman (2012, p. 69).
81. Harel (1975).
82. Bascomb (2009, p. 245).
83. Harel (1975, p. 170).
84. Ibid., p. 179.
85. Ibid., p. 168.
86. Ibid.
87. Bascomb (2009, p. 245).
88. Aharoni and Dietl (1996).
89. Harel (1975, p. 167).
90. Cesarini (2004, p. 232).
91. Harel (1975, p. 178).
92. Aharoni and Dietl (1996, p. 147).
93. Harel (1975).
94. Adolf Eichmann, in Kimmelman (May 9, 2011; p. A1).
95. Cesarini (2004, p. 231).
96. Ibid.
97. Eichmann, in Aharoni and Dietl (1996, p. 152).
98. Harel (1975).
99. Klaus Eichmann, in Harel (1975, p. 164).
100. Malkin and Stein (1990).
101. Harel (1975).
102. Steven (1980).
103. Bar-Zohar and Mishal (2012).
104. Ibid.
105. Raviv and Melman (2012, p. 70).
106. Malkin and Stein (1990).
107. Aharoni and Dietl (1996, p. 162).
108. Ibid., p. 163.
109. Cesarini (2004, p. 234).
110. Aharoni and Dietl (1996).
111. Ibid., pp. 164–165.
112. Walters (2009).
113. Aharoni and Dietl (1996, p. 165).
114. Ibid.
115. Raviv and Melman (2012, p. 70).
116. Aharoni and Dietl (1996).
117. Harel (1975).

Chapter 3

1. Gilbert (1998, 2008; p. 336).
2. State of Israel, Prime Minister's Office (undated).
3. Malkin and Stein (1990, p. 246).
4. Ibid.
5. Ibid., p. 247.
6. Sachs (2001, p. 84).
7. Ibid.
8. Cesarini (2004, p. 238).
9. Ibid.
10. Ibid., pp. 238–239.
11. Arendt, p. 240.
12. Sachs (2001, p. 84).
13. Harel (1975).
14. Cesarini (2004).
15. Ibid.
16. Gilbert (1998, 2008).
17. Sachs (2001, pp. 85–87).
18. Tharoor (April 8, 2011; p. 1).
19. Eichmann, in von Lang and Sibyll (1983, p. 291).
20. Sachs (2001, p, 88).
21. Shirer (1960).
22. Eichmann comrade, in Shirer (1960, p. Shirer 978f).
23. Gilbert (1998, 2008).
24. Sachs (2001).
25. Friedman (1989, p. 278).
26. State of Israel, Prime Minister's Office (undated).
27. Ibid.
28. Aharoni and Dietl (1996).
29. Raviv and Melman (2012, p. 71).

Chapter 4

1. Amos (1980, pp. 144–145).
2. Ibid., p. 144.
3. Herzl (1896, 1998; 157).
4. Ibid., p. 39.
5. Ibid., p. 157.
6. Grainger (2006, p. 178).
7. Balfour, in Woodward and Butler (1952, p. 346).
8. Ibid.
9. Gilbert (1998, 2008).
10. League of Nations (December, 1922; p. 1).
11. Begin (1952, 1972).
12. British officer, in Begin (1952, 1972; p. 221).
13. Ibid.
14. Gilbert (1998, 2008; p. 135).
15. Hirst (1977, p. 110).
16. Bickerton and Klausner (2005).
17. Gilbert (1998, 2008).
18. Einstein, in Jerome (2009, p.187).
19. Ibid.
20. Gilbert (1998, 2008).
21. Ibid.
22. Bar-Zohar and Haber (1983, 2002, 2005, p. 75).
23. Begin (1952, 1972, p. xii).

24. Ibid., p. 46.
25. Gilbert (1998, 2008).
26. Brown (2004, p. 126).
27. Pappe (2006).
28. Ibid., p. 30.
29. Meir, in *The Washington Post* (June 16, 1969; p. A1).
30. Margolick (May 4, 2008).
31. Ibid.
32. Morris (2004, p. 342).
33. United Nations Conciliation Commission for Palestine (1951).
34. United Nations Relief and Works Agency for Palestine Refugees (undated).
35. Hertsog and Gazit (2005).
36. Ibid.
37. Ibid., p. 148.
38. Friedman (1989, pp. 278–279).
39. Gilbert (1998, 2008).
40. Segev (2005, 2007; p. 15).
41. Bickerton and Klausner (2005, p. 151).
42. Ibid., p. 153.
43. United Nations General Assembly (November 22, 1967).
44. Lukacs (1999).
45. United Nations General Assembly (November 22, 1967).
46. Lukacs (1999, p. 99).
47. Karsh (2003).
48. Katz (2004).
49. Ibid., p. 27.
50. Raab (2007).
51. Ibid.
52. Ibid., p. 32.
53. Ibid., p. 34.
54. Ibid., p. 35.
55. Katz (2004, p. 28).
56. Ibid.
57. Amos (1980, p. 142).
58. Hirst (1977, p. 308).
59. Amos (1980, p. 144).
60. Katz (2004, p. 31).
61. Hoffman (2006, p. 164).
62. Amos (1980, p. 221).
63. Hirst (1977, p. 310).
64. Amos (1980, p. 221).
65. Ibid.
66. Ibid.
67. Hirst (1977).
68. Crelinsten and Schmid (1993).
69. British Broadcasting Corporation (May 9, 1972).
70. Ibid.
71. Wilson (March 1, 2013).
72. British Broadcasting Corporation (March 1, 1973).
73. Korn (1993, p. 164).
74. Ibid.
75. Ibid.
76. British Broadcasting Corporation (March 1, 1973).
77. Korn (1993, p. 169).
78. Ibid.
79. Wilson (March 1, 2013).
80. Nimeiry, in Hirst (1977, p. 319).

Chapter 5

1. Officials Ignored (July 23, 2012b).
2. Bar-Zohar and Haber (1983, 2002, 2005; p. 124).
3. Wolff (September 2, 2002).
4. Ibid.
5. Officials Ignored (July 23, 2012b).
6. Ibid.
7. Bar-Zohar and Haber (1983, 2002, 2005).
8. Taylor (2004, pp. 168–169).
9. Reeve (2000, p. 42).
10. Ibid.
11. Latsch and Wiegrefe (June 18, 2012).
12. Klein (2005, pp. 29–30).
13. Ibid.
14. Abu Daoud (July 4, 2010).
15. Moghaddam (2006, p. 2).
16. Large (2012, p. 197).
17. Ibid.
18. Reeve (2000).
19. Al-Jishey, in Klein (2005, p. 40).
20. Wolff (September 2, 2002).
21. Shumar, in Klein (2005, p. 21).
22. Ibid., p. 27.
23. Koppel Report, in Large (2012, p. 195).
24. Hart, in Kelly (April 28, 2012).
25. Large (2012, p. 202).
26. Gutfreund, in Reeve (2000, p. 4).
27. Berger, in Reeve (2000, p. 7).
28. Reeve (2000).
29. Tsabari, in Reeve (2007, p. 18).
30. Ibid.
31. Avraham Melamed, in Ladany (2008, p 303).
32. Ibid., 304.
33. Ibid.
34. Bowerman, in Moore (2006, p. 290).
35. Ibid., p. 290.
36. Bowerman, in Large (2012, p. 206).
37. Lalkin, in Reeve (2002, p. 13).
38. Lalkin, in Klein (2005, p. 47).
39. Officials Ignored (July 23, 2012b).

40. Large (2012, p. 207).
41. Reeve (2000, p. 14).
42. Moore (2006).
43. Marvin (April, 1972).
44. Ibid., p. 81.
45. Ibid.
46. Brundage, in Keinon (August 29, 2012).
47. Taylor (1993, p. 8).
48. Graes, in Reeve (2000, p. 15).
49. Large (2012).
50. Irish athlete, in Reeve (2000, p. 66).
51. Korn (1993, p. 108).
52. Bar-Zohar and Haber (1983, 2002, 2005; pp. 127–128).
53. Korn (1993, p. 48).
54. Klein (2005).
55. Hans-Dietrich Genscher, in Klein (2005, p. 63).
56. Tröger, in Reeve (2000, p. 84).
57. Klein (2005).
58. Reeve (2000).
59. ABC Sports/EPSN (December 20, 2005).
60. Ibid.
61. Klein (2005, p.66).
62. Ibid.
63. Taylor (1993, p. 8).
64. Doust (February 29, 1992).
65. Dobson (1975, p. 92).
66. Kelly (April 28, 2012).
67. Large (2012).
68. Ibid.
69. Klein (2005, p. 72).
70. Reeve (2000).
71. Bar-Zohar and Haber (1983, 2002, 2005; p. 129).
72. Moore (2006, p. 297).
73. Brundage, in Moore (2006, p. 297).
74. Dobson (1975, p. 95).
75. Large (2012, p. 239).
76. Yodfat and Arnon-Ohanna (1981, pp. 89–90).
77. Bohr, et al. (August 28, 2012).
78. Ibid.
79. Reeve (2000).
80. Ibid.
81. Large (2012, p. 241).
82. Klein (2005, p. 94).
83. Reeve (2000, p. 153).

Chapter 6

1. Taylor (1993, p. 14).
2. Jonas (1984, 2005).
3. Munich (2005, 2006).
4. LaPorte (2010).
5. Ibid., p. 395.
6. American Public Media (2013).
7. Jonas (1984, 2005).
8. Ephraim, in Jonas (1984, 2005; p. 79).
9. Klein (2005).
10. Ibid., p. 106.
11. Ibid., p. 107.
12. Ephraim, in Jonas (1984, 2005; p. 88).
13. Bar-Zohar and Haber (1983, 2002, 2005).
14. Venn-Brown (1984).
15. Zwaiter, in Venn-Brown (1984, pp. 216–217).
16. Ibid.
17. Bar-Zohar and Haber (1983, 2002, 2005; p. 147).
18. Tinnen and Christensen (1976, p. 77).
19. Jonas (1984, 2005).
20. Ibid.
21. Mossad agent, in Jonas (1984, 2005; p. 105).
22. Aviv ("Avner"), in Jonas (1984, 2005; p. 105).
23. Venn-Brown (1984).
24. Klein (2005, p. 123).
25. Ledda, in Venn-Brown (1984, p. 115).
26. Ibid.
27. Jonas (1984, 2005).
28. Ibid.
29. Pilot, in Hess (February 24, 1970; p. 1).
30. Aviv ("Avner"), in Jonas (1984, 2005; p, 145).
31. Ibid.
32. Operative, in Jonas (1984, 2005; p, 146).
33. Bar-Zohar and Haber (1983, 2002, 2005; p. 151).
34. Jonas (1984, 2005).
35. Ibid., p. 153.
36. Ibid.
37. Klein (2005, p. 132).
38. Ibid.
39. Jonas (1984, 2005; p. 162).
40. Tinnen and Christensen (1976, p. 84).
41. Bar-Zohar and Haber (1983, 2002, 2005; p. 154).
42. Ostrovsky and Hoy (1990, p. 4).
43. Klein (2005, p. 146).
44. Ibid.
45. Tinnen and Christensen (1976, p. 89).
46. Klein (2005).
47. Jonas (1984, 2005).
48. Al-Kubaisi, in Jonas (1984, 2005; p. 180).
49. Aviv, in Jonas (1984, 2005; pp. 180–181).

50. Klein (2005).
51. Jonas (1984, 2005).
52. Ibid.
53. David Elazar, in Klein (2005, p. 169).
54. Burton and Bruning (2011, p. 173).
55. Ibid., p. 174.
56. Tinnen and Christensen (1976, pp. 95–96).
57. Ibid., p. 95.
58. Burton and Bruning (2011, p. 175).
59. Klein (2005, p. 179).
60. Ibid.
61. Tinnen and Christensen (1976, p. 97).
62. Bar-Zohar and Haber (1983, 2002, 2005).
63. Tinnen and Christensen (1976, p. 105).
64. Ibid., p. 113.
65. Mike Hatari, in Tinnen and Christensen (1976, p. 117).
66. Klein (2005).
67. Reeve (2001).
68. Tinnen and Christensen (1976, p. 187).
69. Ostrovsky (1990).
70. Burton and Bruning (2011).
71. Ibid., p. 177.
72. Mellgren (March 1, 2000).
73. Ibid.
74. Burton and Bruning (2011).
75. Klein (2005).
76. Weiner (2007, 2008; p. 450).
77. Ibid.
78. Burton and Bruning (2011, p. 179).
79. Reeve (2001).
80. Ibid.
81. Witness statement, in Taylor (1993, p. 47).
82. Gunman Kills (January 15, 1991).
83. Youssef (June 10, 1992).
84. Reeve (2001, p. 208).

Chapter 7

1. Hoffman (2006, p. 63).
2. Ibid.
3. Gero (1997, 2009).
4. Mickolus (1980, p. 8).
5. Burkeman (September 27, 2001).
6. Gero (1997, 2009; p. 10).
7. Plane Bombs (May 29, 1962).
8. Koerner (2013).
9. Brent (1996).
10. Koerner (2013, p. 36).
11. Gero (1997, 2009).
12. Mickolus (1980, p. 93).
13. Captain Oded Abarbanel, in Gero (1997, 2009; p. 50).
14. Mickolus (1980).
15. Koerner (2013, p. 162).
16. Mickolus (1980, p. 94).
17. Ibid.
18. Green (July 23, 2013).
19. Gero (1997, 2009; p. 50).
20. Dunstan (2009, p. 5).
21. Mickolus (1980, p. 94).
22. Central Intelligence Agency, Directorate of Intelligence (July 1977).
23. Mickolus (1980, p. 581).
24. Raviv and Melman (1990, p. 218).
25. Ibid.

Chapter 8

1. Passenger, in Stevenson (1976, p. 4).
2. Ben-Porat, et al. (1976, 1977; p. 16).
3. Ibid., p. 16.
4. Ibid.
5. Ofer (1976).
6. Dunstan (2009, p. 11).
7. Passenger, in Ben-Porat, et al. (1976, 1977; p. 18).
8. Ofer (1976).
9. Dunstan (2009).
10. Bacos, in Dunstan (2009, p. 11).
11. Ibid., p. 11.
12. Dunstan (2009).
13. Ben-Porat, et al. (1976, 1977).
14. In Ben-Porat, et al. (1976, 1977; p. 22).
15. Peck (1977, p. 27).
16. Bose, in Ben-Porat, et al. (1976, 1977; p. 31).
17. Mickolus (1980).
18. Martel, in Ben-Porat, et al. (1976, 1977; p. 33).
19. Dunstan (2009).
20. Ben-Porat, et al. (1976, 1977).
21. Ibid. p. 37.
22. Dunstan (2009, p. 13).
23. Ibid., p. 14.
24. Ibid., p. 14.
25. Oded (October 1, 2006; p. 3).
26. Dunstan (2009).
27. Ben-Porat, et al. (1976, 1977).
28. Peck (1977, p. 38).
29. Ben-Porat, et al. (1976, 1977).
30. Ofer (1976, p. 35).
31. Spokesman, in Ofer (1976, p. 27).
32. Ben-Porat, et al. (1976, 1977).
33. Shani, in Dunstan (2009, p. 17).

34. Ibid.
35. Foreign Minister, in Ofer (1976, p. 30).
36. Raviv and Melman (1990).
37. Dunstan (2009).
38. Steven (1980, p. 313).
39. Ibid.
40. Black and Morris (1991).
41. Stevenson (1976).
42. Hartuv, in Melman (July 8, 2011).
43. Ibid.
44. Ben-Porat, et al. (1976, 1977; p. 169).
45. Peck (1977, p. 76).
46. Netanyahu (2002).
47. Stevenson (1976, p. 9).
48. Dunstan (2009, p. 23).
49. Ben-Porat et al. (1976, 1977; p. 162).
50. Ofer (1976).
51. Dunstan (2009).
52. Netanyahu (2002, p. 148).
53. Betser and Rosenberg (1996, p. 323).
54. Netanyahu (2002, p. 160).
55. Shani, in Dunstan (2009, p. 38).
56. Netanyahu (2002, p. 160).
57. Ibid.
58. Dunstan (2009, p. 39).
59. Ofer (1976, p. 120).
60. Betser and Rosenberg (1996, p. 325).
61. Ibid., p. 328.
62. Ofer (1976, p. 120).
63. Ibid.
64. Ibid., p. 121.
65. Dunstan (2009).
66. Betser and Rosenberg (1996, p. 335).
67. Dunstan (2009).
68. Peck (1977, p. 103).
69. Steven (1980, p. 315).
70. Waldheim, in United Nations Security Council (August–September 1976).
71. Van der Vat (June 14, 2007).
72. Verkaik (February 13, 2007).
73. Dunstan (2009).
74. Ibid.
75. British document (June 1, 2007).
76. Parkinson (June 6, 2007).
77. Black and Morris (1991, p. 341).
78. Raviv and Melman (2012, p. 286).
79. Bar-Zohar and Mishal (2012, p. 261).
80. Ibid.
81. Ibid., pp. 261–262.

Chapter 9

1. Keeley (2009).
2. Hamza and Stein (2000).
3. Reiter (July 2005).
4. Shalom (2005).
5. Chubin (1994).
6. Ibid., p. 43.
7. Timmerman (1991, p. 18).
8. Ibid., p. 77.
9. Keeley (2009).
10. Timmerman (1991, p. 46).
11. Hamza and Stein (2000).
12. Claire (2004, p. 38).
13. Ibid., p. 39.
14. Nakdimon (1987, p. 58).
15. Evron (1994, p. 27).
16. Ibid.
17. Wilson (March 1, 2005).
18. Chirac, in Nakdimon, p. 50.
19. Ibid.
20. Ibid., p. 95.
21. Black and Morris (1991).
22. Timmerman (1991, p. 60).
23. Ibid.

Chapter 10

1. Ostrovsky and Hoy (1990).
2. Ibid.
3. Timmerman (1991).
4. Ibid., p. 60.
5. Ostrovsky and Hoy (1990, p. 19).
6. Ibid., p. 20.
7. Ibid.
8. Claire (2004).
9. Timmerman (1991).
10. Claire (2004).
11. Evron (1994, p. 26).
12. Timmerman (1991, p. 58).
13. Benjamin (February 28, 1980; p. A29).
14. In Claire (2004, p. 62).
15. Ibid., p. 61.
16. Nakdimon (1987).
17. Hamza and Stein (2000, p. 133).
18. Ibid.
19. Nakdimon (1987, p. 121).
20. Ostrovsky and Hoy (1990, p. 23).
21. Nakdimon (1987).
22. Claire (2004, p. 64).
23. Ibid., p. 65.
24. Ibid.
25. Obeidi and Pitzer (2004, p. 47).
26. Hamza and Stein (2000, p. 148).
27. Ibid.
28. Claire (2004).
29. Perlmutter, et al. (2003).

30. Claire (2004).
31. Perlmutter, et al. (2003, pp. 56–57).
32. Carter (2006, p. 41).
33. Claire (2004, p. 105).
34. Ibid.
35. Ibid., p. 106.
36. Ibid., p. 107.
37. Mueller, et al. (2006, p. 214).
38. Ibid.
39. Cirincione (May 11, 2005).
40. McKinnon (1987, p. 93).
41. Khadduri (2003, p. 82).
42. Ford (2004, p. 27).
43. Ibid.
44. Ibid.
45. McKinnon (1987, p. 101).
46. Claire (2004).
47. Nakdimon (1987, p. 175).
48. Claire (2004).
49. Ford (2004).
50. McKinnon (1987, p. 110).
51. Raviv and Melman (2012, p. 223).
52. McKinnon (1987, p. 110).
53. Ibid., p. 115.
54. Ibid.
55. Claire (2004, p. 122).
56. Ibid.
57. Solis (2010, p. 182).
58. Raviv and Melman (2012, p. 223).
59. McKinnon (1987, p. 121).
60. Ibid.
61. Kirschenbaum (2010, p. 54).
62. Raviv and Melman (2012, p. 225).
63. Correll (April 2012; p. 61).
64. Raz, in Jackson (June 5, 2006).
65. Ford (2004, p. 35).
66. McKinnon (1987, p. 156.)
67. Ford (2004, p. 35).
68. McKinnon (2004).
69. Ibid.
70. Ford (2004).
71. Perlmutter, et al. (2003, p. 125).
72. McKinnon (2004, p. 172).
73. Styan (2006).
74. McKinnon (2004, p. 172).
75. Ibid., p. 183.
76. Kempster (June 10, 1981).
77. Begin, in *New York Times* (June 10, 1981a, p. A12:4).
78. Louka (2011, p. 392).
79. Feldman (1994, p. 82).
80. Kempster (June 10, 1981, p. B1).
81. McKinnon (2004 , p. 182).
82. Soviets charge (June10, 1981B).
83. Israel Bombs (June 8, 1981, p. B1).
84. Haig, in Claire (2004, p. 219).
85. Kirkpatrick, in United Nations Security Council (June 19, 1981).
86. United Nations General Assembly (November 13, 1981).
87. Ibid.
88. Louka (2011, p. 388).
89. Nossiter (June 20, 1981b).
90. Wilson (March 1983; p. 374).
91. Wilson (Spring 1991; p. 5).
92. Ramberg (May 2012).
93. Reiter (July 2005; p. 361).
94. Chomsky (2006).
95. Ibid. p. 253.
96. Reiter (2006, p. 3).
97. Hasan (March 25, 2012).
98. Reiter (July, 2005).
99. Ibid.
100. Cheney, in *Meet the Press* interview (2003).
101. Feldman (1994).
102. Ramberg (May, 2012).

Chapter 11

1. Shalom (2005, p. 1).
2. Cohen (1998).
3. Gilling and McKnight (1991/1995, p. 34).
4. Cohen (1998).
5. Hersh (1991, p. 27).
6. Cohen (1998, p. 63).
7. Shavit (2013).
8. Cohen (1998, p. 52).
9. Shavit (2013, p. 179).
10. Ibid., pp. 179–180.
11. Shalom (2005, p. 13).
12. Ibid.
13. Hersh (1991, p. 107).
14. Gilling and McKnight (1991/1995, p. 37).
15. Hersh (1991).
16. Ibid., p. 111.
17. Ibid.
18. Shalom (2005).
19. Hersh (1991, p. 79).
20. Ibid.
21. Gilling and McKnight (1991/1995, p. 41).
22. Shavit (2013, p. 186).
23. Gilling and McKnight (1991/1995, p. 41).
24. Ibid., p. 43.

Chapter 12

1. Davenport, et al. (1978).
2. Ibid., p. 40.
3. Eisenberg, Landau, and Portugali. (1978, p. 105).
4. Davenport, et al. (1978, p. 44).
5. Ibid., p. 47.
6. Ibid., p. 43.
7. Ibid., p. 47.
8. Ibid., p. 57.
9. Ibid., p. 63.
10. Ibid., p. 66.
11. Tilney, in Davenport, et al. (1978, p. 70).
12. Eisenberg, Landau, and Portugali (1978, p. 158).
13. Ibid.
14. United States House of Representatives (1954).
15. Shapiro, in Thomas and Santanam (August 28, 2002).
16. Hersh (1991).
17. Ibid., p. 243.
18. Raviv and Melman (2012).
19. Hersh (1991).
20. Cordesman, in *Los Angeles Times* (June 16, 1986).
21. Emshwiller, John R. (November 22, 2013a).
22. Kahana (2006, p. 81).
23. Hersh (1991).
24. Ibid., p. 257.
25. Emshwiller (November 22, 2013b).
26. Security Increases (June 19, 2012).
27. Schaarsmith (March 15, 2014).
28. Emshwiller (November 22, 2013b).
29. Security Increases (June 19, 2012).
30. Cockburn and Cockburn (1991).
31. Emshwiller, John R. (November 22, 2013a).
32. Israeli Spy (June 16, 1986).
33. Halperin, in Cockburn and Cockburn (1991, p. 77).

Chapter 13

1. Shavit (2013, p. 176).
2. Ibid., p. 177.
3. Cohen (2003, p. 7).
4. Snowden, in Greenwald (2014, pp. 47–48).
5. Snowden, in Greenwald, et al. (June 11, 2013).
6. Kessler (March 12, 2014).
7. Toscano (1990, p. 9).
8. Ibid., p. 10.
9. Cohen (2003, p. 31).
10. Toscano (1990).
11. Ibid., p. 13.
12. Vanunu, in Gilling and McKnight (1991/1995, p. 10).
13. Thompson (1988).
14. Gilling and McKnight (1991/1995).
15. Forsberg (2006).
16. Gilling and McKnight (1991/1995, p. 12).
17. Thompson (1988, p. 10).
18. Gilling and McKnight (1991/1995, p. 15).
19. Toscano (1990).
20. Ibid., p. 45.
21. Ibid., p. 52.
22. Gilling and McKnight (1991/1995, p. 15).
23. Toscano (1990).
24. Hounam (1999, p. 41).
25. Ibid., p. 41.
26. Cohen (2003, p. 3).
27. Smith, in Hounam (1999, p. 42).
28. Hounam (1999, p. 43).
29. Ibid.
30. Cohen (2003).
31. Guerrero, in Hounam (1999, p. 12).
32. Toscano (1990, pp. 92).
33. Ibid.
34. Cohen (2003).
35. Ibid.
36. Ibid.
37. Thompson (1988, p. 10).
38. UN General Assembly (December 14, 1977).
39. Hersh (1991).
40. Hounam (1999, p. 78).
41. Hersh (1991).
42. Ibid.
43. Molloy, in Cohen (2003, p. 69).
44. Hersh (1991).
45. Parker, in Hersh (1991, p. 314).
46. Ibid.
47. Toscano (1990).
48. Vanunu, in Hounam (1999, p. 69).
49. Vanunu, in Hounam (1999, p. 68).
50. McKnight, in Cohen (2003, p. 104).
51. Hounam (1999).
52. Toscano (1990).
53. Ibid.
54. Hounam (1999, p. 75).
55. Sunday Times Insight Team (Oct 5, 1986, p. 1).

56. Hounam (1999, p. 75).
57. Thompson (1988, p. 59).
58. Peres, in Toscano (1990, p. 224).
59. Toscano (1990).
60. Ibid., p. 213.
61. Ibid.
62. Feldman, in Hounam (1999, pp. 124–125).
63. Toscano (1990).
64. Ibid., p. 301.
65. Amnesty International (April 19, 2004).
66. Ibid.
67. Avnery (April 24, 2004).
68. Evron (1994, p. 273).
69. Ellsberg (April 17, 2005).
70. Vanunu, in Hasan (January 9, 2014).
71. Amnesty International (June 5, 2014).
72. Hounam (1999, p. 77).

Bibliography

Aarons, Mark, and John Loftus. (1991). *Unholy Trinity: The Vatican, the Nazis, and Soviet Intelligence.* New York: St. Martin's.

ABC Sports/EPSN. (December 20, 2005). *The Tragedy of the Munich Games* (video). New York: Arts Alliance America/Virgil Films and Entertainment.

Abu Daoud (obituary). (July 4, 2010). *The Telegraph.* Retrieved July 3, 2013, http://www.telegraph.co.uk/news/obituaries/sport-obituaries/7871498/Abu-Daoud.html.

Aharoni, Zvi, and Wilhelm Dietl. (1996). *Operation Eichmann: The Truth About the Pursuit, Capture and Trial.* New York: John Wiley and Sons.

American Public Media. (2013). Aviv: Fabricator or Smear Victim? *American Public Media.* Retrieved August 4, 2013, http://americanradioworks.publicradio.org/features/lockerbie/resources/story_aviv.html.

Amnesty International. (April 19, 2004). Press Release: Israel/Occupied Territories—No Restrictions or Conditions Must Be Imposed On Mordechai Vanunu Upon His Release. *Amnesty International.* Retrieved on June 6, 2014, http://www.amnesty.org/en/library/asset/MDE15/041/2004/en/be66e955-d5e7-11dd-bb24-1fb85fe8fa05/mde150412004en.html.

Amnesty International. (June 5, 2014). Press Release: Israel—Supreme Court Must Overturn "Absurd" Travel Ban on Nuclear Whistleblower. *Amnesty International.* Retrieved June 14, 2014, http://www.amnesty.org/en/for-media/press-releases/israel-supreme-court-must-overturn-absurd-travel-ban-nuclear-whistleblower-.

Amos, John W. (1980). *Palestinian Resistance: Organization of a Nationalist Movement.* New York: Pergamon.

Arendt, Hannah. (1963, 1964). *Eichmann in Jerusalem: A Report on the Banality of Evil.* New York: Penguin.

Avnery, Uri. (April 24, 2004). Vanunu: The Terrible Secret—"The Americans, It Seems, Are Very Worried." *The U.S. Campaign to Free Mordechai Vanunu.* Retrieved June 12, 2014, http://www.vanunu.com/uscampaign/archive9/20040424terriblesecret.html.

Bar-Zohar, Michael, and Eitan Haber. (1983, 2002, 2005). *Massacre in Munich: The Manhunt for the Killers Behind the 1972 Olympics Massacre* [Previous title: *The Quest for the Red Prince: Israel's Relentless Manhunt for One of the World's Deadliest Terrorists* (1983, 2002)]. Guilford, CT: Lyons.

Bar-Zohar, Michael, and Nissim Mishal. (2012). *Mossad: The Greatest Missions of the Israeli Secret Service.* New York: Ecco.

Bascomb, Neal. (2009). *Hunting Eichmann: How a Band of Survivors and a Young Spy*

Agency Chased Down the World's Most Notorious Nazi. Boston/New York: Houghton Mifflin Harcourt.

Begin, Menachem. (1952, 1972). *The Revolt*. Jerusalem: Steimatzky's Agency.

Benjamin, Milton R. (February 28, 1980). France Plans to Sell Iraq Weapons-Grade Uranium. *The Washington Post*, p. A29.

Ben-Porat, Yeshayahu, Eitan Haber, and Zeef Schiff. (1976, 1977). *Entebbe Rescue*. New York: Delacorte.

Betser, Muki, and Robert Rosenberg, (1996). *Secret Soldier: The Inside Story of the Israel Defence Force's Operations by Israel's Greatest* Commando. London: Simon and Schuster.

Bickerton, Ian, and Carla Klausner. (2005). *A Concise History of the Arab-Israeli Conflict*. Upper Saddle River, NJ: Prentice Hall.

Black, Ian, and Benny Morris. (1991). *Israel's Secret Wars: The Untold History of Israeli Intelligence*. London: Hamish Hamilton.

Bohr, Felix, Gunther Latsch, and Klaus Wiegrete. (August 28, 2012). Germany's Secret Contacts to Palestinian Terrorists. *Der Spiegel*. Retrieved July 23, 2013, http://www.spiegel.de/international/world/germany-maintained-contacts-with-palestinians-after-munich-massacre-a-852322.html.

Brent, William Lee. (1996). *Long Time Gone: A Black Panther's True-Life Story of His Hijacking and Twenty-Five Years in Cuba*. New York: Crown.

British Broadcasting Corporation. (May 9, 1972). Israeli Commandos Storm Hijacked Jet. BBC. Retrieved June 24, 2013, http://news.bbc.co.uk/onthisday/hi/dates/stories/may/9/newsid_4326000/4326707.stm.

British Broadcasting Corporation. (March 1, 1973). Palestinian Gunmen Hold Diplomats in Sudan. BBC. Retrieved June 24, 2013, http://news.bbc.co.uk/onthisday/hi/dates/stories/march/1/newsid_4209000/4209239.stm.

British Document: Israel Initiated Entebbe Hijack. (June 1, 2007). *Ynet* (*Yedioth Ahronot / Israel News*). Retrieved December 14, 2013, http://www.ynetnews.com/articles/0,7340,L-3407333,00.html.

Brown, L. Carl (Ed.). (2004). *Diplomacy in the Middle East: The International Relations of Regional and Outside Powers*. London: I. B. Tauris.

Burkeman, Oliver. (September 27, 2001). Can We Ever Stop This? *The Guardian*. Retrieved October 7, 2013, http://www.theguardian.com/world/2001/sep/28/september11.usa4.

Burton, Fred, and John Bruning. (2011). *Chasing Shadows: A Special Agent's Lifelong Hunt to Bring a Cold War Assassin to Justice*. New York: Palgrave Macmillan.

Carter, Jimmy. (2006). *Palestine: Peace Not Apartheid*. New York: Simon and Schuster.

Central Intelligence Agency, Directorate of Intelligence. (July, 1977). *International Terrorism in 1976*. Washington, D.C.: Central Intelligence Agency.

Cesarini, David. (2004). *Becoming Eichmann: Rethinking the Life, Crimes, and Trial of a "Desk Murderer."* Boston: Da Capo.

Chant, Chris. (2012). *Special Forces: History, Roles and Missions, Training, Weapons and Equipment, Combat Scenarios*. Bath, England: Parragon.

Chomsky, Noam. (2006). *Failed States: The Abuse of Power and the Assault on Democracy*. New York: Metropolitan.

Chubin, Shahram. (1994). "The Middle East." Chapter Two in *Nuclear Proliferation After the Cold War*, edited by Mitchell Reiss and Robert S. Litwak. Washington, D.C.: Woodrow Wilson Center.

Cirincione, Joseph. (May 11, 2005). Bombs Won't Solve Iran. *Washington Post*.

Claire, Rodger W. (2004). *Raid on the Sun: Inside Israel's Secret Campaign that Denied Saddam the Bomb*. New York: Broadway.

Cockburn, Andrew, and Leslie Cockburn (1991). *Dangerous Liaison: The Inside Story of the U.S.-Israeli Covert Relationship*. New York: HarperCollins.

Cohen, Avner. (1998). *Israel and the Bomb*. New York: Columbia University Press.

Cohen, Yoel. (2003). *The Whistleblower of Dimona: Israel, Vanunu, and the Bomb*. New York: Holmes and Meier.

Correll, John T. (April 2012). Air Strike at Osirak. *Air Force Magazine*, Vol. 95, No. 4, pp. 58–62.

Crelinsten, Ronald D., and Alex P. Schmid. (Eds.) (1993). *Western Responses to Terrorism*. London: Frank Cass.

Davenport, Elaine, Paul Eddy and Peter Gillman. (1978). *The Plumbat Affair*. Philadelphia: Lippincott.

Declaration of the Establishment of the State of Israel. (May 14, 1948). Retrieved May 3, 2013 at Jewish Virtual Library: http://www.jewishvirtuallibrary.org/jsource/History/Dec_of_Indep.html.

Dobson, Christopher. (1975). *Black September: Its Short, Violent History*. London: Robert Hale.

Doust, Dudley. (February 29, 1992). Munich: The Gunfire Still Echoes Today. *The Daily Telegraph*.

Dunstan, Simon. (2009). *Israel's Lightning Strike: The Raid on Entebbe 1976*. Oxford, England: Osprey.

Eisenberg, Dennis, Dan Uri, and Eli Landau. (1978). *The Mossad, Israel's Secret Intelligence Service: Inside Stories*. London/New York: Paddington.

Eisenberg, Dennis, Eli Landau and Menahem Portugali. (1978). *Operation Uranium Ship*. London: Corgi.

Ellsberg, Daniel. (April 17, 2005). Vanunu's Threat to "Ambiguity" and to Israel's National Security. *The U.S. Campaign to Free Mordechai Vanunu*. Retrieved June 6, 2014, http://www.vanunu.com/uscampaign/20050417ellsberg.html.

Emshwiller, John R. (November 22, 2013a). Mystery Remains on Missing Uranium. *Wall Street Journal*. Retrieved April 20, 2014, http://online.wsj.com/news/articles/SB10001424052702304672404579186030152355004.

Emshwiller, John R. (November 22, 2013b). Waste Land: One Town's Atomic Legacy: A $500 Million Cleanup. *Wall Street Journal*. Retrieved April 20, 2014, http://online.wsj.com/news/articles/SB10001424052702304868404579194231922830904.

Evron, Yair. (1994). *Israel's Nuclear Dilemma* (Cornell Studies in Security Affairs). Ithaca, NY: Cornell University Press.

Feldman, Shai. (1994). "Israel." Chapter Three in *Nuclear Proliferation after the Cold War*, edited by Mitchell Reiss and Robert S. Litwak. Washington, D.C.: Woodrow Wilson Center.

Ford, Peter S. (2004). *Israel's Attack on Osiraq: A Model for Future Preventive Strikes*. Washington, D.C.: Storming Media.

Forsberg, Randall C. (Ed.) (2006). "Data 1: Israel Nuclear Fuel Cycle," in *Arms Control Reporter: A Chronicle of Treaties, Negotiations, Proposals, Weapons and Policy*. Cambridge, MA: Institute for Defense and Disarmament Studies.

Friedman, Thomas L. (1989). *From Beirut to Jerusalem*. New York: Farrar, Straus and Giroux.

Geraghty, Tony. (2010). *Black Ops: The Rise of Special Forces of the C.I.A., the S.A.S, and Mossad*. New York: Pegasus.

Gero, David. (1997, 2009). *Flights of Terror: Aerial Hijack and Sabotage Since 1930*. Yeovil, Somerset, England: Haynes.

Gilbert, Martin. (1998, 2008). *Israel: A History*. New York: Harper Perennial.

Gilling, Tom, and John McKnight. (1991/1995). *Trial and Error: Mordechai Vanunu and Israel's Nuclear Bomb*. London: HarperCollins.

Golda Meir Scorns Soviets. (June 16, 1969). *The Washington Post TimesHerald*, p. A1.

Goñi, Uki. (2002). *The Real ODESSA: How Perón Brought the Nazi War Criminals to Argentina*. London: Granta.

Grainger, John D. (2006). *The Battle for Palestine, 1917*. Woodbridge, England: Boydell.

Green, David B. (July 23, 2013). This Day in Jewish History: The First and Only El Al Hijacking. *Haaretz*. Retrieved October 13, 2013, http://www.haaretz.com/news/features/this-day-in-jewish-history/.premium-1.537402.

Greenwald, Glenn. (2014). *No Place to Hide: Edward Snowden, the NSA, and the U.S. Surveillance State*. New York: Metropolitan.

Greenwald, Glenn, Ewen MacAskill and Laura Poitras. (June 11, 2013). Edward Snowden: The Whistleblower Behind the NSA Surveillance Revelations. *The*

Guardian. Retrieved June 15, 2014, http://www.theguardian.com/world/2013/jun/09/edward-snowden-nsa-whistleblower-surveillance.

Gunman Kills 2 Top Arafat Aides in Tunis, PLO Says. (January 15, 1991). *Los Angeles Times*. Retrieved September 14, 2013, http://articles.latimes.com/1991-01-15/news/mn-142_1_abu-nidal.

Hamza, Khidhir, and Jeff Stein. (2000). *Saddam's Bombmaker: The Terrifying Inside Story of the Iraqi Nuclear and Biological Weapons Agenda*. New York: Scribner.

Harel, Isser. (1975). *The House on Garibaldi Street: The First Full Account of the Capture of Adolf Eichmann Told by the Former Head of Israel's Secret Service*. New York: Viking.

Hasan, Mehdi. (March 25, 2012). Bomb Iran and It Will Surely Decide to Pursue Nuclear Arms. *The Guardian*. Retrieved March 20, 2014, http://www.theguardian.com/commentisfree/2012/mar/25/bomb-iran-nuclear-arms-iraq-israel.

Hasan, Mehdi. (January 9, 2014). The Left Lionises Edward Snowden but Who Will Speak Up For Israel's Mordechai Vanunu? *The New Statesman*. Retrieved June 6, 2014, http://www.newstatesman.com/2014/01/who-will-speak-israels-edward-snowden.

Hersh, Seymour. (1991). *The Samson Option: Israel, America and the Bomb*. London: Faber and Faber.

Herzl, Thedor. (1896, 1998). *The Jewish State*. New York: Dover.

Herzog, Chaim, and Shlomo Gazit. (2005). *The Arab-Israeli Wars: War and Peace in the Middle East*. New York: Vintage.

Hess, John. (February 24, 1970). Swiss Curb Entry of Arabs and Ask Air Safety Talks. *New York Times*.

Hirst, David. (1977). *The Gun and the Olive Branch: The Roots of Violence in the Middle East*. London: Faber and Faber.

Hoffman, Bruce. (2006). *Inside Terrorism*. New York: Columbia University Press.

Hounam, Peter. (1999). *The Woman from Mossad: The Story of Mordechai Vanunu and the Israeli Nuclear Program*. Berkeley, CA: Frog. http://triblive.com/x/valleynewsdispatch/s_88361.html.

Israel Bombs Iraqi A-Reactor; U.S. Protests Attack. (June 8, 1981). *Los Angeles Times*, p. B1.

Israeli Spy Visited A-Plant Where Uranium Vanished. (June 16, 1986). *Los Angeles Times*. Retrieved April 20, 2014, http://articles.latimes.com/1986-06-16/news/mn-11009_1_israeli-intelligence.

Jackson, Patrick. (June 5, 2006). Osirak: Over the Reactor. BBC News. Retrieved March 11, 2014, http://news.bbc.co.uk/2/hi/4774733.stm.

Jerome, Fred. (2009). *Einstein on Israel and Zionism: His Provocative Ideas About the Middle East*. New York: St. Martin's.

Jonas, George. (1984, 2005). *Vengeance: The True Story of an Israeli Counter-Terrorist Team*. New York: Simon and Schuster.

Kahana, Ephraim. (2006). *Historical Dictionaries of Intelligence and CounterIntelligence (Book Three)*. Lanham, MD: Scarecrow.

Karsh, Efraim. (2003). *Arafat's War: The Man and His Battle for Israeli Conquest*. New York: Grove.

Katz, Samuel M. (2004). *Jerusalem or Death: Palestinian Terrorism*. Minneapolis: Lerner.

Keeley, James F. (2009). *A List of Bilateral Civilian Nuclear Co-operation Agreements—Volume 3: Germany (Federal Republic of)—Russia (USSR)*. Center for Military and Strategic Studies, University of Calgary. Retrieved January 9, 2014, http://dspace.ucalgary.ca/bitstream/1880/47373/9/Treaty_List_Volume_03.pdf.

Keinon, Herb. (August 29, 2012). After 40 Years, State Releases Munich Papers. *The Jerusalem Post*. Retrieved July 14, 2013, http://www.jpost.com/National-News/After-40-years-state-releases-Munich-papers.

Kelly, Cathal. (April 28, 2012). Munich Massacre Terrorists Helped Unwittingly by Canadians in 1972 Olympic Atrocity. *Toronto Star*. Retrieved July 6, 2013, http://www.thestar.com/sports/olympics/2012/04/28/kelly_munich_massacre_terrorists_helped_unwittingly_by_canadians_in_1972_olympic_atrocity.html.

Kempster, Norman. (June 10, 1981). Israel: Begin Dismisses Criticism Over Attack: Explains Raid on Iraqi Atomic Site as Self-Defense. *Los Angeles Times*, p. B1.

Kessler, Glenn. (March 12, 2014). Edward Snowden's Claim That He Had "No Proper Channels" for Protection as a Whistleblower. *The Washington Post*. Retrieved May 11, 2014, http://www.washingtonpost.com/blogs/fact-checker/wp/2014/03/12/edward-snowdens-claim-that-as-a-contractor-he-had-no-proper-channels-for-protection-as-a-whistleblower/.

Khadduri, Imad. (2003). *Iraq's Nuclear Mirage: Memoirs and Delusions*. Toronto: Springhead.

Kimmelman, Michael. (May 9, 2011). 50 Years After Trial, Eichmann Secrets Live On. *New York Times*, p. A1.

Kirschenbaum, Joshua. (2010). Operation Opera: An Ambiguous Success. *Journal of Strategic Studies*, Vol. 3, Issue 4, pp. 49–62.

Klein, Aaron. (2005). *Striking Back: The 1972 Munich Olympics Massacre and Israel's Deadly Response*. New York: Random House.

Koerner, Brendan I. (2013). *The Skies Belong to Us: Love and Terror in the Golden Age of Hijacking*. New York: Crown.

Korn, David A. (1993). *Assassination in Khartoum: An Institute for the Study of Diplomacy Book*. Bloomington: Indiana University Press.

Ladany, Shaul. (2008). *King of the Road: From Bergen-Belsen to the Olympic Games*. Jerusalem/New York: Gefen.

LaPorte, Nicole. (2010). *The Men Who Would Be King: An Almost Epic Tale of Moguls, Movies, and a Company Called DreamWorks*. Boston: Houghton Mifflin Harcourt.

Large, David Clay (2012). *Munich 1972: Tragedy, Terror, and Triumph at the Olympic Games*. Lanham, MD: Rowman and Littlefield.

Latsch, Gunther, and Klaus Wiegrefe. (June 18, 2012). Munich Olympics Massacre: Files Reveal Neo-Nazis Helped Palestinian Terrorists. *Der Spiegel*. http://www.nytimes.com/1992/06/10/world/plo-says-slain-official-planned-covert-talks.html 7/3/13, http://www.spiegel.de/international/germany/files-show-neo-nazis-helped-palestinian-terrorists-in-munich-1972-massacre-a-839467.html.

League of Nations. (December, 1922). League of Nations Mandate for Palestine (Eretz-Israel) Together with a Note by the Secretary-General Relating to Its Application to the Territory Known as Trans-Jordan. *Mandate for Palestine Organization*. Retrieved May 7, 2013, http://www.mandateforpalestine.org/the-mandate.html.

Louka, Elli. (2011). *Nuclear Weapons, Justice and the Law*. Cheltenham, England: Edward Ellgar.

Lukacs, Yehuda. (1999) *Israel, Jordan, and the Peace Process*. Syracuse, NY: Syracuse University Press.

Malkin, Peter Z., and Harry Stein. (1990). *Eichmann in My Hands*. New York: Warner.

Margolick, David. (May 4, 2008). Endless War. *New York Times*. Retrieved May 5, 2013, http://www.nytimes.com/2008/05/04/books/review/Margolick-t.html.

Marvin, Carolyn. (April, 1972). Avery Brundage and American Participation in the 1936 Olympic Games. *Journal of American Studies*, Vol. 16, No. 1, pp. 81–105.

McKinnon, Dan. (1987). *Bullseye One Reactor*. San Diego: House of Hits.

Meet the Press (transcript). (March 16, 2003). NBC News. Retrieved March 22, 2014, file:///C:/Users/Marc%20Vargo/Documents/~Iraq%20-%20Osirak%20Nuclear%20Reactor/CHENEY%20TRANSCRIPT%20Osirak%20Interview%20with%20Vice-President%20Dick%20Cheney,%20NBC,%20%20Meet%20the%20Press,%20%20Transcript%20for%20March%202016.htm.

Mellgren, Doug. (March 1, 2000). Norway Solves Riddle of Mossad Killing (Israel and the Middle East: Special Report). *The Guardian*. Retrieved September 10, 2013, http://www.theguardian.com/world/2000/mar/02/israel.

Melman, Yossi. (July 8, 2011). Setting the Record Straight: Entebbe Was Not

Auschwitz. *Haaretz*. Retrieved November 10, 2013, http://www.haaretz.com/weekend/week-s-end/setting-the-record-straight-entebbe-was-not-auschwitz-1.372131.

Mickolus, Edward F. (1980). *Transnational Terrorism: A Chronology of Events, 1968–1979*. Westport, CT: Greenwood.

Moghaddam, Fathali M. (2006). *From the Terrorists' Point of View: What They Experience and Why They Come to Destroy*. Westport, CT: Praeger Security International.

Moore, Kenny. (2006). *Bowerman and the Men of Oregon: The Story of Oregon's Legendary Coach and Nike's Cofounder*. New York: Rodale.

Morris, Benny (2004). *The Birth of the Palestinian Refugee Problem Revisited*, 2d ed. (Cambridge Middle East Studies). Cambridge, England: Cambridge University Press.

Mueller, Karl P., Jasen J. Castillo, Forrest E. Morgan, Negeen Pegahi, and Brian Rosen (2006). *Striking First: Preemptive and Preventive Attack in U.S. National Security Policy*. Santa Monica, CA: RAND.

Munich. (2005). DVD. Directed by Steven Spielberg. Universal City, CA: Universal Studios Home Video.

Munich Officials Ignored Attack Warnings. (July 23, 2012a). United Press International (UPI.com). Retrieved online August 11, 2012, http://www.upi.com/Top_News/World-News/2012/07/23/Munich-officials-ignored-attack-warnings/UPI-49361343070002/?spt=hs&or=tn.

Nakdimon, Shlomo. (1987). *First Strike: The Exclusive Story of How Israel Foiled Iraq's Attempt to Get the Bomb*. New York: Summit.

Netanyahu, Iddo. (2002). *Yoni's Last Battle: The Rescue at Entebbe, 1976*. Jerusalem and New York: Gefen.

Nossiter, Bernard D. (June 20, 1981). Israelis Condemned by Security Council for Attack on Iraq. *New York Times*. Retrieved March 20, 2014, http://www.nytimes.com/1981/06/20/world/israelis-condemned-by-security-council-for-attack-on-iraq.html.

Obeidi, Mahdi, and Kurt Pitzer. (2004). *The Bomb in My Garden: The Secrets of Saddam's Nuclear Mastermind*. New York: John Wiley and Sons.

Oded, Arye. (October 1, 2006). Israeli-Ugandan Relations in the Time of Idi Amin. *Jewish Political Studies Review* 18, pp. 3–4. Retrieved November 2, 2013, http://jcpa.org/article/israeli-ugandan-relations-in-the-time-of-idi-amin/.

Ofer, Yehuda. (1976). *Operation Thunder: The Entebbe Raid—The Israelis' Own Story*. New York: Penguin.

Officials Ignored Warnings of Terrorist Attack. (July 23, 2012b). *Der Spiegel*. Retrieved June 30, 2013, http://www.spiegel.de/international/germany/officials-ignored-warnings-of-munich-olympics-massacre-a-845867.html.

Ostrovsky, Victor, and Claire Hoy. (1990). *By Way of Deception: The Making and Unmaking of a Mossad Officer*. New York: St. Martin's.

Pappe, Ilan. (2006). *The Ethnic Cleansing of Israel*. London: One World.

Paris. (1993, 1995). New York: Dorling Kindersley.

Parkinson, Dan. (June 6, 2007). Israel Hijack Role "Was Queried." BBC News. Retrieved December 14, 2013, http://news.bbc.co.uk/2/hi/uk/6710289.stm.

Peck, Ira. (1977). *Raid at Entebbe*. New York: Scholastic.

Perlmutter, Amos, Michael Handel, and Uri Bar-Joseph. (2003). *Two Minutes Over Baghdad*. London: Routledge.

Plane Bombs Kill 200 Since 1949. (May 29, 1962). *Anderson Herald* (Madison, Indiana), p. 9.

Quotation of the Day. (June 10, 1981a). *New York Times*, p. A12:4.

Raab, David. (2007). *Terror in Black September: The First Eyewitness Account of the Infamous 1970 Hijackings*. New York: Palgrave Macmillan.

Ramberg, Bennett. (May 2012). Osirak and Its Lessons for Iran Policy. *Arms Control Today*, Vol. 42. Retrieved March 18, 2014, https://www.armscontrol.org/act/2012_05/Osirak_and_Its_Lessons_for_Iran_Policy.

Raviv, Dan, and Yossi Melman. (1990).

Every Spy a Prince: The Complete History of Israel's Intelligence Community. Boston: Houghton Mifflin.

———. (2012). *Spies Against Armageddon: Inside Israel's Secret Wars.* Sea Cliff, NY: Levant.

Reeve, Simon. (2000). *One Day in September: The Full Story of the 1972 Munich Olympics Massacre and the Israeli Revenge Operation "Wrath of God."* New York: Arcade.

Reiter, Dan. (July 2005). Preventive Attacks Against Nuclear Programs and the "Success" at Osiraq. *Nonproliferation Review,* Vol. 12, No. 2, pp. 355–371.

Reiter, Dan. (2006). The Osiraq Myth and the Track Record of Preventive Military Attacks. *Ridgway Center Policy Briefs* (Matthew B. Ridgway Center for International Security Studies, University of Pittsburgh), Vol. 4, Issue 2, pp. 1–4.

Sachs, Ruth. (2001). *Adolf Eichmann: Engineer of Death* (Holocaust Biographies). New York: Rosen.

Schaarsmith, Amy McConnell. (March 15, 2014). Report: More Dangerous Radioactive Waste Near Apollo Than First Thought. *Pittsburgh Post-Gazette.* Retrieved April 22, 2014, http://www.post-gazette.com/local/region/2014/03/14/Federal-report-finds-nuclear-waste-underestimated-at-Armstrong-County-site/stories/201403140175.

Security Increases Around Pennsylvania Nuclear Disposal Site. (June 19, 2012). Homeland Security News Wire. Retrieved April 22, 2014, http://www.homelandsecuritynewswire.com/dr20120619-security-increases-around-pennsylvania-nuclear-disposal-site.

Segev, Tom. (2005, 2007). *1967: Israel, the War, and the Year That Transformed the Middle East.* New York: Metropolitan.

Segev, Tom. (2010). *Simon Wiesenthal: The Life and Legends.* New York: Doubleday.

Shalom, Zaki. (2005). *Israel's Nuclear Option: Behind the Scenes Diplomacy Between Dimona and Washington.* Tel Aviv: Jaffee Center for Strategic Studies.

Shavit, Ari. (2013). *My Promised Land: The Triumph and Tragedy of Israel.* New York: Spiegel and Grau.

Shirer, William. (1960). *The Rise and Fall of the Third Reich: A History of Nazi Germany.* New York: Simon and Schuster.

Simons, Geoff. (1994). *Iraq: From Sumer to Saddam.* New York: St. Martin's.

Solis, Gary D. (2010). *The Law of Armed Conflict: International Humanitarian Law in War.* Cambridge, England: Cambridge University Press.

Soviets Charge U.S. Was Accomplice in the "Act of Gangsterism" by Israelis. (June 10, 1981b). *New York Times.* Retrieved on March 23, 2014, http://www.nytimes.com/1981/06/10/world/soviet-charges-us-was-accomplice-in-the-act-of-gangsterism-by-israelis.html.

State of Israel, Prime Minister's Office. (Undated). The Eichmann Trial: Fifty Years After—A Behind the Scenes View of the Arrest and Trial of Adolf Eichmann. *Israel State Archives.* Retrieved April 19, 2013, http://www.archives.gov.il/ArchiveGov/Templates/Articals/Article.aspx?NRMODE=Published&NRNODEGUID={BAEF9609-8647-45AC-85D7-D413767C4DDC}&NRORIGINALURL=%2farchivegov_eng%2fpublications%2felectronicpirsum%2feichmantrial%2feichmantrialintroduction.htm&NRCACHEHINT=Guest#2.

Steinbicker, Earl. (1995). *Daytrips France.* Mamaroneck, NY: Hastings House.

Steven, Stewart. (1980). *The Spymasters of Israel.* New York: Macmillan.

Stevenson, William. (1976). *90 Minutes at Entebbe.* New York: Bantam.

Styan, David. (2006). *France and Iraq: Oil, Arms and French Policy-Making in the Middle East* (Library of International Relations). London: I. B. Tauris.

Sunday Times Insight Team. (October 5, 1986). Revealed: The Secrets of Israel's Nuclear Arsenal. *The Times/Sunday Times,* p. 1.

Taylor, Paul. (2004). *Jews and the Olympic Games: The Clash between Sport and Politics.* Brighton, England: Sussex Academic Press.

Taylor, Peter. (1993). *States of Terror: Democracy and Political Violence.* London: BBC.

Tharoor, Ishaan. (April 8, 2011). The Eichmann Trial. *Time Magazine*. Retrieved May 4, 2013, http://content.time.com/time/specials/packages/article/0,28804,2064099_2064107_2064409,00.html.

Thomas, Gordon. (1999). *Gideon's Spies: The Secret History of the Mossad*. New York: St. Martin's.

Thomas, Mary Ann, and Amesh Santanam. (August 28, 2002). NUMEC Made Significant Advancements. *The Tribune-Review*. Retrieved April 18, 2014, http://triblive.com/x/valleynewsdispatch/s_88361.html#axzz3Cw3PI6WS.

Thompson, James. (1988). *Israel's Bomb: The First Victim—The Case of Mordechai Vanunu*. Nottingham, England: Spokesman/Bertrand Russell Peace Foundation.

Timmerman, Kenneth R. (1991). *The Death Lobby: How the West Armed Iraq*. Boston: Houghton Mifflin.

Tinnen, David, and Dag Christensen (1976). *The Hit Team*. Boston: Little, Brown.

Toscano, Louis (1990). *Triple Cross: Israel, the Atomic Bomb, and the Man Who Spilled the Secrets*. New York: Birch Lane.

United Nations Conciliation Commission for Palestine. (1951). General Progress Report and Supplementary Report of the United Nations Conciliation Commission for Palestine—Covering the Period from 11 December 1949 to 23 October 1950. *United Nations Information System*. Retrieved June 9, 2013, http://domino.un.org/unispal.nsf/9a798adbf322aff38525617b006d88d7/93037e3b939746de8525610200567883.

United Nations General Assembly. (November 22, 1967). *Resolution 242: The Situation in the Middle East*. United Nations (Information System). Retrieved June 9, 2013, http://unispal.un.org/unispal.nsf/0/7D35E1F729DF491C85256EE700686136.

United Nations General Assembly. (December 14, 1977). *Resolution 105D: Relations Between Israel and South Africa*. United Nations. Retrieved June 7, 2014, http://www.un.org/en/ga/search/view_doc.asp?symbol=A/RES/32/105&Lang=E&Area=RESOLUTION.

United Nations General Assembly. (November 13, 1981). *Resolution 487: Armed Israeli Aggression Against the Iraqi Nuclear Installations and its Grave Consequences for the Established International System Concerning the Peaceful Uses of Nuclear Energy, the Non-Proliferation Of Nuclear Weapons and International Peace and Security*. United Nations. Retrieved March 16, 2014, http://www.un.org/documents/ga/res/36/a36r027.htm.

United Nations Relief and Works Agency for Palestine Refugees. (Undated). *United Nations Relief and Works Agency*. Retrieved May 5, 2013, http://www.unrwa.org/etemplate.php?id=85.

United Nations Security Council. (August-September 1976). Excerpts from United Nations Security Council Debate on the Entebbe Incident. *UN Monthly Chronicle*, Vol. 13, No. 8. Retrieved on December 11, 2013, http://www.tjsl.edu/slomansonb/Entebbe.html.

United Nations Security Council. (June 19, 1981). United Nations Security Council Resolution 487. *Security Council Official Records, 2288th Meeting*. United Nations. Retrieved March 16, 2014, http://domino.un.org/unispal.nsf/be25c7c81949e71a052567270057c82b/4aed70baa0b37b53052567fd00762f30.

United States House of Representatives. (1954). *Atomic Energy Act of 1954*. 83d Congress, 2d session, H.R. 9757.

van der Vat, Dan. (June 14, 2007). Kurt Waldheim: Austrian President and UN Secretary-General Who Lied About His Service in the German Army. *The Guardian*. Retrieved online December 10, 2013, http://www.theguardian.com/news/2007/jun/15/guardianobituaries.austria.

Venn-Brown, Janet. (Ed.) (1984). *For a Palestinian: A Memorial to Wael Zuaiter*. London: Kegan Paul International.

Verkaik, Robert. (February 13, 2007). Revealed: The Fate of Idi Amin's Hijack Victim. *The Independent*. Retrieved November 20, 2013, http://www.independent.co.uk/news/uk/crime/revealed-the-fate-of-idi-amins-hijack-victim-436181.html#.

von Lang, Jochen, and Claus Sibyll. (1983).

Eichmann Interrogated: Transcripts from the Archives of the Israeli Police. New York: Farrar, Straus and Giroux.

Walters, Guy. (2009). *Hunting Evil: The Nazi War Criminals Who Escaped and the Quest to Bring Them to Justice.* New York: Broadway.

Weiner, Tom. (2007, 2008). *Legacy of Ashes: The History of the CIA.* New York: Anchor.

Wiegrefe, Klaus. (April 1, 2011). The Long Road to Eichmann's Arrest: A Nazi War Criminal's Life in Argentina. *Der Spiegel.* Retrieved December 10, 2012, http://www.spiegel.de/international/germany/the-long-road-to-eichmann-s-arrest-a-nazi-war-criminal-s-life-in-argentina-a-754486.html.

Wiesenthal, Simon. (1967, 1968). *The Murderers Among Us: The Simon Wiesenthal Memoirs.* New York: Bantam.

Wilson, Andrew B. (March 1, 2013). What Did Arafat Get for Killing U.S. Diplomats? *The American Spectator.* Retrieved June 24, 2013, http://spectator.org/archives/2013/03/01/what-did-arafat-get-for-killin.

Wilson, Richard. (March 1983). A Visit to the Bombed Nuclear Reactor at al-Tuwaitha. *Nature,* Vol. 302, No. 31, pp. 373–376.

_____. (Spring 1991). Nuclear Proliferation and the Case of Iraq. *Journal of Palestinian Studies,* Vol. 20, No. 3, p. 5.

_____. (March 1, 2005). Letters to the Editor—Will Iran Be Next? *The Atlantic Magazine.* Retrieved January 24, 2014, http://www.theatlantic.com/magazine/archive/2005/03/letters-to-the-editor/303727/.

Wolff, Alexander. (September 2, 2002). When the Terror Began. *Time Magazine.* Retrieved July 1, 2013, http://www.time.com/time/magazine/article/0,9171,340700,00.html.

Woodward, E. L., and R. Butler. (Eds.) (1952). *Documents on British Foreign Policy 1919–1939, First Series,* Volume IV, Number 242, p. 346. London: HMSO.

Yodfat, Aryeh, and Yuval Arnon-Ohanna. (1981). *PLO: Strategy and Politics.* London: Croom Helm.

Youssef, Ibrahim M. (June 10, 1992). P.L.O. Says Slain Official Planned Covert Talks. *New York Times.* Retrieved September 14, 2013, http://www.nytimes.com/1992/06/10/world/plo-says-slain-official-planned-covert-talks.html.

Index

Abarbanel, Oded 156
Abdallah, Hashi 169–170
Abu Nidal Group 149
Adwan, Kemal 135
Aerbel, Dan 140, 144–145, 233–234, 238
Afif, Luttif "Issa" 93
Aharoni, Zvi 13, 22–24, 29–30, 39, 41–54, 57–59, 66
AK-47 (Kalashnikov rifle) 95, 96, 98, 99, 100, 135, 149, 167, 181, 182
al-Chir, Hussein Abad 128–131, 136
al-Fatah *see* Fatah
al-Kubaisi, Basil Paoud 132–134, 138
al Malhouk, Abdullah 87–88
al-Meshad, Yahya 200–202
al Nasser, Adli 87
Alon, Yosef 139
al-Qas, Rizk 87–88
al Rafai, Zaid 86
al-Tuwaitha Nuclear Research Center 190, 194, 195, 199, 201, 203, 205, 206, 209, 211, 213, 214, 215, 216, 219–220
Amadeo, Mario 62
American Friends of the Fighters for the Freedom of Israel 75
American Jewish Committee 64
Amin, Idi 159, 166–169, 171–172, 176–177, 181–185
Amit, Meir 233
Amnesty International 270–271
amphetamines 96
"anticipatory self-defense" 217
antigay prejudice (Homophobia) 267
apartheid 259
Arab-Israeli War: 1948; War of Independence 76–78, 207, 225; 1956 227; 1967, Six-Day War 79; 1978 98
Arab League *see* League of Arab States
Arafat, Yasser 81, 83–84, 86, 87, 93, 120, 123, 146

Arledge, Roone 108
Arms Export Control Act 218, 271
ar-Ruba'i, Muhammad Najib 190
Ashkelon Prison 266, 270
Asmara Chemie 234, 235, 236, 238
Aswan Dam 277
Atlantic-Richfield Company (ARCO) 242
"Atoms for Peace" (speech) 226
Atoms for Peace Program 226, 239
Auschwitz 49, 173, 182
The Avengers 28
Aviv, Juval 116–117, 122, 128

Baader-Meinhof Gang 104, 137, 158–161
Babcock and Wilcox Company 242
Bacos, Michel 163, 165, 174
Balfour, Alfred 72
Balfour Declaration 72, 74
Barak, Ehud 168
Barbie, Klaus 14
Bar-Lev, Omer 182
Barrow, Peter 237–238
Batista, Fulgencio 154–155
Bauer, Fritz 19, 20, 21
Begin, Menachem 6, 74, 76, 146, 194, 195, 196, 199, 200, 204–210, 212–218, 220–222
"Begin Doctrine" 221
Benaman, Kamal 140–144
Ben-Gurion, David 1, 2, 4, 7, 10, 23–25, 48, 60–64, 66, 86, 124, 190, 225, 226, 228–231, 246, 247, 251, 272
Ben-Gurion Airport *see* Lod Airport
Ben-Gurion University of the Negev 251
Ben-Zvi, Itzhak 66
Beretta (pistol) 122, 134, 143, 181
Bergen-Belsen concentration camp 28, 101
Berger, David 99, 100, 111, 112
Bergmann, Ernst David 226
Bernadotte, Folke 76
Betser, Muki 179–181, 183

295

Bevin, Ernest 75
bin Talal, Hussein *see* King Hussein of Jordan
Biscayne Traders Shipping Corporation 236
Black Panthers 155
Black Power (movement) 139
Black September (historic event) 83
Black September Organization (BSO): Munich massacre 91–111; origin and development 83–86
Bloch, Dora 177, 182, 184
Bolton, August 236
Borochovitch, Ida 182
Böse, Wilfred 161, 162, 163, 164, 165, 173, 182
Bouchiki, Achmed 144, 145
Bouchiki, Torill 144
Bouviet, Antonio Dega 167
Bowerman, Bill 101, 102
Brandt, Willy 106
Brent, William Lee 155
British Intelligence *see* MI-5; MI-6
British Mandate for Palestine 73, 75–78, 204
Brundage, Avery 104, 108, 112
BSO *see* Black September Organization
Bush, George H. W. 221

Caesarea (Kidon) 119
camera, concealed 23
Camp David Accords 204–207
CAPRI 15, 16
"caramel" 6, 199, 200, 212
Carlos the Jackal (Ilich Ramirez Sanchez) 137, 161, 167
Carter, Jimmy 204, 205, 270
Castro, Fidel 154–155
Chambers, Erika 147, 148
Chatila Refugee Camp 94
Chaussepied, Damien 216
Che Guevara Brigade/Gaza Unit (PLFP) 163, 165
Cheney, Dick 221
Chernobyl nuclear disaster 255
Cheryl Bentov ("Cindy Hanin") 261–264, 266, 268, 271
Chirac, Jacques 192, 194
Chomsky, Noam 220, 270
Christians 73, 77, 78, 88, 93, 148, 254, 255, 267
Churchill, Winston 73, 76
CIA 3, 146, 147, 158, 205, 228, 243
Clement, Ricardo *see* Eichmann, Adolf
Clinton, Bill 117, 270
Cockburn, Andrew 244
Cockburn, Leslie 244
Cohen, Pasco 182
Cold War 189, 194, 288
Columbia Law School 99
Committee to Safeguard the Islamic Revolution 203
Committee X 119
Communism 104

Craxi, Bettino 263
Curzon, Nathaniel 73
cyanide 46, 64

Dachau 17
Dani, Shalom 28, 41, 56, 61
Daoud, Abu 88, 93, 94, 95, 96, 149
Dar al–Bayda Airport 156
David, Yitzhak 182
Dayan, Moshe 109–110, 206
Declaration of the Establishment of the State of Israel 1
Deir Yassin, Israel 75, 76
Delilah (biblical figure) 226
d'Estaing, Valérie Giscard 168, 169
diaspora 64, 74
Dimona nuclear reactor/project 227–240, 245–246, 248, 250–253, 255–258, 260–261, 263, 265, 267–271
Disneyworld 147
Doust, Dudley 108
DreamWorks SKG 117
Dulles, Allen 3

Eban, Abba 56
Eichmann, Adolf (aliases Ricardo Clement, Klement) 4–5; in Argentina 13–17; capture 38–59; childhood 11; execution 66; manhunt 17–25; Nazi conversion 11–13; trial 60–65
Eichmann, Dieter 13, 54–56
Eichmann, Horst 13, 54
Eichmann, Klaus 13, 17–19, 54–56, 80
Eichmann, Vera 16, 23, 39, 54
Eichmann in My Hands 33
Eid, Guy 87–88
Einstein, Albert 75–76
Eisenhower, Dwight W. 226
Eitan, Rafael "Rafi" 26, 27, 28, 31, 34, 41, 42, 43, 44, 45, 48, 58, 61, 206, 209, 213, 214, 241
Eklund, Sigvard 219
El Al Airlines 32–33, 37, 56–59, 61, 82, 112, 121, 123, 132, 136, 152, 155, 156, 158–160, 169
el Arja, Jaïl 167
Elazar, David 136
Elian, Yona 29, 38, 41, 46, 47
Ellsberg, Daniel 272
Embakasi International Airport 158
enriched uranium *see* uranium
Entebbe International Airport 166, 168
Eshkol, Levi 233
L'Espresso 120
Etzion Air Base 214, 216
Euratom *see* European Atomic Energy Commission
European Atomic Energy Commission (Euratom) 234, 235, 236, 237
European Common Market 234
Exodus 1947 75
Ezeiza Airport 56, 58

Faht-Information 124
Failed States 220
Fatah (al-Fatah) 81, 83–84, 89, 93, 118, 120–121, 123, 129, 131, 135–137, 157
Fatah-Kuwait 135
FBI 117, 198, 240, 243
Fedayeen 83, 94
Feldman, Avigdor 268–269
Final Solution *see* Holocaust
Fiorelli, Mario 203
Flights of Terror 153
For a Palestinian 120
Fourth Amendment (U.S. Constitution) 247
Fuldner, Horst Carlos 15, 54
Fürstenfeldbruck Airfield 109, 110, 111, 113, 114

GAO *see* General Accounting Office
Garibaldi Street 22, 23, 30, 35, 40, 42–44, 54
Gat, Yaacov 57, 58, 59
gay *see* homosexuality
Gaza Strip 78, 80, 163
Gazit, Shlomo 194
General Accounting Office (GAO) 243
genocide 11, 12, 18, 51, 64
Gente 92
Gestapo 17
Giavanna C 15
Gilinsky, Victor 244
Girard, Yves 193
Gladnikoff, Marianne 140, 142, 143, 144, 145
Golan Heights 80, 157, 179–180, 183, 250, 259
Goldfinger 40
Graes, Annaliese 105
Grant, John 154
Groupe des Ecologistes Français 198
Guerrero, Oscar 256, 258, 259–260
Gur, Mordechai "Motta" 170, 176
Gutfreund, Yossef 98, 99, 112

Hadad, Wadia 174, 186
Haganah 2, 27, 28
Haig, Alexander 218
Halperin, Mort 244
Hamshari, Amina 123, 126, 127
Hamshari, Mahmoud 123–127, 129, 130
Hamshari, Marie-Claude 123, 126, 127
Hamza, Khidhir 201, 203
Harari, Mike 119, 145
Harel, Isser 3, 4, 5, 10, 20, 21–30, 32, 33, 36–39, 41, 42, 44, 48, 49, 51, 52, 56–57, 59, 60, 62, 63, 66
Harris, Erwin 155
Hart, David 97, 109
Hartuv, Ilan 173
Hawaiian islands 147
Hercules C-130 (transport aircraft) 168, 175, 177, 178, 179, 180, 181, 182
Hermann, Sylvia 17, 18, 19
Hermann, Lothar 17, 18, 19, 21
Hermoni, Avraham 240, 241

Hersh, Seymour 240
Hershkowitz, Henry 101
Herzl, Theodor 72
Hewlett-Packard 195
Himmler, Heinrich 15
hippies 140
hit squad (Mossad), structure 128
Hitler, Adolf 3, 11, 14, 17, 51, 52, 54, 55, 91, 102, 104, 167
Hofi, Yitzhak 171, 194, 196, 200, 203, 206, 209, 214, 222
Holocaust ("Final Solution") 4, 5, 10, 12, 13, 15, 16, 18, 19, 20, 23, 24, 25, 27, 28, 45, 48, 52, 53, 60, 62, 64, 65, 66, 74, 75, 78, 79, 98, 168, 173, 174, 184, 208, 227, 231, 239, 247, 254
Homophobia *see* Antigay prejudice
Homosexuality 201, 267
honeytrap 261, 262
Hounam, Peter 254, 255, 256, 257, 260, 265, 266, 273
Hudal, Alois 14
Humint (Human Intelligence) 67
Hussein, Saddam 189, 190, 192, 196, 198, 207, 212, 220, 222
Hussein bin Talal *see* King Hussein of Jordan

IAEA *see* International Atomic Energy Agency
IAEC *see* Iraqi Atomic Energy Commission
Ilani, Efraim 29, 30, 48, 61
International Atomic Energy Agency (IAEA) 188, 193, 194, 219, 220, 226, 229, 230, 246
International Committee of the Red Cross (Red Cross) 14, 103
International Olympic Committee (IOC) 102, 103, 104, 105, 106, 112
IOC *see* International Olympic Committee
IRA *see* Irish Republican Army
Iraqi Atomic Energy Commission (IAEC) 189, 190, 213
Irgun 74, 75, 204
Irish Republican Army (IRA) 137
Iron Curtain 154, 155
Isis nuclear reactor 193, 197, 199, 208, 213
ISORAD *see* Isotopes and Radiation Enterprises, Ltd.
Isotopes and Radiation Enterprises, Ltd. (ISORAD) 241
Israeli Defense Forces (IDF) 6, 134, 136, 151, 170, 173, 175, 177, 178, 179, 180, 181, 183, 205, 206, 209, 210, 213, 216, 222, 228
Iyad, Abu 93, 149

Jaaber, Faiz Abdul Rahim 167
James Bond 40, 260
Japanese Red Army 104, 137
The Jewish State 72
Jews: Ashkenazi 249, 250; Sephardic 249, 250, 252, 267
Jonas, George 116
Judaism, Orthodox 29, 239, 250

Kafkafi, Jeruham 240, 241
Kaiser-Franz-Josef School 11
Karoline Café 142, 143, 144
katsa 131, 200
Kennedy, John F. 190, 229–230, 231, 272
Kennedy, Robert 88
Keshet 125, 126, 130
KGB 67, 129, 130, 137, 221
KH-11 satellite imagery 205, 219
Khaled, Leila 82, 83
Kidon *see* Caesarea
Kierkegaard, Søren 254–255
King David Hotel 74, 204
King Faisal of Iraq 133, 189–190
King Hussein of Jordan (Hussein bin Talal) 81–83, 215
Kirkpatrick, Jeanne 218
Kissinger, Henry 146
Klement, Ricardo *see* Eichmann, Adolf
Knesset 60, 151, 230–231, 246, 268
Koppel Report 97
Korbut, Olga 95
Körner, Peter 237
Kristallnacht 28
Kuhlmann, Brigitte 161, 163–164, 165–166, 182

Labor Party (Israel) 206, 218
Ladany, Shaul 101–102
LAKAM 232, 240, 241
Lalkin, Shmuel 97, 102
League of Arab States (Arab League) 1, 86
League of Nations 73
Ledda, Romano 123
Legacy of Ashes: The History of the CIA 146
Le Moine, Jacques 163
Leonardo da Vinci Airport 136, 155
Leventhal, Paul 239
license plate (revolving) 40, 45
Likud Party 218
Lillehammer, Norway 142–146, 233, 238
Lod Airport (Ben-Gurion Airport) 86, 104, 133, 164, 178
Lodge, Henry Cabot 61
Lufthansa Airlines 109, 110, 111, 113

M-84 *see* Mark–84 bomb
Machon 2 250, 251, 252, 271
Magalle, Marie-Claude 201–202
Malkin, Zvi 3, 9, 28, 31, 32, 33, 34, 35, 36, 40–46, 48, 50, 57, 61, 125
Mandate for Palestine *see* British Mandate for Palestine
Manning, Chelsea 273
Mapai Party (Israeli Workers' Party) 227
Marine Corps 102
Mark–84 bomb (M–84) 209, 216
Martel, Patricia 165–166
Maxwell, Robert 7, 260
Meet the Press 221
Meir, Golda 5, 24, 48, 62, 67, 70, 77, 96, 103, 104, 106, 115–116, 117, 119, 131, 144, 145, 229, 230, 252
Mengele, Josef 14, 16, 49–50
MI-5 172
MI-6 67
Mitterrand, François 7, 212
Mokhsi, Ziad 136
Molloy, Michael 260
Moore, George Curtis 87, 88
Mulago Hospital 178
Munich (film) 17
Munich massacre *see* Black September Organization
Muslim Brotherhood 86
Mussolini, Benito 55

Nakaa, Abdel Hadi 136
Nasser, Gamal Abdel 3, 79
Nasser, Kamal Butros 135
National Liberation Front (Algeria) 156
National Security Agency (NSA) 205, 240, 243, 247, 248, 273
National Socialism 11, 28, 50
Nautilus 239, 240
Nazi hunters 15, 17, 62, 66; *see also* The Avengers
Nazism *see* National Socialism
Nazzal, Yusuf "Tony" 93
Negev Desert 7, 207, 211, 212, 225, 226, 229, 246, 248, 249
Negev Nuclear Research Center *see* Dimona nuclear reactor/project
Neo-Nazis 63, 94
Nesher, Yitzhak 29, 31, 36, 45, 48, 50, 61
Netanyahu, Benjamin 151
Netanyahu, Iddo 179, 180
Netanyahu, Yonatan 151, 179, 180
New Orleans 147
New York Times 76
Nike, Inc. 101
Nimeiry, Gaafar 89
Nissiyahu, Yehudith "Judith" 29, 38, 48, 50, 61
Nixon, Richard 89, 114, 244, 272
Noel, Cleo 87, 88
Noga 258
Notes on a Controversy 117
NPT *see* Treaty on the Non-Proliferation of Nuclear Weapons
NRC *see* Nuclear Regulatory Commission
nuclear landmines 259
Nuclear Materials and Equipment Corporation (NUMEC) 233, 239–245
Nuclear Regulatory Commission (NRC) 210, 242, 243
NUMEC *see* Nuclear Materials and Equipment Corporation
Nuremberg Trials 117

Obeidi, Mahdi 203
Occupied Territories 157, 172, 183, 214, 251, 259

Index

Olympiastadion Berlin 91
Olympic Games, Berlin (1936) 91–92
Olympic Games, Munich (1972) 5, 67, 69, 91–115
Olympic Hotel (Cyprus) 129, 130
One Thousand and One Nights 120
Operation Big Lift 197, 203
Operation Eichmann (book) 47
Operation Iqrit and Biri'm 95, 112
Operation Plumbat 232, 234–239
Operation Spring of Youth 134–136
Operation Uganda 161, 164
Oppenheimer, Robert 261
Osirak nuclear reactor 197, 199–200, 202–204, 206, 208–211, 214, 216–222; *see also* Osiris nuclear project
Osiraq 197, 199; *see also* Osiris nuclear project
Osiris nuclear project 192–193, 194, 195, 196, 197, 213
Owens, Jesse 102, 112

Pahlavī, Mohammad Rezā 79
Palestine Liberation Organization (PLO) 81–90, 93, 112–114, 116, 118, 119, 120, 123, 124, 126, 127, 128, 129, 132, 134, 135, 136, 140, 141, 145, 146, 147, 149, 156–158, 167, 172, 185
Palmach 28
Pentagon Papers 272
Peres, Shimon 168, 169, 206, 209, 212–213, 218, 226–228, 230, 246, 257, 258, 260, 262–263
Perón, Juan 14, 15
PFLP *see* Popular Front for the Liberation of Palestine
PLO *see* Palestine Liberation Organization
The Plumbat Affair 234
plumbate 237
plutonium 6, 220, 228, 243, 250, 252–253
poison 46, 47, 50, 64, 202–203, 241
Popular Front for the Liberation of Palestine (PFLP) 82–84, 118, 133, 134, 137, 152, 158–159, 160, 161, 163, 165, 166, 167, 169, 170–176, 181, 182, 184, 185, 186; *see also* Che Gueverra Brigade/Gaza Unit
"preemptory self-defense" 217
pressure bomb 130, 138
Principal Allied Powers 73
Proskauer, Joseph 64

Qassim, Abd al-Karim 190

Rabin, Yitzhak 164, 169, 170, 174, 176, 183, 185, 194
Ramberg, Bennett 221
Ramleh Prison 66
Rasool, Abdul-Rahman Abdul 202–203
ratline 14
Reagan, Ronald 205, 217–218
Red Cross *see* International Committee of the Red Cross
Red Prince *see* Salameh, Ali Hassan
Reid, Ogden 229–230
Republican Palace (Baghdad) 201, 215
Revolution Day 9, 32
Revolutionäre Zellen 161
Rickards, Byron 152–153
The Rise and Fall of the Third Reich 65
Rizak, Georgina 147
Romano, Yossef 101, 107, 123
Rothschild, Walter 72
Russia 27, 72

Sadat, Anwar 106, 108, 204
Sagan, Carl 269
Saguy, Yehoshua 206, 222
SAICA *see* Società Anonima Italiana Colori e Affini
St. John's Anglican Church 254, 255, 256
Salameh, Ali Hassan ("Red Prince") 93, 137, 140–144, 146–149
SAM *see* Surface-to-Air Missile
Samir (BSO informant) 131
Samson (biblical figure) 226
The Samson Option 240
Sanchez, Ilich Ramirez *see* Carlos the Jackal
Sassen, Willem 53
Sayeret Golani *see* Sayeret Matkal
Sayeret Matkal 134, 164, 177–179, 181–183
Scheersberg A 236
Schmidt, Bill 102
Schoklitsch, Armin 15
Schreiber, Manfred 103, 104
Schulz, Brigitte 160
selection process (Third Reich) 173
Sertorio, Francesco 235
SGM *see* Société Générale des Minerais
Shalom, Avraham 28, 30, 41, 44, 45, 48, 58, 61, 241
Shamir, Yitzhak 76, 206, 213, 260, 266
Shani, Joshua 168, 180
Shapiro, Zalman 239–45
Sharon, Ariel 117, 156, 206, 213
Shayetet 13 134–135
Shibi, Abdel Hamid 136
Shin Bet 26, 27, 28, 29, 132, 185, 241, 251, 271
Shirer, William 65
Shomron, Dan 179, 180, 181
Shumar, Arie 97, 102
Sieber, Georg 92, 101
Sinai Peninsula 80, 157, 179, 180, 183, 214, 216
Sirhan, Sirhan 88
"Situation 21" 92, 93, 101
Six-Day War *see* Arab-Israeli War, 1967
Skyjacking 86, 114, 151–167, 185; "Skyjack Sunday" 82–84
SNIA Technit 203
Snowden, Edward 247–248, 249, 272–273
Società Anonima Italiana Colori e Affini (SAICA) 235
Société Générale des Minerais (SGM) 235
Sokolovsky, Tuvia 98, 99, 100

Solitary confinement 8, 269, 270
Soreq Nuclear Research Center 226, 227, 242
Spector, Arlen 243
Der Spiegel 93
Spielberg, Steven 117
Spitz, Mark 102, 105
SS (Nazi force) 11, 14, 15, 21, 44, 47, 53, 54, 55, 64, 65
Stern Gang 75, 76
Strike Team (Operation Eichmann) 27–29
Suez Canal 158, 227, 228, 230
Sunday Mirror 260, 261, 263, 264
Sunday Times (London) 256, 258, 259, 260, 263, 264, 265, 266, 268
Surface-to-Air Missile (SAM) 159, 169, 192
The Sydney Morning Herald 256

Tacuara (fascist youth group) 55
Tammuz I and II *see* Osiris and Isis nuclear reactors
Tavor, Moshe 28, 39, 40, 41, 42, 43, 45, 46, 48
Taylor, Theodore 261
Tel Aviv Museum 1
telephone bomb 125, 126, 127
Thatcher, Margaret 8, 218, 263
Third Reich 4, 10, 12, 15, 52, 66, 91
Three Mile Island nuclear accident 198, 245
Tilney (First Officer) 237
Treaty on the Non-Proliferation of Nuclear Weapons (NPT) 190, 193
Tröger, Walther 103, 104
Tsabari, Gad 99–100
Tulane University 99
Tutu, Desmond 270

U-2 spy plane 228–229
UNESCO *see* United Nations, Educational, Scientific, and Cultural Organization
Union de Banque Suisse 118
Union of Soviet Socialist Republics (USSR) 113, 129, 190–191, 228
United Arab Republic 79
United Nations 1, 2, 3, 6, 62, 73, 77, 77, 80, 146, 184, 185, 218, 219, 259; Conciliation Commission for Palestine 78; Educational, Scientific, and Cultural Organization (UNESCO) 124; Relief and Works Agency for Palestine Refugees in the Near East (UNRWA) 78; Resolution #181 76–77; Resolution #242 80; Resolution #487 7, 219
U.S. Arms Export Control Act 218, 271
U.S. Atomic Energy Commission 189, 230, 231, 240, 246
U.S. Department of Homeland Security 243
U.S. Department of Justice 117
U.S. Department of State 77, 218, 219, 220, 221
U.S. House of Representatives 270

U.S. House Subcommittee on Energy and the Environment 243
U.S. House Subcommittee on Oversight and Investigation 243
Universal Declaration of Human Rights 269
Universal Pictures 117
UNRWA *see* United Nations, Relief and Works Agency for Palestine Refugees in the Near East
uranium 193, 199, 206, 209, 212, 216, 226, 231, 232, 233, 236, 239, 240, 242, 245; enriched 6, 7, 193, 199, 239, 240, 243; yellowcake 7, 223, 234, 235, 236, 237, 238
USSR *see* Union of Soviet Socialist Republics

Vacuum Oil Company 11
Vanunu, Mordechai 7, 8, 248–273
Vatican 14
Vengeance 116, 117
Venn-Brown, Janet 121, 123
Vichy, France 228
Vietnam War 272

Waldheim, Kurt 167, 184
Wall Street Journal 243–244
War of Independence *see* Arab-Israeli War, 1948
Washington Post 77
Watergate scandal 256
Weapons of Mass Destruction (WMD) 200, 208, 216, 221, 223, 229, 242, 245, 246, 237, 251, 252, 257, 261, 265, 266, 268, 271, 272
Wehrmacht 184
Weinberg, Moshe 99, 100, 101, 102, 103, 112
Weizman, Ezer 206
West Bank 78, 80, 120, 121
Westinghouse Corp. 239, 242
Where Eagles Dare 143
whistleblower, motives 248–249
Wilson, Richard 193, 219, 220
WMD *see* Weapons of Mass Destruction
World Trade Center 153

Yadin, Yigael 206
Yarisal, Burham 236
Yariv, Aharon 117
yellowcake *see* uranium
Yeshiva Ohel Shlomo 250
Yom Kippur War 183
Yussuf, Abu 135

Zamir, Zwicka "Zvi" 103, 108, 109, 111, 115, 117, 125, 126
Zionism 72, 73
Zionist Organization of America 239
Zwaiter, Wael 120–123, 127, 128, 129, 133
zyklon-B gas 12

www.ingramcontent.com/pod-product-compliance
Ingram Content Group UK Ltd.
Pitfield, Milton Keynes, MK11 3LW, UK
UKHW041925140426
5217IPUK00014B/325